Islam in the Middle Ages

Islam in the Middle Ages

The Origins and Shaping of Classical Islamic Civilization

Jacob Lassner and Michael Bonner

Praeger Series on the Middle Ages
Jane Chance, Series Editor

PRAEGER
An Imprint of ABC-CLIO, LLC

A B C 🝢 C L I O

Santa Barbara, California • Denver, Colorado • Oxford, England

Library of Congress Cataloging-in-Publication Data
Lassner, Jacob.
  Islam in the Middle Ages : the origins and shaping of classical Islamic civilization / Jacob Lassner and Michael Bonner.
    p. cm. — (Praeger series on the Middle Ages)
  Includes bibliographical references and index.
  ISBN 978–0–275–98569–1 (hard copy : alk. paper)
  ISBN 978–0–313–04709–1 (ebook)
1. Civilization, Islamic. 2. Islamic Empire—History—661–750. 3. Islamic Empire—History—750–1258. 4. Islam—History—To 1500.   I. Bonner, Michael David. II. Title.
DS36.85.L37   2010
953'.02—dc22   2009034494

14 13 12 11 10   1 2 3 4 5

This book is also available on the World Wide Web as an eBook.
Visit www.abc-clio.com for details.

ABC-CLIO, LLC
130 Cremona Drive, P.O. Box 1911
Santa Barbara, California 93116-1911

This book is printed on acid-free paper ∞

Manufactured in the United States of America

Contents

Preface

There is an old Egyptian proverb, "the fingers of the hand are not of equal length." Although this book on Islam is part of a multivolume effort dealing with a wide range of medieval religious civilizations, it may differ greatly in approach, tone, chronological reach, and even length from the other works of the larger project. There is, for one, the vastness of the domains so rapidly conquered by medieval Islamic armies. Tens of thousands of Arab tribesmen, initially from the Arabian Peninsula, came to rule over tens of millions of peoples in a world that extended from current-day Spain and Portugal to Central Asia. One also has to consider the relative openness of the Muslim conquerors to absorbing and redefining for themselves local and regional customs and institutions, as well embrace, promote, and advance the philosophy and science of the ancient Greeks, Persians, and peoples of the subcontinent of India, all of which served to create an extraordinarily complex and diverse medieval civilization. It comes as no surprise then that to produce a single volume on the origins and formation of medieval, or as we would prefer to say, classical Islamic civilization is incredibly taxing on the abilities of an individual scholar, or in this case two scholars working in tandem.

Any responsible author or authors writing a volume on medieval Islam, especially one that is primarily intended for a general reading audience is immediately faced with a number of problems. Not the least of these is producing a book that is in some way different from the numerous other books that have appeared on the subject ever since the study of Islam became a discipline worthy of "scientific" investigation in the great universities of the West. With the recent resurgence of Islam in the Near East and elsewhere, the number of books that appear regularly on the tables and shelves of bookstores has seemingly grown beyond measure. The availability of so many books for readers anxious to learn about Islam and the Islamic world is, however, a mixed blessing, because here as well, the fingers on the hand are not of equal length. Not all who write about the Islamic world have the knowledge to grapple with so large a subject, even when limited to the formative centuries of Islamic civilization. Because of recent advances in the various subfields of Islamic learning, it has become virtually impossible for any scholar, however erudite, to command firsthand all the disciplines to produce a readable and informative survey. There are multi-authored volumes but, valuable as they are, they tend to represent the conventional wisdom of an earlier age rather than bold new thinking. Moreover, with so many collaborators, such books can appear disjointed and hence jarring to some readers.

Searching about for models that might be suitable for our own project, we found it remarkable that in so many respects the best single English language survey of medieval Islam (at least regarding the development of religious thought and institutions) remains *Mohammedanism*, a work published nearly seventy years ago by the British orientalist H. A. R. Gibb (Oxford, 1940). Gibb, whom some scholars went so far as to proclaim the greatest living interpreter of Islam in the Western world, was entrusted with producing an up-to-date survey without footnotes but with a brief but well-chosen bibliography. That the author did with consummate skill, an elegant style, and a conviction of view that sometimes skirted the ambiguities of the situations he described. While one could have wished Gibb had provided a broader and more detailed historical context for the development of Islam, history in narrative form has never been a central focus of this and similar early surveys, except for accounts of the life of Muhammad, perhaps the most difficult of all moments of Islamic experience to historicize. One would have to regard this as a pity, especially in Gibb's case, because his unusually acute observations of early Islamic history were never published in book form, but instead circulated in a few articles and an oral tradition handed down by scholars who had the privilege of partaking of his lectures and classroom discussions. Some eight decades since Gibb first articulated his ideas on historical developments in the early centuries of Islam, they remain for those historians familiar with them a launching pad for present and future research. It might have been somewhat of an intellectual conceit to single out Gibb out as the greatest interpreter of Islam in the Western world, but his distinction as a historian of immense learning and perception has to be trumpeted even now.

In 1946, the University of Chicago Press published *Medieval Islam*, a rather different kind of survey by Gustave E. von Grunebaum. Unlike Gibb, who remained fully rooted in the traditional orientalist outlook in which he was reared, von Grunebaum cast his intellectual net far beyond the medieval Islamic world, as he was both interested in and familiar with developments in the social sciences, as well as European literature and thought. He deliberately cultivated an audience for whom knowledge of Islam would be of comparative value. Readers of *Medieval Islam* are treated from the outset to an impressive display of erudition in which references to and quotes from all sorts of Near Eastern and other sources are sprinkled generously throughout the text. Despite many fascinating insights, *Medieval Islam* can be an elusive read, for the author does not always supply his audience with the necessary infrastructure to fully absorb the range of his intellectual curiosity. No doubt, that is due in part to the origins of the book, a series of academic lectures given at the University of Chicago where the prestigious Committee on Social Thought brought together learned partners representing a wide spectrum of disciplines. By the author's admission, he had written a book on Muslim values rather than a more straightforward narration of political, or for that matter institutional, history. In a more recent age, the book would have been described as a history of mentalities.

A decade later, von Grunebaum would publish a second book: *Islam* (Routeledge & Keegan Paul, 1955). Its subtitle, *Essays in the Nature and Growth of a Cultural Tradition*, hints at a continuation of the approach in his previously published lectures. Although the format of the book more closely resembles the standard surveys of Islamic civilization, the author's primary concern is the formation of cultural consciousness in Islam, a story which he takes to modern times. As before, von Grunebaum is reaching out to a broader audience than his orientalist colleagues or individuals searching for an informed introduction to Islamic civilization. He seeks to engage reflective intellectuals more generally interested in the formation of cultural consciousness and problems of cultural transmission and absorption, that is, of cultural self-definition and influence. In this book, the author emerges as a thought-provoking cultural anthropologist manqué, but, like most surveys of medieval Islam, his study tends to shortchange extended narrative history.

As if to compensate for that missing narrative, a book published originally by von Grunebaum in German was translated some seven years later into English as *Classical Islam: A History 600–1258* (Unwin & Allen, London, 1970). As we were in writing our book, von Grunebaum was concerned about giving the term classical Islam a meaningful definition and an appropriate time frame. By classical he decided on the past that Muslims in subsequent generations re-appropriated and sought to relive to accommodate the realities of the present. For the end of the classical period, he chose 1258 C.E., the year in which the Mongols captured Baghdad and put an end to a caliphate that had lasted for half a millennium, and which despite a weakness of many generations was regarded by the majority of Muslims as part of God's grand design. The year 1258 was in that respect a major watershed in the history of the Muslim faithful and therefore a convenient historical marker. Nevertheless, von Grunebaum is well aware many of the classical institutions of the Islamic world were already shaped in the first four Islamic centuries, a point we have emphasized in defining the chronological parameters our own project. As in his earlier books, von Grunebaum's main concern remains the formation of Islamic consciousness, but in this publication it is integrated within a tightly packaged historical framework. Indeed the ground covered is so vast, and the narrative so densely detailed, some readers will find it difficult to keep track of all the linkages between political history and the history of religious and cultural developments. Moreover, the author chooses not to interrogate the historical sources; rather he uses them as a platform with which to discuss the larger issues of Islamic culture. Readers curious about social and political developments may find themselves yearning for an analysis more closely linked to the Arab chroniclers and the problems they present in recovering elements of an Islamic past that is both real and imagined. These reservations aside, *Classical Islam* strikes us as being a book of extraordinary interest as it is of great learning. And yet, it seems to have drawn less attention than his earlier essays. For whatever reason, it seems to have completely disappeared from the syllabi of courses on Islamic civilization as well as the discourse of current Islamicists. The same can be said for his stimulating Chicago lectures published a decade earlier.

Although still cited from time to time, *Islam*, perhaps his most popular work, has also become somewhat of an intellectual curio. While it remains a stunning read, it too is now largely unappreciated and even disparaged by some Islamic scholars, even more so by social scientists, the very intellectual community the author was intent on reaching. We suspect the real reason this book does not continue to receive the attention it still deserves is the manner in which the author time and again boldly confronts the question of why Muslims were unable to sustain their cultural achievements of the Middle Ages; adjust more nimbly to changing historical circumstances; and, as did the West, develop a continuing sense of curiosity in other civilizations. Merely posing the question seems to rankle politically correct voyeurs who today turn their gaze on Islam and the Near East. But von Grunebaum cannot be so casually dismissed. His incisive treatment of the tension between traditional Islamic societies and the invasive challenge of the West, and more generally his treatment of how both civilizations evolved and welcomed or rejected innovation, has lost none of its original significance.

Gibb, although also neglected today, retains his reputation as a sensitive and sympathetic interpreter of Islam. Reading Gibb, one can imagine oneself entering into a dialogue or at least discussion with medieval as well as modern Muslims. He was a great admirer of Arabs and their culture and more generally of Islamic achievements. In his later years, he was highly critical of what was happening to the discipline in which he was raised and which he helped define with such great authority. When, in the 1960s, a group of American scholars proposed a marriage of sorts between traditional oriental studies and the rapidly evolving social sciences, Gibb was an uneasy patron of the enterprise. He openly expressed contempt for some social scientists writing about Islamic societies, as he did not at all recognize in their elaborate paradigms and broad generalizations anything that resembled the Islamic world he knew so intimately and in such detail. To put it differently, there was no Islam in the Islamic world of their conception. In his view, they simply lacked the necessary linguistic and analytical tools to examine the roots of a great civilization that then commanded the allegiance of hundreds of millions of followers and over a geographical landscape that matched if not exceeded that of any premodern empire. For Gibb, as with other orientalists well schooled in philology and the close reading of primary texts, true understanding of Islam began with engaging the rich literary heritage medieval Muslims bequeathed to subsequent generations of the faithful—not exactly the strong suit of most political scientists and anthropologists who entertained thoughts about traditional Islamic culture, nor of a budding generation of historians trained in departments of history rather than textually oriented departments of oriental, or Near Eastern, studies as they were sometimes known.

One could hardly accuse von Grunebaum of not being able to engage Muslim sources. Like Gibb, he was trained as an orientalist; his early work was dedicated to Arabic literature and literary theory. But his demeanor was forged in cosmopolitan Vienna and not the common rooms of the elite British colleges. The medieval Islamic world von Grunebaum describes has a decidedly more elusive feel than that of Gibb. Where Gibb sought clarity and decisive statements, there is an almost teasing quality to the manner in which von Grunebaum wielded arcane references to illustrate a given point, as if inviting his reader to partake of an intricate intellectual game. There is, moreover, that judgmental tone to von Grunebaum's writing we have mentioned. In both his first two popular books, the great cultural accomplishments of the medieval Muslims are seen as an ephemeral moment. From his perspective, there is something in the very nature of traditional Islamic culture that limits the extent to which Muslims who remain truly faithful can adapt to innovative concepts and/or break with the historic past that was said to govern Muslim self-consciousness. There is nothing meanspirited or intentionally demeaning about his view of a cultural sclerosis afflicting a once-vibrant Islamic civilization, nor can his view be as easily dismissed as some decidedly less-learned scholars declare, especially in light of what has transpired since the Islamic world was overtaken by the West. Nevertheless, his notion of Islam being unable to sustain the great civilization of the Middle Ages strikes us as requiring a more refined historical context, or in any event has to be somewhat modified given materials that have since come to light, particularly in the areas of Islamic philosophy and science.

By the mid 1960s, there was a perceived need that Muslims ought to speak for themselves, and so the same press that published von Grunebaum's aforementioned lectures, produced *Islam*, a primer for students of Islamic civilization written by Fazlur Rahman, a devout Muslim born and raised in the India of the British Empire. His book, though it ranges into modern times, generally follows the format and guidelines of Gibb's earlier work in that it is largely concerned with the formation of classical Islamic civilization. Discussing this book, a reviewer in the prestigious *Times Literary Supplement* proclaimed somewhat crankily: "Serious 'scientific' Islamic studies have been left to Western orientalists and their pupils, who have made great contributions but have analyzed Islam 'merely' as a historical datum, as a dead body, so to say," a judgment that may say more of the reviewer than the book reviewed. After having received a traditional Muslim education and university degree in India, Rahman took his Ph.D. at Oxford where Gibb was the Laudian Professor of Arabic. That is to say, Rahman's graduate training was traditional Oxbridge rather than the advanced Islamic curriculum of al-Azhar, the great Muslim institution of higher learning in Cairo. The subject of his dissertation and his most serious intellectual pursuits thereafter was medieval Islamic philosophy, a subject which was linked in medieval times to science, and which occasioned the engagement of Muslims with the worlds of the ancient Greeks and Persians as well as ongoing intellectual contacts with learned non-Muslims of medieval times. One simply cannot embrace this highly technical field of study and be parochial in training and outlook. Rahman writes like the Western-trained orientalist he is, but he also has an agenda that derives from his Muslim upbringing. There is a tinge of apologia in his criticism of Western scholars when they doubt the historicity of various Islamic traditions; above all, like his teacher Gibb, the quintessential orientalist of his time, Rahman envisions an Islam that accommodates itself to the scientific advancements of the modern West, but does so by evolving out of its own creative past.

As with the books of Gibb and the essays of von Grunebaum, there is a paucity of historical background; only the life and times of the Prophet Muhammad are subjected by Rahman to a general review. There is a chapter on sectarian developments, but it needs to be fleshed out more fully against the background of the intricate politics of the occasion. To be sure, Rahman was not overly absorbed by history for its own sake; as noted, his scholarly and personal concerns lie elsewhere. His book, which has gone through several printings, is still widely read more than forty years after its initial publication, and remains standard fare in many classrooms. In effect, his book has displaced Gibb's *Mohammedanism* as the survey of choice for many serious teachers of Islam. As a useful survey of Islamic religion and religious institutions, the book remains important until this day, but it needs to be updated in light of important research since his death, especially in what medieval Muslims labeled "the religious sciences" where a younger generation of scholars has broken new ground.

There have been, to be sure, a number of general surveys published in English over the ensuing decades, certainly too numerous to mention. Among the more reflective and detailed is Jonathan Berkey's *The Formation of Islam* (Cambridge, U.K., 2003) which deals with religion and society in the Near East from 600 to 1800. The virtue of Berkey's work is twofold. For one, it brings to the direct attention of the reader scholarship that has been published since the old masters; it also offers richer historical detail than one finds in other surveys, save von Grunebaum's *Classical Islam*, which it resembles in breadth of interest. As we do in our own project, Berkey seeks to capture a broad audience of students and lay people, but, again as we do, he hopes it will prove useful as well to professional scholars in the field. Catering to all these constituencies is no easy task, as we have discovered. Berkey's is a very ambitious book, to say the least. He moves beyond the world of Islam to tell his story against the backdrop of a larger Near Eastern canvas, in our opinion a brave and certainly correct decision. But in doing so he sometimes falls back on secondary sources that are either suspect or outdated.

There is at times a need for a more critical and informed judgment of the scholars on whom he relies, Islamicists and non-Islamicists alike. There are pitfalls in relying on reflective and extended essays written by scholars who base their views largely on secondary readings. One can only admire the author's reach and the need for a detailed book that sees the formation of Islamic civilization as part of a larger picture that extends from late antiquity until the outset of modern times in the Near East, but with a picture so vast, so intricate, and so complicated by the need to make judgments well beyond the sphere of his own learning, however wide it may be, there are occasions when consultation and cautious language might have better served Berkey and his audience. Despite these concerns, there is indeed much to admire in Berkey's volume. Because it paints on so broad a canvas, it occupies a unique place among the more recent surveys available in English to general reading audiences. Others are more derivative of the old classics and none carry the authority of their learned predecessors, thus leaving a serious and disturbingly large gap to be filled.

We have cited the relative absence of historical context from many of the standard surveys of medieval Islam. Although there is no lack of chronicles in Near Eastern languages that describe in various ways the events of the times, in the world of medieval Islamic scholarship, history never attained the prestigious status of the religious and philosophical sciences. It was at best an ancillary discipline that focused on the lives of great men and collective groups whose behavior might set guidelines for Muslims contemplating their own actions. In fact, Islamic history only became a truly independent discipline in the Western academy during the last half of the twentieth century, that is, late in the development of the modern orientalist project. Most of the early orientalist works surveying the medieval period merely paraphrased the historical sources then known, producing, thereby, histories that repeated the medieval narratives as if they were a true reflection of events past.

The first survey of Islamic history intended for a broad English reading public that offered a truly reflective presentation of medieval Islamic history was Bernard Lewis's *The Arabs in History*, a short volume written in the elegant and highly readable style that has become the hallmark of all his many published tomes. First written in the 1940s, this work has been reprinted many times and was revised somewhat in an edition published some fifty years later. Now in his 90s and considered the doyen of Near Eastern historians, Lewis managed to compress a prodigious amount of learning and historical analysis into a series of chapters that stimulate the imagination of seasoned specialists as well as introduce the novice reader to the history of the Arab Near East. Most of the book is taken up with the medieval environment and as such it became over the years perhaps the single most read introduction to medieval Islamic history in and out of the classroom. Much has been written of the history of those times in learned articles and densely annotated monographs, but to date, Lewis's work still holds up as a primer for those interested in the history of medieval Islam as opposed to merely the development of its religious thought and institutions.

In 1995, Lewis published a more expansive work, *The Middle East: A Brief History of the Last 2,000 Years* (Weidenfeld & Nicholson, U.K. Scribners, U.S.). By its very title, it is clear the book was intended to deal with an extended history of the region from ancient to recent times. Like von Grunebaum whose works were written nearly a half century earlier, Lewis is concerned with the formation of historical consciousness, but as he also discusses history as it unfolded in successive eras, the reader is able to establish a clearer view how over extended generations Muslims (and also their subjects) came to define themselves in the present, interpret the past, and anticipate the future. Above all, Lewis has captured with great clarity the indebtedness to the past that still haunts traditional Near Eastern societies, Muslim or non-Muslim. He is much too astute to claim that these societies, particularly Muslim society, are incapable of breaking with all of established precedent and as a result have remained essentially static, but he has too much integrity to pander to the notion that debts to the past do not exist.

We have no idea what audience this book has attracted, but the fluid writing, enriched with anecdotes drawn from primary sources, and spiced with no small amount of irony and humor, is a model of how to combine great learning and readability to attract the attention of both scholars and a general reading public. Scholars steeped in the historiography of medieval times can appreciate, if not indeed envy, the manner in which Lewis applied his vast knowledge and razor sharp historical intelligence to produce surveys of Islamic history written in such fluid prose it could be absorbed by the intelligent reader who had absolutely no knowledge of the world of Islam. Islamic studies are blessed with any number of learned scholars and historians of keen insight, but, among living historians, Lewis remains *sui generis* in communicating complex ideas to the general reader.

With models such as Lewis, Gibb, von Grunebaum, and Rahman, the authors of this tome have found shaping their own project to be a humbling experience, as have no doubt other scholars attempting to write surveys of Islamic civilization. As historians, we would be remiss if we did not note the effort of our contemporary Hugh Kennedy, whose book *The Prophet and the Age of the Caliphates* (Longman/Pearson, Harlow UK, 2004) is an excellent survey that roughly covers the chronological period which frames our work. The strength of Kennedy's book is the manner in which it sums up the general state of our historical knowledge based on an intimate familiarity with both primary and secondary sources. But Kennedy, by his own admission, shies away from speculative interpretation bearing in mind the needs of readers who approach the history of the Near East for the first time and who thus require the basic framework of chronological narrative.

In preparing our own primer for understanding the Islamic Middle Ages, we sought a less straightforward narrative. We were constantly aware of how difficult it is to strike a balance between political and social history, and religious institutions and scholarship, especially as we were obliged to present readers with a text that does not sacrifice scholarly integrity and is, at the same time fully accessible not only to scholars of the medieval Islamic world but also to a broad audience curious about Islam and the Near East. In effect, we have attempted to emulate the best of our learned predecessors within a single volume. That is to say, we have tried to provide an understanding of medieval Islamic civilization that addresses its myriad intellectual and religious achievements within the framework of an evolving political and social history that both was shaped by and helped shape how medieval Muslims understood themselves and the larger world beyond. To that end, we initially included four chapters on monotheist minorities in the lands of Islam: the world of Islam's Jews and Christians, a subject which, oddly enough, has never received a proper place of its own in any of the surveys of medieval Islam. The discussion of Christian-Muslim relations also enriched greatly our treatment of the Umayyad dynasty (661–750 C.E.), a polity that some readers may feel has received less attention than it deserves in our current narrative. We also included a double chapter on Islamic philosophy and science, subjects closely linked to intellectual cross-pollination with a more ancient world of scholarship in which medieval Jews and Christians played an active role along with the Muslims. All of this made for much too long a book and considerable material has been excised for a future tome including these five chapters and a lengthy segment on the formation of oriental studies in the West.

Specialists of the region and period will note its strong suit was intended to be its treatment of history; that is hardly a surprise, as both authors are primarily historians of the medieval Near East. Where we have departed from most past surveys is not only in spending more time and effort supplying the historical background of the events discussed, but in alerting readers as to how difficult it often is to fashion a coherent historical narrative from the very complex and often contradictory primary sources at our disposal. As we shall have recourse to say, perhaps more times than our readers will want to be reminded, the story of the Islamic Middle Ages, as told by the chroniclers, is more often than not the story that should have been, or might have been, rather than the story that was. We felt obliged to inform our readers of this salient fact by interrogating various Muslim traditions as we weighed the historical evidence and drew our conclusions, sometimes confidently, and sometimes being forced to speculate because of the ambiguous evidence at our disposal.

As historians of political and social history, we are forced to admit our treatment of Islamic religion, religious institutions, and scholarship is more derivative than we would like; we have been obliged to rely heavily on the researches of a number of scholars who have helped reshape our own understanding of the aforementioned subjects by challenging the conventional wisdom of earlier generations. Our debt to them is clearly acknowledged. We shamefully admit as well a neglect of belles-lettres and artistic production but our mandate to produce a book about religious civilization has at least given us a lame excuse not to pretend knowing more than we know, let alone expose what we do not know to our reading audience. In any case, our cup was already overflowing. Given the complexity of bringing so much material together in the manner we have chosen, what has emerged is a book far lengthier than the earlier surveys devoted either to religion and religious institutions or to historical developments alone. We trust readers of all sorts will appreciate what this book attempts to say rather than what it does not.

We began the Preface by noting this book is a part of a larger project that falls under the rubric of medieval religions. The very concept of the Middle Ages, generally understood as the period following ancient times and preceding momentous historical developments that eventually led to the shaping of modern Europe, is a thoroughly European invention that articulates European (and Byzantine) experience seen in retrospect by historians of the West. Conventional wisdom emanating from the Western academy has always placed Islamic civilization within this wider picture of the Middle Ages. At first glance, there is every reason to do so. The Prophet Muhammad began his mission in the seventh century. In the decades that followed the Arabs conquered the Byzantine lands of the Fertile Crescent and North Africa. In 711 they invaded the Iberian Peninsula, establishing a foothold in Europe that they maintained until 1492 and the fall of Granada. They suffered the encroachment of Christian Europe during the Crusades, contested control of the Mediterranean with European navies, and engaged the distant Christians in commerce and trade either directly or indirectly. The Islamic world also served as a conduit by which the classical traditions of learning that had languished and then all but disappeared in the Latin West were reintroduced via extensive translation activity emanating from lands of the Islamic east and Spain. In all these circumstances, the Islamic world that occupied the Fertile Crescent, the southern rim of the Mediterranean, territories conquered from the Byzantine heartland, and on occasion Sicily and other islands within the great sea was part and parcel of what we now broadly define the world of the Middle Ages.

When, however, one examines the development of Islamic religious thought and institutions, with their great debt to a more ancient monotheist past, and the formation of Islamic philosophy and science that continued and advanced the great traditions of the Hellenistic world, much of which took place in the first four Islamic centuries, one could just as easily consider the civilization forged by the Muslims within the time Europeans labeled the Middle Ages (certainly the Low Middle Ages), as the last great civilization of Late Antiquity. Moreover, the Islamic world did not undergo the sort of reformation that changed the political landscape of Europe, nor did it quite experience anything that resembled the European Renaissance at a comparable time. In that respect, one could argue that medieval Islam, using a descriptive label originating in the Western academy, continued well beyond the chronological parameters of Europe's Middle Ages. For many historians of the Islamic world, or in any case the Arab world, the Middle Ages really end and the modern age begins only with Napoleon's invasion of Egypt in 1798, signaling thereby the weakness of the Muslims in the Near East and the beginnings of the imperial encroachment of the West.

There was also a vast Islamic world that extended far beyond the direct or even indirect reaches of European influence in what Westerners describe as the Low Middle Ages (600–1050 C.E.). The lands of Islam situated further to the east, extending from current-day Iran well into Central Asia were hardly an integral part of the Latin West, nor were the early Islamic polities that were created in Afghanistan and later in the subcontinent of India, or in sub-Saharan Africa. On the other hand, it seems a bit churlish to deny Islam a place in a series on medieval civilizations. The question remains how the Muslims themselves understood their civilization at the time and indeed how they continue to understand it today. That brings us to the important problem of establishing meaningful periods in Islamic history, and why we have chosen to begin and end our account of medieval Islam as we have, namely from roughly the seventh and tenth centuries C.E.

Scholars who teach medieval Islamic history and culture in the universities of the West have divided their courses in different ways, each determined, at least to some extent, by limits set by academic calendars, the number of teachers available and their competencies, and the demands of the larger programs in which those courses are situated. Virtually all surveys of medieval Islam begin in sixth century C.E. Arabia and the life of the Prophet Muhammad, but there are sharp divisions as to how organize the subsequent material. In each case, the individual course begins and ends with what instructors would label a major watershed in the history of the Islamic peoples—a moment of history where historians perceive a dramatic break with the past. One can of course appreciate the all too apparent significance of particular moments in history, but many historians of the West have come to understand these seemingly dramatic breaks as the end of ongoing processes that are long in the making, thus blurring the lines between one era of history and another and rendering the notion of watershed itself somewhat problematic. Muslims of the times were well aware that momentous events shaped their destinies and that of Muslims and civilizations past. A close reading of the more reflective medieval chroniclers would seem to indicate they were also conscious that long-developing trends played a role in historic events that unfolded, but their basic means of interpreting the past, understanding the present, and anticipating the future was to imagine history as God's will made manifest in the affairs of humankind and the natural order. Needless to say, that took them only so far. To give further explanation to events, they turned to the behavior of individuals and more inclusive groups. In sum: in so far as history was God's invention, it remained a mysterious process that defied definitive explanation; but in so far as it was also the result of human activity, it allowed for moral judgment based on the behavior of individual rulers and more inclusive groups. It comes as no surprise that historical writing in the medieval Islamic world is heavily biographical, ranging from the biographies of noteworthy figures arranged according to chronological layers (in Arabic *tabaqat*) to historical and belletristic works arranged according to dynasties. By the tenth century C.E., Arabic chroniclers had invented a novel way of dividing historical time by recording the events of successive years within the dynastic arrangement. One cannot determine from the world view of contemporaneous Muslims any descriptive label or series of labels that would enable current Western scholars of Islam to divide the experience of the Muslims and chart the growth of Islamic civilization in a manner that would satisfy intellectual sensibilities forged in the Western academy. In that sense, to speak of medieval Islam is to refer to a label of convenience which is no worse and no better than any other.

Our book is largely concerned with historic and cultural developments that molded early Islamic civilization, a process that began in pre-Islamic Arabia and continued through parts of the tenth century C.E. It was during that period that the basic political, legal, and religious institutions of Islam first developed into a more or less coherent whole that was to serve as a paradigm for many if not most Islamic societies until the onset of modern times and beyond. This does not imply that Islamic civilization remained static, that it was or is incapable of assimilating new ideas and forms, or of giving rise to new institutions or shifts in religious attitudes. But those aforementioned times shaped and continue to shape in fundamental ways the historical consciousness of the Muslim faithful, especially in the Near East where Islam was born and first embarked on the path to becoming a world religion. Those four centuries were in every sense the formative period of Islamic culture and civilization and thus serve to explain why our subtitle reads: *The Origins and Shaping of Classical Islamic Civilization*.

The main text of the book is divided into three major parts, each of which contains chapters of varying length. Part One deals with the Prophet Muhammad and the origins of the Islamic community, in Arabic the *ummah*. Here we analyze a complex story which has shaped Muslim self-consciousness for some 1,300 years; namely the creation of a universal religious community that recognizes no distinctions among the believers. The narrative of our sources mixes traces of an apparent history with demonstrable legends, always a difficult mix for the serious historian. The second part deals with the transformation of the ummah into a polity that commanded a historical stage equal to that of the Roman

Empire at its height. We trace the development of that polity in and beyond the Arabian Peninsula, which gave birth to Islam with a special emphasis on the consequences of the ummah's inner contradictions: the claim to true universality for all its constituents versus residual tribal sensibilities and other lingering loyalties to kinship groups, as well as local and regional ties that claimed the allegiance of Muslims old and new. Were that not enough to compromise the idealized community of the faithful, there was also conflict between leading elements of the Prophet's household, which, from time to time, undermined the legitimacy of his successors. And yet, in their heyday, the Muslim successors to the Prophet, particularly the Abbasid caliphs of the eighth and early ninth centuries, were able to establish the solid foundations of a centralized authority that led in turn to effective rule. Alas, the regime began to crumble under the weight of declining revenues and what had become overly centralized governance. The last chapter of Part Two thus deals with the emerging cracks within universal Islamic empire and the incipient decline of the caliphate. Part Three deals with the religious institutions and scholarship that gave sustenance to the state and set boundaries for the religious behavior of Muslims regardless of where they were situated. Here we investigate the central role of the Qur'an and its interpreters and note the inventiveness of Muslim scholars having to legislate in ever-changing conditions and venues, a task made difficult as true revelation was said to have ended with Muhammad, the last of God's prophets. Their capacity for innovation under these circumstances is a truly remarkable story, as is the intellectual sophistication invoked by Muslim scholars. We also note the existence of popular forms of religion, the reaction of Muslim ascetics and pietists to what they considered the dry fare of theologians and legal scholars. All this has made for a complex and highly engaging study.

Acknowledgments

The ancient Jewish sage Rabbi Akiba reportedly said that he had learned a great deal from his teachers, more from his colleagues, but most of all, he profited from discussions with his students. There can be no question that our intellectual debt to others is widely distributed—so much so it would have been impracticable and perhaps an injustice to list all those to whom we owe special gratitude, not only because that list would have been exceedingly long, but also for fear we would have inadvertently omitted any number of individuals.

A leading Islamicist once remarked to his students that "scholarship is a lonely business." By that he meant one bears a personal and heavy responsibility to uphold the standards and intellectual integrity established by earlier generations of scholars. In authoring this book we have always been keenly aware of that great burden, and as with all our writings we had always to consider what our mentors, official and unofficial, might think, be it from their position in the current academy or from the celestial academy into which they have entered over the passing years. With that in mind, this book is dedicated to Bernard Lewis and M. J. Kister; and to memories of S. D. Goitein, David Ayalon, and Franz Rosenthal *z"l*.

According to tradition, Rabbi Akiba was immensely indebted to his wife for her encouragement and support. In similar fashion, we acknowledge the supportive role of our wives Phyllis Lassner and Daniela Gobetti, formidable scholars in their own right. Their insightful and constructive criticisms, born of literary studies and political theory along with a healthy dose of common sense, has persuaded us, albeit at times somewhat reluctantly, to rethink elements of our intellectual framework and presentation of ideas. Being able to share intellectual concerns with them has made our scholarship and writing a less of a lonely business; indeed, it has made our vocation as historians a joy.

As regards the editing and production of this volume, our thanks go out to the staff of the Praeger Press. Finally, readers should be aware that the markers that signify long vowels in Arabic as well as the diacritical marks that distinguish certain Arabic letters from others have been omitted from our transliteration of Arabic words. Readers familiar with Arabic will have no problem because of the absence of these marks; those unfamiliar with the language will not notice their absence, nor will their absence change the meaning of any text.

PART I

MUHAMMAD AND THE ORIGINS OF THE ISLAMIC COMMUNITY (UMMAH)

Arabia on the Eve of Islam

One may harbor the impression that the Arabian Peninsula, a vast expanse of some million square miles, was until the birth hour of Islam a hostile and remote land. In truth, pre-Islamic Arabia was not a single geographical environment cut off from all other neighboring civilizations. Much as it is today, the peninsula was marked by diverse landscapes formed by mountain ranges, different types of water beds, underground cisterns, and—in some regions—vast arid zones. Each of the different landscapes gave rise to its own ecosystem and, where human habitation was possible, to diverse patterns of settlement and networks of communication.

To the south, mountain peaks, which reach as high as 14,000 feet, intercept heavily seeded clouds that produce seasonal monsoon rains. Too heavy to pass over the mountains, the clouds jettison their waters, causing torrential downpours. In ancient times, water thus made available on a regular basis permitted widespread cultivation. Failure to control water resources and distribute them proportionately could have resulted in disaster for settlements along the entire irrigation system. As a result, the south, in its heyday, was ruled by kings and petty dynasts whose combined influence extended over significant domains.

The kingdoms of the south were also enriched by trade involving other regions of the peninsula and by contacts with lands in East Africa and also the Fertile Crescent, the geographical arc extending from Egypt through ancient Mesopotamia. By the early decades of the sixth century C.E., the century in which the Muslim Prophet Muhammad was born, much of Arabia had been penetrated by external elements. The south in particular was subjected to foreign stimuli—political, economic, and cultural. Abyssinians, crossing the Red Sea from Africa, settled in Yemen, the southwestern region of the Arabian Peninsula. They brought with them Christianity and the potential to promote the interests of the Christian rulers from whose land they came. In the southeast of the peninsula, subjects of the Sasanian monarchs, the inheritors of the ancient kingdoms of Persia, established colonies and married with the local population, thereby creating pockets of foreign political influence that would later spread to other areas of the south. Beyond Arabia to the northwest loomed the Byzantine Empire, a polity generally supportive of their Christian Abyssinian brethren.

The presence of foreign elements in the south gave rise to new cultural and material tastes. In the areas of Christian penetration, it also diminished the political and moral authority of the local pagan dynasts and their allies. Religious missions representing various branches of Christianity took root. Jews were also part of the local landscape, although the structure of their communities in south Arabia and the nature of their beliefs and observances remain largely unknown. In any case, it was the spread of Christianity that occasioned concern among the southern rulers. Central authority established by pagan rulers had been slowly unraveling amidst political and economic conditions that are yet to be ascertained in detail or reconstructed with certainty. There are reports of a major decline in cultivatable lands and with that there was tension among groups competing for living space. In such circumstances, it is not likely that systems of governance escaped unscathed or that established beliefs and religious practices went unchallenged.

Cognizant that the old paganism was in retreat, the southern rulers seemingly viewed Christian missionaries, regardless of their religious persuasion, as a vanguard for powerful forces from abroad: the Abyssinians across the Red Sea and the Byzantines to the north. In an apparent move to counter the growing influence of Christianity, the Yemenite monarch Dhu Nuwas embraced Judaism, or, put somewhat more cautiously, he embraced religious beliefs and practices that might have resembled local forms of Judaism in some way or another. As regards Dhu Nuwas's understanding of Judaism and his genuine sympathy for that faith, we know little and are unlikely to learn much if anything more. Be that as it may, the Jewish communities of south Arabia, whatever their numbers and whatever their beliefs, were apt to remain loyal to whosoever ruled them, because for the Jews there was no external power that might make claims on their allegiance. Lacking any foreign patrons, they could turn only to their God and their temporal rulers for support. As was the case wherever Jews were then settled, the Jews of Arabia represented no danger at all to established authority.

As champion of his new faith, Dhu Nuwas reportedly invoked stern measures against the Christian settlers of his domains. Some scholars have suggested that these actions were in reprisal for well-documented policies against the Jews of the Byzantine Empire. It seems more likely that the objective of Dhu Nuwas's policy toward the Christian settlers was to break their southern enclaves. But Christianity was already rooted in the Yemen, and that was enough of a pretext for the powerful Abyssinian ruler to intervene. Within short order, Abyssinian forces reduced much of the Yemen to an Abyssinian protectorate and, having gained supremacy in the south, they then sought to influence events further north. As one moved northward in Arabia, geography was less hospitable to human settlement, and so history tended to run a different course. As in the south, there is rain, but the northern Mediterranean rains are intermittent, so the average yearly precipitation is not all that meaningful; years, indeed decades, may pass without significant rainfall. Then suddenly there may be a great downpour that causes violent flooding. The residue of water may give rise to some form of vegetation, but the flora will be short-lived as the land dries between distant rains. In the most arid regions, vast desert areas that are marked by perennial drought, even the most devastating flash floods are quickly absorbed. Beyond the southern rim, extensive sand dunes cover literally half the remaining peninsula. The enormous Rub' al-Khali or "Empty Quarter," an expanse of several hundred thousand square miles, is for the most part uninhabitable even for herdsmen and was not passable before the introduction of modern transport.

Nevertheless, some desert zones do permit settlement. There are sites within the desert landscape that retain water at the surface or trap water in underground cavities, water which can then be brought to the surface. One finds patches of land with sufficient vegetation to maintain herds, at least for part of the year, and, where water is more abundant, extended areas of green appear in the form of oases, sites that may allow for the cultivation of variegated crops including fruit-bearing trees and life-sustaining cereals. Some oasis dwellers engaged in agriculture, others were active in handicrafts and/or other commercial enterprises. The Hijaz, the birthplace of Muhammad in western Arabia and the starting point of his religious mission, was an area marked by oasis settlements and adjoining lands inhabited by neighboring Bedouins.

The Hijaz on the Eve of Islam

By all accounts, the Hijaz oases on the eve of Islam were narrowly circumscribed living environments. Although the number of inhabitants of any given oasis cannot be determined with assurance, in all likelihood, the smaller settlements contained populations numbering in the hundreds, at most. Where the oases were, however, clustered within a larger area, such as at the Prophet's adopted city Medina, a site that extended over some twenty miles and allowed for large-scale cultivation of dates, the number of inhabitants was likely to reach a thousand and more. But these settlements too might be held captive to competition for living space. On the whole, areas for cultivation and pasturage beyond the south of Arabia were limited. The shortage of lands on which to settle and graze was presumably exacerbated by the breakdown of agriculture in the south, a critical turn that purportedly led over time to increasing nomads and migrations northward, particularly in the sixth century c.e. That wholesale shift of societal units produced a ripple effect. Groups that had moved on because they were unable to find land to sustain themselves, contested hitherto remote units for pasturage and water, circumstances that led as a matter of course to feelings of tension and instability throughout the oasis regions.

Separated from one another by desert zones without natural links, many oases were, before the migrations, relatively isolated from the nearest areas of extensive settlement. As a result, the oasis tribesmen and the Bedouins who were situated in the surrounding lands came to value self-reliance tempered by a strong sense of collective responsibility. The absence of natural links to serve as highways or waterways created a margin of safety because opponents had to travel great distances in order to engage the oasis dwellers and their immediate neighbors in combat. The risks and energy required for that kind of fighting were better saved for an absolutely critical moment. Raiding was not uncommon in the desert areas, but it was more sport than warfare. As a rule, tribal warriors concerned with demonstrations of manliness preferred posturing to life-threatening engagements. When issues had to be decided by force of arms, the tribes might resort to ritual champions in single combat rather than mobilize for all-out war.

However, circumstances had seemingly changed. The general decline in living space throughout the peninsula was likely enough an incentive for tribal groups to negotiate long distances and engage in the uncertainties of warfare. With increased tensions, the oasis dwellers and their nearby Bedouin allies were compelled to enter into far-flung alliances so as to protect their environment from the encroachment of predators displaced from their native lands by force or natural circumstances. One generally refers to the oasis dwellers and the Bedouins as tribesmen because their societal units were organized along tribal lines. Modern social scientists are inclined to regard the very notion of "tribe" a highly problematic concept, and so a word of explanation is in order. We refer to tribe as it is conventionally referred to by historians of the Near East and as it was and continues to be understood by the Arabs themselves. That is, a tribe refers to tightly concentrated kinship structures made up of immediate blood relatives and non-blood relations who are allowed to join the group by complex and highly variegated formulas of adoption. By their very nature, groups closely related by blood ties tend to be at first self-contained units with clearly defined markers of identity. The internal markers are maintained by extensive marriage within the group, preferably among first cousins so as to keep the blood lines pure. The external markers can be distinctive dress, battle standards, calls to arms, and, above all, territorial boundaries staked out by the kinsmen and their allies. Where significant distances separate different kinship groups, identities and tribal boundaries tend to remain, more or less, intact. But when boundaries are traversed and territory is contested, circumstances may forge a need for temporary alliances against invaders. Agreements may then be established between proud groups not related by blood but equal in prestige and fighting strength. Newly minted alliances might also reflect the soliciting of weaker, less prestigious clients, to bolster strong military forces that seek to become even stronger. In such circumstances, weaker groups, unable to go it alone, but retaining residual fighting strength, might be inclined to ally themselves with patrons anxious to bulk up their own military might. With many warriors in tow, larger more powerful alliances could dissuade potential aggressors from encroaching upon their lands. Military strength could thus be used for deterrence as well as territorial expansion. Groups of equal standing brought together for purposes of mutual protection (*tanasur*) might eventually merge through arranged marriages, thus creating a larger blood unit over time; clients of lesser standing could also became part of prestigious kinship groups, but generally not in circumstances that afforded them equal prestige and hence social standing. Their daughters might be married off to the younger sons of their patrons but not to the first-born. When it came to the eldest son, the patron would seek a paternal cousin from among his woman kinfolk. Nor would patrons be inclined to marry off their daughters to clients of lesser social standing.

When still more fighting men were needed, auxiliary troops or hired mercenaries could fill the ranks of newly forged and powerful tribal armies. Neighboring Bedouins or bands of tribally organized misfits were often employed for such purposes, but the allegiance of these marginal elements to the larger group was tempered by the misfits' powerful ethos of independence and their clearly defined sense of self-interest. There was always the danger that these bands of fighting men would desert their allies when circumstances proved expedient. The formation of tribal alliances of various sorts offered seemingly rational solutions to tensions brought on by increased competition, but the creation of more inclusive groups was bound to weaken the ideological foundations of Arab tribalism. Individual units demanded that blood ties be kept as pure as possible, and, related to that, that kinsmen should not have to answer to any but their own folk. Given the tense conditions of sixth- and seventh-century Arabia, the desert Arabs found themselves in a quandary. There was the need for larger and larger groups to protect joint interests, but that forced individual tribal units to compromise their blood lines and, beyond that, their much-cherished independence.

Moreover, the tribal associations could eventually reach a theoretical limit that made them too large, too diffuse as regards bloodlines, and ultimately too unwieldy to command allegiance from all segments of the alliance, particularly the more distant allies. Internal squabbling inevitably eroded that sense of esprit de corps that made tribal armies effective fighting units. Seeking greater influence through greater numbers, the largest tribal associations could be stretched thin over too large a geographical landscape. Such alliances would then become extremely cumbersome, especially when the central actors, the tribes at the fulcrum of power, were forced to react quickly to events in distant locations where their influence might be marginal at best. Because of the anarchic sensibilities that pervaded tribal life, the more remote elements of any alliance might become embroiled in conflicts that were not in the best interests of the major partners, including conflicts with other remote members who might have been occasional adversaries, if not former enemies of long standing, prior to joining the alliance. In such circumstances, the powerful tribes or kinship groups at the center of the alliance would be hard pressed to choose sides among quarrelsome groups at the periphery. Worse yet, they might respond halfheartedly on behalf of one or another contesting party; either response would likely be seen as an act of betrayal by the other party, in any case an act occasioning a loss of honor. At that, offended units situated on the periphery might well take leave of the larger alliance and abandon their erstwhile confederates. That would have been especially true of tribal units that reluctantly joined the alliance, that is, tribesmen who had been more or less coerced into recognizing the hegemony of more powerful partners attempting to extend their influence over an increased territorial arc. Whatever the circumstances, the propensity for anarchy that so dominated kinship groups in the oasis regions meant that, at any moment, elements of a particular tribal alliance might be inclined to break away and pursue their own course of action.

No individual family unit, certainly no larger association of blood relatives, willingly recognized the authority of an external group, nor would they voluntarily obey the dictates of non-kinsmen. Put somewhat differently, they would not offer allegiance to another clan or tribe because in their hearts they recognized that group's authority. To be sure, when reality intervened, individual tribal units could be forced to reckon the calculus of power. With survival at stake, they could be compelled, if not coerced, into acknowledging the material wealth and military superiority of those more powerful than themselves. Faced with that overwhelming reality, they would compromise their precious independence and become part and parcel of larger tribal associations, even if such arrangements reduced them to mere clients of more prestigious patrons. Despite the salving effect of tribal diplomacy, a kind of formal political theater designed to mollify reluctant partners by allowing them to retain a mock independence and hence dignity, clients so obtained rendered their allegiance grudgingly. Patrons could claim no legitimate authority; they compelled allegiance by demonstrating their power, whether apparent or real, to those who saw themselves as vulnerable and in need of protectors. But allegiance obtained in this way could never be taken for granted. Compelled by circumstances into a demeaning relationship, disgruntled clients waited only for the opportune moment to reclaim their much valued independence and self-esteem, most likely when patrons whose networks of carefully cultivated alliances had reached a point of diminishing returns.

As constituent units broke away, and the large tribal associations began to unravel, smaller, more cohesive groups espied the situation like scavengers circling their prey. And then, at the opportune moment, they acted resolutely. Increasing their own fighting strength, and hence prestige, the smaller more cohesive groups attracted allies equal to themselves as well as displaced remnants of sundered alliances, small tribal units that were now at risk without proper protection and therefore in need of new patrons. These newer augmented tribal groupings then became dominant until such a point when they too would become too large and too unwieldy, setting into motion once again the breakdown of tribal organization. The large tribal configurations beyond the south were not constant entities; they were forever changing in a climate of great instability and shifting allegiances. Whatever advantages there might have been to establishing some sort of centralized authority—as the southern kingdoms did before events eventually overtook them—these advantages were stifled by deep-rooted tribal anarchy and the rejection of formal institutions of rule. Therein lay the paradox of a society simultaneously threatened by centripetal and centrifugal forces. The tribal associations faced the dual threat of being forced to give ground to other more powerful groups or imploding because of internal stresses.

There was, however, one area that offered considerable promise to large-scale cooperation among tribesmen—the potential of lucrative trade with lands situated beyond the peninsula and regions within it. Wider and more effective control of local environments was possible when two or more associations linked by geography promoted common economic interests. Because long-distance trade allowed all groups situated along the trade route to share in the profits, there was an impetus for oasis dwellers and Bedouins to form arrangements that would be mutually enriching. Suppressing the urge to interfere with caravans passing through their tribal domains, Arabs benefiting from long-distance trade instead allowed free passage to caravans transporting a wide variety of sought-after items. This cooperation, born of immediate economic interests, led to larger tribal associations sharing common values and even religious sentiments. Ultimately, these cooperative efforts gave way in Islamic times to a new societal paradigm in which religious ties supplemented and then replaced blood as the most significant marker of identification within the extended social unit.

The emergent Islamic community (*ummah*) disavowed—at least theoretically—distinctions of ethnicity, geographical origins, and even social status. All Muslims were equal in the eyes of their Prophet and the one and only God. In reality, the birth and subsequent growth of the Islamic community was much affected by prevailing tribal ideals and by social cleavage. The ummah may have been conceived by Muslims as an egalitarian religious community born of a particular moment and geographical environment, but it evolved within a larger tribal setting of complex social and economic change. In Arabia, and later in the surrounding lands, the Islamic community continued to be directly affected by the lingering effects of Arab tribalism. Indeed, the initial shaping of the Islamic community and the subsequent growth of Islam must be explained, at least in part, as a consequence of tribal societies subjected to the stresses of transformative change caused by instability throughout the Arabian Peninsula.

Multi-Tribal Cooperation: The Expansion of Tribal Politics

Even before the rise of Islam, Muhammad's kinsmen, the clans of Quraysh, attempted to link, albeit loosely, religion, trade, and tribal politics. Their objective was the creation of a larger and more effective association of tribal units in which they themselves would play the dominant role. The geographical center of this unfolding plan was Mecca, an ancient and much revered shrine site in the Hijaz region of West Arabia. There was great prestige in administering its pagan shrine and thus much could be gained by Quraysh from evicting its guardians, the tribesmen of Khuza'ah. At first, the clans of Quraysh lived as herdsmen in the bleak lands surrounding Mecca. Sometime, probably on the eve of the sixth century, they managed to enter Mecca and displace the Khuza'ah as guardians of the Ka'bah, its holy shrine. Some of the Quraysh settled in the hollow near the water supply and Ka'bah, a choice location, while others occupied the slopes of the surrounding hills. The clans of the inner city (*bitakh*) became responsible for the administration of Mecca and its dealings with the world beyond; the inhabitants of the slopes, the outer areas (*zawahir*), were in turn more depended upon for their fighting skills. Seemingly united against the external world, the clans of Quraysh nevertheless quarreled among themselves; various factions, seeking advantage, established alliances that even broke down family lines. In that sense, the Quraysh were a microcosm of a much larger tribal phenomenon. But in the end whatever acrimony existed among individual and extended families was not allowed to compromise the evolving economic and political interests of Quraysh as a whole. These interests were linked to developing Mecca, promoting its shrine in the religious life of Arabia, and, related to that, fostering newly established political and economic networks based on long-distance trade.

In tribal societies, which tend to anarchy, there can be no formal institutions of government. Still, the Quraysh, having understood the importance of cooperation among themselves, established a consultative assembly (*mala'*) in which the leading notables of the clans participated. At first glance, the work of the mala' would seem to have been entirely deliberative; the assembly could not formally administer the affairs of Mecca by directing the individual clans to act, as they were nominally autonomous units within the larger society of Quraysh. That being the case, the only effective decisions taken by the mala' would have been those agreed upon unanimously by all the participants. Nevertheless, tribal politics allowed for, indeed encouraged, back channels in which to manipulate decision making. For no clan among the various clans of Quraysh could dictate policy. Nor could any single clan defy a decision taken by all the others. Even the most powerful clans could not expect to retain their influence, based as it was largely on wealth acquired through long-distance trade. The enterprising merchants of Quraysh always feared unexpected misfortune, the worst scenario being the loss of an entire shipment of goods due to natural disaster or one occasioned by human intervention. There was also the possibility that fluctuating prices at a particular time might deny merchants expected profits. As a result, the relative strength of the clans shifted from time to time, giving rise to realignments in clan politics. The less-powerful clans sought alliances among themselves to prevent the dictates of their more powerful kinsmen. High marks were thus accorded to those leaders who were capable of manipulating the current situation to their clan's advantage. In the end, it would appear that the Quraysh as a whole maintained the self-discipline to promote their larger objectives. The responsibilities for attending the affairs of the shrine site and transforming Mecca into a commercial center were negotiated without serious disturbance among themselves. Where the Khuza'ah lived in makeshift dwellings, the Quraysh, now fully sedentary within Mecca itself, built permanent housing. The water supply was expanded and civic improvements were in evidence throughout the site. In time, Mecca became a vibrant area of settlement. It never was a place of agricultural production like the great oases of western Arabia—foodstuffs had to be imported. Mecca's new fame, and indeed its growth, rested with the marriage of its sacred status as a shrine to pagan gods to its strategic position close to the caravan routes. The defining moment in the transformation of Mecca from bare shrine site to commercial and religious-political center occurred during the lifetime of Hashim, the progenitor of the clan bearing his name, and a direct ancestor of the Prophet Muhammad.

It was Hashim, the great-grandfather of the Prophet, who attempted to take over the ancient trade routes controlled by Yemenites. At first, when the Quraysh were mere herdsmen living in the vicinity of Mecca, their function was to supply the southerners with the camels required for caravans. At a later point, they led the caravans themselves, but their trade was largely confined to areas not all that distant from Mecca. Finally, they attempted to play the dominant role in the international trade controlled by the Yemenites, a move that elicited a failed invasion by an Abyssinian-led expeditionary force from the south. Running the caravan trade was not simply a matter of keeping the southerners at arm's length. The dominance of the Quraysh in long-distance trade and the subsequent emergence of Mecca as an important commercial center were the result of skilled negotiations between the Qurayshites and the authorities who controlled the commercial distribution centers in the lands adjacent to the Arabian Peninsula. First Hashim and then his brothers obtained trading charters (*ilaf*) giving Qurasyh and their caravans free passage and privileged status beyond the frontier. With that, the Quraysh could conduct business at caravan terminals in Syria-Palestine and other locations. This was an opportune moment for tribesmen who had raised camels but a few generations earlier.

Prolonged warfare between the Byzantine and Sasanian empires had destabilized the borders separating the imperial states north of Arabia. As a result, the major trade routes transporting wares from the east became hazardous and filled with risk for most merchants. Even in times of peace, the Byzantines were dependent on their Sasanian neighbors for materials arriving from the east, as both the major inland waterways and great overland trade routes first traversed regions ruled by the emperor of Iran. An alternate path that led to the caravan terminals of the Byzantine Empire had obvious advantages. Following a pattern established earlier by the Yemenites, Hashim and his fellow Qurayshites organized a route that bypassed the war zones. Wares transported by ocean craft to Arabia, as well as local products (dates, clarified butter, leather goods and the like) made their way via large caravans to northern terminals. As a result of the enterprising merchants of Quraysh, Abyssinia and the Yemen were connected with Syria-Palestine and Iraq.

Obtaining safe conduct for caravans beyond the frontier did not guarantee, however, freedom of passage within the peninsula itself. The Bedouin tribes and oasis dwellers who straddled the interior routes had to be made cooperative partners with the larger venture so that they would resist the urge to pillage the caravans passing through their tribal domains. In return for safe passage and assistance, these groups would be partners in the profits the caravan trade might yield. In addition, the Quraysh would peddle the wares or produce of their newfound partners in the bustling markets of caravan terminals beyond the frontier. Given these profitable enterprises, the outlying tribes balanced their tribal ethos, with its emphasis on self-reliance, fierce independence, and raiding for sport, against the advantages of a newly discovered prosperity. The month in which the annual pilgrimage to Mecca took place was declared a period in which there would be no fighting. In time, the period of truce was extended still further. An elaborate agenda for the pilgrimage was established in which different tribal units within and external to Quraysh assumed different responsibilities.

Societal units that, as a rule, valued anarchy over central authority and self-reliance over dependence were being driven into a larger cooperative venture that was bound to compromise traditional tribal values. We would have to regard this development as one of those experiments that took place from time to time among the Arabs, experiments at creating a larger political framework that emphasized economic and military cooperation. Without going into excessive detail, we could say that in this case, the economic and military cooperation negotiated by the leaders of Quraysh was paralleled by cooperation in religious matters linked to the centrality of Mecca as a pagan shrine center and place of pilgrimage. Among the leaders of Quraysh, there was a growing awareness of the importance of diplomacy and self-control, and they linked those values to religious sentiments and practices. In effect, there was large-scale religious and political cooperation among discrete Arab tribal associations even before the rise of Islam. It would be left to Muhammad to successfully weave all these strands together into a durable fabric by adding one more thread to the mix: A belief in monotheism and more particularly in his prophetic vocation and message.

Muhammad Prophet
of Islam: Origins

There are literally thousands of terse Muslim legal statements and lengthier historical accounts that describe the life and times of the Prophet and the origins and development of the Islamic community. The wisdom that has evolved in the universities of the West is that these "authoritative" traditions, which were first introduced in writing well after the dawn of Islam, reflect by and large circumstances of an age and place removed from the Prophet and his milieu. Almost all Western scholars now agree that the pithy and highly formulaic legal statements attributed to the Prophet (*hadith*) mostly represent a massive effort to Islamize non-Muslim practices that had been rooted in lands beyond Arabia even before Muhammad began preaching. Unable to disavow or otherwise overcome entrenched practices stemming from Roman and Jewish law, or popular religious observance among the different mono-theists, Muslim scholars linked what was palpably foreign to the Arabian Prophet and his environment. In such fashion, legal and social practices borrowed from a non-Muslim world were given Arabian-Muslim origins and with them a sense of legitimacy.

The lengthier historical accounts (*akhbar*), including major bio-graphies and detailed accounts of the early Muslims in battle, are also regarded by Western scholars as back projections. In the case of these accounts, however, the tendentiousness is rooted in political rather than legal concerns. Many accounts of Muhammad and the early faithful reflect a historiography carefully crafted by propagandists of the existing ruling house and/or their opponents. The task of the hired pens was to legitimate the Prophet and his community, the *ummah*, by linking them to legitimate prophets and monotheist communities of previous ages. Muhammad was described as the Qur'an pronounced him to be: "The Lord and Seal of the [monotheist] Prophets"; the nascent Muslim community in turn was made heir to the monotheist heritage of the ancient Israelites and depicted as basically without corruption, a pristine model of a religious society that later Muslims were enjoined to emulate.

In professing these views, propagandists sought also to enhance the images of their generous patrons, rulers or would-be rulers wishing to legitimize their own position and that of their extended families. They did this by claiming links to the Prophet and the original Islamic ummah, just as Muhammad himself had claimed links to the biblical past. Thus, the politics of the present was always described in a manner that conformed to an idealized history, often with considerable inventiveness. Where such links could not be made to fit comfortably with existing realities, the process of harmonizing past and present was reversed. An earlier history was then reshaped, however obliquely, to resemble the politics of more recent times. Confronting such artful narratives, Western scholars have long concluded that the Muslim versions of Muhammad's life and the gripping story of his emerging community reflect a history that has been greatly embellished, and when necessary even invented out of whole cloth, for political as well as strictly religious purposes. As they have come to see it, early Muslim historiography is a chronicle of events that should have been rather than events as they were or even as they might have been. Clearly, the Islamic tradition is not the stuff from which to write a rich and deeply textured history. Even those scholars who believe that some traditions reflect the early history of the ummah are hard-pressed to find a safe point of entry into the material. That is to say, there is as yet no sure method with which to sift the genuine from the contrived, or, better put, the majority of current historians are as yet unwilling to embrace any method that makes such claims. Some scholars have cautiously shied away from producing anything that might resemble a descriptive narrative of the Prophet and his times. Others less constrained by epistemological concerns have tried their hand at biography, often with little or (at best) insufficient attention to the problems inherent in the project. One scholar even contemplated a psychobiography of Muhammad, an effort that would have put a literary tradition rather than a patient on the couch. Clearly, one would prefer a descriptive account of the dawn of Islam that is both scholarly and balanced, that is, a version of events marked by highly nuanced judgments and by language that is sufficiently circumspect as to allow readers to appreciate how difficult it is to speak of events in a responsible fashion.

Keep in mind that there are no Arabian archives bearing materials from the period in question; nor are there incidental documents from the peninsula. Indeed there are no prose texts at all from the birthplace of Islam or conclusive archeological data. Almost all that we know from Muslim sources about Muhammad and the rise of Islam is contained in the problematic accounts of later times, a critical point that we will be forced to emphasize time and again. To be sure, there is Muslim scripture that most Western scholars accept as the authentic public utterances of the Prophet. But the Qur'an offers no extensive historical framework, nor does it contain material that can be traced directly to conventional forms of historical writing, as do, for example, various books of the Hebrew Bible.

The lack of historical Muslim info.

Muslim scripture does share with the Hebrew Bible a moral vision of the world, one that is also rooted in monotheist belief. But on reading the Qur'an, one gets little if any sense of the tight narrative structures that are part and parcel of biblical historiography or even the accounts of the Gospels. The Qur'an reminds us less of the storied books of Samuel and Kings and the accounts of Jesus's life than of Hebrew prophetic literature, with its explosive linguistic cadences and its ambiguous historical referents. For the most part, the style of the Qur'an is clipped and highly allusive, as one might expect of Muhammad's public utterances, pronouncements consistent in all respects with what we expect of prophetic declarations. Of all the segments of the Qur'an, only the twelfth surah, the story of the biblical Joseph son of Jacob, has a beginning, middle, and end that hang together as a coherent narrative. That is not to say Muslim scripture is entirely devoid of historical content. As with the works attributed to the more ancient Hebrew prophets, the Qur'an is informed by contemporaneous events as well as more distant historical memories. To begin with, there is mention of several people who reportedly played roles in the earliest history of Islam, but these names appear rather infrequently. Even Muhammad occurs only four times—five if we include Ahmad, considered by scholars medieval and modern to be an alternate name of the Prophet. Mecca, the birthplace of the Prophet and the site of his revelation and early mission is mentioned but once; Medina, the birthplace of the Islamic state five times. Sites of famous battles fought by the Muslims are mentioned—such as Badr and Hunayn.

These are, however, passing references; so many other major battles described in detail by the later historical sources have no place at all in Muslim scripture as we have it. There are, to be sure, oblique references to events more clearly spelled out by the Arabic chroniclers of future generations and also references to historical developments beyond the Arabian Peninsula: the contemporaneous war between the Byzantines and Sasanians that begins the segment of the Qur'an called al-Rum, "The Byzantines," as well as many ancient tales based loosely on biblical events and persons, albeit with "Arabicized" names. There are also hazy references to a real or invented ancient Arabian past. No doubt, Muhammad's audience and the next generation of his followers could piece together a coherent story of sorts from these scattered fragments of narratives, but in the end there was much that was left to the imagination of later Muslim commentary.

In other words, Muhammad's public utterances are not history, if by history we mean tales which explain human experience as related to events progressing in time—a story told in an orderly fashion and then informed by an overarching perspective that gives it literary or intellectual as well as moral coherence. Such as it is, history, or, if you prefer, echoes of historical events, are often spliced together in the Qur'an with references to legislation or moral pleadings and admonitions, usually without a defined or even definable historical context. When examined individually and as a whole, the discrete divisions and verses of Muslim scripture often appear disjointed with little if any evidence of sustained or unified composition, let alone a larger detailed picture of Muhammad and his times. After collating various fragments and taking oral testimony, the Muslim editors responsible for the authoritative version of the Qur'an arranged the 114 surahs according to length and not chronological order. The only exception to that scheme is the opening surah, which serves as an introduction to the rest of the text. It happens that many of the shortest surahs are considered by Qur'an scholars to be among the earliest revelations.

To be sure, various surahs are introduced with a superscription indicating them to be prophetic pronouncements from either the Meccan or Medinan period of Muhammad's mission. But the editor's marking the surah as Meccan or Medinan may refer only to part of a larger segment, cobbled together, all too often, from highly diverse statements reflecting very different moments of Muhammad's career. There is simply no way of reconstructing with any degree of certainty the chronological history of the Qur'anic text. In any event, no such reconstruction has satisfied or will satisfy the majority of Western scholars. Quite obviously, a failure to establish the sequence of Muhammad's public utterances complicates the modern historian's task no end. There are a myriad of commentaries on the Qur'an, but one is rarely, if ever, sure whether the commentary captures scripture as Muhammad's contemporaries understood it or as a puzzled later commentator and his generation struggled to find meaning in it for themselves. All these matters will be investigated further in our more comprehensive discussion of Muslim scripture.

In the end, Western historians investigating the origins of Islam are forced to return to the historical texts, that vast range of belles lettres, chronicles, and more narrowly defined biography that describes in seemingly minute detail the life and times of the Prophet. As there is no apparent reason to have invented all of these accounts, at least none discernible to skeptical historians, some are likely to contain kernels of the historic past; but, more often than not, there is no reasonably sure way of identifying these truths. That considered, these familiar materials should be interrogated with full recognition of the problems that they inevitably pose for reconstructing even the broadest outlines of a distant and hazy past.

The Origins of the Prophet Muhammad

Anxious to recover the background of Muhammad's life and times, we find ourselves continuously asking questions we cannot answer to our satisfaction, certainly not by relying on the vast biographical data of the Middle Ages, both Muslim and non-Muslim. Christian sources are highly polemical and largely given to fantasy, particularly the visions of Muhammad and his life that circulated in the Latin West. Jewish references to the Prophet are few and far between with virtually no data on his activities as prophet or statesman. As we have noted, the Muslim sources, however detailed, are extremely problematic. From the perspective of the medieval Arabic authors, the person of Muhammad looms considerably larger than the events that brought him to power and enabled him to serve as a prophet and political leader able to unite tribesmen from disparate regions of Arabia under the banner of Islam. As regards many critical points of Muhammad's career, we find ourselves lacking firm ground on which to begin an informed discussion, let alone imaginatively reconstruct the past.

For example, despite the many extant traditions about the Prophet's origins, we are left in the dark as to the year and circumstances of his birth. Most standard modern histories of Islam tell us that the Prophet was born in or around the year 570 C.E. But for this fact, the authors of these modern histories generally rely on one another and on a peculiar from of circular reasoning. There is a well-known Muslim tradition, reported in many versions, that the Prophet began his mission at or around the age of forty. Since it was assumed by some scholars that this mission commenced around 610 C.E., one had only to subtract forty years from that date to arrive at 570. But the best evidence that Muhammad began to preach in 610 is also based on the tradition of his having been forty at the time of his mission. Reversing the arithmetic, scholars simply add forty years to the conventionally accepted date of his birth in order to determine the beginning of his career, hardly convincing or even presumptive evidence. Moreover, as we shall have cause to see shortly, in this case, as in other literatures and other civilizations, the age of forty is a well-known literary trope that denotes a certain kind of maturity and not at all a specific age.

In the medieval sources there is no date according to any known calendar that lists the Prophet's birth. The earliest Muslim calendar, which only saw the light after Muhammad's death, reckons time from the Hijrah, the moment when the Prophet left Mecca for Medina, allegedly some ten years after he began to preach. Prior to promoting this calendar, the Arabs of Quraysh reckoned time according to primitive time-fixing artifices, such as linking chronology to events of an unusual nature that electrified a particular age and then served as useful pegs on which to hang extended historical memories. Thus, the Prophet was said to have been born in the dramatic Year of the Elephant, that is, the year in which the Abyssinians in south Arabia attempted to retake the trade routes traditionally dominated by the Yemenites but more recently controlled by Muhammad's ancestors, the clans of Quraysh. The Arabic historical sources, all written long after the reported event, speak of an ill-fated expeditionary force led by one Abraha and spearheaded by elephants, awe-inspiring animals never before seen in the Hijaz. But as best we can determine, the miraculous salvation of Mecca, which is described obliquely in the Qur'an, actually took place around 540, a date much too early for the birth of the Prophet, as that would put him in his 70s when he is likely to have started to preach, in his 80s when he vigorously pursued his religious and political agenda, and in his 90s when he emerged victorious over his Meccan enemies. It is of course possible the Year of the Elephant mentioned in connection with the Prophet's birth reflects a later incursion not yet accounted for in any historical record, but that is a bit of a stretch. The question of why Muslim tradition bothered to link the Prophet's birth with the aforementioned event is a complicated issue that does not concern us here. Suffice it to say, the tradition that the Prophet was born at a time when his kinsmen were saved by divine intervention was considered a harbinger of his future vocation.

Indeed, Muhammad's birth is embellished with all sorts of legendary details in an attempt to promote the authenticity of his prophetic calling. Even before Muhammad was conceived, there were reported rumblings among learned Christians and Jews that a prophet was soon to be born. The Jews in particular were said to be excited at the prospect because they believed the Prophet would be one of them as in the past—an expectation later dashed much to their consternation when God's messenger turned out to be an Arab of Quraysh. Some Christians were more receptive once they could ascertain the future. A woman of Quraysh whose brother Waraqah ibn Nawfal had reportedly converted to Christianity and was familiar with the sacred writings and oral traditions of both Jews and Christians, offered 'Abdallah, Muhammad's father to be, a magnificent gift. If he were willing to bed her [so that she might have the honor of giving birth to the designated prophet of God]; he could have a number of camels equal to those that were sacrificed at the time of his birth. But 'Abdallah's father had other designs. 'Abdallah was soon married off to Aminah, one of the most noble women of Quraysh with a prestigious genealogy on both the maternal and paternal sides of her family—in sum, a worthy mother of God's ordained messenger (*rasul allah*).

As Aminah's pregnancy advanced toward term, strange occurrences were observed. A (sacred) light emanating from her pregnant belly illuminated the castles of Bostra in distant Syria-Palestine. The miraculous light was interpreted as evidence that the mother was carrying the very special child that Waraqah's sister hoped she would bear. Then, at the time of birth there were cosmic disturbances that signified the long-expected event of God's design. In addition devils were stoned and idols were toppled, all telltale signs of a new prophet arriving. Neither mother nor father was destined to see the moment of Muhammad's revelation. Tradition has it that Aminah died when Muhammad was a small child and that his father expired around the time of his birth. Like all the newborn of Quraysh, the boy was nursed by Bedouin women. Being fatherless, he was in the care of his paternal grandfather, and following the latter's death was raised by his uncle Abu Talib, the leader of the clan of Hashim. In effect, Abu Talib became, in accordance with tribal custom, the boy's surrogate father and hence protector. Although Abu Talib never himself became a Muslim, he was honor-bound by tribal codes to protect his nephew in all circumstances. While he still lived, Abu Talib shielded the Prophet from serious harm, for any serious threat to Muhammad was regarded as a challenge to the honor of Abu Talib and by extension to the entire clan of Hashim.

The young orphan, deprived from an early age of parents and a beloved grandfather, is portrayed as clinging to his uncle, so when Abu Talib embarked on a journey to Syria, he took the boy with him indicating the two would never part, or words to that effect. The trip proved an eventful moment in the future Prophet's life. As the caravan reached Bostra (the very settlement whose castles were illuminated by the light emanating from the pregnant Aminah's belly), a Christian monk by the name of Bahira broke custom and sought out the entourage of Qurayshite Arabs. Hitherto, Bahira had taken no special notice of the Arab caravans coming and going. As a rule he confined himself to his cell where he read sacred Christian writings, as did consecutive generations of monks who inhabited that very same cell and read the same texts before him. Islamic tradition thus suggests the Christian monks handed down a received wisdom from generation to generation, and as they were not about to communicate with the world beyond their monastery, that wisdom was not likely to have been polluted by external influences.

Bahira's behavior in this account and others like it is then unusual, to say the least. Not only did he take notice of the Qurayshites, he invited them to a lavish meal, hardly what one would have expected from a monk living in relative if not complete solitude. What could explain this behavior? We are led to believe it was something that Bahira had seen as the caravan approached, something startling that exercised his imagination. One of the travelers was shielded [from the hot sun] by a cloud that hovered over him alone. When that person sat under a tree, the branches drooped to shade him as did the cloud. It was in recognition of that extraordinary happenstance that Bahira extended his invitation to "young and old, slave and free alike."

Alert readers would have already begun to assemble the missing pieces of the puzzle and sort out the events about to unfold in the story. The invitation to the "young" was clearly a reference to the youngest of the group, the boy brought along by his uncle Abu Talib. The person shaded by the cloud and drooping branches of the tree (while others sweltered in the heat) was likely favored by God, for how else can one explain this miraculous treatment. Muslims familiar with the tradition were thus likely to suspect that the individual referred to was none other than young Muhammad and that the signs of his religious vocation were evident to the monk as they had been to Waraqah ibn Nawfal's sister at the time of the Prophet's birth. These suspicions were borne out by the unfolding narrative.

When the caravan people from Quraysh arrived, the monk inquired if all were present, for he did not notice the mark of prophecy on any of those attending. He was well aware of the prophetic signs because they were discussed in the book that he and the Christian monks before him had studied for generation upon generation. The only one missing was the boy left behind to look after the baggage, that is, young Muhammad. When Muhammad was ushered in, Bahira examined him closely to see if his general appearance matched that of God's anticipated messenger (in the book). Bahira then posed a series of questions to ascertain whether in fact the lad was indeed the prophet whose coming was foretold in his Christian text. The boy refused to acknowledge the legitimacy of the idols housed in the Ka'bah, the ancient shrine of his native city—a proper response. Bahira then questioned the boy about his likes and his habits. The lad answered all these queries to the monk's satisfaction. Finally, the Christian discovered on the boys back the prophetic markings described in the Christian holy book. All that remained was to ascertain that the child was in fact Abu Talib's nephew. When asked about the child, Abu Talib replied he was his son, but when questioned further he revealed Muhammad was actually his nephew. With that, the monk knew the miracles of the cloud and of the tree were the harbingers of what he learned after the banquet. The learned Christian monk had encountered the child who would become the last of God's messengers when he came to reach full maturity some thirty-five years later. Abu Talib is then advised by Bahira to return with the boy to his native land and guard him carefully, for "if the Jews see him and know about him what I know [a likely situation as they too knew of a prophet's coming from their own holy books], they will do him evil."

What are we to understand from this account, a story told in many sources and with considerable variation? Or to put it somewhat differently, what did medieval Muslims derive from this tradition? At a surface level, they were informed how Muhammad's prophetic future was already foreseen in his childhood, if not indeed even before he was born. But there is a deeper thrust to the story as it unfolds here and in other accounts. The story of Bahira the monk is a clever Muslim polemic against those Christians and Jews who denied the legitimacy of the Prophet's claims. If Bahira was able to ascertain Muhammad's future calling on the basis of his own religious tradition, surely other learned

Christians and also Jews could have and should have done the same. Hence Bahira's advice to Abu Talib: Guard the boy lest the Jews knowing of his existence and future calling plan doing him harm. As interesting as these accounts are, they leave us begging for details of a historic Muhammad's early life. Unfortunately, the reports of his early manhood and standing in society are no more illuminating.

We are told that at the age of twenty or thereabouts, Muhammad wed Khadijah, a wealthy divorcee and widow twice his age. She had only recently employed him as her agent in the caravan trade. Again, we are not dealing here with actual ages but with well-known tropes: twentyish is the time of life at which one begins to make one's mark, fortyish, the age in which genuine maturity complements still vigorous energy. What is peculiar to this tradition is the nature of the marriage. Men of standing married shortly after entering pubescence; their intended brides often chosen for them from among first cousins were younger still and assuredly chaste. Given the tender age of the bride, and at times the groom, it sometimes took years for the bride to move into her husband's house and for the marriage to be consummated. In contrast, here was a man destined to be a prophet, indeed *the* Prophet, remaining unmarried until full manhood, and then taking as his wife an older woman who had been both divorced and widowed. In sum, she had been rejected by man and deprived of male companionship by God. However obliquely, the story suggests to readers that Muhammad had not the means or prestige to take on a proper bride of proper social standing, even though he himself came from a well-known family of a well-established clan.

Because we know nothing of the social dynamics of such May-December marriages among the Quraysh, it would be irresponsible for us to declare the union of the young man of apparently modest means and his older but extremely wealthy employer as an arrangement borne of obvious convenience. But it is not we alone who are puzzled by the marriage. The Islamic tradition is also troubled and goes to lengths to justify the rather unusual relationship. Despite her age and despite her having been previously married—not once, but twice—Khadijah is portrayed as turning down one suitor after another. Be that as it may, the framers of these traditions clearly understood that in their time and setting the marriage of Muhammad to Khadijah would have raised a few eyebrows. In some medieval accounts, we are informed that Khadijah's father vigorously opposed the union as unsuitable; in others the father was already dead at the time of the nuptials, a subtle hint that he would have opposed the marriage had he lived. How then could one explain the seemingly strange course of events? What better reason than to link the unusual marriage to authenticating Muhammad's prophetic mission? Indeed the accounts linking the two events are an extension of the earlier stories of the Prophet visiting Syria with his uncle Abu Talib. On this occasion, the narrative projects Muhammad some fifteen years or so into the future. He does not go to Syria as a young boy clinging to his uncle, but as a young man leading the expedition.

There are accounts that Khadijah, having heard of Muhammad's honesty and acumen, employed him to lead one of her caravans to Palestine-Syria. He was accompanied by her slave Maysarah. As events unfolded, it was clear this was to be no ordinary business enterprise. According to one account, when the caravan reached its destination, Muhammad sat himself in the shade of a tree (presumably to shield himself from the searing sun). The tree was near the cell of a Christian monk. The Christian asked Maysarah who was resting beneath the tree, for, as the monk pointed out, none but a prophet ever sat there, a rather casual and unexplained observation obviously pregnant with meaning. On the return journey, the caravan was beset by the blistering heat of high noon, but Maysarah observed that the Prophet was shaded from the sun's rays by the wings of two angels that hovered over him. When Muhammad returned with profits that had doubled her initial investment, Khadijah was delighted that he had managed the transaction in so stellar a fashion. But it was not young Muhammad's business acumen alone that so impressed her, but rather Maysarah's report of the monk's words and the miracle of the angels shielding Muhammad from the sun. Having heard Maysarah's testimony, she immediately sought out her kinsman Waraqah ibn Nawfal, the alleged Christian steeped in Christian and Jewish lore. Waraqah confirmed that Muhammad was to become the long expected prophet. Other accounts have Khadijah seeking the opinions of other learned monks, always with the same result: recognition on their part of her husband's destiny. With Muhammad's glorious future confirmed by the learned Christians, Khadijah, allegedly the richest woman of Quraysh, took the initiative and proposed marriage to her youngish kinsman, an unusual act, as marriage is generally proposed by spokesmen from the groom's household. Clearly, she understood what was at stake in marrying Muhammad. Based on the information obtained from Waraqah, she sought to be the wife of the Prophet, just as Waraqah's sister (presumably based on similar information from her brother) sought to be the Prophet's mother some twenty years earlier.

There are then numerous versions of Muhammad's trip to Syria on behalf of his rich employer but the essential point in each and every one of the accounts is the same. The miracles surrounding the journey are meant to demonstrate the legitimacy of Muhammad's prophetic claims. More important yet is the recognition of his (future) prophetic calling by a learned Christian, a monk who in one variant had confined himself to his cell where generations of monks had read the same holy books portending the future. How is it then that this monk was able to conclude that Muhammad was indeed the quintessential prophet whom God had planned to send to humankind? The tradition in fairly sparse language would have us understand that the monk probably read of this prophet's future coming in his own sacred writings, texts which he and other learned Christians pored over in successive generations.

Whichever gloss one may wish to give to the most unusual marriage of Khadijah and Muhammad, Muslim tradition makes it clear, time and again, that Khadijah was a source of unquestioned support once he embarked on his religious mission. He shared his first religious experiences with her, and it was she who went (once again) to her learned kinsman Waraqah to confirm the authenticity of her husband's very first revelation. While Khadijah lived Muhammad took no other wives, even though she bore him no male offspring, certainly none that survived. In normal circumstances, a male without a proper heir might have called for taking a second wife or a slave with whom to cohabit in an attempt to perpetuate the line, as in Abraham's taking Hagar, the maidservant of his then barren wife Sarah. Or one might seek other women from the extended family household as did Jacob when his favored Rachel died after giving birth to two sons and his other wife, her sister Leah, ceased to produce further offspring. Indeed, the later history of Muhammad's clan is replete with stories of favorite first wives unable at first to produce a male successor to the master of the extended household. Muhammad's decision not to seek a partner while Khadijah still lived was unusual in the social milieu of contemporaneous Mecca. Her death, at a critical point of his career, was clearly a serious blow.

Although he later took ten other wives, mostly diplomatic unions, only Khadijah bore him children who survived. She was the mother of his four daughters, only one of whom, Fatimah, bore offspring. He is credited with four sons: Ibrahim, who was the son of a Coptic concubine and who died in infancy, and three other sons, al-Qasim, al-Tayyib, and al-Tahir. But the matter of the birth of these three sons is obscure, and in all likelihood they are later inventions to answer nagging doubts about the last and quintessential messenger sent by God to humankind. For how could a human being so blessed by God be unable to a produce a single surviving male heir. The three boys are rarely mentioned in the vast literature devoted to the Prophet (the tradition presumes that all died very young) and the very names chosen for them are related to regnal titles taken by caliphs beginning only in the middle of the following century. Once again, Muslim tradition seemingly shaped the past to legitimize Muhammad and his prophetic vocation, this time by making him father to male offspring.

The beginnings of Muhammad's prophetic vocation are similarly shrouded in mystery. The tradition is seemingly less concerned with a description of circumstances as they were or might have been and more with establishing the truth of Muhammad's claims while at the same time denigrating his opponents. As we shall see in the following segment, the accounts of Muhammad's prophetic calling, like those of his childhood visit to the monk and his business trip to Syria at the behest of his future wife, masks a discernible polemic against those monotheists (read Christians and Jews) who, unlike Waraqah ibn Nawfal, could not bring themselves to declare that which they knew only too well, namely that Muhammad was a true prophet in the chain of past monotheist prophets sent earlier by God to do His bidding.

The Prophet's Mission: Mecca

There is by now a voluminous literature on Muhammad's prophetic career. There are tens of thousands of pages devoted to the Prophet and the origins of the Islamic community in both Muslim and Western writings. Among the many medieval Arabic sources, the most systematic and detailed accounts are found in books dealing with Muhammad's military campaigns (*maghazi*) and the biographical literature (*sirah*) focusing on him and his companions. A good deal of this material was integrated into later Arabic chronicles and all sorts of literary texts rich in historical anecdotes. As often as not, narrowly focused individual accounts are inserted randomly in works of literature to entertain as well as enlighten the Muslim reader. But at other times, as is the case with the more comprehensive histories, there is enough material to create a sustained historical narrative; all the more so when variants and even conflicting reports based on testimony from different authorities are juxtaposed within the same text. Confronted by a number of accounts based on different perspectives, medieval and modern readers have been able to piece together a larger and more coherent story of Muhammad's mission.

Many biographical works dealing with the Prophet and his followers are arranged according to generation (*tabaqah*, pl. *tabaqat*). Each individual and/or extended family is accorded an entry as part of the more inclusive whole. That kind of encyclopedic format gives rise to many individual stories but no seamless narrative of Muslims interacting among themselves and the world beyond. In contrast, there is the *Sirah*, the massive biography of the Prophet written by Ibn Ishaq (d. 767 C.E.), a sweeping work of history ranging from ancient legends to details of the Prophet's life and an extended description of his military ventures and diplomacy. Unfortunately, there is no scientific edition of the *Sirah*. The first part of the biography, which deals with a pre-Islamic past far removed from the age of the Prophet, is known only from fragments scattered throughout medieval Arabic literature. The remaining segments, originally preserved in an edition assembled by the ninth-century historian Ibn Hisham (d. ca. 830 C.E.), represent the single largest and certainly most important biography of the Islamic Middle Ages. Accounts of the Prophet's career attributed to Ibn Ishaq and his informants are also preserved by other later authors, especially Muhammad ibn Jarir al-Tabari (d. 923 C.E.) whose great chronicle spices up Ibn Ishaq's narrative with alternative versions of various events. The added material allows today's historians a means of measuring the original account for accuracy. By comparing and contrasting the discordant elements of many different versions, astute modern scholars develop a feel for specific messages cleverly concealed within the text.

The *Sirah* of Ibn Ishaq is not an innocent account of critical moments in the history of the Muslims and Islam. Commissioned as it was by the newly established Abbasid dynasty around 750 C.E., its description of the past does not reflect a neutral presentation of persons and events. Quite the opposite, the most exhaustive description of the Prophet's life is politically driven, a brilliantly conceived account to legitimate Muhammad's prophetic calling by linking him to the authentic monotheist prophets of earlier times, and then validate the rule of the author's Abbasid patrons by linking them and their extended house to the Prophet and his household. All this, especially the valorization of Muhammad's Abbasid kinsmen from the clan of Hashim, required the reshaping and at times reinventing of the past.

Revelation and the Beginnings of Islam

With the accounts of Muhammad's birth and those of his meeting with the monk Bahira portending the future, Muslim biographical literature turns to the long expected moment: the revelation that marked the beginnings of his Prophetic mission. The *Sirah* (among many sources) reports that when Muhammad reached the age of forty, God sent him out of compassion to the world at large (*'alamin*) "as an evangelist (*bashir*) to all men (*kafatan li-l-nas*)." Straightforward as it seems, this terse statement calls for considerable explication. We have already noted that reaching the age of forty is a literary devise and not necessarily a historical fact. Truth be told, other Arabic sources indicate Muhammad was in his early forties when he began his career, in any case a proper time of life to take on so large a burden and at God's behest no less.

Among the ancient Greeks, forty was the age at which one combined physical prowess with the accumulated experience to lead men forcefully but more important wisely, a sentiment that is seemingly echoed in the Qur'an (Surah 46:15). But there is more to this linkage than that which is suggested by ancient Greek sensibilities. More likely, this is the echo of a Jewish tradition with which Muslims had greater familiarity, as they were in direct and early contact with learned Jews and Jewish converts. The Talmud, that vast compendium of ancient Jewish law and lore, also stresses the importance of being forty. Most important is the well-known tradition that Moses was forty years of age when he began his prophetic vocation after having been overcome by a supernatural occurrence, a bush in an isolated wilderness that burned and burned but was never consumed. Any possible link between the first and greatest of the prophets in Jewish (and also Christian) tradition and the last and quintessential prophet of Muslim tradition bears close watching.

As did Aminah, Jochebed (Moses's mother) also experienced a strange pregnancy, a happenstance trumpeted by Jewish tradition as foretelling her son's future greatness. Admittedly, the significance of being forty and supranatural pregnancies for the mothers of persons chosen for greatness could well fall within the framework of universal folklore. There is then no compelling need to declare and with much certainty that for whatever reason Islamic tradition favored well-known stories from Jewish tradition. However, there is more to the respective histories of the two great monotheist prophets and lawgivers. There are accounts in both Jewish and Islamic tradition that do indeed suggest deliberate cultural borrowing. Jewish and Muslim tradition alike maintain both prophets were born and died on the same day of the same month. It would be absolutely remarkable if this were mere coincidence. Nor can it be a coincidence that both Jewish and Islamic traditions declare their greatest prophet was born without foreskin (thus making the obligatory rite of circumcision unnecessary). Ever since God instructed Abraham to remove the foreskins of his entire male household, circumcision has marked the passage of newborn and converted males into the Jewish community. It is perhaps the most identifiable marker of Jewish identity and more particularly it is *the* sign of Abraham's covenant with God, the agreement in which the progeny of Israel's forefather were declared God's chosen people. Among Jews, God's covenant and the rite of circumcision are rendered by the same word (*b'rith*, or as regards circumcision, more correctly *b'rith milah*).

But what, if anything, do references to Jewish tradition tell us about Muhammad's being born without a foreskin? According to Jewish lore, Moses was not the only Jew to be born fully circumcised. The rabbis maintain that many of Israel's prophets were born that way and so they did not have to undergo the Jewish ritual performed ordinarily on the eighth day following birth. That held true also for kings David and Solomon, both of whom were regarded by Muslims as prophets sent by God and not merely temporal rulers. In claiming the same for Muhammad, the Islamic tradition seems to suggest that their prophet was indeed the legitimate successor to Moses and all the Israelite prophets sent by God in previous ages and circumstances, a claim made time and again in the Qur'an and subsequent Muslim writings.

Having informed us that Muhammad was sent to deliver God's message at the age of forty (to be seen now in light of Moses's career), the *Sirah* goes on to link Muhammad directly to God's previous messengers. This is accomplished by offering a commentary to a well-known verse of the Qur'an, the so-called Covenant of the Prophets. (Surah 3:75). The verse relates that each and every time God was about to send a prophet to deliver His message, he asked the prophet to make a covenant with Him. This was an agreement in which that prophet pledged himself to take the scripture and wisdom that God imparted to him and relay it to his people. In doing that, the prophets would also pave the way for a future messenger (that is, Muhammad) whose appearance would confirm for their people all they had been told about his future coming. In such fashion each and every monotheist prophet would express his faith in Muhammad and assist him by laying the groundwork for future generations of their people to accept him and his religion. When asked by God whether they accepted the terms of the covenant, they replied positively. Then both God and the prophets-to-be bore witness to the transaction.

It all seems fairly clear at first glance: the monotheist prophets of old were all obligated to tell their peoples of the future coming of Muhammad so that when the last and most perfect Messenger of God appeared, he would by accepted by one and all alike. That message was duly recorded in every monotheist version of scripture and received wisdom. The Qur'anic verse would then seem to indicate that Muhammad was not sent by God to the Arabs of the Quraysh alone, or even to all the Arabs but no other people. Rather, his mission was universal in nature, or as the *Sirah* was wont to put it: "the world at large," an evangelist to "*all* men." But we are still left to wonder who are these prophets and their peoples, and whether the prophets actually fulfilled their part of the bargain and spoke about Muhammad's future coming. For the Qur'anic text only tells us that they took the pledge. It does not explicitly state if all or at least some prophets sent by God carried out their obligation. Islamic tradition is anxious to leave no doubt this was the case. The brief for Muhammad's legitimacy imbedded in the Qur'anic verse as well as the targeted audience of its hidden and censorious message had to be made crystal clear to all readers.

Paraphrasing and fleshing out Muslim scripture, Muhammad's biography provides us with a more complete picture of events, a version which serves as a commentary to the original verse of the Qur'an. As described in the *Sirah*, the earlier monotheist prophets "all" carried out their obligation to transmit what they knew of Muhammad's future coming, information which then became part of their people's tradition. The *Sirah* also identifies the aforesaid recipients of the prophetic messages as the "people of the two books," meaning the Old and New Testaments. All that remained for the Muslims was to demonstrate that the predictions of Muhammad's mission that were transmitted by all the preceding prophets were actually understood by Jews and Christians receiving this message. The continuing saga of Muhammad's prophetic vocation makes that point clear; certainly no less clear than the traditions of the Prophet's birth, his encounter with the learned Christian monk in Syria, and his marriage to Khadijah.

The text goes on to describe events surrounding the revelation. Muhammad, as he often did in pagan times, performed religious devotions in the isolated hills surrounding Mecca. There, he reportedly experienced supernatural experiences. The last of these experiences has Muhammad hearing a voice call out: "O Muhammad! You are the Messenger of God and I am [the angel] Gabriel." He looked up and saw the angel straddling the horizon. No matter how hard he tried, Muhammad was unable to avoid this overwhelming vision. There Muhammad stood stupefied and unable to move for the longest period of time. For Christian polemicists of the Latin West, the account indicated the Muhammad the imposter was having an epileptic fit. For Muslims, it was evidence that Muhammad encountered in an isolated area of Mecca a vision such as Moses witnessed in the wilderness of Sinai.

When Muhammad finally made his way back to Khadijah, she inquired where he had been and after he informed her of all that had transpired she expressed hope this meant he would (finally) be "the prophet of this people." To verify her suspicion, she went to her learned kinsman Waraqah who had mastered not only the scripture of Jews and Christians, but was familiar as well with the broad range of their religious learning. As he did when Khadijah first consulted him, that is, after Muhammad returned from his trip to Syria, Waraqah affirmed Muhammad's prophetic vocation, this time indicating that the moment of revelation had taken place: "The archangel (or greatest revelation) that had previously come to Moses has already come to [Muhammad]." Somewhat later, when Muhammad himself related to Waraqah what he had seen and heard, the learned Christian repeated what he said to Khadijah and then added that Muhammad would be called a liar, treated disdainfully, cast out of his community, and opposed in battle, a prediction that Muhammad's claims to prophecy and all that implied would be rejected by some to whom he was being sent with God's message.

What are we to make of this extended account? By tying Muhammad to Moses, both at the beginning and at the end, the author leads his readers to believe the Prophet of Islam is a link in a long chain of monotheist prophets. By citing the Qur'anic verse on the Covenant of the Prophets and then commenting upon it as it does, the *Sirah* makes it clear that the future coming of Muhammad was foretold in Jewish and Christian religious texts. By having the learned Waraqah verify that to be the case, our source confirms that persons acquainted with Jewish and Christian scripture and lore were familiar with the prediction of Muhammad's prophetic vocation and thus should have endorsed the Prophet when he began his mission. But as Waraqah predicted, Muhammad would in fact be opposed when he took his message to the people.

If the truth of Muhammad's calling is found in earlier monotheist traditions and if that truth was so readily available to other monotheists, why should there have been opposition to him and his message by Jews and Christians? We might also ask why should there have been opposition to him by his pagan kinsmen from among the Quraysh? What is it about his message and his followers that so exercised the polytheists among his people? The first question is answered from the very outset and explicitly by Muhammad and the Muslims. If Jews (and Christians) of the time did not follow the Prophet, it is because they deliberately falsified their scripture by denying what they knew to be true. The second, which asks us to explain the pagan opposition to Muhammad, is not so explicitly stated and requires a nuanced reading of difficult medieval sources that link the composition of Muhammad's early following and the nature of his missionary activities at Mecca to important social and economic undercurrents of the time.

Muhammad's Mission at Mecca

As did medieval Muslim authors, most modern orientalists were inclined to examine the Prophet and his message largely in religious terms. Some nineteenth-century biographers showing the prejudice of their age regarded him as a *poseur* who deliberately or unwittingly bore a false message; others gave him passing marks for religious sincerity but were nevertheless suspicious of his learning and critical of his behavior when he assumed the role of statesman—the words "ignoramus" and "opportunist" were employed. Admittedly, the focus on Muhammad's religious sincerity and the setting of his religious activities are crucial to an understanding of the rise of Islam, but so too is the social and economic environment that marked his life and times, a subject that most Western scholars of earlier generations were not prepared or inclined to engage.

At the least, the early modern biographies tend to paraphrase the available medieval sources; at most they give a detailed analysis of religious phenomena based on a more critical reading of the very same sources plus comparative materials drawn from Jewish and Christian tradition. Only the Belgian Jesuit Henri Lammens wrote in great detail about the socioeconomic condition of Mecca on the eve of the Prophet's mission, but his 1910 study in which he labeled Mecca a "merchant republic" and went on to describe the desert town as a commercial hub with all the material and cultural sophistication of an Italian city-state was roundly criticized for being thoroughly unreliable and misleading. Critics also noted the manner in which he disparaged the religion of Islam. In the end, Lammens, who imposed a modern European vision on historical phenomena of another place and time, left many unanswered questions about the political economy of Meccan tribal life.

It was not until the 1950s, when W. Montgomery Watt published *Muhammad at Mecca* (Oxford, 1953) and *Muhammad at Medina* (Oxford, 1956) that Western biographers of the Prophet would turn full attention to the ground originally explored by Lammens and examine more responsibly and in great detail specific links between the beginnings of Islam and developments in the social and economic milieu of sixth- and seventh-century Arabia. In his two-volume biography, Watt presents his readers with an imaginative framework with which to consider the genesis of the new faith. That framework was explained more fully in a later work, *Islam and the Integration of Society* (London, 1961), a reflective and highly stimulating book that addressed the theoretical concerns of sociologists as well as the traditional interests of Watt's orientalist colleagues.

Whether writing as a sociologist or an orientalist, Watt, like all of us, remains caught on the horns of a dilemma: how to handle the difficult Arabic sources, all of which were compiled a century and more after the death of Muhammad. Knowing full and well that much of the biographical material concerning the Prophet is an invention designed to defend Islam against unbelievers (Jews and Christians) and certain Muslims against other believers (the Abbasid caliphs versus their opponents and the reverse), Watt is forced to pick through a politically driven literature in search of kernels of historical truth. He assumes, no doubt quite correctly, that among the later historical narratives there may be, indeed are, accounts or segments of accounts that are not complete fabrications. But it is not always clear why he privileges certain reports over others. One has the impression that he has conceived a broad picture of Islamic origins and, by employing a hunt and peck method, has isolated individual traditions in order to buttress his model. We are often asked to reject the sum of a particular account as fictitious but accept elements within it as likely truths culled from an elusive past. One can surely quibble with if not oppose outright many of Watt's conclusions, but fifty years after publication his work remains a useful launching pad to explore the composition of the earliest Muslim community; the nature and impact of Muhammad's early preaching; and the subsequent opposition to him and his prophetic mission.

During the first Islamic century or thereabouts, prestige among the Muslims was derived in large part from personal or family service to the Prophet and the community of the faithful. Among the factors considered were the moment of conversion (early converts were more noble); participation in military campaigns (the earlier the better); valor on the field of battle (glorious death in combat had its merits); and the like. With much at stake, those who preserved tribal memories tended to shape their picture of Muhammad's world in accordance with personal and group interests, as did compilers of accounts promoting rival claimants who sought to lead the Muslims at a later time, writers such as Ibn Ishaq, the hired pen of the Abbasid house, and the various historians who took up the cause of the Shi'ites, the party (*shi'ah*) favoring the progeny of 'Ali, the son of Abu Talib. How then are we to determine the actual composition of the early Muslim group at Mecca? Perhaps the safest course is to trace in detail the background of each and every early convert found on the lists of Arab authors.

The medieval sources would have us believe that Muhammad did not actively seek converts until three years after he was visited by the angel Gabriel. At that point, Muhammad had few followers. All are agreed that Khadijah was the first among them; some say 'Ali, the son of Abu Talib, was next (most probably a tradition to legitimize Ali's later claim to leadership of the Islamic community and by extension the claims made by 'Alid supporters on behalf of his offspring). Also mentioned is a freed slave of Muhammad's household and Abu Bakr, the first of the caliphs (that is, the successors) chosen to lead the Muslim community after the Prophet's death. Abu Bakr, it was said, actively recruited fellow Qurayshites to join Muhammad's following, and, as a result of his efforts, dozens of men and women entered the fold, forming the nucleus that was to later become the first Islamic community.

There is no reason to doubt that most of the important Muslims were recruited at this time and thus derived great prestige and in certain instances great political leverage for themselves and their families. The four "righteous caliphs" picked to lead the ummah after Muhammad's death all came from this group, as did the various candidates passed over. But the lists of early converts also includes a number of individuals who played no important role in subsequent developments, leading us to believe that this roster of Muhammad's first supporters may actually reflect the composition of his early following. There would have been no reason at all to include the names of nonentities on any list which had been fabricated at a later time to promote the importance of the early converts. If the list is indeed authentic, as Watt surmised, there is a narrow opening for measuring the Prophet's early following. For Watt this meant tracing the family and clan affiliation of each and every convert mentioned.

After doing just that, Watt was able to conclude that Muhammad's early following broke along the following lines: younger sons of the best families from the leading clans of the Quraysh; a large number of mostly young men from the other clans; and finally a few individuals unrelated to any clan by blood, including persons nominally outside the formal protection of the clan system. That breakdown of the early followers coincides with a medieval author's description of them as "young men" and "those considered weak (*mustad'afun*)," that is, those who had no blood relatives to protect them. Counting individuals, Watt was able to conclude that some early Muslims were recruited from the leading families of the most prestigious clans; the majority originated, however, with leading families of lesser clans. A few early Muslims, without proper blood ties to Quraysh, were only affiliates of established clans, but still worthy of their support; a smaller number yet were without any formal arrangement for protection within the clan system. The last were therefore likely to be at risk if threatened for whatever reason.

This picture of Muhammad's early following is a far cry from the group described by previous generations of Western scholars. Those scholars imagined Muhammad first appealed to the flotsam and jetsam of unraveled tribal societies, individuals and small families that somehow made their way to him. Without support of influential blood relations, these down-and-outs were said to have gravitated to the Prophet whose social message appealed to the underprivileged, gave them dignity and, above all, provided the dispossessed with a sense of belonging. Many such people joined the Prophet's cause later in his career when he actively sought allies of all sorts to strengthen his position within his newly adopted home at Medina and combat his various enemies beyond it. But Medina, where Muhammad came to settle a decade or so after the purported start of his mission, was a vastly different environment. At the outset of his preaching, his followers would seem to have been mostly young men around the age of forty, or younger still, virtually all of them solidly entrenched in well-established kinship groups that were honor bound to give them full support and protection. What is it about Muhammad and his message that attracted people of this sort? Here were individuals with bright futures turning to Islam in a pagan society brimming with self-confidence, thereby risking criticism from their own kinfolk, and in certain instances economic and social boycott.

There is a temptation to see the early Muslims as being increasingly conscious of the growing disparity in wealth and prestige between the likes of themselves and the older and more affluent members of Quraysh. Seen from this perspective, they chose Islam hoping to close the gap between the "haves" and themselves, the "have some that would like to have some more." Comparing apples of the seventh century with oranges of the twenty-first is generally not a good tack for serious historians, but there just might be some profit in juxtaposing Muhammad's Mecca with modern Riyadh, the capital of Saudi Arabia. Whereas the founder of the Saudi dynasty was considered one of the people, his successors have created, through their enormous wealth, an unbridgeable gap between themselves and a newly formed middle class. Such as it is, the antagonism toward the royal family and its rule results not from its subjects living in abject poverty or because their welfare is neglected or their safety is arbitrarily put at risk by excessively cruel and capricious security agencies. Rather, they are put off by open displays of opulence from a fabulously wealthy element of society, while they themselves are dishonored by having to advance through a corrupt and highly degrading system that stifles their initiative and robs them of their ambitions. Would a similar situation explain why the younger men of middling clans embraced Muhammad and his faith fourteen hundred years ago? Was there no other way of expressing their resentment except taking up a new faith and strange religious practices? Surely, there was something about Muhammad's evolving message that spoke directly and powerfully to concerns of a spiritual nature. Lest we forget, resentment against the current Saudi government also focuses on the ruling family's debasement of true spiritual values.

One can readily imagine how the dramatic changes taking place in and around Mecca affected tribal ideals. Relatively isolated kinship groups living in marginal oasis areas stressed collective responsibility; indeed, assuming the burden of a fellow kinsman was at the core of individual and group behavior. Survival of the group itself was seen as linked to the welfare of each and every blood relative. When the Quraysh were camel breeders, there were always dangers lurking in the environs of Mecca. The loss of a herd to natural causes or different kinds of predators could immediately alter one's capacity to carry on in life. The hair of the animals was used to make clothing, the skin to make shelter, and the milk and meat to provide nourishment. Because at any time the same might happen to any of the victim's kinsmen, the clans of Quraysh were obligated to make up the loss without taking advantage of another's distress. Similarly, the loss of a father placed an enormous burden on the other close male relatives to look after the widowed mother and any surviving offspring. The story of Muhammad and his uncle Abu Talib is a case in point. Obligations of this sort were not considered an unwanted burden but a clearly defined responsibility sanctioned by generations of communal behavior. To do otherwise was to visibly stain the honor of the extended clan.

The emergence of Mecca as a major commercial center, with the Quraysh playing a lead role in long-distance trade and local commerce, represented an environment quite different from that of the past. Mecca's commercial interests were protected by a network of alliances that brought relative peace to west Arabia and beyond. Under the circumstances, life became much less marginal for the Qurayshites. The lives of individuals and their immediate families were less subject to dramatic change that threatened immediate or long-range hardship, let alone survival. The enterprising men of Mecca, having become liberated from camel breeding, were bound to regard their new situation with great confidence. This caused an apparent shift in social relationships and in certain ways changed attitudes toward clan responsibilities. On the fringes of the oases, no camel breeder would have lent an item or animal desperately needed by a blood relative and then demanded interest on the loan. That would have meant taking advantage of a blood relative, a definite breach of tribal etiquette. Investing in large caravans for purposes of long-distance trade or even selling wares at fixed locations within Mecca required a more sophisticated approach to borrowing and lending. New financial arrangements thus bent the prohibition against charging interest.

With marginal life an experience of the past, collective responsibility gave way to more narrowly defined self-interest. Smaller family units tended to act more independently; business partnerships cut across family and clan lines challenging traditional loyalties; and loyalties to more inclusive groups competed with incipient individualism. Such changes were likely to invoke a sense of nostalgia among those of the Quraysh who yearned for a return to familiar and time-tested values. It is most likely therefore that Muhammad's appeal did not derive from any single concern experienced by his followers but by a cluster of grievances that could be addressed through belief in a religion that embraced their social values while at the same time demanded dedication to a single God prepared to reward or punish humans in accordance with their worldly behavior.

We should be careful not to exaggerate the alleged malaise of growing individualism. The basic unit of society was still the larger association linked by blood. The Quraysh became preeminent in west Arabia precisely because they were able to soft peddle individual and group differences for the sake of the common good. Nothing was allowed to interfere with the long-distance trade and the elaborate alliances that made it possible. There was, to be sure, a certain subcurrent of tension among the Meccans and their allies. The very nature of tribal association with its emphasis on absolute autonomy remained the theoretical ideal that informed tribal sensibilities. But large-scale cooperation clearly had its advantages for the Quraysh and their partners. The accumulated wealth and the absence of serious conflict over an extended period of time were not easily dismissed. No doubt, there was always the potential for problems that might cause the intricate network of alliances to collapse;

tribal xenophobia (*'asabiyah*) could always reassert itself. But for the present, the framework that provided the Meccans with their wealth and prestige seemed secure.

So why did Muhammad and his relatively small following attract opposition from the oligarchs presiding over the affairs of Mecca? What was so threatening about belief in the God of Heaven and about a day of judgment when all of humankind will be held accountable? Would this have led to an economic boycott of Hashim, the Prophet's clan, and its close associate Muttalib? Does it explain the physical abuse of certain Muslims, let alone the reports of a grandiose plot to take the Prophet's life and his subsequent flight to Medina? Several views have been advanced by modern scholars to identify his opponents and the nature of their antagonism to him and his mission.

According to one theory, the Meccans concluded that Muhammad's embrace of monotheism implied an end to the pagan shrine at Mecca. With that, the spiritual core that held the Qurayshite alliances together would unravel. The great fair and the pagan pilgrimage that brought countless visitors to the shrine site enriched the coffers of the Quraysh while sustaining the tribe's prestige as guardians of the Ka'bah. At first glance, this may strike us as a compelling argument, although to think such views could have led to an attempt on Muhammad's life seems a bit of a stretch, as we shall see later. Be that as it may, it is not clear that Muhammad was entirely inflexible about the shrine and various pagan idols at the early stages of his career. Faced with opposition bred of a long-standing custom, he seems to have espoused a live-and-let-live attitude toward unbelievers (*kafirun*), or so we can ascertain from the Qur'an: "You have your religion (*din*) and I have mine." (Surah 109: esp. 6). The segment of scripture known as "The Star" (Surah 53:19–20) states: "Have you seen [the two pagan goddesses] al-Lat and al-'Uzza, [19] and Manat the third and other? [20]" It is clear from an extensive and wide variety of early sources Surah 53:20 continued the thought with "*high-flying cranes whose* [divine] *intercession is to be hoped for.*" At a loss for how to deal with these revelations, which clearly contradicted everything they knew the Prophet stood for based on verses later revealed in the Qur'an, Muslim commentators groped for an explanation. When he said, "I have my religion and you have yours." Muhammad was understood as making overtures not to the pagans of Mecca but to the Jews of Medina, monotheists like himself (the authorities are clear, nevertheless, that these words of seeming accommodation did not exempt the Muslims from combating the Jews as the verse was abrogated by harsher revelations to follow).

The verse that originally praised the goddesses was decidedly more problematic, and so Muslim authorities held that in this instance Satan had clouded the meaning of Muhammad's words, as he had indeed clouded various words of all the previous prophets sent by God. In any case, the Prophet's early concession to polytheism bore no fruit.

If Muhammad was in a conciliatory mood toward the polytheists early in his career, what reason would there have been for the Qurayshites to bring pressure on the Prophet and his fledgling group of supporters? Watt argues that the leaders of Mecca realized already at this time that the creation of a community based on religious ties and a prophet chosen by God meant that prophet would control its politics as well as its religious life. Given the logic of his religious beliefs, Muhammad was likely to insist on holding political authority in perpetuity. For leadership that God bestows only God takes away. This notion runs counter to traditional tribal politics. As a rule, tribesmen recognize authority grudgingly and only when compelled. The heads of clans and more inclusive tribal groups ruled at the behest of the notables who could at any moment withdraw their favor and seek another from among their own. Realizing that control of their affairs would be dominated by Muhammad and his Muslim followers, the oligarchs of Mecca were said to have been galvanized into action, going so far as to concoct an elaborate plan for the Prophet's death. Admittedly, there is logic to this line of reasoning, but it presupposes ever so much. We are being asked to believe that the Meccans foresaw with astonishing clarity the events that transpired years later when Muhammad moved to Medina, gathered a large army of diverse tribesmen, and used that oasis as a base from which to challenge the Quraysh, politically and militarily. Modern scholars who promote this view of the Meccan opposition have the benefit of hindsight; they write with full knowledge of Muhammad's astounding successes at Medina. It is doubtful that the Meccans had any inkling, let alone foresaw in detail, the events that would later overtake them.

What then was the nature of the opposition to Muhammad; on what grounds was it based; and how serious was it? Given what we know of the early community and given what we know of tribal life at the time, one could argue that the opposition to Muhammad as a religious leader was actually mild during his years in Mecca, and that neither he nor the vast majority of his followers were in any kind of real danger. Indeed, one can make the case that Muhammad took off for Medina not because his life was at risk, as our sources indicate, but because his mission at Mecca had failed. His effort had, more or less, run its course and without the expected success. As regards the opposition, whatever moves were directed against him and various other Muslims were not simply in reaction to his religious message but were colored by larger political agendas dictating relations between clans at the time.

In any case, all scholars are agreed that by 620 C.E., the Prophet's career at Mecca had reached an impasse. His wife Khadijah, a great source of financial and emotional stability had died, as had his uncle and surrogate father Abu Talib. Abu Talib had been the leader of his clan and as long as he lived the clan of Hashim was honor bound to look after Muhammad. But after Abu Talib's death the clan leadership went to a younger uncle, more or less the same age as the Prophet. The latter, Abu Lahab by name, was quite ambitious and anxious to restore good relations between Hashim and the leading clans of Quraysh whose leaders had conspired to impose a boycott of all the Quraysh against Hashim and its close ally Muttalib. It appears the latter two groups had been at the forefront of an alliance of lesser clans to stem the influence of the leading oligarchs. Isolating them economically and socially was a lesson to any who would tamper with the current order. The apparent price for the ending the boycott was the jettisoning of full support for Muhammad on the pretext of an alleged slur cast by him against his deceased polytheist grandfather. It cannot be said that Muhammad was thrown to the wolves and that his position had become precarious, but it was now clear that he had absolutely no leverage with which to continue his floundering mission.

There are various reports that the Muslims were much damaged by social ostracism and economic boycott and that a number of them had left the fold because they were physically abused. These reports seem to coincide with a plan of action against the Muslims developed by Abu Jahl, one of the leading Meccans who was strenuously opposed to Muhammad and his mission. When encountering men of high birth, that is Muslims from among the leading clans of Quraysh, Abu Jahl suggested the Meccans cast aspersions on their honor; when confronting merchants (the majority of Muslims from the middling clans, especially Hashim), he suggested they impose an economic boycott; those Muslims who lacked proper clan affiliation were to be beaten (as they would have no supporters to protect from their adversaries). While this policy would have been enough to seriously weaken the Muslims, most of whom were susceptible to the boycott, it would hardly have been enough to cause Muhammad's followers to defect en masse. Any social and economic boycott would have been difficult to sustain. Muslims were no doubt involved in partnerships with non-Muslims and were married to partners from non-Muslim families as business interests cut across clan lines. On the one hand, non-Muslim friends, relatives, and business partners might try to pressure the Muslims into compliance so as to make life easier for all; on the other they could have eventually harbored resentment against the call for a boycott. In either case, Muhammad's mission was not likely to succeed without the full support of his own kinsmen. And so he sought a change of venue.

Initial negotiations with outlying tribes and with leaders from the nearby oasis of Ta'if produced no positive results. However, talks with Medinese tribesmen arriving in Mecca during the pagan pilgrimages of 621 and 622 proved fruitful. The first meeting paved the way to recruit converts in Medina, an oasis three day's journey from Mecca and then known as Yathrib. The next year a larger group of pilgrims met with the Prophet to lay the groundwork for settling him and his followers in Medina. Several hundred Muslims then made their way to the oasis, but the Prophet, 'Ali, and Abu Bakr remained behind waiting for permission to emigrate.

The medieval sources would have us believe the Meccans now saw Muhammad as a serious threat. By moving to Yathrib, he would be in position to rally the local Medinese behind him and take up arms against his former tribe. It is said he had already decided to engage the Qurayshites in open combat. And so, they assembled in the council chamber where they made collective decisions of grave importance. Attending the meeting were representatives from the all the clans save Hashim and Muttalib (as these two closely linked clans would be dishonored to discuss taking action against one of their own). Also attending was the Devil disguised as a sheikh from the distant highlands of Arabia. He had come to offer them council and was invited to enter. Not surprisingly, his carefully crafted advice gave rise to the elaborate scheme by which the Meccans hoped to dispose of God's Prophet.

It is not at all likely that the notables of Quraysh, who prided themselves on their independence of thought and action, would have invited a total stranger to advise them in so important a matter. The Devil can be charming and seductive, but his very presence in this account makes us suspicious that the events discussed therein ever took place as related here. Nevertheless, the story is of immense interest because it suggests ever so strongly that, contrary to Muslim tradition, the Prophet's life was never in danger. Someone attending the conclave argued that Muhammad be cast out of the community. In tribal societies habitual troublemakers who lowered the honor of their kin could be declared "undesirable" (*makhlu'*) and set adrift from their society. With no formal protection, such individuals would have to scrounge about for survival, hardly circumstances suitable for promoting a prophetic mission. There is another reason that favored this solution. Not only would Muhammad's life be spared, no one could be accused of doing him bodily harm. Under the circumstance, his own clan and its ally Muttalib would hardly be compelled to retaliate against the rest of Quraysh to salvage their honor. But the Devil saw a flaw in this intelligent scheme. He reminded the Meccans of Muhammad's eloquence and how he could win adherents to his cause and then return to Mecca to "attack them and rob them of their authority [exactly what he later did from his new base in Medina]."

Another speaker spoke of putting him in chains and leaving him imprisoned [without food or water] until death overtakes him. There is an interesting, indeed compelling logic to this method of dealing with Muhammad. There is, to begin with, a real sense of ending to the affair; the Prophet will not survive and with that his challenge to the oligarchs of Mecca will be ended. Moreover, the burden of his death will not fall heavily on the perpetrators of Quraysh. By the curious laws of homicide then practiced by the desert Arabs—at least as seen from the prospective of later Muslim authors—primary responsibility for Muhammad's death would have fallen on the chains that bound the Prophet and not the jailors who fettered him. At most, the jailors might be accused of man-slaughter, in Arabic "something like homicide" (*shibh 'amd*) but not "homicide" (*'amd*) which always requires drawing blood from the victim with a sharp instrument that penetrates the body. At worst, the Meccans would be obliged to pay Hashim heavy blood money to compensate Muhammad's clan for his death, probably an agreed upon number of camels. But that would be a relatively light price to pay for restoring pagan Mecca to normalcy.

And yet, this second rather ingenious plan did not meet with the Devil's approval. He pointed out that Muhammad's friends might release him from his confines, and when their numbers grew, they could return to Mecca and destroy "your authority." Finally, a suggestion wins the Devil's approval. It is offered by no less than Abu Jahl, the implacable enemy of Muhammad who had designed the earlier strategy for weakening Muhammad and the Muslims. Muhammad would be assassinated by blows from a sharp sword. But how could one carry off so audacious a plan with homicide written large all over it? Such a move would surely have compelled Hashim to seek revenge from the clan of his attacker, creating thereby an extensive opening for blood feud, precisely the kind of civil conflict the Quraysh wanted most to avoid. Each of the clans (save Hashim and Muttalib of course) would designate a young assassin of impeccable genealogy (and hence fully protected by their status). Armed with sharp swords, they would strike the Prophet simultaneously "as if with one blow." With that, the Prophet's blood would be spread evenly among the participating clans making it impossible for his kinsmen to seek revenge from all of them. Nevertheless, to allow Hashim to retain its honor and bring it and Muttalib back into the fold, a very large payment of blood money would be offered.

The clever plot was then set in motion, but the angel Gabriel intervened. Muhammad, made aware of what was afoot by God's protective angel, cast a spell over the would-be assassins leaving them in a trance outside his dwelling. 'Ali slept in Muhammad's place, having been assured by the Prophet that no harm would befall him, while the Prophet fled to Medina with Abu Bakr, his trusted friend and future father-in-law. As told by the medieval sources, the Prophet's emigration (Hijrah), described as a flight, was a harrowing experience portrayed in the best tradition of the battle-day narratives of later tribal historians.

What are we to make of all this? Was there really a plot to kill the Prophet; were there any realistic circumstances that would have called for such an act and in which such an act could have been seriously considered? It is abundantly clear that this medieval tradition has gone to great lengths to dramatize the danger faced by Muhammad and the divine intervention that saved his life and validated his mission. Clearly, the medieval writers were hard pressed to find a single scenario that could realistically put Muhammad at risk. It is likely he went to Medina peacefully as did several hundred of his followers before him. The oligarchs of the Quraysh were probably glad to get rid of him as at the moment they regarded him as no more than a self-righteous dissident. Their real concern was his clan, which riled the political waters they sought to keep calm to their own advantage. Muhammad's loss of standing within his own clan was the likely price that Hashim had to pay to return to the good graces of the other clans of the Quraysh. His emigration to Medina might then be seen as the consequence of that sequence of events. Clearly the Meccans did not anticipate how Muhammad would change his situation and of course theirs, once he was firmly settled in his new environment.

The Prophet's Mission: Medina

The move to Medina, however arranged and carried out, proved to be the major watershed in the Prophet's career. At Mecca, Muhammad was the leader of a relatively small group of believers whose identity was defined, not only by their loyalty to him and their embrace of his religion, but also by extremely powerful ties to the families and clans that embraced and protected them. Religion was an expression of belief; one's public face was determined by all-important blood ties, the essential markers that accorded individuals and groups their identity and status within a larger tribal society.

Our sources indicate that at Medina, Muhammad became the unquestioned head of a powerful religious community (ummah). The constituents of that community owed their primary allegiance to the Prophet and the ummah as a whole. In many respects, the ummah took on the characteristics of a familiar tribal polity, except that, in theory, ties of religion replaced those of blood. As did powerful tribes, the Prophet's newly formed community had an army, conducted war and "foreign policy," levied taxes, and adjudicated disputes among those tribesmen who fell within its political sphere. The critical actor in this unfolding drama was the Prophet himself. While at Mecca, Muhammad was a religious leader with moral authority over the relatively few who, out of religious conviction, were inclined to recognize his prophetic vocation. At Medina, he became, as well, a political leader over those who found it in their interest to accept Islamic authority or who had been compelled to accept it by economic circumstance or military pressure.

In Medina Muhammad became powerful.

Borrowing W. Montgomery Watt's formulation, Muhammad became a statesman as well as a prophet.

Unable to convince his fellow Qurayshites by verbal persuasion, the Prophet would utilize the political leverage acquired at Medina to compel the Meccans to accept his message, using armed force if necessary. To deal with the Quraysh in this way, Muhammad would have to construct broad alliances of the sort the Meccans had assembled, and, along with that, undermine and then dismantle the alliances that allowed Mecca to engage in long-distance trade. As a result, a mission originally limited to kinsmen in Mecca would evolve over time into a mission for all of western Arabia, and, following that, all the Peninsula. When, following the death of Muhammad, Arab armies conquered vast lands well beyond the frontiers of Arabia, Islam began to emerge as a world religion—in the words of Ibn Ishaq previously cited, a religion for "all humankind." By any yardstick, the expansion of Islam and the transformation of the ummah into an imperial polity were exceedingly rapid. Within less than a hundred years, Muslims had carved out a state that extended from eastern Iran to the Iberian Peninsula. It is hard to believe, indeed it is almost inconceivable, that these developments were planned or even foreseen by the Prophet and his immediate entourage. One could go a step further. It is not likely that Muhammad even foresaw how events would favor him so rapidly in Medina when he arrived there in 622. The likely objective of his move was to secure a place for himself and his followers rather than directly challenge Mecca and its allies. Securing an arrangement with the Medinese was no small matter. In tribal societies, guarantees of safety always called for delicate negotiations. Before talking with representatives of the Aws and Khazraj, the leading tribes of Yathrib (as Medina was then known), the Prophet had tried and failed to secure a place for himself and his followers at two other locations. Any agreements that would have allowed Muhammad and the Muslims to relocate had to be reached with the expectation they would be fully honored and, most important, at terms that satisfied the Prophet and his followers.

The negotiations between Muhammad and the Medinese that preceded the Hijrah are then critical to an understanding of the events that purportedly followed. But as with every eventful moment in the Prophet's life, we are stymied by the historical license of our tendentiously driven sources. Once again we are forced to interrogate descriptions of events that should have been and not events as they were or might have been. Our questions are clear enough: Did the Prophet anticipate the larger or even broad contours of his eventual struggle with the Quraysh?

That is, did he go to Medina knowing full and well that he would establish a community based on religious rather than blood ties, and then engage in numerous political alliances to challenge the Meccans and their confederates? What did the Medinese make of their invitation to the prophet from Mecca? Put somewhat differently, why did they invite a stranger with more than a hundred, perhaps several hundred, followers to enter their midst—a highly unusual act? What was the substance of these secret negotiations, the last of which was held in the dead of night and away from prying eyes and curious ears?

These are not questions that we can answer with any sort of confidence. There is, to be sure, no dearth of material on the negotiations and the Hijrah that followed. Seen in retrospect, Muhammad's move to Mecca was recognized by the Muslims for what it turned out to be: a major if not *the* major turning point in the history of the Prophet and the early Muslim community. The enormous importance of the event moved the early Muslims to reckon time from the date of the Hijrah, thus establishing the Islamic calendar that has continued until this day. So what may we say about this crucial moment in the formation of Islam, or, to be more precise, what might we be willing to conjecture?

Moving to Yathrib the Future Administrative Center (Madinah) of the Prophet

Unlike Mecca, Yathrib/Medina was a series of agricultural settlements stretched like a ribbon over some twenty miles, with water and vegetation appearing, disappearing, and reappearing as one traveled the route. The early history of the settlement is obscure. About a half century ago, D. S. Rice, the Islamic art historian and archeologist, uncovered a paving stone in the Hauran region of Syria, an area that was in ancient times, part of an extensive trade network. On the reverse of the paving stone was cuneiform writing from the time of the last Babylonian Empire, a thousand years before the rise of Islam. When deciphered, the text seemed to reflect a trade route of some sorts, which included among the various locations a place called Yathrib. There is no reason to doubt the inscription refers to Medina, as there is more than ample evidence in ancient sources of Babylonian incursions into the Arabian Peninsula.

Rice's discovery revived interest in an old theory that Jews came to Arabia after being exiled from the Land of Israel by the Babylonian king Nebuchadnezzar (ca. sixth century B.C.E.), coincidentally a view that is expressed in medieval Arabic sources. Yathrib was allegedly settled by a number of Jewish tribesmen, the major groups being the Nadir, Qurayzah, and Qaynuqaʿ. Who these Jews were, how they got to Yathrib, and what they might have known or practiced of normative Judaism, cannot be answered with certainty. In any case, with the decline of living space in south Arabia and migration of tribes northward, pagan Arab tribesmen moved into the unoccupied lands of the oasis, originally as the clients of the Jews. But in time—probably mid-sixth century C.E.—the clients became more powerful than their original patrons. Roles were now reversed as the major Jewish tribes became in effect clients of the Aws or Khazraj, pagans who had migrated from the south. Lesser Jewish and pagan tribal units were also situated at Yathrib.

The Aws and Khazraj, who frequently feuded (perhaps because the oasis was now overcrowded) engaged one another in open combat, drawing into the conflict the Jews linked to their clans. And so, the Aws and Khazraj, who stemmed from the same southern tribal configuration, the Banu Qaylah, and the Jews who were clients of one or the other Arab tribe, became involved in open conflict that threatened the stability of the oasis. A halt in fighting, occasioned by inconclusive combat, did not end with a formal declaration of peace and a return to normalcy. Neither party was apparently willing to concede anything of substance. Watt assumes, perhaps correctly, that the situation of no war but also no formal peace drove the tribesmen into their protective forts and kept them there, causing neglect of the agricultural economy. With that, there would have been need of an outside arbitrator, thus explaining why individuals of the Aws and Khazraj approached Muhammad. Unable to resolve the dispute themselves, they sought the man with claims to prophecy, but more important, a man of well-known moral virtue.

Muhammad did, in fact, become a sort of arbitrator shortly after arriving in Medina, but in describing the negotiations leading up to the Hijrah, the major Arabic sources do not mention arbitration, at least not explicitly. As a rule, medieval writers seeking to explain history favored religion over politics. To be more precise, they tended to give political phenomena a religious gloss. In this case, religious sensibilities were depicted as the ultimate engine that drew individuals and groups to the Prophet and led them to accept Islam.

Our sources would have us believe that some Medinese, members of the Khazraj, met with the Prophet at one of the periodic fairs in Mecca and embraced him and his message. Although pagans, they knew something of monotheism as they were linked to Jewish tribesmen in what is described as an uneasy situation. Faced with occasional humiliation, their erstwhile Jewish allies had boasted that a prophet was soon to appear and that they (the Jews) would rally to this prophet and with his assistance would turn against the pagans (who had displaced the Jews from prominence and compromised their honor). Having heard Muhammad speak, it was clear to these pagans that he was indeed the prophet of whom the Jews had spoken and that it would be wise to preempt the Jewish plan by accepting Muhammad and his message before the Jews rallied to him and enlisted him on their side. There is in this description of events a melding of political and religious motives. Satisfied that Muhammad was indeed the prophet (mentioned in Jewish scripture), the pagan visitors became Muslims. They pledged to seek possible converts from among their tribe and hoped that acceptance of Muhammad and Islam could lead to unity among their warring clans (perhaps a hint of arbitration?) and the defeat of any potential action taken by the Jews emboldened as they were by the expectations of a new prophet and change of fortunes. Muhammad's fame subsequently spread throughout the habitations of the Khazraj (and presumably the Aws).

This tradition has a familiar ring; it conjures up polemical texts previously encountered in our narrative of Muhammad's life. As in the case of Muhammad's birth, his trips to Syria, and the events surrounding his first revelation, we are informed the older monotheists knew of the prophet's imminent arrival (as they had read predictions of his coming in their sacred writings and absorbed such wisdom in oral traditions that were handed down from generation to generation). The description of events also anticipates Muhammad's attack on the Jews, a brazen policy that embarrassed the Jews' Medinese patron whom Muhammad wished to bring down—but more about the Jews and local politics later. The polemical thrust of this account notwithstanding, it may indeed preserve a genuine echo of the past. The pagans speak of uniting their warring factions through an embrace of Muhammad and Islam. Although that assuredly took place following the Hijrah, there is no specific mention here of arbitration or, more important yet, there is no inkling of Muhammad and his Meccan followers taking up residence among the Medinese.

During the pilgrimage of 621, twelve members of the Aws and Khazraj, soon to be known as the Ansar or "helpers" (of the Prophet), reportedly met with Muhammad at al-'Aqabah, the isolated mountain pass near Mecca that served as venue for the first meeting. There, at al-'Aqabah, the Medinese formally swore allegiance to God's Messenger and pledged to uphold a set of universal principles which (later) became known as "The Pledge of the Women" (after the women of Quraysh who took the pledge when Mecca capitulated to the Muslims). The pledge taken by tribesmen of the Aws and Khazraj enjoined them to give allegiance to Muhammad and foreswear polytheism. In addition, they pledged not to steal; fornicate (with another's woman); engage in the (ritual) killing of offspring; slander neighbors (an invitation to reprisal and feuding); or disobey Muhammad in what was clearly right. Fulfilling these obligations would reserve a place for them in Paradise; disobeying would bring punishment in this world or, barring that, on the Day of Resurrection when God decides whether to punish or forgive. They then returned to Medina with a man sent by the Prophet to instruct them and the other converts in how to practice Islam. Again, there is no firm indication that Muhammad would immigrate to Medina in order to arbitrate their internal disputes, let alone that his Meccan followers would take up residence with him. Moreover, there is not the slightest hint that the Medinese would take up arms on his behalf, a point the medieval authorities are only too anxious to stress.

The issue of Muhammad's settling in Medina and taking up arms only surfaced during a third meeting at al-'Aqabah in which the Prophet met with seventy-three men and two women from the Ansar, all but one converts to Islam. According to our source, the non-Muslim, a leading figure at Medina, was brought along because the Ansar wished to convert him and thus spare him of hellfire for his pagan beliefs. If there is any truth to this report, it is more likely the need to convert him was because his approval was needed to sell any agreement made with the Prophet to those who remained polytheists at Medina. The Ansar had not yet paved the way for the Prophet to transfer his mission to the troubled oasis; there were still details to work out. Not coincidentally, the encounter between Muhammad and the Ansar is portrayed as a clandestine meeting that took place in the middle of the night. Apparently, the Prophet did not wish to be observed by either his own kinsmen or the nonbelievers of the Aws and Khazraj who had come to Mecca as pilgrims.

The Prophet's medieval biographer Ibn Ishaq begins his account of the deliberations with a statement by Muhammad's paternal uncle al-'Abbas. Though not a Muslim himself, al-'Abbas is pictured as most anxious to defend his nephew's interests. He informs the Muslims of the Aws and Khazraj that for Muhammad to settle among them they would have to guarantee his safety "as we [Hashim] do." There is something most odd in Ibn Ishaq's description of the meeting. In most sources, Muhammad's uncle is pictured as an implacable opponent of his nephew; a recalcitrant pagan who sided with the oligarchs of Quraysh, and who only converted at the eleventh hour after the Meccans had all capitulated and accepted Islam. When they finally recognized Muhammad's authority, many early opponents, certainly the sons of his opponents, became active in the ummah, but not al-'Abbas. There is no clear indication that he sought or was given responsibility for promoting the new faith. How then might we explain the seeming anomaly of the uncle supporting his nephew at this delicate meeting which was to be kept secret from the polytheists, and what might al-'Abbas's presence at al-'Aqabah tell us about the historical accuracy of this particular report if not the rest of the account?

It is apparent that, in this case, a critical moment of Islamic history has been reshaped, if not invented, by Ibn Ishaq to make it consonant with later political developments. As the official propagandist of the Abbasid dynasty, our author was compelled to rewrite the life of al-'Abbas because Abbasid claims to rule rested on descent from their ancestor, the Prophet's oldest surviving paternal uncle (see Part Two). Ibn Ishaq could hardly claim that the progenitor of the Abbasid house was an early Muslim; that ran counter to received wisdom. But he could argue that, unbeknownst to the majority of Muslims, al-'Abbas supported Muhammad. Speaking on Muhammad's behalf at a secret meeting attended by no other Qurayshites save the Prophet was a telling case in point. Not surprisingly, claims by the Abbasids and their supporters on behalf of al-'Abbas were treated with skepticism and even disdain by their opponents. To be sure, such claims also raise a few eyebrows among modern scholars of the West.

As the story continues to unfold, the Medinese ask Muhammad to speak for himself. He invites them to protect him as they "would protect their women and children [that is, if he were nothing less than one of their immediate blood relatives]." One of the Ansar stresses the martial tradition of his tribe and pledges to protect Muhammad as requested. But there are doubts about the long-range consequences of such an alliance. A second speaker interrupts the proceedings and questions whether the Prophet will remain at Medina "after God has given [him] victory." What is meant by "victory" is anything but clear, especially if we share the assumption of most Western scholars that Muhammad went to Medina as an arbitrator whose task was to calm passions and restore normalcy among warring parties. The speaker goes on to explain that in making league with the Prophet, the Ansar will have to sever their current ties to others. The others are unspecified but Muslim authorities understood them to be the Jews of Medina with whom the Prophet later went to war on no less than three occasions even though they were clients of different Medinese clans and thus entitled to the protection of these clans.

Faced with these concerns, the Prophet reaffirms his obligation to the Ansar. He is prepared to wage war on any who would wage war against them and make peace with any who would make peace with them. At face value, the account seems to tell us that the Muslims and the Ansar had entered into a verbal agreement of mutual protection; nothing more, nothing less.

Muslim tradition gives the episode a more dramatic meaning. The second pledge taken by the Medinese was reportedly a "Pledge of War" which implied combat against the insolent Quraysh. God had finally unfettered the shackles that had bound Muslims to endure insults and persecution from their Meccan kinsmen. The Muslims who had been forced into exile will now fight the polytheists until "God alone is worshipped." In this understanding of events, the Ansar meeting with Muhammad at al-'Aqabah actually committed themselves to support him in his future campaigns against Mecca and perhaps his later break with the Jews. If this last reading is correct, it presupposes the Ansar foresaw the Muslim attack on the Jews, who were at the time clients of the Aws and Khazraj, and, more startling yet, it declares the Ansar were prepared to accept Muhammad's throwing down the gauntlet to the Meccans. We are thus asked to believe that even before the Prophet left for Medina, the talk of war against Mecca was in the air. That is quite an assertion. Given the power and prestige of the Quraysh and their allies, the Ansar might have been more than a bit reticent to take up arms against them. At the time of these reported negotiations, the Medinese would have had much too much on their plate to even consider so wild and dangerous a scheme as warring against Mecca and the grand alliance, especially as the Ansar had not yet put their own house in order.

If we do not read more into these accounts than is already there, the present story of the negotiations, written long after the incident, is meant to reflect later developments, obscuring thereby the sum and substance of what went on at this last meeting between Muhammad and the converts from Medina. We know for sure only that Muhammad was prepared to take up residence in the oasis. There is no specific reference of his Meccan followers (*muhajirun*) in our account, but as they are said to have preceded him en masse, we can assume the emigration of the entire community had to be part of the discussion. We can certainly assume that the Prophet and the Muslims would not have made the trek without firm guarantees of protection, the sort of guarantees that are described by our author. We may also assume that the Prophet went to Medina to serve as an arbitrator as there is firm evidence he did just that after he arrived at his new home.

The Prophet at Medina

For self-reliant Arab tribesman who jealously guarded their autonomy, arbitration was a last resort. As they ordinarily resisted the intervention of outsiders, they would have to perceive an extraordinary threat to themselves and their community before allowing a person unrelated by blood to sort out clan or intertribal affairs. In tribal societies, entering into and conducting proceedings of arbitration were part and parcel of an extremely complicated process. All the parties to the dispute had first to agree to arbitration and then select an acceptable arbitrator. Upon reaching the scene of the negotiations, the arbitrator would be given a surety by the contesting parities, hostages or moveable property, to insure there was no breach of faith. If one party acted in bad faith during the proceedings, the arbitrator could declare the property, say a large number of camels, forfeit to the other. If that breach of faith caused the spilling of blood and in an extreme case the death of a tribesman, the arbitrator could declare licit the blood of the offending party's hostage or the equivalent thereof. Such sureties compelled serious negotiations and, more to the point, compliance with the arbitrator's decision. When the contesting parties settled on an agreement formally ending the dispute, the property and/or hostages were returned, the arbitrator was rewarded for his effort, and then he returned from whence he came. Over time, the decisions of arbitrators might become widely known and enshrined as precedent for tribesmen who might follow the broad or specific outlines of previous decisions without having to actually invite outside intervention—that is, if the parties to the dispute were not so heated as to preclude their agreeing on anything.

This is not the sequence of events we encounter in our sources. Muhammad did not come alone or with a few assistants to Medina. Several hundred Muslims are said to have taken up residence with him, settling initially in the lands of those who invited them. Nor did the Medinese who invited his intervention foresee his leaving once he achieved his objective. They are reported as wishing him to stay. Above all, there is an assumption that the Ansar will all convert to his faith. With that, Muhammad is more than a mere arbitrator; he is a Prophet with powers that transcend even those of a tribal sheikh, for in theory the believers must accept not only his religious guidance but also his political authority. In effect, the nascent Muslim ummah was to have become a tribe-like configuration in which powerful bonds of blood were replaced by even more powerful bonds of faith. That was, to say the least, a radical departure from the political organization of Arab tribes, so radical indeed that some Medinese accepted Muhammad and his authority grudgingly and then spoke openly against some of his policies, particularly Muhammad's eventual decision to challenge the pagan Quraysh and its powerful allies. That challenge began in 623 with a number of raids against Meccan caravans that had to travel along routes in the broad general vicinity of Medina.

According to our sources, the first of these raids was carried out on unsuspecting and lightly escorted caravans by a relatively small number of warriors (eight to twelve), all drawn from the ranks of the emigrants, who had allegedly been given secret instructions, to be opened only after they left Medina—a seeming indication that the Prophet was reluctant to involve the recent Medinese converts to Islam in this risky venture. In view of their later behavior, some of the Medinese leaders would have been extremely worried about antagonizing the greatest military power in western Arabia, especially because the most notable of the raids was carried out during the holy month of Rajab when the Arabs of the peninsula abstained from all fighting. Later assaults involved larger numbers of raiders, and, in March 624, the Meccans heavily reinforced a major caravan headed for Syria; the Muslims assembled a force that reportedly consisted of some three hundred fighting men, including a significant number of Medinese converts who were no doubt now willing to risk battling Quraysh for the spoils of victory.

The circumstances surrounding the event, the so-called Battle of Badr, are difficult to sort out. What can be said is that the Battle of Badr was by all Muslim accounts a stirring victory for the believers and was thus marked for all time as the first great triumph of the faithful, the quintessential victory that would lead to the eventual conquest of Mecca; the Islamizing of the Arabian Peninsula; and the eventual Arab/Muslim conquest of the lands beyond. Our sources indicate that the results of battles in which the Muslims acquired considerable booty enhanced the Prophet's position among his hard-core emigrant followers and the Medinese converts, but it also raised fears among certain leaders of the Aws and Khazraj about Meccan reprisals.

Muhammad surely could not have initiated raids against the Quraysh upon his arrival in Medina two years earlier, nor could joining the Prophet in these raids have been a condition agreed upon by the Medinese during the negotiations with him at al-'Aqabah. At the time, the risks for all concerned were much too high to plan let alone undertake such a course. Before feeling free to turn against his Meccan kinsmen, the Prophet had to define and solidify his personal position and that of his Muslim followers in Medina. Our best source for how he and the Muslims functioned among the Medinese is a document that has become known as the "Constitution of Medina." Many modern scholars specializing in the early Islamic period tend to accept the document as an authentic statement of the times. They base this on both the style and content of the Arabic text. There is, however, considerable disagreement as to whether the constitution in our possession is a unified document agreed upon at a particular moment by all the parties settled in Medina, or whether it is cobbled together from a number of sources reflecting different moments in the early history of Muhammad and his companions. Most modern Arabists believe the text reflects an early stage in the history of the ummah as there are references to the Jews, whose major tribes were expelled between 625 and 627. Others maintain that as the Nadir, Qaynuqa', and Qurayzah, the major Jewish tribes, are not explicitly mentioned, the Jews of our document may be some minor tribal groups who were allowed to remain. Were that so, the document would most likely have been composed after the expulsions. Written in what can be described as clipped Arabic, the text is difficult to fathom, and so there is also disagreement among learned Arabists as to the meaning of specific phrases. Nevertheless, a general consensus emerges among scholars who accept the historicity of the document; with that consensus, the new arrangements by which the Medinese managed their disputes are abundantly clear.

If we assume for the sake of argument that these arrangements do reflect an early stage of Muhammad's activities at Medina, the agreement, which was binding on all the major parties mentioned, would have provided for the following situations: (1) Should there be problems between the aforementioned parties, they were to be brought to Muhammad for adjudicating. In such fashion, the possibilities for renewed conflict would be seriously reduced. (2) No party to the agreement is permitted to enter into external alliances without the Prophet's explicit permission, thus preventing uncontrollable shifts of influence that could upset the newly established balance of power. (3) Disputes within families and extended blood relations are to be settled in traditional fashion, that is, by the leading members of the families and clans, without having to come before Muhammad. Were all this an accurate reflection of conditions in Medina, the agreement would have made the Prophet the leader of a large community with powers theoretically greater than that of any tribal leader. And yet, the agreement also recognizes the force of tribal sensitivities in so far as internal disputes were to be resolved as before.

The agreement and the relocation of many Muslim families in a safely controlled environment presented Muhammad with an opportunity to think once again of his original objective, that of converting the Qurayshites to Islam. In his private and more ambitious thoughts he might have extended that vision to all the Arabs of the peninsula, and in specific moments, particularly after numerous successes, to the world beyond the northern frontier of Arabia. At the least, one can assume the humiliation at the hands of Quraysh had taught Muhammad a lesson. To gain a foothold among the tribesmen of Mecca, it would be necessary to acquire the prestige that comes with military power. Without that power, there was no prospect of religious reform. When the opportunity presented itself at Medina, Muhammad seized the initiative. By process of trial and error, he cemented his hold on the Medinese factions and set into motion events that would create major alliances and a significant counter force with which to face the Meccans. Eventually, he would take the field of combat against his own kinsmen and challenge them for political supremacy and, having done that, he would lay the foundations of a larger religious community that would embrace the entire peninsula.

But establishing control of Medina was far from simple. The ummah had to function in a world of tribal realities. The carefully crafted community was held together by the requisite needs of its different constituencies, but these needs were born of the necessities of the moment. There was no guarantee that once the chaotic world of the Medinese became more settled, the less committed among the Aws and Khazraj and the more independently minded Jews who remained separate from the ummah would not subvert or even reject Muhammad's hard-won authority. After all, about what manner of community are we talking? The conglomeration of various groups that comprised the larger population of the oasis, particularly the most powerful of these units, the Aws and Khazraj, could at any given moment stress loyalty to tribe over any allegiance to a religious leader unrelated to them by blood. That would have been particularly true if, in challenging Quraysh, Muhammad would have raised fears among his new associates that the Meccans would seek retaliation against all the inhabitants of Medina. However small scale, and carried out by emigrants, the early raids against the Meccan caravans beginning in 623 must have had a disquieting effect on certain leaders of the Muhammad's host, especially Ibn Ubayy, who is depicted in our sources as being particularly concerned. How then did the Prophet solidify his control over the oasis that had become his new home and the center of his religious mission?

Solidifying Control

Any assessment of power, based on the available sources, reveals that Muhammad began his mission at Medina with clear assets. For one, he held the trump card of arbitrator, a position the Medinese were only too willing to grant, given their current circumstances. He also had unquestioning supporters, the Meccan emigrants who had been with him in difficult times and resisted various types of pressures to abandon him. To the contrary, rather than leave the Prophet, they abandoned their larger families and their place of origins to join Muhammad in "exile" in Medina. They found the ummah in Medina to be a parallel community to that of their kinsmen in Mecca. While kin remained of great importance, for them religious ties had transcended ties to blood relatives—at least they were as important. But the emigrants who were not sufficiently powerful to prevent the collapse of the Prophet's mission in Mecca were also not powerful enough to allow him to carry on without concern in Medina. Their support alone hardly guaranteed success. An additional prop would have to be found to support Muhammad's political activities, thus allowing his moral and religious authority to grow now that it had taken root. Who would be his initial allies?

At first glance, one might think he should have won over the Jewish tribes who shared with the Prophet a monotheist vision and a sacred history based on the world of the Hebrew Bible, albeit in different narratives. If Muhammad thought the Jews would accept him fully, he was sorely mistaken. The Jews, with a highly developed sense of their own history and religious practices, would not bend—at least that is what the Muslim sources, including the Qur'an, indicate. For Jews—that is for those Jews who practiced normative Judaism—prophecy ended with the destruction of the Temple in Jerusalem and was thereafter left to imposters, mutes, and small children. Muhammad was the most eloquent of men and he was surely no child when he undertook his mission. Moreover, the differences between Muslim religious practices and those of the Jews must have been a source of great tension, particularly as it affected matters as basic as sharing meals. Assuming that the Jews of Medina followed kashruth, the highly restrictive dietary laws of the Talmud, they would have found difficulty eating in Muslim houses. That might very well have been the case as the Qur'an states the overly complicated Jewish dietary laws were no less than a punishment inflicted by God.

Whereas Muhammad initially accepted Jewish practices, it would seem in an effort to win them over to his side, he soon adopted the distinctly Muslim observances that continue until this very day. And so the fast of Ashura', the equivalent of the Jewish fast day of Yom Kippur, an event observed one day a year from sundown to sundown, was relegated to lesser importance. Instead, Muslims favored the Fast of Ramadan which takes place over an entire month from sunrise to sunset with feasting in the evening. Similarly, the number of prayers during the day which might originally have been three, as proscribed by Jewish law, was fixed at five; and the orientation of prayer that was at first in the direction of Jerusalem, as among the Jews, was later redirected to Mecca. Moses, the great Hebrew lawgiver, is the dominant figure of Muhammad's early preaching, but he is overtaken by the patriarch Abraham in subsequent revelations. Abraham, judged by Muslims an early monotheist (*hanif*), was correctly seen as a precursor of the Israelite religion; and because he was the father of Ishmael as well as Isaac, he was the progenitor of the Northern Arabs, whom Islamic tradition linked to Ishmael, the alleged ancestor of Quraysh, Hashim, and the Prophet himself. The Muslim embrace of Abraham and his progeny through Ishmael rather than the latter's half brother Isaac enabled Muhammad to claim a genuine monotheism that skirted the Jewish notion of the chosen people and rooted monotheism in the Arabian Peninsula instead of the Fertile Crescent as in the biblical narrative.

While all these moves reflect the changing attitude of the Prophet toward his fellow monotheists, they do not seem to portend the physical attacks on the Jews that followed later. There is nothing to suggest that what befell the Jews was from the outset part of a carefully designed policy. What then occasioned the initial break with the Jews? Was it merely their outright rejection of him and his claims of being a legitimate prophet, as were Moses and the prophets of Israel in earlier times? Would that have been sufficient to war against the Jews of Medina, confiscate their lands and goods and force them into exile, the fate that was to befall the Qaynuqa' and the Nadir, two of the leading Jewish tribes? It surely would not explain the later decision to exterminate the adult males of the Qurayzah, a cruel and extraordinarily unusual act of collective punishment that still defies explanation. Should we be looking then for political links that brought the wrath of the Muslims upon all the major

Jewish tribes of Medina and later against their brethren at the oasis of Khaybar, the last Jewish settlement of importance outside of south Arabia? It could very well be that the fate of the Jews in Arabia was conditioned by more than one factor. Certainly, there was animosity generated by their denial of the Prophet's mission, but the Jews might also have suffered because of a larger game of political power that was soon to unfold within Medina and beyond. Not only had the Jews rejected Muhammad, some were clients of Muhammad's detractors among the so-called hypocrites (*munafiqun*), important Medinese tribal figures like the aforementioned Ibn Ubayy of the Khazraj who grudgingly accepted Islam out of convenience, but, given lingering tribal sentiments and loyalties, were prone to oppose the Prophet's policies from time to time, especially when Muhammad initiated action against the Meccans, a course that would have appeared to some Medinese foolhardy, indeed most dangerous.

The hypocrites represented a more potent challenge to the Prophet's authority than their Jewish clients. Muhammad needed the full backing of the Aws and Khazraj. Without the continuous and full support of these most powerful Arab tribes there was not the slightest hope of solidifying the ummah, let alone engaging the Quraysh and spreading Islam beyond the limited geographical area of Medina's influence. Arguably, Muhammad's relations with the Jews reflect his need to shore up his somewhat tenuous hold on the Ansar and prevent any shift of alliances that could undermine the Prophet's future plans elsewhere. Muhammad's turn against the leading Jewish tribes may have been occasioned by these larger political issues.

The physical attack on the Jews, which reflected the evolving needs of the Muslim community, was not sudden but part of a gradual breakdown of relations between the Jews and the Prophet. These needs may be defined as follows: (1) Consolidating as much control over the disparate tribal elements at Medina as tribal sensitivities would allow, particularly among the Aws and Khazraj, the most powerful political actors. (2) Insuring adequate living space and the means to satisfy the economic needs of the emigrants from Mecca. This was a complicated problem as the Meccans were not agriculturists who could work the date plantations that dotted the oasis even if such plantations fell into their hands. (3) In similar fashion, the Prophet would later have to secure dwelling space for new converts making their way to the oasis. By converting to Islam, it was theoretically possible for small family units and even individuals to gain full acceptance within the ummah, as it was the tie of religion and not blood that constituted the basis of membership in the community of the faithful. Ordinarily, tribes would seek alliances with units that provide significant numbers of warriors. As a result, individuals and small societal units seeking safety could never negotiate an advantageous or even attractive position within the tribal system. Muhammad, in search of fighters to augment the ranks of his forces, was less discriminating and brought those disadvantaged by the tribal system fully into the fold. Because their standing was determined entirely by their position within the ummah, these new converts turned out to be fierce advocates of the Prophet and his cause.

Where do the Jews fit into this picture of conversion? With the increasingly strained relations between the Muslims and Jews, the Prophet might have contemplated an oasis without their major tribes. The Jews possessed the choicest agricultural lands, many strongholds, and in the case of the Qaynuqa', they were prosperous merchants and artisans. The Qaynuqa' were settled in a place in Medina that the Meccan immigrants would certainly have coveted. Indeed, the first attack on the Jews, an event that took place in 624 after the victory at Badr, is directed against those who supplied the oasis's non-agricultural needs. The forced expulsion of the Jews and the loss of their lands, weapons, and tools are, to say the least, puzzling as there is nothing in the description of the events leading up to the armed conflict that gives proper explanation to the turn of events. The Muslim tradition itself is at great pains to offer a meaningful explanation.

The Arabic sources would have us believe the break with the Jews all began because of an incident that took place in the market of the Qaynuqa', a prank that compromised the modesty of a Muslim woman. Upon witnessing the event, an outraged Muslim struck the Jew dead and the Jews retaliated taking the Muslim's life in turn. As described, the incident has an understandable logic in a world of tribal sensibilities. Compromising the modesty of a woman, even if only lifting her skirt to expose her body parts, was a grave insult. The Muslim's response to this outrage was then perfectly understandable as was the subsequent reaction of the Jews to the death of one of their own. Situations of this sort could easily lead to blood feud and ultimately the destabilization of the community's carefully brokered truce. The so-called constitution of Medina was specifically designed to ameliorate the bad blood occasioned by incidents such as the one that took place in the market of the Qaynuqa'. How is it then that the initial spilling of blood did not result in Muhammad's intervention and settling the dispute by payment of blood money, however that payment might have been arranged given the complexity of the case? Both parties would seem to have shared some of the responsibility, although clearly the Jews initiated the event by acting in so insulting a fashion to a Muslim woman.

It is then surprising that there is no call for arbitration. The Jews, fearing the worst, withdrew to their strongholds and Muhammad rallied the Muslims to besiege them. After two weeks, the Qaynuqaʿ were forced to surrender and go into exile, leaving behind their arms and some tools, although they could collect the debts owed them and exit their lands with that. This was a considerable victory for the Prophet and the Muslims. It is said that the Qaynuqaʿ could muster some 700 fighting men and possessed 400 coats of arms. Perhaps equally important, whatever tools were left behind could be used by the Muslims who would replace them as the artisans and shopkeepers of the oasis. Some scholars have argued the Jews' safe exit with their wealth, negotiated by their patron Ibn Ubayy, is a sign of the latter's great prestige. One can, however, give a rather different interpretation of the unfolding event. There was hardly any provocation that merited a physical reprisal since the Jews signaled they would surrender. Such a reprisal would have been inconsistent with tribal norms given the circumstances of the dispute between the Muslims and Jews. In any case, what is of importance here is not the weakness of the Jews in defending their strongholds or the strength of the Muslims, but the failure of the hypocrite Ibn Ubayy, as patron of the Jews, to come directly to their defense with his associates. No doubt, he read the situation and assessed that any blow to his prestige occasioned by his failure to assist his clients in battle would have been easier to sustain than an armed confrontation with the Muslims in which he and his fellow hypocrites might have fared badly. Given his reluctance to risk a fight with the Muslims, it is no wonder Ibn Ubayy was seriously concerned Muhammad might draw his people into a confrontation with the powerful Meccan alliance, a potential disaster for all the Medinese.

In reacting to Muhammad's raids, particularly after Badr, the most provocative act against the Meccans to date, Ibn Ubayy was expressing a real concern shared by more than a few influential figures in the oasis. The grand alliance in which the Meccans played the central role was perceived by them if not indeed by all Arabs as the most powerful force in western Arabia. Nor did the Medinese who warned against the possible consequences of Muhammad's aggressive stance express their opposition with words alone; given the opportunity to participate in the raid at Badr, they allowed prudence to dictate their action and declined to join the attacking party. Ibn Ubayy and the others clearly foresaw the likely reaction of Quraysh. As it was, the incident at Badr cost the Meccans dearly in both men and material. A number of their notables had fallen in battle, losses that would have to be avenged to preserve the honor of families as well as maintain the widely held impression that Quraysh and its many allies were capable of brushing aside any challenge to Meccan supremacy when the situation demanded it. And so the Meccans responded; an expeditionary force was organized by Abu Sufyan, whose family, the House of Umayyah, would, in an ironic turn of events, eventually displace Muhammad's successors from power some three decades later, although long after they too had all converted to the new faith.

5

The Meccan Response and the Triumph of the Ummah

Under Abu Sufyan's leadership, the grand alliance invoked by the Meccans reportedly assembled a fighting force of some three thousand men. As with all battlefield accounts written in Arabic, there is much confusion in the sources—all were written well after the event in question and are given to a kind of storytelling that glorifies the bravery and martial skill of the Muslim fighters at the expense of others. Nevertheless, by all accounts, the fighting, known as the Battle of Uhud, was a stinging defeat for Muhammad and his followers. Had the course of fighting been otherwise, the Muslim chroniclers would have trumpeted the success of their ancestors instead of searching for evidence that the Muslims had held their own despite their considerable losses and their seeming disarray at critical point of the engagement. In any case, when the Muslims retreated from the field of battle, Abu Sufyan did not press the advantage held by his forces; instead he withdrew his large army, satisfied, it would appear, that they had punished the enemy who would abandon the policy of interfering with the long-distance trade.

In warfare between tribes and/or clans, the line between victory and defeat is often ambiguous. Winners can claim victory only if all who participate in battle perceive the outcome as decisive. One only loses an engagement by being killed and/or exiled, or by publicly acknowledging defeat. Even when humbled into formally recognizing objective realities, the defeated party is, more often than not, soothed by the balm of diplomatic niceties; a sort of staged theater agreed upon in advance by the warring factions. At Uhud, the Meccans may have won the battle, but by failing to resolve the issue between them and the ummah to their satisfaction, they could not be declared outright winners. As a result, the Prophet was able to regroup his forces, consolidate his position among the Medinese, and lay plans to win the campaign of the future. Immediately after the setback at Uhud, the Medinese opposition to the Prophet grew more vocal, particularly Ibn Ubayy and some other notables of the Ansar. They had doubts about confronting Mecca from the outset, but when attacked by Abu Sufyan they felt compelled to defend their lands against the invaders. Though they succeeded in keeping the Meccans at bay, the results of Uhud only confirmed their fears of the Prophet's recklessness. Muhammad suffered other setbacks later that year as Muslim raiding forces sustained losses against groups other than Quraysh, and in regions further removed from the friendly confines of Medina.

Faced with changing fortunes, particularly the aftermath of Uhud, the Prophet had to reestablish his authority fully. A few individuals from families sniping at the Prophet were assassinated without reprisal, a sign that the opposition was incapable of, or perhaps better put, unwilling to mount a direct challenge despite the blow to their personal prestige and that of their kinfolk. Assassination, a method of dealing with political adversaries, would have been considered counterproductive if not unthinkable in the Prophet's first two years at Medina. Eliminating an opponent at that time would have aroused passions possibly leading to blood feud and the destabilization of the newly established ummah; it now became a weapon in Muhammad's political arsenal. Somewhat earlier, a figure linked loosely to the Jewish tribe of Nadir, a poet who defected to the Quraysh and ridiculed the Prophet in his verses, was killed amid unlikely circumstances. Even more improbable is the description of what was to befall the Jewish tribe that had sheltered that poet Ka'b al-Ashraf, namely the expulsion of the Banu Nadir, not coincidentally a tribal unit also allied to Ibn Ubayy and the hypocrites as were the exiled Qaynuqa'.

Six months after Uhud, the Prophet reportedly went to the Nadir to receive blood money with which to settle a dispute. The Nadir are described as having been prepared to resolve the issue amicably and invited Muhammad to partake of a meal with them at which point he and his companions sat with their backs to a wall. Before the meal was served and the business concluded, the Prophet slipped away, to be followed later by his companions. According to Muslim sources, the angel

Gabriel (the very same heavenly being who had protected Muhammad when the Meccans plotted taking his life on the eve of the Hijrah) appeared before the Prophet and alerted him to an assassination planned by the Nadir. The wall where Muhammad sat was to be collapsed over his head and elements of the structure were to fall upon him killing him. Forewarned once again by divine intervention, the Prophet, as before, sought safety by exiting quickly lest the plotters carry out their scheme.

One almost has the feeling that this story, like the account of the Meccan assassins ready to pounce and strike God's messenger as if with one blow (at the Devil's prodding no less) reflects a theoretical discussion of retribution for different types of attempted murder in tribal society. Whatever the case, the ensuing story told in the Arabic sources troubles modern historians, as indeed the attack on the Jews seems to have troubled medieval Muslim authors. Having determined through divine intervention that the Jews were about to kill him through a seemingly ingenious scheme (although no attack had actually taken place and therefore no blood was spent), the Prophet reportedly demanded that the Nadir leave Medina within a narrowly prescribed period of time or face death. Should they choose to leave peacefully, they would retain ownership of their palm trees and receive part of the produce (meaning perhaps receipts from the sale of the dates). This is all very strange but perhaps not altogether unfathomable to readers acquainted with tribal conventions as they were perceived by our authors. The Muslim chroniclers are apparently hard pressed to explain why the Prophet acted against the Jews as he did when there did not seem to be any demonstrable provocation on their part (other than their continued recalcitrance at accepting the legitimacy of the Prophet's mission). Hence, the report of the bizarre plot in which the Prophet would have been killed without the assassins shedding his blood directly (let alone with a sharp instrument that would have made the act a homicide worthy of exacting blood revenge). That being the case, the Prophet could insist only that the Jews abandon their lands (the equivalent of paying blood money, though, as noted, in this instance no blood was actually shed).

Rather than capitulate to the Prophet's demands (what had they done to merit this brazen threat that sullied their honor?) the Jews withdrew to their strongholds; the Muslims in turn set about destroying their rich plantations. All this took place as Ibn Ubayy, the patron of the Jews, offered them little in the way of assistance, just as he did little if anything to defend his other Jewish clients, the Qaynuqaʿ. Faced with an insurmountable situation, we are told the Nadir capitulated and prepared to accept the original conditions offered them. But Muhammad, sensing their weakness, and given Ibn Ubayy's response, or rather lack thereof, changed the rules of the game. The Nadir would abandon their lands, leaving their weapons behind and would receive nothing from the sale of their dates. Their lands would then be occupied by the Muslim emigrants and their weapons made part of Muhammad's arsenal. The event shamed Ibn Ubayy and the hypocrites; their status among their kinsmen was greatly diminished and a new leadership for the Aws and Khazraj, long cultivated by the Prophet, prepared to fill the gap. In a brilliant display of tribal politics, combined no doubt with sincere religious conviction, Muhammad humbled his most outspoken rivals at Medina, expelled another major Jewish tribe that denied his legitimacy as a monotheist prophet, and secured additional living space for his loyal followers who came with him as strangers to the oasis and previously lived as guests on the lands of others. The Nadir, humbled by the circumstances, made for their estates in the Jewish oasis of Khaybar. At Khaybar, they intrigued against the Prophet until he conquered the oasis in 628.

All this political maneuvering did not end Muhammad's concerns. By 627, the caravan trade, the source of the Meccans' immense wealth and political influence, had ground to a halt. At that time, realizing the gravity of the situation, the Meccans summoned the entire confederacy of tribal units that fell within their commercial and political orbit. An army of some ten thousand warriors, including tribal units recruited from outside the grand alliance, descended on Medina in an attempt to crush the Muslim challenge once and for all. In this venture, the Meccans were supported, at least politically and financially, by the expelled Jews of Medina and their coreligionists at the wealthy oasis of Khaybar.

The attacking army would seem to have outnumbered all the potential fighters among the Medinese, which included individuals from the Aws and Khazraj who were quite naturally still reluctant to engage so powerful an enemy in battle. Some reportedly held discussions with the Meccans and were therefore asked to leave the oasis before the battle commenced—a puzzling description of events to say the least. Why allow the fainthearted neutrals the possibility of assisting or even joining forces with the Meccans, if only on an individual basis? We should note that by then the political capital of the hypocrites, whose heart was not in the conflict with the Quraysh, was diminished, if not largely spent. Under any circumstances, individuals who hesitated to follow the Prophet could be dealt with more easily; only one group might have been considered a problem by Muhammad if they chose to defect. The last of the major

Jewish tribes, the Qurayzah, represented a significant fighting force, and in the end they did refuse to band with the defenders of Medina, declaring neutrality instead.

At face value, the Meccans and their allies had a significant advantage, but in the end they were denied success. The account of what happened is, if nothing else, murky. We are told that a Persian convert to Islam named Salman advised Muhammad to dig a trench (*khandaq*) around the oasis, a defensive stratagem well known among the Persians but unknown to the Arabs of Arabia. Faced with the obstacle before them, the opposing cavalry troops were befuddled and unsure of how to proceed, and so they merely besieged the oasis rather than attempting an all-out assault. Our sources tell us that at some point of the siege, the Meccans held talks with the Qurayzah, in an attempt to gain some advantage against the Medinese defenders, but, as reported, the effort came to naught. The Qurayzah refrained from joining the battle (or agreeing to any arrangements that would have compromised their Medinese neighbors). Finally, the large attacking force withdrew without engaging Muhammad and his allies in extended combat.

A closer look at the sources suggests a somewhat more complex picture of what might have transpired. The large Meccan force consisted of many disparate elements, not all committed allies within the grand alliance, but bought off [some reportedly with Jewish wealth from Khaybar] to do battle and share in the glory and the spoils of war. The failure to initiate the kind of combat that would reflect the chivalry of desert warriors and earn the lucrative booty of a victorious campaign, had to have a highly negative effect on the invading force. Under the circumstances, significant elements of the attacking army broke off from the main body and returned to their tribal lands. The so-called Battle of the Trench was in effect not much of a military engagement. But it demonstrated that the grand alliance served as no deterrent to an ambitious and crafty enemy. Even after the Meccans mustered all their possible allies to form a single army, that force was, because of tribal considerations, too unwieldy to serve as a highly motivated fighting unit. The Meccans hardly lost the battle, but not having decisively won any battle, as no real battle took place, they squandered their perceived advantages. Their reputation for invincibility sullied, they became vulnerable to the Muslims who grew bolder as their strength in warfare and diplomacy became more and more apparent.

The first outcome of the Meccan failure was the extermination of the male adults of the Banu Qurayzah, a cruel punishment that had no precedent and was very much at odds with tribal codes of chivalry. As a rule, tribes sought to avoid shedding excessive blood, even against their most bitter enemies; for such actions could give rise over time to violent retaliation by groups linked either by blood or treaty to tribesmen that had been put to the sword indiscriminately. Full-scale fighting was a last resort; even when large forces were assembled, it was at times deemed preferable to have individual fighters engage in ritual combat. What then explains the seemingly unusual fate that befell the Qurayzah following a battle that was not even bitterly contested, and in which it could not be said they took a fighting role? Surely, something had to explain why Muhammad acted as he did. Julius Wellhausen, the famous biblicist who also wrote about Islam, was of the opinion that the very possibility the Qurayzah might turn against the Prophet caused him so much dread that he reacted with uncalled-for and truly unusual brutality.

As did Wellhausen, many orientalists were quick to blame the Prophet as being cruel and vindictive to the Jews once he repelled the threat of his pagan adversaries. Trying to imagine why the Prophet acted in so capricious a manner, they saw the extermination of the Qurayzah through the lens of Islamic tradition. And so they envisioned Muslims fathoming the Jewish rejection of Muhammad, an individual who shared broadly the Jews' monotheist sensibilities, as an act of betrayal, not only of the Prophet but of the Jews' own tradition, which reportedly foretold of his coming. Others scholars saw the elimination of the adult males of the Qurayzah as a carefully calculated act undertaken for political advantage, although what advantage could be gained by killing the Jews rather than expelling them as had been the policy with the Qaynuqa' and Nadir is anything but clear. One could, of course, argue that having taken refuge in Khaybar, the Jews previously exiled from Medina were in league with the enemy and that the Prophet was unwilling to allow a strengthening of the Jewish opposition to him. The answer to why Muhammad went so far as to have the men of Qurayzah exterminated and the women and children enslaved remains, in any case, a riddle without adequate explanation. Even the Muslims were puzzled by this unusual turn of events.

Like modern scholars of the West, Islamic tradition is hard pressed to find a proper reason for the unprecedented severity unleashed upon the Jews. There are reports that the Prophet had a special pact of mutual assistance with the Qurayzah which they renounced unilaterally, tearing up the document on the advice of Huyyay ibn Akhtab, a well-known opponent of the Prophet from the Nadir. It is hard to imagine why the Prophet would have singled out the Qurayzah for a special pact, let alone how the Qurayzah could have entered into such an agreement while at the same time they were the clients of the Aws, patrons who guaranteed their protection. And why should they have been influenced to renounce the alleged agreement on the advice of one whose own tribe was exiled from Medina in disgrace? These traditions surely explain why the Prophet might have wished to exterminate the Qurayzah but they hardly seem credible nor do they reflect the dominant thrust of the Islamic narrative which, unlike the scholars of the West, attempts to distance the Prophet from the actual decision, precisely because it seems so damning to his character. Some modern Muslim writers, apologetic about the event, argue, albeit with little or no evidence, that not all the males of the Qurayzah were put to death. One thing appears certain: the Prophet in allowing for the mass killing did not do so to eliminate the last vestiges of Jews in the oasis, as smallish Jewish family units not linked to the major tribes remained scattered about Medina. Hence, the failure of the Jews to convert to Islam could hardly have been the overriding reason effectively to annihilate a leading Jewish tribe. Nor do our sources describe the decision as easy to implement. The chroniclers make it clear that the action taken against the Qurayzah was not only without precedent, it required an elaborate strategy based on tribal patterns of behavior.

As were the Qanuqaʿ and the Nadir, the Qurayzah were formally allied with one of the tribes of the Ansar—in this case they were clients of the Aws. That presented the Prophet with no small problem. Leading figures from the Aws, compelled to look after the Qurayzah by tribal codes of honor, intervened on behalf of the Jews, who, after all, had remained neutral during the celebrated siege of Medina. As our Arabic authors understand the unfolding events, Muhammad could not under any circumstances initiate a plan of action that would have so compromised the Ansaris whose support he required. We are not speaking of expulsion, the fate of the Qaynuqaʿ and Nadir, but of mass killing. Clearly, the tribal honor of the Aws demanded that they and they alone shoulder the responsibility for the extermination of their adult male clients and the enslavement of the women and children. But the Jews had not actually intervened on behalf of the invading force. If there were even the slightest hint that they took up arms for the grand alliance, or in any other way directly assisted the Meccans and their allies, the chroniclers would have not only described such actions in detail, they would have magnified them to enhance the accusations against the Jews and justify the Prophet's actions.

According to our sources, the Prophet, realizing he could not compel the Aws into giving up their clients to be killed and enslaved, left the decision to them, but for that purpose he chose Saʿd ibn Muʿadh of the Aws who lay near death from wounds sustained during the battle. Saʿd ibn Muʿadh was the same man Muhammad had been promoting as a replacement for Ibn Ubayy as leader of all the Ansar, thus ridding himself of the meddlesome Ibn Ubayy who from the outset attempted to limit the Prophet's power and curtail his ability to engage the Quraysh and their allies. There is logic of sorts to this scenario portrayed by the chroniclers. We are seemingly led to believe that Saʿd, the noble warrior, lying on his deathbed from having participated in a battle without the assistance of his erstwhile clients and allies, was bitter over their choice to remain neutral and thus sought revenge for his own impending death. In such circumstances, his decision to exterminate the males of the Qurayzah would be understandable to his kinsmen who, following the Prophet's suggestion, allowed the mortally wounded Saʿd to decide for all of them, albeit without fully realizing that Saʿd might go so far as he did. In such fashion, Islamic tradition makes it clear the Prophet had no direct hand in the action and was therefore not directly responsible for this seemingly incongruous act of brutality. Nor for that matter were the Aws collectively responsible. If anyone were to be held accountable, it was Saʿd, but his decision was guided by revenge driven by tribal sentiments one could readily understand. The chroniclers may have absolved the Prophet of any questionable behavior as regards the extermination of the Qurayzah, but we are still left seeking a plausible reason for this drastic act of collective punishment.

Be that as it may, the failed siege of Mecca, the elimination of the Qurayzah, and the seeming collapse of the last vestiges of internal opposition within Medina allowed the Prophet to devote all his energies to breaking the Meccan hold on Western Arabia. It was, however, one thing to keep the Meccans at bay—no small triumph at that—and quite another to produce the military and political strength to successfully replace Quraysh and their allies as the political linchpins of the region, let alone convert the pagans among them to the new faith.

The Path to Triumph

The failure of the Meccans to deal decisively with Muhammad changed the political calculus in the region. With the retaliatory power of the grand alliance seriously compromised and the caravan trade essentially brought to a halt, Muhammad's adversaries became increasingly vulnerable. The Prophet now undertook a diplomatic initiative to drive a wedge between the Quraysh and their allies, while at the same time he reinforced and expanded his own network of alliances. The balance of power, at the outset so favorable to Quraysh and Mecca, slowly shifted to the Muslims and Medina. In 628, Muhammad felt sufficiently bold to undertake an expedition to Mecca accompanied by some fourteen hundred men. According to Muslim tradition, the Prophet decided on this course as a result of a dream referred to in the Qur'an (58:27) in which he was informed by God to "enter the sacred mosque (*al-masjid al-haram*)," an act that would have transformed a pagan rite of pilgrimage to the Ka'bah into a Muslim rite and Mecca into an Islamic sanctuary. In such fashion, a pagan ritual that generated enormous religious and political prestige would have been reconstituted into an act celebrating the one true God. But sometime before reaching his destination, the Prophet had second thoughts of confronting an enemy who had sent an advanced party of two hundred cavalry to block his path. The situation was now reversed. The failure of the grand alliance to put an end decisively to the Muslim threat had greatly undermined its prestige and room to maneuver. An offensive against Mecca that produced less than the capitulation of its inhabitants would have had a similar effect on the Islamic ummah.

By any yardstick of measurement, Quraysh remained a most formidable opponent. Moreover, as did the Muslims in Medina, the Meccans would be fighting in defense of their own lands and the sanctity of their shrine; they could thus be expected to offer maximum resistance. Any perception of failure in engaging the enemy would be a major setback for the Prophet and his mission, as it would lower his prestige and make it difficult for him to hold together what had become his much expanded but still loosely knit alliance. It would appear that the Prophet was not alone in his doubts; various Bedouin tribes in the vicinity of Mecca refused to join in the venture. The failure to rally others to attack Mecca may have been what convinced the Prophet to reconsider a full-scale assault.

Rather than confront the Meccans, given the uncertainty of the moment, Muhammad agreed to a ten-year truce known as the Truce of Hudaybiyah, perhaps after a place of that name situated near Mecca where the pact was concluded. According to the chroniclers, the original plan to take Mecca by force was to be aborted and the Muslim force would withdraw. Instead Muslims would be allowed to undertake a minor pilgrimage (*'umrah*) to the holy city unimpeded; fighting between the parties would cease; any Qurayshites who had become part of the ummah without the permission of their patrons or masters (presumably slaves, women, and children) would be sent back to those patrons and masters; both the Muslims and the Meccans were free to build their own network of alliances, but Muhammad could not (actively) recruit followers from among the Quraysh. When the treaty was finally concluded, the Muslims undertook ritual sacrifices to the God in heaven.

The tradition's description of this event explains away the difficulty facing the Prophet at his moment of truth, namely the realization that his long-anticipated triumph would have to be delayed and at some cost. The Prophet's dream in which God commanded him to pray "in [what was to become] the sacred [Muslim] mosque" (Surah 48:27) was conveniently cited to explain why Muhammad was willing to settle for a ten-year truce that allowed for a minor Muslim pilgrimage rather than risk a military defeat or even stalemate. The historical narratives that describe the event make it abundantly clear that the Prophet had indeed expected the Bedouins to rally to his side but as they failed to do so, he had no recourse but to settle for a truce. As reported, the stipulations of the truce gave the Muslims a religious stake in the holy city, but in the end, Muhammad would have been left with no real sense of triumph; at the least there would have been serious disappointment. If the truce were to be observed, he would be no closer to converting his polytheist kinsmen than he had been at the outset of his career, a time of weakness when he felt compelled to make conciliatory gestures to their pagan beliefs in the vain hope they would eventually come over to him of their own accord. The agreement to cease all raids on the caravans of Quraysh while giving the latter a free hand to negotiate alliances as they saw fit, might have resulted, in the long run, in resuscitating the grand alliance. Looking beyond the explanation proffered by Islamic tradition, the Truce of Hudaybiyah was a setback for Muhammad and completely unanticipated. The Prophet, ordinarily so brilliant in seizing the moment, was apparently guilty of overreaching. Not only had he not forced the capitulation of the Meccans, he had mobilized a fighting force that no doubt anticipated the glory of battle, to say nothing of the booty following a Meccan defeat. Our sources report that once the negotiations were under way, Muhammad was compelled to exact a pledge from those who accompanied him, so as to hold them in line and bind them to any decision he was about to make. Muhammad understood he had to regain the initiative.

Within six weeks a Muslim force set out to attack Khaybar, the rich Jewish oasis a hundred miles to the east of Mecca, a settlement which sheltered many of his former enemies and which helped fund the siege of Medina, though the Jews of Khaybar supplied no fighting forces of their own. One may suppose that with such a history, and with Muhammad's general antagonism toward the Jews, unaccepting as they were of him and his message, sooner or later the Prophet would have moved against Khaybar. In this case, one suspects the timing of the attack was linked to the aborted expedition against Mecca and, related to that, the need to satisfy an Arab army ready and anxious to do combat and to enjoy the spoils of war. The Jews were apparently caught by surprise. The truce should have made for a more relaxed atmosphere in the region. Moreover, Khaybar was nearly 100 miles distant from Mecca. Any foray against the oasis was bound to take considerable planning and, one would have expected, time to execute. The rapid deployment of the Muslim attacking force seems to have been unexpected. As the Muslim army arrived, the Jews of Khaybar took to their forts and initially the Muslims made no headway. After some six weeks of skirmishes—there do not seem to have been any large-scale engagements—the Jews were forced to capitulate. According to an agreement between the warring parties, the Jews retained their lands but were compelled to assign half the produce from their farms to the Muslims. Our sources report the other Jewish settlements along the route to Syria-Palestine were soon brought under Muslim control. Seeing what had happened at Khaybar, the Jews of the Wadi al-Qura and Tayma' made similar agreements with the Prophet, sharing the revenue of their date harvest with the Muslims. Tradition has it that the caliph 'Umar ibn al-Khattab (634–644 c.e.) ended these arrangements when he evicted all the Jews from the Hijaz. That tradition, which became the accepted narrative of what befell the Jews of the region, is contradicted by correspondence from the Jews of the Wadi al-Qura preserved in the cache of letters and documents known as the Cairo Geniza, a repository of Jewish writings dated several centuries after 'Umar's alleged ethnic cleansing of the Hijaz. If there is any truth to the reports of 'Umar's expelling the Jews, it applied in all likelihood to only part of the Hijaz, particularly the holy cities: Mecca and Medina, and their environs. In any case, the victory over the Jews of Khaybar marked the end of Jewish political influence in western Arabia and the last time Jews took up arms against Muslims in major combat until the modern state of Israel came into being.

According to some seemingly apocryphal reports, the victory did not come cheaply. A Jewish woman from the oasis—a refugee whose male relatives of the Qurayzah had been exterminated—poisoned the Prophet as the Muslims were celebrating their hard-won triumph with a victory feast. While the other Muslims ate donkey meat, she offered the Prophet his favorite dish, shoulder of lamb (donkey meat was ritually unclean according to Jewish dietary laws). Tradition has it that the morsel was delicately seasoned with a deadly potion. One could readily understand, given tribal sensibilities, why she would have chosen to avenge her murdered kinfolk. However, in this case, the meat would appear more seasoned with irony than any deadly substance. So delicate was the poison applied, the Prophet only succumbed to eating the tainted meat some four years later. For those Muslims who were inclined to believe the Jews actually killed Muhammad, or, to be more accurate, set his eventual death into motion, a more convincing account was required. Four years is, after all, a rather long time for a man to linger after having been administered a deadly potion. A second tradition thus maintained that another woman, this time from the exiled Nadir, administered the tainted morsel to the Prophet. The Prophet, sensing something was wrong with the first bite, spit it out. As the would-be assassin later explained her plan, she was merely testing to see if Muhammad was indeed a legitimate Prophet. If that were in fact so, he would have detected the poison as he did. And so the woman now convinced of Muhammad's legitimacy married the Prophet of God and converted to Islam. Still other accounts report variations on this theme. The historicity of all these accounts was, needless to say, dubious; clearly even the Muslims had their doubts. They are well-known tropes that attempt to link the Jews to treacherous behavior, thus explaining what befell the Jews of Arabia.

The Truce of Hudaybiyah did not last. The Meccan opposition to the Prophet was riven by internal strife allowing Muhammad to seize the opportunity and bend the rules that forced him to send Meccan converts back to their owners and masters. When the Meccans bridled at the turn of events, the Prophet assembled a large army that marched against Mecca in 630. After some initial light resistance, the badly divided Meccans decided to capitulate leading to Muhammad's triumphal return to the place of his birth and early life. The so-called conquest (*fath*) of Mecca was a much different affair from that of Muhammad's other triumphs. A general amnesty was declared; even the most vociferous of the Prophet's opponents, some with the blood of Muslims on their hands, were spared; there were no spoils of war; and no pillaging of the Meccan wealth. In effect, the Meccans accepted Muhammad and Islam so that life might more or less return to normal. They felt assured they could live their lives as before, although their status within an evolving Muslim society had been seriously tarnished by their opposition to the Prophet and his message. In time, they would reestablish themselves as significant players in the expanding ummah, especially after the Islamic conquest, in which they and their relatives played a significant role.

In many ways, Mecca remained as it was, but it was also much transformed. The Ka'bah, the pagan holy shrine was cleansed of its idols and became the quintessential religious monument of the ummah. The pilgrimage, central to the religious and political life of the region, was transformed into a Muslim sacred ritual. In such fashion, there was no dramatic break with perhaps the most significant customs and institutions of the past; the transition from paganism to Islam in Mecca was reasonably smooth. After all, the Quraysh were all kinsmen and certain timeworn institutions were so familiar they could not easily if at all be abandoned. And yet, the political and religious landscape had been significantly altered. In opposing the oligarchs of Quraysh, Muhammad's main task was to keep his community intact and to slowly but surely undermine the elaborate alliances that created the allusion of Meccan invincibility. Having driven a wedge into these alliances, the Prophet now had to establish a new network of alliances in order for the ummah to become preeminent in western Arabia and beyond. The very hard core of Muhammad's followers—the emigrants from Mecca, the loyal Ansar, the individuals and small family units that found true security and social status within the ummah, and all the others who had converted to the new faith as a result of moral conviction, even the self-serving former opponents within Quraysh—could be counted upon to back the expansion of the ummah.

Elsewhere, in more distant regions and among the more anarchical Bedouin tribes, relationships to Muhammad and more particularly to the ummah were complex and potentially hazardous. The same strains that appeared in the grand alliance could easily appear among the ummah's most recent allies. Any doubts as to the viability of the ummah might occasion wholesale defections from tribesmen whose allegiances tended to be volatile and all too often determined by self-interest rather than any sense of religious conviction. Some scholars maintain that Islam provided for a significant void in the spiritual life of the polytheist Arabs and thus had widespread appeal. They argue that not only Mecca but virtually the entire Arabian Peninsula had become engulfed with a spiritual malaise for which the belief in the one and only true God was the answer. It is, of course, true that other Prophets also made their appearance in the Arabian Peninsula, but it strikes us that claim of Islam's wide spiritual appeal is based on a rather naïve view of polytheism and an even more naïve view of the power generated by the anarchic sensibilities of the Arab tribesmen. If the Prophet succeeded it was because he knew how to leverage the political realities of the moment for the benefit of his core community of true believers. Our sources tell us of widespread conversion to Islam all over the peninsula; but there is little evidence that either the tribal leadership or the tribes at large saw the light as did the Prophet, that is "like the crack of dawn." Muhammad made it clear to tribal leaders that their personal conversion to Islam was essential to their position within the new political configuration that was displacing the old grand alliance. To demonstrate how this conversion suited their self-interest he waged a series of successful campaigns against the unbelievers. In the last years of his life following the conquest of Mecca, Muhammad welcomed a series of delegations from regions far and wide. The capitulation of the hitherto powerful Meccans warranted diplomatic initiatives by all sorts of groups. However, not all were destined to become loyal followers. The Prophet's insistence that some tribes show their obeisance by paying tribute to the authorities in Medina did not sit well with them. "False" prophets appeared in different regions, religious figures that had to be disposed of in battle. One may wish to argue that at the time of the Prophet's death in 632, the issue of whether an Islamic ummah centered in Medina would dominate all of Arabia was far from settled. What the Prophet accomplished in his lifetime was surely remarkable. As regards marrying faith to religion, he was no doubt the equal to any of the monotheist messengers before him, at least as can be determined from the tendentious sources produced by Jews, Christians, and Muslims alike. The real question was whether the ummah as an ideal or reality could successfully withstand his death.

PART II

THE TRANSFORMATION
OF THE ISLAMIC UMMAH

6

Succession, Conquest, and Expansion: The Ummah Becomes an "Arab Kingdom"

In 632 the Prophet Muhammad died after having been seriously ill for a period of time. His possible death, though a source of obvious concern to the inner circle of the Muslim community, reportedly came as a surprise; indeed, various sources describe him as seemingly recovered or on his way to recovery shortly before he expired. These accounts, like so much of what has been written of this traumatic moment in the history of the early ummah, are likely inventions of later times, as once again the political factions governing or seeking to govern the community of the faithful rewrote or reinterpreted the past to legitimize their claims. What seems certain is that the Prophet's death, unexpected or otherwise, presented the nascent Islamic polity with a serious quandary. As the Prophet lay ill and incapacitated—at the least unable to attend prayers at his own mosque—the leading Muslims must have been aware that sooner or later they would have to replace him at the helm.

But how does one replace the last of a kind? Muhammad was, as the Qur'an put it: "the seal of the prophets," that is, the quintessential and last of a long line of messengers sent by God. No future leader of the ummah could lay claim to God's direct revelation and, lacking that, no future leader could directly receive divine instruction, or the divine mandate with which the Prophet ruled. As the Muslims did not contemplate the dissolution of the ummah after the Prophet's death, there was an anticipated and then real crisis to surmount. There was no successor who could muster universal acclaim and there was no established mechanism by which to replace the irreplaceable.

Left without any precedent for establishing a new leader or defining the nature of his authority, and without any candidate who could immediately command the allegiance of the entire inner core of the ummah, the Muslims fell back on the tried and familiar and approached the issue of succession as if they were choosing the sheikh of a clan or more extensive tribal unit. The Aws and Khazraj actively promoted their own candidate. There is reason to suspect there was also support of some sort for the Prophet's first cousin, son-in-law, and "adopted" brother, 'Ali ibn Abi Talib. Claims for 'Ali's candidacy at the time are found in later sources trumpeting his worthiness and that of his descendants, the offspring of his marriage to Muhammad's daughter Fatimah. Because she was the only one of the Prophet's progeny to bear children, the continuity of the Prophet's bloodline rested with the aforementioned union. At some point, the continuity of the Prophet's bloodline took on special meaning for a segment of the faithful as did the close relationship between the Prophet and 'Ali and 'Ali's father Abu Talib, who was in effect Muhammad's surrogate parent. Outside the inner core of the ummah were the old Meccan oligarchs, now converted to the true faith. No doubt, they entertained thoughts of a comeback in the political arena, but the Meccans lacked the credentials and the opportunity to press their claim. Their early and in certain instances sustained opposition to the Prophet and his message disqualified them in the eyes of the faithful, and so they were forced to bide their time until a more opportune moment.

As the inner-core Muslims argued among themselves without reaching any agreement, Abu Bakr, the Prophet's father-in-law, and two close companions discretely solicited the support of major political leaders within the ummah. In what amounted to a hastily assembled tribal election (*shura*), they secured the vote (*bay'ah*) for Abu Bakr (r. 632–634). Choosing Abu Bakr in this fashion established two precedents that guided Muslims for nearly a thousand years: First, the successor to the Prophet, who would eventually become known as *khalifah* or caliph, had to be chosen from Quraysh, the Prophet's tribe, most often from his immediate kinsmen, the Hashimites. Second, the mechanism of succession would be the equivalent of a tribal election with the formal vote for the caliph to be taken by the leading notables of the ummah on behalf of the community as a whole.

Later 'Alid claims to the contrary, the Prophet did not favor anyone to succeed him, let alone his first cousin. Nor was Abu Bakr, the first of the so-called "righteous" or "rightly guided" caliphs (*Rashidun*) the undeclared heir apparent, as some anti-'Alid writings suggest. Abu Bakr, perhaps desirous of a seamless transition, broke with the Prophet's precedent of not naming a successor and chose his close associate 'Umar ibn al-Khattab (r. 634–644). By all accounts, 'Umar turned out to be the correct choice to command the faithful. The second of the righteous caliphs was an extraordinary administrator, and while many of his alleged innovations might very well be back projections of later developments there can be no doubt that the expansion of the ummah was largely due to him. Abu Bakr may have brought the entire Arabian Peninsula under Islamic control and may have sent raiding contingents to probe the soft spots along the frontier separating Arabia from the lands beyond, but it was 'Umar who set into motion events that paved the way for the Arab conquest and the subsequent expansion of Islam.

After ten years at the head of the ummah, 'Umar was assassinated by a seemingly deranged individual unhappy over his tax burden. As the caliph lingered between life and death, he reportedly pondered his own succession calling attention to the two precedents that had previously guided the ummah: Muhammad's reluctance to name his successor for whatever reason and Abu Bakr's decision to arrange for an orderly transfer of power by choosing a successor in advance. Our sources indicate that 'Umar expired without designating anyone to replace him thus opening the door to forming a new shura drawn from the early companions of the Prophet. The group caucused among themselves but they were unable to reach a unanimous decision. 'Ali was said to have remained steadfast in his desire to assume the mantle of the Prophet; other candidates had the wherewithal to block 'Ali but not to insure their own election. After much discussion within the shura, one of the leading claimants withdrew and was given the task of suggesting a candidate upon whom all could agree. Ironically, but perhaps not surprisingly, the nod was given to the least likely of all the contenders, 'Uthman ibn 'Affan, an elderly individual with no experience at warfare and a lineage that linked him to the clan of Umayyah, steadfast opponents of the Prophet and, according to the anti-Umayyad chroniclers, also opponents of the Prophet's ancestors.

'Uthman was in all likelihood a compromise choice with which all the leading players were willing to live. As he was in his late sixties, there was every reason to expect his tenure was likely to be short and the process of selection would soon begin anew. The caliph lived on, however, for another twelve years. The disgruntled aristocrats from the Prophet's inner circle, sensing the old man's lack of resolve, pressured him politically and, more generally, made his life difficult. As a result, he increasingly turned to relatives from his hitherto discredited clan. Whereas 'Umar made it a policy to rotate provincial governors so that none would challenge the authority of his rule in Medina, 'Uthman increasingly chose his relations to run the emergent Islamic polity, much to the chagrin of the old inner circle of Muslims. Then, in a dramatic and unexpected development, the commander of the faithful was assassinated as his predecessor had been. A new shura was convened, but on this occasion 'Ali carried the day. It turned out to be a pyrrhic victory.

Almost immediately after 'Ali became caliph, Talhah and al-Zubayr, early followers of the Prophet and members of the shura, broke ranks with the newly elected caliph. They made for Basrah, a major garrison town in Iraq, to raise the necessary military forces with which to contest 'Ali's rule. The reasons for their rebellion, so soon after they had elected 'Ali, are anything but clear; it is not likely that the available sources will provide us with a satisfactory answer. Some scholars see the rupture as having been occasioned by 'Ali's concern over vast fortunes the two rebels had acquired in the lands conquered by the armies of Islam, but that explanation remains a matter of conjecture. Talhah and al-Zubayr were accompanied in this venture by the Prophet's widow A'ishah, the daughter of Abu Bakr. Her participation in the rebellion reportedly stemmed from a personal grudge. 'Ali had argued vociferously that the Prophet divorce A'ishah after an alleged scandal involving a young warrior. The Prophet refused and 'Ali was shamed. With the rebels mobilizing in Basrah, 'Ali went to Kufah, the other Iraqi garrison town, to raise an army of his own and then defeated the triumvirate in the Battle of the Camel, so named because the fighting swirled around a camel upon which A'ishah was mounted. The murder of 'Uthman and, more particularly, the failure of the Prophet's inner circle to assist him actively, compromised the moral authority of the caliphate itself. As we shall see shortly, the ummah would soon find itself beset by another civil war that culminated in the assassination of 'Ali and the ascent of Islam's first dynastic order, a form of governance hitherto foreign to the Arabs of west Arabia and their political sensibilities.

Medieval Muslims who were not supporters of the 'Alids tended to look nostalgically at the early caliphate. They saw it as a more or less pristine institution forged at an idyllic time before dissension within the ummah led to civil war and the corruption of traditional Islamic values.

After the Rashidun, various individuals and partisan groups were described as acting in a self-serving fashion at the expense of what had been a commonly shared communal responsibility. Later caliphs and would-be caliphs were thus accused of compromising the values of the universal Islamic ummah founded by the Prophet. In modern times, traditional Muslims searching for authentic forms of governance have declared the period of the "righteous" caliphs as representing a form of primitive democracy, one rooted not in the experience of the ancient Greeks or in the slogans of the Western Enlightenment but in a truly Islamic setting, and hence a legitimate model for those Muslims who seek a more equitable rule but are generally inclined to reject the encroachment of the West and Western values.

Reality presents the detached modern scholar with a somewhat different picture of the righteous caliphs and the ummah. As we have noted, three of the first four caliphs were assassinated and the other was imposed upon the community in an election engineered by a minority of three, including the future caliph himself. By any yardstick of comparison, the righteous caliphs and their associates were beset by the same human frailties that afflict all leaders, even the best leaders in the most just societies. Given the structural imbalances, indeed the fractures within the larger ummah, none of the Rashidun could have ruled as effectively as they did without resorting to political innovation that at times undermined the traditional and idealized notion of the early Islamic community. What is striking above all is the residual appeal of the concept of the ummah, an appeal so powerful that it called for a re-visioning of early Islamic history in an effort to tone down negative images of rifts among the faithful. Even as the Islamic state expanded into the vast territories beyond the historic Arabian homeland and counted among its new constituents myriads of non-Arab converts; and even as these converts were treated as second-class Muslims and their regions had to pay obeisance to the political and religious authority emanating from the Hijaz, the notion that the ummah represented a vast tent in which all Muslims were in fact equal and were at one time unsullied by shabby politics had enormous emotional appeal. The continued belief in the ideal of a universal and pristine community of all Muslims, a community that recognized no meaningful distinctions of ethnicity, language, or geography, might seem in retrospect as a template with which to mold a contemporary society, but it ultimately served and continues to serve as a detriment to real and effective innovation in forms of governance. Although the idealized Islamic polity never existed, not even in the time of the Prophet, the very idea of that polity overwhelmed any attempt at decentralizing Islamic rule in an expanding Islamic state. Since the outset of Islam, there has been a profound tension between the sense of a tightly knit community generated by the aforementioned notion of the ummah and the realities of a history occasioned by local Arab politics, the Arab conquest, and the subsequent expansion of Islam, events that brought disparate peoples and regions under the umbrella of Muslim rule. As long as Muslims embraced the ideal of a universal ummah, no local autonomy or separate regional authority could be declared legitimate by those responsible for upholding Islamic law and tradition. The result was an uneasy relationship between the center and the periphery of Muslim rule.

Conquest and Expansion

Acclaiming Abu Bakr as the Prophet's successor did not resolve the problems facing the nascent Islamic polity after the latter's death. The ummah of the time was by no means joined at the hip and united in outlook and politics. Whatever pacts Muhammad had established after the conquest of Mecca were linked directly to his own person. More often than not, the death of a partner to an agreement among Arab tribesmen rendered that agreement null and void. There was no expected continuity as with nations entering into formal treaty arrangements. To be sure, any agreement between individual tribal leaders could be renegotiated by interested parties following a leader's death, but that was subject to a show of good will by all the participants. The Arabic sources would have us believe the Prophet converted virtually the entire of the Arabian Peninsula to the new faith and that those new Muslims took to Muhammad and his message enthusiastically and without reservation. It is more likely, based on a close reading of these texts, that the negotiations tied only the leaders of the outlying tribes to the Prophet and the Prophet alone, and that his death occasioned second thoughts as to whether their conversion to Islam called for continued support of the Medinese center. Aligning with Medina was the equivalent of aligning with Mecca in the past, a marriage of temporary convenience born of political necessity and possible economic advantage. One notes in this respect how quickly the grand alliance of the Meccans dissolved when the presumed military and financial strength of the Quraysh was called into question. Considering the mood of the times, one could easily exaggerate the unifying power generated by the concept of a religious community embracing a common political cause and a religious faith calling for uniformly prescribed observance.

The emergent Islamic ummah did not put an end to Arab tribalism or even reduce substantially the anarchic sensibilities that formed the political outlook and behavior of the Arab tribesmen. Blood was seemingly as thick as faith, and in certain instances more so.

No sooner had Abu Bakr taken control of the ummah than he was confronted by strong tribal insurrections. The chroniclers would have us believe that Muslim armies then took the field against Arab converts who abandoned Islam. The fighting that followed was known as the war of the *riddah*, meaning the battle against apostasy, but it would appear the campaigns initiated by Muhammad's successor were waged to strengthen the very tenuous hold the Muslims had over areas far and wide. The riddah wars were nothing more than a campaign to Islamize all of Arabia. Ironically, the very success of the Muslims in rapidly consolidating their hold on the rest of Arabia might well have been a prescription for later disaster. The logic of joining forces with the Muslims was similar to that of joining forces with the Meccans a generation earlier. Any alliance with a powerful polity that was capable of mobilizing a massive coalition of fighting forces would discourage enemies from taking the field against a particular tribe. But it also forced all the disparate groups of the ummah to remain at peace with one another. There could be no raiding for sport or, more important yet, no warfare to offset economic hardship. With diminished grazing and agricultural lands, and the entire peninsula brimming with armed groups, but with no longer any substantial enemies against whom to campaign and relieve distress, Arabia came to resemble a boiling pot about to spill its contents. Had nothing changed, there is the possibility, indeed the probability, that the ummah would have imploded.

There was, however, the porous frontier between the Arab domains and the Byzantine and Sasanian empires to the north. Long engaged in a debilitating conflict, the major powers beyond Arabia, inheritors of an imperial tradition that went back centuries and more, lacked the capacity to defend their southern borders as before. Arab tribes that had in earlier times settled along the frontier and had been in the employ of their imperial patrons to protect them from other Arab raiders became disaffected when their usual subsidies were not maintained. As a result, raiding tribesmen from the peninsula, Muslim and non-Muslim alike, probed the Byzantine and Sasanian defenses and raided the settled territories beyond, first for economic gain and then to settle permanently.

Here we face a series of related questions. When did the early Muslims first set their sights on the invasion and conquest of regions beyond

Arabia—the lands of the Fertile Crescent that in ancient times comprised Egypt, Greater Syria (current day Syria, Israel, Lebanon, Jordan, and the lands of the Palestinian Authority), and Mesopotamia (more or less modern Iraq)? What were the perceived objectives of the nascent Islamic polity when its forces first crossed the frontier? To be more specific: Did the Muslim authorities in Medina dispatch Arab armies beyond Arabia with the intention of settling in the new territories and converting the indigenous peoples to the new faith? Beyond that, how did Greater Syria, the land referred to by the Arabs as al-Sham or "the North," replace Arabia as the political center of the Muslim world in the seventh century, only to be replaced in turn by Iraq in the eighth?

Determining the character of the Arab conquests and Islamic expansion is no easy matter. As with the life and times of the Prophet, we are faced with wide-ranging problems of historicity and historical interpretation. The data, such as they are, tend to be found in chronicles first assembled in the ninth century, that is, works compiled long after the events in question. Indeed, many important narratives are found in sources still further removed in time. More important yet, accounts were fashioned—often deliberately—to reflect the religious and political views of later generations. Later Muslim writings speak of Muhammad's kinsmen, indeed of the Prophet himself, visiting and trading in Byzantine-ruled lands to the north. There are also reports of military probes by Arabs along the frontier region. But none of that enables us to draw a vivid, let alone detailed, picture of the Muslim strategies as the early Islamic ummah evolved. Still, there are many interpretations of the Arab-Muslim conquest, Muslim and non-Muslim alike. So significant an event in world history compels comment even when the evidence is exceedingly fragile.

Past and present discussions of these events have always given rise to powerful religious sensibilities; they have also shaped patterns of political behavior. Throughout the course of history, evocative memories of the Islamic conquest have moved the Muslim faithful to action and created expectations among them for a glorious future. For the world of Christendom, the very same events have occasioned a rather different response. Throughout the Middle Ages, Christians, mostly men of the cloth, sought meaning from what seemed to them the onslaught of a perniciously false religion. Writing before modern oriental studies took root in the great European universities, these learned and not so learned men of the West took a religiously inspired and rather jaundiced view of early Islam. They saw the Arab expansion as a planned effort to propagate a new and false faith and by brutal means. At the extreme, this model of conquest made its way into popular tales and schoolbooks that took on an extended life of their own: a distorted narrative describing mounted Arab tribesmen charging wildly out of the desert into a more civilized world. Having conquered vast new territories, the Muslims were portrayed as offering the local inhabitants the unhappy choice of Islam or the sword. This dramatic reading of events seems to imply a massive and rapid conversion to Islam under the most menacing form of duress, the very threat to one's life.

In truth, the indigenous peoples of the conquered lands were given a less worrisome choice. They could surrender without conflict, in which case they would retain their property, and their personal and religious freedom, subject only to discriminatory legislation that was relatively mild. Or, choosing armed resistance to the Muslim invaders, they could risk having their lives and property declared licit, in effect becoming martyrs to their religious and/or political convictions. In any event, the conversion of the populace in the conquered territories would seem to have been a gradual process that in certain areas extended over centuries. Allowing for this corrected view of the Arab conquest, we are left with a nagging question. If conversion, forced or otherwise, was not the primary reason for Arab warriors to cross the frontier and ultimately settle in the lands beyond, what indeed was?

The Causes of the Expansion

By the end of the nineteenth century, modern orientalists drew a more complex picture of the Arab conquest. The religious motivation of the Islamic expansion was modified, if not jettisoned altogether in favor of a conquest necessitated by economic factors. According to a theory first proposed by Hugo Winckler, the incursions across the border were caused by rapid and extensive desiccation throughout Arabia, a land already marked by vast uninhabitable spaces. That Arabian tribesmen crossed the frontier to extort and plunder before settling permanently is clearly attested in the Muslim accounts. But that alone hardly vindicates Winckler's grand theory. There is not a shred of scientific evidence to support his view. There is no data to suggest a substantial change of climate in Arabia during the period in question, the kind of change that would have led, of necessity, to extremely arid conditions; a decline in living space; raids beyond the frontier; and ultimately, large-scale immigration. Still, a refined economic model, without Winckler, remains the regnant paradigm of Islamic expansion. As noted, scholars now believe that attempts to consolidate Islamic rule in all of Arabia created enormous pressure on its disparate tribal associations. In order to relieve that pressure, Arab tribesmen resorted to time-honored pursuits. They crossed the frontier to raid the settled territories beyond. There was at first no intention of actually seizing territory for an expanding Islamic state. The campsites of Arab warriors took on the semblance of permanent settlements only after local resistance crumbled and the tribesmen looked for further worlds to conquer and exploit. In sum, the story of the conquest is the all-too familiar story of the desert versus the sown. From this perspective, the Islamization of the conquered territories was the by-product rather than the primary cause of the Arab conquest—the result, so to speak, of unplanned consequences. But is that the whole story?

Some thirty years ago, Fred Donner, a young historian, resuscitated the importance of religion while fashioning yet another paradigm with which to explain the Islamic expansion. His views are detailed in a massively documented work, *The Early Islamic Conquests* (Princeton, 1980). On the whole, Donner tends to reject the deterministic (read economic) causes of the conquests as well as accidental historical processes (that is, Arab tribesmen initiating the conquest inadvertently when, following their anarchic inclinations, they moved beyond the border to raid and plunder, a spirited pursuit that might be described, however whimsically, as the national sport of the Arabs). Instead, Donner sees the conquest as inextricably linked to a more deliberate process, namely the expansion of an evolving Islamic state in the Arabian Peninsula, or, to be more specific, in the Hijaz, the region that gave birth to the Prophet and his faith-based community. From his perspective, the Arab migrations and the success of the conquests were the direct result of an emerging Islamic state's capacity to integrate Arabia's tribesmen and to organize them to attain well-defined military and political objectives.

Readers are thus led to believe that the early Arab incursions and the subsequent migrations of entire tribal groups were by design an Islamic expansion. The purpose of this bold enterprise was to strengthen Islam and the foundations of the newly established Islamic state in western Arabia. Because Islam provided the moral cement binding the anarchic tribesmen to the state authority evolving in Medina, the early Arab expeditions led, of necessity, to an Arab-Muslim expansion and then to the formation of a Muslim imperial polity that destroyed a Persian empire of long standing and forced the Christian Byzantines from the Fertile Crescent and then from the lands beyond. In addition to Arab tribesmen from Arabia, that nascent imperial polity soon embraced local Arab and non-Arab converts to Islam. The victorious Muslims also established procedures to govern the large indigenous communities that were as yet reluctant or unwilling to accept the new faith because of residual loyalties to their own venerable traditions. In Donner's view, the Islamic ummah, by his definition a viable state already in this time, was the apparent force behind Islamic expansion and the beginnings of a future Islamic empire. The conquests of the seventh century were, from the outset, a Muslim as well as an Arab achievement. His readers might then conclude that crossing the frontier was, at the least, a religiously inspired act. In any event, that is how it certainly would have seemed to Muhammad's successors, the early caliphs in Medina as well as the early Muslim community that evolved in their lifetime. That is also the outlook embraced by the medieval Arabic historians although they present ample evidence for contradictory views.

The very sources meticulously examined by Donner can lead, however, to a somewhat different conclusion. Islam may well have been the moral cement that united the tribesmen beyond the frontier and the original Muslims ruling from Medina, but what does it mean to concede this point? Donner's claim that the Arabian center was fully capable of imposing centralized authority seems at best problematic. Our sources indicate the caliphs were always playing catch-up with events rapidly unfolding beyond the frontier. By all accounts, the Arab tribes had their own interests to consider, most of them not of a strictly religious nature—some warriors had not yet converted to Islam even as they served the Islamic ummah. There is no evidence that the area commanders expanded the arc of military activity out of Islamic sentiments, let alone in coordination with the central Islamic authorities in Medina. To the contrary, the tribesmen fighting in the lands beyond presented the caliphs in Arabia with unexpected new situations, many unplanned and some risky. These impromptu agendas were regarded with suspicion, even disapproval by the central authorities. Even after large-scale migrations beyond the frontier and the consolidation of Muslim rule there, relations between the center and periphery were testy, to say the least. Within three decades (by 661 c.e.), the center gave way and the administration of the Islamic state—it was by then a real state in all but name—moved to Damascus and the conquered territories.

Although in retrospect this realignment of power seems to have been inevitable, most of the old circle of Muslims retained and jealously guarded the Hijaz and in particular Mecca and Medina as the religious and political fulcrum of the ummah. Real power shifted, however, to the lands beyond Arabia where large Arab tribal units were concentrated and where there was ample booty and taxes for independent minded governors to buy their loyalty. While most Arabs were good Muslims, however one might wish to define a good Muslim, the anarchically inclined tribesmen were capable of turning a deaf ear to commands, even from a centralized religious authority. Religious loyalty, or, to be more precise, loyalty to the Islamic leadership in Medina, competed with powerful loyalties to immediate and extended kin and, beyond that, allegiances to tribal configurations, as well as formal and informal ties of clientage and patronage.

Against these multiple loyalties, the Muslim aristocrats remaining in the Hijaz had little with which to compete. The tribesmen would not break with Islam, but they could in all good conscience subvert the authority of the Muslim government in Medina when they saw it as conflicting with their own interests. Facing potential if not actual disobedience from independent field commanders who led large and mobile forces, 'Umar, the second commander of the faithful, sought to play games of musical chairs with those who led the armies and served as governors *pro tem* of the lands they conquered. Replacing independent and battle-tested generals respected by the warriors with bland administrators trusted by the central authorities served only to complicate the relationship between Medina and the tribesmen in the field.

Conditions were exacerbated when the tribesmen saw themselves acquiring less and less of the fruits of their conquest. According to a formula reportedly established by the Prophet, the tribesmen were entitled to the lion's share of the booty, but the tax revenues of the lands conquered, which exceeded by far the combined monies and kind available to the fighting forces, went to the central authorities in Arabia who in turn supplied the provincial governors with funds to administer local needs. As the pace of the Islamic conquest slowed against stiffening resistance by the Byzantines in lands bordering the Mediterranean and against the Sasanians in the mountainous areas of Iran, there were fewer opportunities for acquiring extensive booty. The days of rapid victories immediately beyond the frontier were past. The tribesmen now saw themselves receiving a smaller portion of the riches acquired by the new Islamic polity. They were still granted their base salaries, food allotments, and occasional bonuses. But given the ever-increasing tax revenues, it took little imagination to see that the lion's share of the total revenue went into the coffers of the state. As the more primitive tribesmen had to contend with an economy based on money that was subject to sudden fluctuations of price, they quickly came to understand that their incomes, which were largely fixed, were not sufficient recompense for their service. In addition, the slowing pace of the conquest and the settlement of tribal units in close proximity to one another gave the Arab warriors ample opportunity to revert to their anarchic sensibilities and feuds that could destabilize nascent Islamic governance.

Should they have chosen to plunder the provincial treasuries, disaffected tribal forces could have laid their hands on the resources needed to resist the early caliphs and their handpicked governors. For other than their moral authority, the Medina-based Commanders of the Faithful lacked the means to bring their tribal armies to heel. The levers of political power were now in the conquered provinces. A century later, a politically astute caliph based in Iraq received word of an insurrection against his rule. Upon hearing that the rebellion had broken out in Medina he quipped, "A land without wealth, devoid of human resources and [lacking adequate] weaponry." The caliph was, needless to say, much relieved that he did not have to face large, well-armed, and well-financed contingents. When he later discovered that a second revolt had broken out in Iraq, he was not so dismissive of the challenge to his rule. A revolt in the Hijaz was one thing; an insurrection in Kufah, one of the garrison towns established by the conquering Arab tribesmen, was another. Despite its religious preeminence, west Arabia and its holy sites had become a backwater of Muslim politics.

The Shift of the Political Epicenter to the Provinces: The Umayyads in al-Sham

The defining moment in the shift of political power from Arabia to the provinces was the first great civil war among the Muslims (656–661 c.e.). A contingent of disgruntled Arab fighting men set out for their provincial base feeling their grievances had been resolved at an audience with the caliph 'Uthman. While en route, they discovered they had been betrayed (it would appear without the caliph's knowledge) and that their lives were suddenly at risk. And so they returned to Medina and killed 'Uthman as the pious and aged caliph read the Qur'an besieged in his quarters and without support from any of those who voted him Muhammad's successor twelve years earlier. The shameful death of 'Uthman cried out for vengeance, all the more so after his bloodied garments were smuggled out of Medina and sent to a prominent relative,

Mu'awiyah ibn Abi Sufyan, the governor of Syria. Reacting in typical Arab fashion, Mu'awiyah sought satisfaction on behalf of himself and his extended family, the house of Umayyah. The spilt blood of his kinsman the caliph had to be avenged; the regicides had to be brought to justice.

As the new commander of the faithful, 'Ali ibn Abi Talib was unwilling or unable to produce the culprits—he himself was tainted by failing to offer effective assistance to 'Uthman—relations between Medina and the great province to the north deteriorated. 'Ali now attempted to force Mu'awiyah from the provincial seat he had held for a dozen years and more. The governor refused and 'Ali was left with no recourse but to remove him by force of arms. Lacking adequate military forces in the Hijaz, the new caliph set off for Iraq in order to raise a proper army with which to challenge Mu'awiyah's battle-tested and highly disciplined Syrian contingents. As the confrontation unfolded, Mu'awiyah laid no claims on the caliphate—he had never been considered by any shura as a likely candidate to succeed the Prophet. He merely insisted that as 'Ali could not or would not bring to account those responsible for the death of his murdered relative, the current caliph should step aside and allow the Muslims to determine who should command the faithful. Only later did the governor of Syria finally declare himself the successor to the Prophet, a ceremony that did not take place in Medina as before— the city was still under 'Ali's control—but in Jerusalem, a venerated place with its own sacred credentials.

The events giving rise to the conflict as well as the conflict itself are detailed in the chronicles, but, as with most major moments of early Islamic history, they are shaped by later events and political circumstances. What is clear is that the murder of 'Uthman, which sparked the outbreak of intercommunal hostilities in 656, was a major watershed in the history of the ummah. True, he was not the first of the righteous caliphs to be assassinated, nor would he be the last. His predecessor, 'Umar, had been killed; his successor 'Ali was also destined to lose his life at the hands of an assassin. But as reported, 'Umar's death came at the hands of a deranged individual. Tragic as it might have been, his death hardly represented a broad assault on the moral or political authority of the ummah's leader. The deaths of 'Uthman and later of 'Ali reflect altogether different circumstances. As reported by our Arabic authors, these assassinations were deeply entwined with contemporaneous politics that affected the very institution of the caliphate. Regarding 'Uthman, it was a complicated series of events that were brought to a head when some disaffected tribesmen took his life while the Hijazi Muslim notables stood aside and did not come to his assistance. Whatever their reasons for not supporting 'Uthman, it could be said the old notables bore responsibility for the death of a blameless Muslim who was one of the Prophet's staunchest followers. 'Ali was assassinated in turn by a former supporter who, along with others, broke with the caliph when he submitted his dispute with Mu'awiyah to arbitration. Known as Kharijites, that is "those who secede," the secessionists were brutally dealt with by the 'Alid loyalists on the field of battle and were destined to remain throughout Islamic history a strident sect and periodic thorn against established authority.

The debilitating five-year war pitted old allies and families against one another. As the conflict dragged on with no end in sight, the ummah grew weary and by all accounts willing to consider compromise. The unexpected death of 'Ali was thus seen by many Muslims as an opportunity to bring the civil war to an end. When 'Ali was assassinated, his son al-Hasan reportedly had 40,000 loyal warriors to carry on his behalf and that of the family, but al-Hasan was unwilling to continue the struggle, whereupon Mu'awiyah sought and now received the acclaim of the entire ummah as the new Commander of the Faithful. Simply put, the time was ripe for bringing the hostilities to a formal close. Mu'awiyah's first task was to declare a general amnesty for the participants on both sides; he then set out to restore order while legitimizing al-Sham as the new center of Arab rule.

During the forty years or so that he ruled from Damascus, first as provincial governor and then as caliph, Mu'awiyah might have been described as the quintessential tribal sheikh. Realizing that he could not compel loyalty from the Hijazi aristocrats or impose absolute control over the Arab tribesmen, he sought gentler but highly effective methods of persuasion. His way of conducting state policy was based on traditional tribal politics of clientage and patronage. He took insults form the Prophet's kinsmen, the Hashimites, with forbearance and flattered and bought off potential rivals among them and their allies. Only when forced by what he considered extraordinary circumstances, did the caliph take up arms against fellow Muslims or otherwise seek severe punishment for those opposing him. Although he was the son of Abu Sufyan, an opponent of the Prophet, Mu'awiyah was reportedly a crypto-convert to Islam even before the capitulation of the Meccans and, subsequent to that, a confidant of the Prophet, facts that had to be balanced by the anti-Umayyad chroniclers. Mu'awiyah was a person of too many accomplishments to be treated lightly by those who recorded history in retrospect. Given the caliph's active and often successful warfare against the

Byzantine Christian enemy, and the orderly rule he restored to the burgeoning Islamic state, there was little for which even the most rabid pro-Shiʻite authors of later generations could fault Muʻawiyah, but fault him they did when rendering their final judgment. On the one hand, they were forced to admire his capacity to administer the rapidly evolving Islamic ummah; but having done so, they accused him of preferring the temporal world (*dunya*) to that of the spiritual (*din*). By no means did they imply the caliph was a bad Muslim, let alone that he harbored anti-Muslim views. They complained instead that he relished politics and was totally consumed by the administration of the state, as opposed to the descendants of ʻAli who are described as foreswearing the politics of the moment for the common good of the community. There were, to be sure, given episodes in Muʻawiyah's career that elicited a stern rebuke from the anti-Umayyad historians, none more condemnable than for his having arranged the succession of his profligate son Yazid, described as a somewhat indifferent Muslim. With the choice of Yazid, Muʻawiyah set into motion events that would deny leadership of the ummah to the Prophet's family and clan for the better part of ninety years. Had there been an Umayyad historiography, or at least remnants of a surviving historical tradition that favored Muʻawiyah and his successors, we might have a rather different picture of the house of Umayyah, one that granted them considerable credit for keeping the Byzantines at bay along the frontier with Syria while expanding the Islamic realm beyond Iraq and into North Africa and Spain. But such is not the case. Denying the Hashimites their proper place for so long a period of time was an outrage that could not be reconciled by the only historians of record, those broadly favoring the Prophet's house.

Muʻawiyah's decision to name his son successor while he, that is the caliph, still lived, certainly broke with all past precedent. The leading notables of the ummah no doubt assumed that following Muʻawiyah's death, they would take up the issue of succession once again. As happened following the death of the previous caliphs, a new shura of Hijazi Muslims would be convened and a new leader chosen, presumably from among their own, the families most closely linked to the Prophet by blood and past loyalty. Muʻawiyah's decision to name a son to succeed him suggested that the profligate Yazid and successive generations of unworthy Umayyads might similarly arrange the succession of their own offspring, perpetuating thereby the rule of a clan other than that of the Prophet, a clan that had been tarnished by dishonor when they opposed Muhammad at the outset of his mission. Truth be told, succession did not go quite so smoothly within the house of Umayyah, but despite internal feuds and armed conflicts they managed to retain rule from 661 until 750. For the aristocrats of the Hijaz and indeed many others, there was something obscene about the continuous rule of a clan that had initially rejected the Prophet and even opposed him in dramatic fashion. Readers of the Arabic chronicles were familiar with the report of Mu'awiyah's mother chewing on the liver (i.e. licking the blood) of the Prophet's uncle Hamzah as he lay slain on the field of battle, an act which earned her the sobriquet "The Eater of the Livers (*akilat al-akbad*)." Whether or not the event actually took place, it would have been rightly understood for what it was meant to be: a symbolic gesture by which Hind, the wife of Abu Sufyan and mother of Mu'awiyah, exacted revenge for the blood of one of her own relatives killed in an earlier foray. The Prophet granted Hind and her husband amnesty after the conquest of Mecca, but, as she reportedly came to the Prophet disguised and fearing repercussions, the gravity of her alleged act and more generally the responsibility of the house of Umayyah in opposing the Prophet were self-apparent, at least to readers of the Arabic chronicles describing the events of the time.

With such moments etched in memory—it made little difference if they were real, shaped, or invented—it is not surprising that some leading Hashimites and indeed other early Muslim notables are pictured by Muslim historians as refusing to take the oath of allegiance to the future caliph at Mu'awiyah's court. Some reports have them escaping to the Hijaz in fear of their lives; but as best as we can ascertain, the initial response to Mu'awiyah's brazen initiative was rather muted. The Hashimite antipathy to Umayyad rule had not yet congealed as to allow for discrete groups to seriously contemplate, let alone draw up a plan of action for, the overthrow of the existing regime. The anti-Umayyad sources portray the Hashimites, and in particular the 'Alids, as reluctant to take up arms because the relatives of the Prophet recognized the dangers of dividing the ummah once more. Truth be told, time and again the Prophet's family and their Hijazi supporters were bought off by Mu'awiyah's largesse and easily outmaneuvered by his deft handling of tribal politics. It was not until the abortive revolt of 'Ali's son al-Husayn (see below) that the Hashimites attempted the overthrow of the Umayyad house, but even then, some twenty years after Mu'awiyah declared himself caliph, the descendants of 'Ali lacked the organizational talent and vision for concerted and effective action.

As we shall see in a later discussion of the Hashimites, al-Husayn's rebellion shortly after Mu'awiyah's death in 680 was a rather quixotic affair that ended with needless tragedy. A more serious revolt against Umayyad rule was that of 'Abdallah the son of the Qurayshite notable al-Zubayr. 'Abdallah ibn al-Zubayr was related to the Hashimites through his mother, the daughter of the first caliph Abu Bakr; his illustrious father was one of Muhammad's early companions and had been one of those responsible for choosing the third and fourth righteous caliphs. The son of al-Zubayr thus had impressive credentials, more impressive than those of the reigning caliphs of the time. But as 'Ali had learned some twenty years earlier, credentials alone could not stem the Umayyad challenge, nor could the Hijaz provide the human and financial resources for a successful campaign. What was required was a grand alliance that extended beyond the spiritual heartland of Islam. That the counter-caliphate of the Zubayrids lasted for more than a decade (681–692) despite serious internal challenges from the Kharijites and other erstwhile allies may be attributed to two factors: dissension within the house of Umayyah, which opened the gates to local insurrections, and the political marriage of the Iraqi Arab tribesmen to the Hijazi notable. The Iraqis, who chafed under Syrian domination, and the old Hijazi Muslims, grieved by the continuous rule of the Umayyad parvenus, joined forces to common purpose. The Iraqis provided the military muscle to launch and sustain the challenge; the Hijazis, the descendants of Muhammad's early circle of followers, gave the revolt its sense of legitimacy. It is doubtful that the Iraqis had a vested interest in the personal claims of the Hijazi pretender. Such as it is, the evidence indicates they would have been satisfied with any Muslim notable who could properly claim the mantle of the Prophet. Having supported 'Ali against Mu'awiyah, they were prepared to declare for al-Husayn against the Umayyad's son and handpicked successor Yazid. For the Iraqis, 'Abdallah's claim to the caliphate was merely the most recent opportunity to remove the yoke of Damascus. They were surely aware a Muslim government centered in Medina with limited human and financial resources would have given them greater license to govern their own affairs than the Syria-based caliphs. The Iraqis exercised considerable independence in their dealings with the Zubayrids, but they served their cause well before their regionally based revolt collapsed.

The Umayyads, often led by extremely capable rulers, managed to regroup as they often did. Over time, they reduced the danger from Iraq by dispatching large numbers of Arab tribesmen from the provincial garrison towns to partake in campaigns far to the east in the distant regions known as Khurasan. In order to bring Iraqis to heel, the Umayyads also built an administrative center, Wasit, midway between

Kufah and Basrah, hitherto the twin capitals of Iraq. The new provincial center was garrisoned with large, well-trained, and loyal Syrian forces commanded by prestigious governors with powers to act decisively, if not ruthlessly. But such efforts could not survive the structural imbalances of Umayyad rule. The loyalty of tribal armies, even the Syrian contingents that were generally accustomed to taking orders from respected leaders, be it the Umayyad caliph or his appointed governor, were susceptible to anarchic sensibilities and self-serving actions when the leadership of the Umayyads was contested within the ruling house and its close circles. When sensing the state was adrift, the army, its commanders, and the provincial authorities grew exceedingly cautious and were slow to respond to external threats as they unfolded. In the end, the tribal foundations of the Muslim armies and the unresolved contradictions of the very nature of the so-called Arab-centered kingdom brought the Umayyad polity to an end. Ironically, the transfer of Iraqi tribesmen and then other powerful military forces to consolidate the Muslim hold on Khurasan planted the seeds of massive defection among the tribal armies stationed there. The Khurasan army would be the vanguard of a Hashimite revival that challenged and then overthrew the house of Umayyah in 750.

Some close relatives of the Prophet, assimilating the lessons of the past, also regrouped, and out of the various movements that sought to overthrow the standing regime a new and more adroit leadership emerged. The descendants of the Prophet's uncle al-'Abbas, first cousins of the 'Alids, created a clandestine and tightly knit revolutionary apparatus and were wise enough to wait before openly challenging the existing regime. Laying the groundwork for a successful campaign, the rebels delayed unfurling their banners until they succeeded in raising a powerful army capable of holding its own and more with the seasoned veterans of the Umayyads. Abbasid agents, taking advantage of dissension within the ranks of the Khurasan army and more generally the revolutionary climate of the times, declared an open revolt when the house of Umayyah, torn by dissension in its own ranks and distracted by rebellions closer to home, was unable to fully recognize let alone meet the new challenge in time. With that, a branch of the Hashimite clan restored the Prophet's house to its proper role as leaders of the ummah and ushered in a new era in which Islamic governance would cater less to tribal sensibilities. Had the Umayyads been granted an extended lease on life it is conceivable they might have undergone a successful transition from an Arab-centered polity to a relatively stable ruling order free from the debilitating effects of Arab tribalism; that is, a polity with a more universal outlook and basis of rule. As often as not, the Umayyad caliphs were figures of keen political intelligence and considerable resolve. The area they came to rule in some fashion or other extended from the Iberian Peninsula in the west to the borders of central Asia in the east. Above all, they enjoyed considerable success against the Byzantines. It would appear, however, that the Umayyads were more able to expand Muslim rule than to consolidate it. In the end, the very foundations of their rule eventually did them in.

Like the early caliphate, the Umayyad regime privileged a small Arab segment at the expense of an ever expanding non-Arab population of the Islamic ummah. As they lacked the capacity to overthrow the Syrian-based regime without the backing of a real army and as they had no authority to elect a caliph from among their own, the non-Arab converts, mostly settlers or descendants of settlers who flocked to the garrison towns to supply services needed by the tribal contingents, tended to be partisans of the family of 'Ali and/or other Hijazi notables not identified with the ruling regime. We are obliged to ask had conditions been more settled toward the end of the Umayyad caliphate, might it have been possible for the ruling regime to make a truly respected place for non-Arab clients who, as Muslims, were equal, at least in theory, to their Arab patrons. Related to that, could the house of Umayyah have decentralized rule from Damascus so as to allow local governors more license in administrating the needs of their broadly based constituencies? Any such decentralization might have given the governors of distant regions greater freedom to react to evolving circumstances, and, above all, make more rapid use of the Arab military that had been sent them from the heartland of Islamic rule.

These questions are far reaching and the answers they occasion are at best speculative; that is always the case when one looks at history through a counterfactual microscope. Allowing our minds to wander, we can imagine that over time, the Umayyads might have reined in the Arab tribal armies and made circumstances easier for the non-Arab Muslims. As regards decentralization, one can point to the establishment of the city Wasit and then Madinat Ibn Hubayrah, Umayyad administrative centers that allowed the regime's governors in Iraq to take considerable license in exercising their own judgment. Controlling the unruly province required a shortened time to respond to new situations. But the larger problem of Islamic governance still remained and would have continued if the Iraqi model had been followed everywhere and at all times. The point of the administrative centers was not to give the regional populace a freer hand in setting their own agenda, but to allow the governor to administer the often stifling policy of the authorities in Damascus. In the best of situations tensions between the center and the outlying provinces could and did become dicey. Given what has transpired in the Arab world over the last 1,400 years, it does not seem likely that an Umayyad state, however flexible in outlook, could have reconciled the idealized conception of a truly universal Islamic ummah with the urgent need to legitimate some forms of decentralized authority, such as the creation of provinces linked by Islam but formally recognized as independent political units. Throughout the Middle Ages, and even until this very day, the inherent contradiction between an ideal community that transcended the bonds of ethnic, linguistic, and geographical particularities and Islamic societies seeking to celebrate their own sense of community and local space produced tensions that constantly threatened to undermine the foundations of rule at both the center and the periphery.

The Hashimite Restoration:
A Revolution Shaped by Images
of an Idealized Past

Following three decades of clandestine revolutionary activities (718–747 C.E.), the descendants of al-'Abbas, the Prophet's last surviving paternal uncle, co-opted a provincial insurrection in Khurasan, recruited a revolutionary army, and three years later overthrew the dynasty that had displaced the Prophet's family from power. Having disposed of the Umayyads, they established a polity that would endure for more than five hundred years. The medieval chronicles and belletristic works that focus in compelling fashion on the events of the times are a problem for modern scholars, particularly the description of the first two centuries of Abbasid rule. In addition to debasing the Umayyad interlopers, the detailed written record of the early Abbasids often preserves echoes of a carefully articulated bias favoring the new dynasts, so much so that at times the portrayal of individuals and circumstances raises doubts about the historicity of specific episodes. As with the accounts of the Prophet, the early caliphate, and the Umayyads, the embellished record of the Banu 'Abbas presents us with a history that should have been rather than the history that was. This comes as no surprise to discerning readers as some medieval historians were the hired pens of the new dynasty; others reflected, however, the views of their kinsmen and rivals, the 'Alids, fellow Hashimites who savored rule as their sacred right, but were denied it time and again. Having opposed the Umayyads in the past, the ʿAlids and their supporters now opposed their Abbasid cousins, occasionally in armed revolt, more often in wars of propaganda. Present-day scholars seeking a more accurate review of the times are thus encouraged, indeed required, to recognize the difficulties in using these sources.

The very language of medieval Arabic historiography presents difficulties. When reading classical Arabic texts, modern scholars may falter over particular words and expressions. That is particularly troubling when the precise reading of a passage is critical to the larger understanding of the text and with that the historical issues reflected therein. As a rule, scholars then turn to the multivolume Arabic-Arabic dictionaries of the Middle Ages. But these works, useful as they are in presenting readers with so many lexical entries, are not historical dictionaries like the *OED* (*Oxford English Dictionary*), which traces English vocabulary and expressions as they appear in successive periods. More often than not, readers having recourse to the medieval dictionaries cannot specify what words and/or phrases might have meant in specific times and places. Lacking precise meanings for words and expressions at a given place and time inhibits our ability to speak knowingly of events far removed from us. The so-called Abbasid Revolution is a case in point. Probing the history of the medieval Islamic world, and in particular the Abbasid dynasty, Western scholars must explain what they mean when referring to the Abbasid "revolution," their label of choice. If one thinks of the overthrow of a previous regime, the following questions come to mind: How did a clandestine and relatively small group of conspirators manage to overthrow a still-powerful standing regime? If one thinks of the Abbasid revolution in a broader sense, how did the new Islamic polity differ, if at all, from its predecessors going back to the origins of the caliphate and even the ummah at the time of the Prophet's death? In other words, why regard the change of regime as nothing less than a revolution, comparable, say, to the great upheavals of modern Europe to which it has been compared by scholars of the West?

With the unsettled state of medieval Arabic historiography, it is not surprising that the manner in which the Abbasids came to rule and the very nature of their dynastic order have been subjected to different scholarly interpretations. Earlier generations of orientalists concerned with the formation of the Abbasid state, its political institutions and social structure, and the rich civilization to which it gave rise relied on a conventional wisdom derived from European thought and scholarship of the nineteenth century. Until the 1970s and even today there were and continue to be scholars who tailor their data to fit a conceptual framework strongly influenced by the growth of modern European nationalism and along with that theories of race and society that were invoked to support the creation of the newly minted nation-states of Europe—some created in the wake of revolutions against existing imperial authority. These scholars of the Islamic world, whether orientalists of the old school, more recent historians seemingly influenced by revolutionary politics of the 1960s, or Iranian nationalists locked in conflict with modern Arab regimes and the West, depict the emergence of the Abbasid dynasty as the culmination of a long struggle between the "Arab kingdom" of the Umayyads and the conquered population of a recently shattered Iranian empire. The conflict they perceive was between a ruling institution predicated on the special privilege of a relatively small Arab ruling caste and a more broadly defined coalition of revolutionary forces whose Iranian/Persian ethnic origins were rooted in the vast Iranian province of Khurasan.

An exaggerated emphasis was thus given to the role played by the indigenous population of the eastern province during the years of clandestine operations and, especially, during the open revolt that followed. Concurrent with this enlarged role for the native Khurasanis, there developed the rather seductive notion that Islamic government and society became increasingly Iranized under the aegis of Abbasid rule. Seen in this light, the victory of the revolutionary armies over the Umayyad state signified more than a resounding military achievement; it heralded the creation of a new order in which the narrow political orientation and rigidly defined social structures of Arab tribal society were replaced by new modes of thought and behavior and a new polity of universal outlook and composition—in short, a polity that more fully integrated the non-Arab elements of Islamic society as well as pre-conquest Arab settlers who had become clients subordinate to their conquering Muslim Arab patrons.

One supposes that those arguing this point of view could have maintained the Abbasid triumph recreated or at least claimed to recreate the idealized ummah of the Prophet's time, that community that allegedly drew no distinctions among the faithful. There would have been much truth to an argument linking Abbasid universalism with the outlook of the Prophet. There can be little doubt the Abbasid propagandists trumpeted their patrons' links to the Prophet and their dynasty to the community of the Prophet. But that is not how evolving historic developments were read by scholars over the last hundred years and more.

A long line of historians maintained that the universal Abbasid state, although ruled by Arabs, was essentially a new Iranian empire with familiar Iranian institutions, a traditional Iranian style of rule, and occasionally residual Iranian religious beliefs and practices. In sum, the culture, certainly the political culture, of the Abbasids was borrowed from Iran. Except for the widespread use of Arabic (and even that was challenged by native speakers of Persian dialects), Abbasid society, although rooted in the religion of the Prophet, was said to resonate in the most profound way with political institutions and cultural artifacts of a venerable Iranian civilization. One can hardly deny that Iranian civilization and culture affected the outlook of those Arabs who came into contact with it, just as Jewish and Christian thinking and practices were absorbed by Muslims, but it would be entirely misleading to think of the Abbasids as having somehow produced what was in essence an Iranian state and civilization dressed for appearance sake in formal Muslim attire.

A thorough review of the literature, especially sources discovered and analyzed since the 1960s, has forced some modern historians of the Abbasids to revise, indeed to abandon, the old conceptual framework. Although some scholars are yet to be persuaded, it is now clear that the Abbasids, Arab aristocrats who originated in the Hijaz, were brought to power not by local Iranians, nor by Iranized Arabs long settled in Khurasan, nor by the marginalized Arabs and non-Arabs of Iraq, but by a provincial standing army of disaffected Arab tribesmen led by hand-picked Arab commanders who had been part of the clandestine revolutionary movement since its inception. Moreover, the emerging Abbasid state, while increasingly centralized like the great empires of antiquity, can hardly be depicted as little more than an Iranian style polity that was acceptable to the Muslim faithful because its underlying structures, the residue of an earlier Iranian civilization, were embossed with a familiar and traditional Islam. To better understand the shaping of Abbasid rule and society, we have to focus a critical eye on the language and thoughts of our medieval witnesses who hold the key to understanding the Abbasid rise to power and the nature of the civilization and culture that evolved as they ruled.

Contemporaries referred to the advent of the Abbasids as the *dawlah*, a word Arabic lexicographers endowed with a wide range of meanings, including a "turn" that signifies changing times or fortunes. For the new dynasts and their supporters, dawlah meant, more specifically, victory over their predecessors, the house of Umayyah, and, concurrent with that triumph, the formation of an entirely new order. The new commander of the faithful was not seen as carrying on in the tradition of his predecessors. The dawlah was no rebellion of ambitious kinsmen in search of gain for themselves and their extended family; nor was it a coup engineered by restless praetorians seeking their own aggrandizement with a change of political leadership. No parochial interests were championed. No simple rotation of palace occupants was anticipated. Eagerly awaited by a significant cross-section of Islamic society, the onset of Abbasid sovereignty was looked upon by contemporaries as a substantive break with the immediate past. Broadly speaking, the expectations of dramatic change, at times cloaked in messianic imagery foreign to the Arabs of the desert, were fulfilled by events seemingly orchestrated by the emergent dynasts.

The exemplary way in which the first Abbasid caliph attempted to eradicate the last traces of Umayyad rule, which included mutilating the body of the last Umayyad caliph, the brutal killing and wholesale execution of leading members of the ruling house, and, were that not enough, violating the graves of the Umayyad caliphs in the family cemetery, signaled for readers of the chronicles a politics previously unknown among the leading Muslims. There was no precedent whatsoever for the wholesale punishment meted out to the deposed regime; they were, after all, fellow Qurayshites and hence broadly affiliated by bonds of kinship with the Prophet and his extended family. When Mu'awiyah was declared caliph, he made sure to declare a general amnesty for all his opponents and saw to it that 'Ali's sons al-Hasan and al-Husayn , potential rivals for the leadership of the ummah, could live in peace and quite comfortably at that. Why should he have done otherwise? When the Prophet took power in Mecca, he made it a point to spare Mu'awiyah's mother and forgive Mu'awiyah's father, at one time a prominent leader opposed to the Muslims. What then explains the reported ferocity of the Abbasids? No doubt, they felt a deep personal antipathy to the Umayyads to act as they did; that profound resentment awaits, however, further explanation.

As we shall see in the following chapter, the changes initiated by the new order went far beyond a settling of scores, whatever they might have been. The enormity of the changes instituted by the Abbasids represent a truly ambitious departure from both the style and substance of Umayyad rule, whether one speaks of new networks of social relationships that allowed non-Arabs positions of prominence within the inner circles of Abbasid rule; or a complete overhaul of the military structure in which Arab armies, organized along tribal lines and subject to tribal sensitivities, gave way to highly professional regional forces and, following that, ethnic contingents tied more directly to the person of the caliph; or the creation of a highly centralized and massive bureaucracy, encased by truly monumental architecture and reflected in signs of courtly rank and a highly stylized court ceremonial. In this sense, Arabic dawlah, derived from a root meaning "to turn" or "come about" is the semantic equivalent of the English word "revolution," which, since the time of the Renaissance, has come to mean political upheaval as well as rotation. Did this change mean the Abbasids and the Muslim faithful of Arabian origins consciously embraced an older Iranian-style government and in full stride boldly absorbed Iranian culture and institutions, or was the Abbasid revolution initiated with a rather different agenda in mind?

It would seem the far-reaching changes, which completely overturned the existing political and social order, tend to mask another meaning of dawlah, a meaning that extends beyond the semantic range of revolution when it is used as a political term. As regards the Abbasids, dawlah had the additional nuance of a historical process that had come "full turn." There is perhaps no text where this is explicitly stated, but it is implied all so often in official Abbasid historiography where the victory of the Banu 'Abbas is embellished with apocalyptical symbols and heralded as a return to the halcyon days of early Islam when the Prophet ruled a pristine community with religious rectitude and justice. Seen from this prospective, the Abbasid revolution and the Abbasid polity to follow were not to bring about transformative change, let alone restore the political culture of a shattered Iranian Empire; the great upheaval occasioned by the rise of the new dynasty was actually a restorative process. For all the emphasis modern historians have placed on radical change, the central theme of official Abbasid propaganda before and after they came to power was the regeneration of Islamic society by returning to the ethos of the age when the Prophet guided the community of the faithful. In such fashion, the nostalgic memories of a not so distant past were wedded to the social and political realities of the moment and were, as a result, instrumental in shaping the political outlook and culture of the Abbasids in the formative years of their dynasty and in times to follow. No ruler and no regime in the Islamic world could claim legitimacy without heralding a connection to the Prophet and the ummah of old.

Even as they promoted the onset of a new era, apologists for the new dynasty focused their attention on earlier times, though clearly not on an Iranian past. Starting with pre-Islamic times and continuing until the present day, they carefully searched the historic record for inspiration, guidance, and, above all, evidence with which to link the Abbasids to the monotheist prophets of old and, more particularly, to the Arabian Prophet who brought monotheism to its quintessential and final form. With that, they sought to establish their patrons' case for legitimacy. The hired pens of the ruling house portrayed the current Abbasids and their forebears as authentic models of proper moral and political behavior, and conversely they found their adversaries and their ancestors as unfit for leadership in the past or rule of the ummah in the present. The Abbasids were portrayed as analogues to their kinsman, the Prophet, and the recent revolutionary age was proclaimed as a return to the early Islamic community. But history often has a way of creating difficulties for those who invoke it on behalf of a partisan cause that is hotly contested. The Abbasid performance during the Umayyad interregnum— the ninety or so years in which the Prophet's family had been displaced from the leadership of the ummah—was unimpressive, to say the least. Their opposition to the Umayyads, such as it was, often seemed muted if that and thus elicited caustic comments from those who put a high premium on principle and personal courage, the kind of courage valued by Arab tribesmen and reflected in stories of 'Ali's son al-Husayn entering into combat with several dozen companions against 4,000 cavalry of the Umayyad usurpers. Al-Husayn had prepared an insurrection against the established regime and was en route to Kufah to enlist an army but the plan was exposed. With no prospects of rallying the Iraqis to his side as he intended, al-Husayn still could have returned to Arabia from his camp at Karbala'; at worst he would have been humiliated and put under temporary house arrest. But he took up his sword and became a martyr instead. The 'Alids had a record of still other rebellions against an unwanted and (from their perspective) illegitimate Umayyad rule. The record of 'Alid resistance, however badly advised and futile in the end, was nevertheless forged on the anvil of an authentic and highly visible history. On the other hand, the Abbasid revolt seemed forever delayed by cautious and highly secretive preparations. Even after the Abbasid revolution was proclaimed, and even after their armies succeeded in liberating Iraq, the family was unwilling to surface in public and directly take the reins of the force they had unleashed.

As a result, the new dynasty's apologists had to reshape history to make it consonant with the ideals of an earlier age; not the foolish bravado of Arab tribal warriors, but the cautious approach of the Prophet to delay operations against the Meccans until he thought the moment propitious. Those who scoffed at the Abbasids and their seeming lack of courage were reminded time and again in stories real or invented that the Prophet himself cautioned patience when necessary. They pointed out that the Prophet and some of his less fortunate followers had been subjected to numerous indignities over an extended period of time before the historic migration to Medina. Even as he was about to leave Mecca, the Prophet did not call for a military campaign against the pagan oligarchs of his native town. Such a request would have been inappropriate and counterproductive considering the preponderance of power that his opponents, among them the ancestors of the Umayyads, could have brought to bear against him. A politically astute leader knows the wisdom of delaying gratification, even revenge, and thus designs a policy that discourages risky ventures for the sake of long-range gains. The Prophet fully understood the value of quiet overtures and secret meetings. The description of his clandestine encounters with the Medinese in the middle of the night was emblematic of that understanding and was used as a model for Abbasid revolutionaries to conduct their business—or so their apologists maintained.

Caution had its place, but the Abbasid dynasts fully understood that memories of active resistance against the Umayyads roused great fervor among certain elements of the faithful. The Abbasids would not have been well served if their official chroniclers pictured them as less willing than others to confront the descendants of the Prophet's enemies than their 'Alid cousins. The dynastic apologists thus argued that Abbasid family leaders had indeed suffered at the hands of the Umayyads, but the stories they told at best embellished the truth and more probably were outright inventions. In any case, how could one compare the martyrdom of defiant 'Alid rebels to an Abbasid notable being banished from the Umayyad court for what appears, at worst, a social indiscretion? The Abbasid claims strained credulity. The lines were thus set for a conflict among the Hashimites of the *ahl al-bayt*, the extended family or the "Prophet's house," each seeking to take advantage of calls for change, a conflict that would ultimately lead to the Shi'ite-Sunnite split that has compromised the unity of the ummah for more than a millennium. In addition, the Abbasids had to contend with more marginal sects that made their appearance from time to time, as well as the religiously austere Kharijites whose more militant advocates lurked in the background ready to assert themselves at given moments and places.

The Abbasids and Radical Sectarians Within the Ummah

As Umayyad rule began to unravel, there was a seeming rise in messianic expectation. The earlier anticipated date for apocalyptical change, the turn of the first Islamic century, had come and gone, but the house of Umayyah remained in power. Nevertheless, the notion of a new era bringing about dramatic changes remained strongly engraved on the imagination of numerous Muslims. Such as they were, the apocalyptical meanderings of the times are more likely the residue of messianic speculation that was part and parcel of the pre-Islamic Near East, particularly among Christians and Jews, but no doubt also among other religious or ethnic groups about whom much less if anything is known. A number of radical sects, identifiably or nominally Muslim, but with what must have seemed rather strange beliefs and practices, attached themselves to the cause of bringing down the house of Umayyah and, following that, supporting or opposing the incipient Abbasid regime. The marriage of a radical messianic message to revolutionary expectations is not unusual nor was it without its advantages to the house of 'Abbas. There was, after all, nothing to prevent Abbasid propagandists from assuming a multitude of poses during the period of clandestine operations; they could thus appear as embracing all things to all peoples. But the Abbasids had to be cautious lest their more freewheeling agents and followers expose them to risk by publicly exhibiting bizarre behavior that would attract attention.

One of the most notable cases of this sort was their agent Khidash who operated among the villagers of Khurasan where he spread extremist views associated with the so-called Khuramiyyah, a loose label for splintered sectarian groups who believed in violating cardinal rules of social and moral behavior (as that would no doubt hasten the onset of the messianic age). Various sources report that Khidash was seized by the local Umayyad authorities and after being brutally tortured was killed and his body parts hung in public display; other accounts suggest that the Abbasids themselves did away him for fear his actions would have led to exposing elements of the clandestine revolutionary network. The bill of particulars the Abbasid apologists drew up against Khidash, included propagating views and encouraging forbidden social practices that he endorsed in the name of the hidden leader (*imam*) of the Abbasid family without seeking the latter's approval (implying thereby that, had he known of Khidash's intentions, the imam would have withheld his permission). In any case, the Abbasids, given their initial need for anonymity, and their later need to appear as properly orthodox Muslims, would have felt it necessary to distance themselves from more radical leaders and sects. Some disappointed followers of Khidash were said to have rebelled against the new Abbasid regime, which was then forced to suppress them with decisive force.

Before and after the revolution that brought them to power, the Abbasids had to contend with a broad spectrum of what may be described as radical proto-Shi'ite groups, all of whom were sure that the overthrow of the past regime would usher in the messianic age. Among them were the Rawandiyah, men of Khurasan, who like Khidash and his followers held heterodox views, including the belief in metempsychosis, that is, the transmigration of souls from one corporeal body to another (*tanasukh al-arwah*). At the time Khidash was still active, a Rawandi propagandist, one al-Ablaq—reportedly a leper who spoke in hyperbolic language— maintained the spirit (*ruh*) attached to Jesus passed on to 'Ali ibn Abi Talib and then to each of the divine imams (of 'Ali's offspring and perhaps the Abbasids as well). It is highly unlikely that so dubious a character as al-Ablaq might have known the identity of the hidden Abbasid leaders; he might not even have been familiar with operatives of the clandestine revolutionary movement. Unlike Khidash, there is nothing to link him directly to the secret cadres in his province. What is certain is that al-Ablaq's Rawandiyah espoused extreme libertine views, and as did other radical proto-Shi'ite groups, they felt obliged to indulge in acts that were reprehensible under ordinary circumstances. Al-Ablaq is pictured as perfectly willing to combine traditional Near Eastern hospitality with an extreme form of communalism that ran counter to the social mores of the time; he shared his wife with his fellow believers as well as his food and drink. Not surprisingly, he too was put to death in a brutal fashion, report-edly by the same Umayyad official who made an example of Khidash. One cannot be certain whether the description of al-Ablaq's demise does not in fact conflate the two groups and their leaders. It is not unusual for medieval Muslim historians to meld different individuals and moments of history. One thing is clear, however, the sudden end of al-Ablaq may have deprived some of his associates of free meals and unusual carnal pleasure, but it did not put an end to this loosely organized sect as a whole.

After the emergence of the Abbasids, some Rawandiyah proclaimed their allegiance to the new order. With the Abbasid caliph unveiled, it would have been no problem to declare the divine soul of Jesus had now entered the new commander of the faithful. And so, several years after the change of dynasty, the second Abbasid caliph al-Mansur (754–775) took his turn as the object of their unusual veneration. The Rawandiyah came to the caliph's court hoping to partake of his food and drink. Although there is no indication they also expected to roam freely about the women's quarters, their public acclaim of al-Mansur's divinity, which was certainly heretical, and their generally unruly behavior, which sparked a riot, forced the entry of the security forces. The latter barely rescued the beleaguered Abbasid caliph from a crushing mob of overzealous admirers. The event led to the arrest of various sect leaders and then an attempt to liberate them. Large-scale intervention resulted in a widespread slaughter of the group. A number of sect members fleeing the carnage reportedly leapt from the heights of the caliph's palace (perhaps expecting a meaningful transmigration of their own). As was the case with various followers of Khidash, segments of the Rawandiyah rejected Abbasid rule, and, having rebelled openly against the regime in their native Khurasan, they invited a lethal response from the central authorities.

Some proto-Shi'ite groups were linked to Abu Muslim, the charismatic paymaster of the Khurasan army, who was treacherously murdered by his Abbasid patrons after they achieved power, when they deemed him a possible liability rather than an asset. Other groups linked to apocalyptical expectations were said to have been highly eclectic sects that combined elements of Judaism, Christianity, and Iranian religions with Islam, a sort of religious syncretism wrapped in messianic expectations. There is a distinctive literature in Arabic that mentions all these groups, a body of texts that falls under the general rubric of heresiography. As described in these writings, the aforementioned sects seem to have an amoeba-like quality; that is, they are marked by constituencies that are constantly dividing and subdividing but apparently without substantial growth or power. Few of these sects are mentioned in the extensive accounts of the time reported by the major chroniclers, and when mentioned—usually as fomenting rebellion—the details are so sparse one may assume they played little role if any in Abbasid politics and society. In the end, or even the beginning, they were no serious threat to the unity of the Islamic ummah, or to the sense of what it meant to be a Muslim for the overwhelming majority of the faithful. It almost appears that the heresiographers had to invent groups and position them at different moments of the historical spectrum in order to fill out the requisite mythical number of some seventy heresies—a number that applied as well to Jewish and Christian sects, the secret names of God, and any number of associations with the number seventy going go back to more remote times.

To be sure, there is a profound difference between these groups and the more normative schools of thought that concerned themselves with theological and/or legal issues. One has to distinguish as well the line between heretics or seeming heretics, apostates, and those who retained in Islamic times Iranian beliefs that were deemed heretical as well by the Sasanian authorities. Muslim heretics might be tolerated as cranks as long as they refrained from challenging the regime, their behavior and influence remained limited to their own circles and their deviance from social mores and religious observance did not negate the basic foundations of an evolving Islamic law. Apostasy was a rather different matter, especially if the apostate not only abandoned Islam but converted openly to another faith, even a monotheist faith. Such an open denial of Islam and its Prophet's message was punishable by death.

A gray zone was reserved for those who, having strayed from the Zoroastrian faith, were declared heretics by the Sasanian authorities. Jews and Christians were genuine monotheists and were thus entitled to protective status under Islam; Zoroastrians were similarly protected as they had a revealed scripture that Muslims considered legitimate for its time and place. But the heretics (*zindiq* pl. *zanadiqah*) of pre-Islamic Iran who believed in Mani, a prophet who allegedly emerged from a Judeo-Christian background sometime in the third century C.E., did not quite fit the official paradigm that governed relations between Muslims and the nonbelievers living among them. Al-Mansur's successor al-Mahdi (r. 775–785) aggressively pursued the Manicheans, rooting them out and persecuting them because it was thought various outwardly observant Muslims had become crypto-followers of Mani. Aside from this particular episode, the Manicheans were generally ignored by Muslim officials as they presented no particular threat to Islam, and unlike some later militant Iranian movements, posed no danger to established authority. The term "zindiq," borrowed from Middle Iranian, was broadly applied over time to all sorts of individuals and groups castigated as heretics and even apostates.

As is the case in many religious communities, the most serious threat to the unity of the ummah came from within what might be considered the mainstream of the faithful: the party (*shi'ah*) of the 'Alid family that would crystallize into what has become known as the Shi'ites. The Abbasids who denied the 'Alids their place at the head of the community were ultimately transmogrified into Sunnites (*ahl al-sunnah wa-l-jama'ah*), that is the "orthodox" or, if you prefer, the more correct but odd-sounding "catholic" community within the Islamic ummah. As a rule, the Sunnites tended to be less innovative religiously than their Shi'ite rivals and certainly less given to heterodox influences than were some Shi'ites within the ummah who travelled along the shoulders of the right path. The latter were influenced by ideas that probably would have seemed foreign, if not even offensive, to the Prophet and his generation of Muslims. They certainly seemed so to the Sunnites who favored traditions established by the Prophet, his companions, and the righteous caliphs. As their world evolved, the Sunnites came to regard the Abbasid commanders of the faithful as temporal rulers, but held they were most deeply inspired and motivated by religious ideals. The Abbasid caliphs in turn gave considerable license and support to the religious authorities they appointed.

In theory, the judiciary and the scholars of the religious sciences were independent of the dynasty; in fact, they were beholden to it. A partnership of sorts was formed. The regime kept order and looked warily at any innovation that might offend the religious establishment. The guardians of the faith did not value change for its own sake; in Arabic, the words for innovation and heresy are one and the same (*bid'ah*). Backed by the state in matters that concerned them most, the religious establishment had reason to reciprocate the relatively free hand dealt them; they used their pulpits to deliver the loyalty of the general populace to the regime. In this partnership, the Abbasid dynasts, who appointed the Sunni religious bureaucrats, almost always held the upper hand.

The Split between the Hashimites: 'Alids versus Abbasids/Shi'ites versus Sunnites

The most explosive issue originally dividing Shi'ites and Sunnites, the two main factions of the ummah, was not abstract religious doctrine and law, but the right to don the Prophet's mantle, grasp his scepter, and actually rule the community of the faithful as it had been ruled in an allegedly idyllic past. Despite the long-awaited fall of the Umayyad state and the return of authority to the Prophet's house, events greeted with widespread approval in the eastern provinces and Iraq, denying rule to the 'Alids at the moment of triumph gave rise to bitter resentments among them and those who had labored long and hard on their behalf. The decisive Abbasid victory, which came on the heels recent and of crushing 'Alid defeats—the 'Alids had failed once again in an effort to dislodge the usurpers in the 740s—left the 'Alid pretenders and their hard-core supporters in a state of bewilderment and political disarray, a not uncommon circumstance for them. There was no guarantee, however, that a more militant 'Alid leadership would not reassemble its following and attempt to topple the new order at some propitious moment. The two closely linked branches of the Prophet's house, which had shared broad political objectives during the Umayyad interregnum, now entered into an extremely complex relationship in which both factions fought to command the same stage and thus became political rivals for supreme leadership of the ummah.

While their political instincts failed them time and again, the 'Alids still merited serious attention. They were the closest blood relatives of the Prophet, in fact, the only descendants of Muhammad's line, as he had no male offspring, and among his four daughters only 'Ali's wife Fatimah gave birth. Moreover, ever since the death of al-Husayn their credentials as martyrs to the cause against the Umayyads were absolutely impeccable. Al-Husayn's tragic end on behalf of the faithful came to generate a powerful emotional appeal that crossed space and time. The incident at Karbala' has become a recurrent theme of Shi'ite apologists and has been commemorated in different ways throughout the course of Islamic history. Where did that reverence for 'Alid sacrifice leave the Abbasids as they focused on solidifying their rule? There was already sufficient uncertainty surrounding their claims. By what rights did they obtain leadership of the ummah? Before it was barely established, the new dynastic order had to address this last question and other concerns that tended to compromise their legitimacy. They also worried about retaining the allegiance of the army that brought them to power without the rank and file even knowing the identity of the hidden Abbasid *imam*, the so-called "chosen one from the house of the Prophet (*al-rida min ahl al-bayt*)." Many supporters of the revolution, unaware of its supreme leadership, might have supposed that when they displayed the black banners, first unfurled in Khurasan, and backed the unnamed "chosen one" they were in fact laboring on behalf of a worthy descendant of 'Ali ibn Abi Talib.

Forced to indicate why indeed they were entrusted with restoring the ummah, the Abbasids staked out their official claim, and then as the 'Alids and others contested this claim the new dynasts shifted to other positions only to be countered again and again in a exchange of claims and counterclaims. At first, the Abbasids accepted that leadership of the ummah had come to rest with 'Ali's family; but not with al-Hasan or al-Husayn, the sons borne him by the Prophet's daughter. Following the lead of some radical Shi'ites, they maintained that after 'Ali's death, the authority to lead his house fell to his eldest son, named Muhammad no less. This Muhammad was born to a captive woman from the tribe of Hanifah. Although he harbored no illusions about the Umayyads and resisted formally recognizing their dynasty, 'Ali's eldest, known as "the son of the Hanifite woman (*ibn al-Hanafiyah*)," had no established alliance with his Fatimid half brothers. Nor does he seem to have harbored any overwhelming desire to rebel against the regime. However, that did not stop some proto-Shi'ite groups from invoking his name when planning or indeed actively rebelling against the house of Umayyah. The partisans of 'Ali who embraced Ibn al-Hanafiyah were known collectively as the Kaysaniyah, after one of their militant organizers. Unlike the Abbasids, they disappeared from view in the eighth century. Their greatest legacy, other than a history of failed rebellion, was the promotion of a radical idea that would later be adopted by some mainstream Shi'ites. After Ibn al-Hanafiyah departed from this world, some of his followers insisted his death was an ophthalmic illusion. He was in a state of occultation, that is, he was safely tucked away in a mysterious place, waiting to reappear and initiate the messianic age. The concept of a hidden leader (imam) destined to fulfill a messianic role had become accepted doctrine among partisans of 'Ali's house as it had earlier among their Hashimite rivals.

Seeking legitimacy, the recently minted Abbasid caliph, like the Kaysaniyah, also invoked the Hanifite line, but in a rather different fashion that served the new Commander of the Faithful and his family's interests. His supporters claimed that when Ibn al Hanafiyah died (for them his death was no mere illusion), the authority to command 'Ali's [and the Prophet's] house allegedly shifted to Muhammad's son Abu Hashim, who alas had no child to succeed him as leader of the family or of the secretive revolutionary cells he had put together. Considering the tragic history of 'Alid resistance to unwanted rule and its dramatic appeal to so many Muslims, it was only fitting that this obscure figure should have been given a martyr's death by Abbasid apologists, but not confronting the Umayyads on the field of battle as did al-Husayn. One could not invent such stirring martyrdom out of whole cloth and expect that it would resonate among the multitudes. Rather, Abu Hashim was reportedly poisoned by the Umayyads who were so impressed with his virtues during a visit to their court, they saw him as a threat to their rule, albeit without being the least aware that he already headed a revolutionary group destined to bring them down.

Not wishing to administer the potion in one lethal dose, the Umayyads positioned vendors of a subtly poisoned frozen yogurt along the route of the journey back to his estate in Humaymah, a hot and dusty place in what is today the Hashimite Kingdom of Jordan. Providentially, Humaymah also contained the estates of Abu Hashim's Abbasid cousins who had lived there continuously since being banished from Damascus by the Umayyads. Abu Hashim fell ill during the journey but lingered long enough, or so the Abbasids claimed, to reach Humaymah and transfer both his authority and his revolutionary cadres to his close friend Muhammad, the great-grandson of the Prophet's last surviving paternal uncle al-'Abbas. Muhammad in turn passed both on to his son Ibrahim al-Imam. After the latter's untimely death on the eve of the Abbasid triumph, the inner circle of the Abbasid family entrusted them to Ibrahim's younger brother 'Abdallah, who was destined to become the first Abbasid caliph, the one bearing the regnal title al-Saffah allegedly "The Shedder of Blood." Needless to say, that story of how the Abbasids inherited the right to command the community of the faithful did not satisfy all who awaited the restoration of the Hashimites, least of all the surviving family of 'Ali ibn Abi Talib and their supporters.

Even before they took power, the Abbasids are described as facing a potential rift in the ranks of their followers. Although the revolutionary army had defeated the Umayyad forces in Khurasan and had entered Iraq liberating Kufah, 'Abdallah, the anonymous "chosen one," remained incognito in adjoining Hammam A'yan, this despite demands he reveal himself to his faithful followers. With the Abbasids in hiding nearby, their agent in the city Abu Salamah effectively controlled much of the day-to-day policy decisions, including those affecting the revolutionary army, which technically passed to his jurisdiction once it left Khurasan. The geographic scope of Abu Salamah's authority included all the major districts between Egypt and Iran, making him a most formidable ally of the Banu 'Abbas, but also a potential enemy capable of inflicting untold damage to their cause. His loyalty to the revolution was bound by a personal oath to Ibrahim, the recently deceased imam; however, Abu Salamah is said to have had serious reservations about the younger brother. In the end, the Abbasids felt compelled to assassinate their client just as they would later do away with Abu Muslim, the trusted paymaster and political commissar of their Khurasan army, as well as a number of other operatives who had served them in the field during the long period of clandestine activity. As with so many revolutions, the new regime cleared the revolutionary stable of its lead horses and entrusted governing to members of its immediate family and the caliph's clients who formed the backbone of the burgeoning state bureaucracy.

The dramatic action taken against the old revolutionaries, particularly the most visible ones, had to be explained to posterity if only to absolve the Abbasids of any wrongdoing. Not surprisingly there are conflicting reports of why Abu Salamah was eliminated despite his many years of faithful service to the Banu 'Abbas and their cause. We are led to believe that having witnessed the collapse of the Umayyad regime, Abu Salamah was inclined to break ranks with the Abbasids and invoke an old precedent by calling for still another shura with which to choose a new commander of the faithful. With that, we are given to understand that Abu Salamah was well aware the choice of the electors might fall on someone outside the house of 'Abbas, presumably one of the prestigious 'Alids. No small wonder the new rulers took action against him. These traditions, while meant to whitewash the Abbasids, could be turned, however, against them. For if Abu Salamah had indeed defected to the 'Alids or, at the least, considered doing so, some might have considered it a sign the old revolutionary had come to his senses and realized the 'Alids were indeed worthier of rule than al-Saffah and his Abbasid relatives.

According to Ibn Tabataba (ca. thirteenth century C.E.), perhaps the most partisan of all Shi'ite historians, certainly the most partisan of those describing the events in question, Abu Salamah was prepared to make common cause with any of three 'Alids whose support he solicited in a series of secret letters: Ja'far al-Sadiq, a descendant of al-Husayn ibn 'Ali; and 'Abdallah al-Mahd and 'Umar al-Ashraf, descendants of al-Hasan. After reading his letter, the first immediately disassociated himself from Abu Salamah and, as if to reinforce his rejection of Abu Salamah's offer, he burnt the missive on the spot, the cautious act of a man displaying none of the impulsiveness of his lamented forebear. The third, 'Umar, it would seem even more cautious, returned his letter unopened, saying he could not acknowledge a communication from a person with whom he was not directly acquainted. On the other hand, 'Abdallah al-Mahd was not given to such prudent behavior; unlike his ancestor al-Hasan who accepted political retirement and a life of ease rather than continue the struggle against Mu'awiyah, this 'Alid was prepared to act. He would respond on behalf of his son Muhammad, the so-called "Pure Soul (al-Nafs al-Zakiyah)" whom he promoted as the long-awaited messianic figure (*mahdi*) destined to restore the Prophet's family to power and redeem the ummah. 'Abdallah found no support, however, from Ja'far al-Sadiq. To the contrary, when approached by his cousin, the latter confessed that he too had received such a letter, and felt obliged to point out to the Hasanid that he ('Abdallah) was in no position to gain the support of the Khurasan army or even neutralize it, a telling comment that pointed to the real impotence of the 'Alids. Without the backing of a loyal and highly professional fighting force, any confrontation with the new regime would be destined for failure. Ja'far's negative response was surely informed by the misfortune of his own uncle Zayd, who in defiance of an older and wiser brother and the family's quietist position, undertook a disastrous rebellion against the Umayyads in 740. The sagacious Husaynid could also cite a failed rebellion declared some fours years later in the name of a descendant of 'Ali ibn Abi Talib's elder brother, another Ja'far. In the latter case, the rebel, one 'Abdallah ibn Mu'awiyah, escaped the battlefield by fleeing to Khurasan, where he was put to death by Abu Muslim shortly after the start of the Abbasid revolution. Abu Muslim's patrons had no need of any 'Alid rivals at this critical juncture.

In an ironic twist of history, the Hasanids, descendants of 'Ali's son who capitulated to the usurpers, had become and would continue to be the promoters of active rebellion against unwanted authority, while the Husaynids, the offspring of the gallant and martyred son of 'Ali, generally opted for a quietist response, preferring to wait for the messianic moment that would return the ummah to its rightful leaders and the world to the righteousness and justice that accompanies such a turn. As divisions among the mainstream 'Alids crystallized over the years, a number of sharply defined factions would emerge, all under the same broad umbrella, and labeled collectively Shi'ites. Lest we forget, however, Shi'ite identities and alignments were considerably more fluid when 'Abdallah al-Mahd weighed backing his son to challenge the house of al-'Abbas.

Once apprised of what had transpired, the Abbasids forced Ibrahim and Muhammad, the sons of 'Abdallah al-Mahd, into hiding; they emerged, calling for a general revolt against entrenched Abbasid rule in 762 C.E. Developments gave the revolt of the brothers a certain sense of urgency. As did the Umayyads, the new ruling house had no need for prolonged and potentially divisive tribal elections. It soon became clear that leadership of the faithful would be kept in the house of 'Abbas and, to insure orderly successions, it would be limited to the progeny of its second caliph Abu Ja'far al-Mansur, who was in many respects the great architect of Abbasid rule. It was then evident that the 'Alid branch of the Prophet's house would be destined to forego that which it coveted and rightly claimed: leadership of the ummah. That the more militant 'Alids like the sons of 'Abdallah al-Mahd would be inclined to act in such circumstances, despite long odds, is not overly surprising. Looking at their revolt in retrospect, it seems clear that it was carried out largely by civilians and paramilitary forces against the standing professional army of the state, a confirmation, so to speak, of Ja'far al-Sadiq's earlier warning. Once the battle-tested Abbasid army returned from the east to engage al-Nafs al-Zakiyah in Iraq and, following that, set upon the rebels led by his brother Ibrahim in Arabia, the results were inevitable.

The 'Alid challenge had failed, but there was an emerging Shi'ite movement that as a matter of principle would never recognize the legitimacy of any leader of the ummah, other than one chosen from the progeny of 'Ali and Fatimah.

One of the most interesting tidbits found in medieval accounts of the aforementioned revolt is a series of deftly crafted letters exchanged between al-Mansur and the rebellious 'Alid leadership. There is every reason to believe the sentiments expressed in the letters genuinely reflect the circumstances of the moment even if the letters themselves might have been subject to later literary shaping. The communications indicate the caliph hoped to end the dispute amicably, which meant for him 'Alid recognition of his claims, based as they were on inheriting the authority first vested with Muhammad ibn al-Hanafiyah and his son Abu Hashim. In return, the 'Alid and his followers would receive a pledge of amnesty. The Abbasid claim of an inherited authority via Abu Hashim was open to all sorts of criticism from those who took time to examine it seriously. Who would believe the fantastic story of how Abu Hashim was poisoned, and even if one did, how could one be sure that the childless son of Muhammad ibn al-Hanafiyah actually transferred his authority and his revolutionary cadres to his Abbasid cousins? Were there any reliable witnesses to this alleged transfer, an event that had taken place a half-century before there was any mention of it? And even if the story was in fact true, at least as regards the transfer of 'Alid authority to the Abbasids, who is to say 'Ali's authority rested with Muhammad ibn al-Hanafiyah and then Abu Hashim? Who were the son and grandson of 'Ali by way of a Hanafite captive to be compared with the offspring of 'Ali and Fatimah, daughter of the Prophet?

In a tone that deliberately mocked the Abbasid caliph al-Mansur, the rebel pointed to the noble lineage of his ancestor al-Hasan ibn 'Ali on both maternal and paternal sides (a claim also made by Muslims on behalf of the Prophet). In contrast, he reminded al-Mansur that his mother had been low born. (The Abbasid was the offspring of a Persian slave; virtually all his successors were similarly the sons of concubines rather than noble Arab women). Was it not more likely, indeed correct, that the leadership of the ummah should reside with a direct descendant of the Prophet himself? Who other than a Fatimid who could make such a claim? As regards an amicable settlement that would result in amnesty for the rebel and his followers, the 'Alid was quick to remind al-Mansur of the treacherous manner he disposed of people after offering them guarantees of safety, among them the Abbasid's (faithful) servant Abu Muslim.

He also pointed out with no small degree of sarcasm that in essence the Abbasids (who remained unknown and in hiding) came to power on the backs of (deceived) 'Alid supporters.

Put on the defensive, the Abbasids boldly shifted their position. They presented a second claim to rule, one that not only promoted their legitimacy but undermined completely that of the rebel leadership. They reminded the 'Alids that the Prophet was without living male offspring to inherit the authority of his family. Muhammad had four daughters, all born to his beloved Khadijah, Fatimah among them. All were thus of noble birth and were acclaimed by all the Muslims, but that was largely irrelevant when it came to the transfer of family authority, for women, although entitled to inherit property were denied political power (*wilayah*). With no designated male successor, family rule went as a matter of course to the oldest surviving paternal uncle, a time-honored tribal custom. The 'Alids proudly proclaimed that when the Prophet was orphaned at an early age, their ancestor, his paternal uncle Abu Talib, took responsibility for him, and raised him as he did his own sons. Lest we be confused that any mention of paternal uncles spoke well for Abu Talib, and hence 'Ali and his offspring, al-Mansur was quick to remind his adversary (and hence all who read this letter) that the Prophet had four paternal uncles, two of whom had become Muslims. Readers were well aware of the history of these uncles. One, Hamzah, died a martyr's death for Islam on the field of battle; another, Abu Lahab, was an outspoken opponent during the early years in Mecca; and a third, Abu Talib, however much he looked after the Prophet, never became a Muslim in contrast to al-'Abbas who converted to the faith. Readers were also aware that as Abu Lahab, Hamzah, and Abu Talib all predeceased their illustrious nephew, at the time the Prophet lay on his deathbed the only remaining paternal uncle was al-'Abbas. The force of al-Mansur's argument was inescapable. With the death of the Prophet, the leadership of his family went by long established custom to the oldest surviving paternal uncle. It was then transferred in turn to al-'Abbas's male offspring until it came to rest with the current caliph, Abu Ja'far, who bore the regnal title al-Mansur "The Victorious." As regards the claim the low-profile Abbasids hijacked an 'Alid revolution (already rich in martyrs), al-Mansur was quick to point out the numerous failed attempts of the 'Alids to unseat the Umayyads (in contrast to the stunning success of the Banu 'Abbas).

Conventional wisdom among modern historians is that this second claim of the Abbasids became official political doctrine during the reign of al-Mansur's son and successor Muhammad al-Mahdi.

There is, however, no compelling reason for us to doubt that throughout al-Mansur's caliphate both claims, the inheritance via Abu Hashim and inheritance via al-'Abbas were promoted simultaneously by propagandists of the Abbasid house. In that way, the Abbasids, as always, could appear all things to all peoples, in this case all Shi'ites. Nevertheless, there were serious weaknesses in claiming that when the Prophet died his authority went to the oldest surviving uncle. No doubt, the most difficult hurdles to surmount were al-'Abbas's failure to become a Muslim prior to the capitulation of Mecca and the wholesale conversion of Quraysh, and, perhaps related to that, the nondescript role he was allowed to play in the affairs of the ummah after he finally converted to Islam. From all appearances, he had no part in evolving politics of a rapidly expanding Islamic polity; his most important role was largely honorific. The second caliph, 'Umar, gave al-'Abbas responsibility for maintaining the well of Zamzam in Mecca and for providing water at the time of pilgrimage (*siqayah*), a religious function that carried over from pre-Islamic times. To make this appointment sound more impressive than it was, al-Mansur, in his letter, claimed the 'Alids coveted these honors and brought their case before 'Umar, only to be denied.

Al-'Abbas's late conversion a full ten years after the Prophet became politically active could not be dismissed so easily. Hence, the career of the Prophet's only surviving paternal uncle had to be rewritten to make it consonant with 'Abbasid aims at a later point in the history of the ummah. The scholar Ibn Ishaq (d. 767 C.E.), suspected of shoddy scholarship at assembling oral testimonies, was brought to the Abbasid court for the express purpose of writing a full-length biography of the Prophet. As previously noted, the work is designed to authenticate the Prophet's claims by linking him to a monotheist history of old as well as to authenticate Abbasid claims by linking them and their regime to the Prophet and the early ummah and by reinventing al-'Abbas, so that he appeared as a strong promoter of the Prophet's interests at a time when the nephew and his followers were most vulnerable in Mecca.

This argument did not put an end to series of claims and counterclaims. By invoking the old tribal custom of succession within a family, the Abbasid apologists left the door ajar for rebuttal. True enough, when a man dies without male offspring, his authority goes as a rule to his oldest surviving paternal uncle, but that is only when he chooses not to name a successor from other blood relatives. A massive literary industry among the Shi'ites attempted to demonstrate that the Prophet had in fact handpicked his first cousin and adopted brother 'Ali son of Abu Talib to succeed him, a story that strained credulity at the other end of the political spectrum. To accept the 'Alid claim one would have to believe that so many of the early Muslims, including those companions of the Prophet situated in positions of prominence, acted in bad faith and with full knowledge of the Prophet's wishes when they denied 'Ali his rightful place at the head of he ummah. Moreover, they denied him not once but thrice. Not acknowledging 'Ali's right to succeed the Prophet would have amounted to a conspiracy of monumental proportions. The tradition that 'Ali had been chosen by the Prophet may be, however, quite early, perhaps as early as the reign of the Umayyads, if not the civil war that brought Mu'awiyah to power. At the latest, it stems from early in the reign of al-Mansur, as Ibn Ishaq addresses that 'Alid claim and demolishes it in a beautifully subtle account intended to leave his readers with the impression that not only was 'Ali not chosen by the Prophet but he feared that if the Prophet made any choice at all, it would not be he who was worthy of being chosen.

All these arguments gloss the irreconcilability of the 'Alids and Abbasids following the rebellion of 'Abdallah al-Mahd. Among the Shi'ites, two major camps emerged, each with a distinctive reaction to having been denied leadership of the ummah. One faction followed the course of Ja'far al-Sadiq, and his predecessors going back to al-Husayn's only son to survive the events at Karbala', the one known as Zayn al-'Abidin "Ornament of the Worshippers." The Husaynids, who stressed passivity until the coming of the messianic redeemer, came to be known as the Imamiyah or Imamis, as they believed 'Ali's authority had passed down through his son al-Husayn and his offspring, a series of specially designated leaders (imam), the last of whom would assume the messianic role of "redeemer" (mahdi) of the ummah. As political events did not favor the Shi'ites, imams came and went without the appearance of the mahdi. The theory of a Shi'ite imam emerging to set a new course for the ummah, remained, however, intact. All in all there were twelve imams, thus giving rise to the designation "Twelver Shi'ites (Ithna 'Ashariyah)." Following his father's death in 874, the last imam of the line, Muhammad ibn al-Hasan was said to have gone into a state of occultation (ghaybah) and thus came to be recognized by his Imami followers as the future redeemer. At first this Muhammad al-Mahdi was said to have communicated with his followers through four successive emissaries, presumably the only ones to know of his secret hiding place. This was declared a period of minor occultation as the imam still was in contact, however indirect, with the broad Imami community.

Then in 941 (non-Imamis might say the likely date of his death), it was said he entered into a period of major occultation and would remain safely hidden until he returned to carry out the mission that went with his title. In the meantime, the Imamis remained passive, waiting until such time when they would receive instructions from the redeemer of the ummah. They remained politically quiescent throughout the entire reign of the Abbasids and beyond because the twelfth imam continued to remain in occultation; like the Jewish and Christian messiahs the hidden twelfth imam has yet to reappear. The prolonged absence of the imam left the group with a bit of a problem, because, in theory, the authority that accrued to the imams was unique among the Muslims. As did the death of the Prophet for the earliest ummah, the hidden imam's extended state of final occultation forced the Imami community to rely on less authoritative leaders. Just as God would send no messengers after the Prophet; no rightful imams would appear to carry on in wake of Muhammad al-Mahdi. There would be no links to add to the extended chain of Shi'ite authority that began with 'Ali and lasted twelve generations.

Having been chosen directly by the Prophet, or so the Imamis claimed, 'Ali was divinely preordained to lead. And so it was with the later imams, as son followed father. Moreover, from the outset, the imams claimed a sense of infallibility, making them immune from error and thus unique guides for the faithful regarding religious matters. They could of course make no claims to prophecy; Islamic tradition was clear that Muhammad was the last of God's messengers, the last able to receive direct revelation. But the angels might speak to the imams without revealing themselves as Gabriel did to Muhammad. In such fashion, the imams were sort of prophets manqué. They were therefore proper substitutes for God's final messenger. In that important respect, they were far different from the caliphs who were mere temporal rulers of the ummah. As a result, the words and actions of the imams could become a source for Islamic law as were the Qur'an and the sunnah, the precedent of the Prophet. Over time, the Imamis produced a corpus of their own religious scholarship, a voluminous body of work unfortunately neglected by most Western scholars of today. At the heart of this intellectual enterprise, which included legal tracts and Qur'an commentary and exegesis, was a work called the *Nahj al-balaghah*. Current printed editions comprise dozens of thick volumes recording various sayings of 'Ali and numerous incidents of his life and times. The historicity of the material, like that of the pro-Abbasid apologists, is dubious, perhaps even more so, but those who peruse the work are treated to a cornucopia of material with which to reconstruct, however tentatively, the evolution of Shi'ite attitudes and the manner in which they reshaped the past in order to conduct themselves in the present and anticipate the future.

Privileging the unique religious authority of the imams meant those who disagreed with them on doctrinal and political matters were in error. That company of misguided individuals came to include a virtual "who's who" of Muslims: those who prevented 'Ali from taking his rightful place after the death of the Prophet, Abu Bakr who handpicked his own successor when leadership of the ummah should have gone instead to 'Ali, and those who denied him once again after a shura or narrow electoral body was convened to choose a successor to 'Umar; to be sure the hated Umayyads stand out; and those responsible for the cruelest cut of all, their cousins within the Hashimite house, close relatives who cheated them out of the reward that was rightfully theirs. We are not speaking here of hair splitting legal niceties or minor distinctions in scriptural interpretation. Imami doctrine totally rejected the religious authority of Sunnite Islam. One might go so far as to say they considered the Sunnites unbelievers, but such a charge, publicly declared, would have called for the intervention of the Sunnite polity and, in the end, compromised the safe space carved out by the cautious Husaynid imams.

In a gesture to the entire ummah, Imamis maintained those who acknowledged the one and only God and the legitimacy of his Prophet Muhammad were in fact Muslims in good standing, the Sunnites among them. However, the true believers were those devoted to the teachings of their divinely chosen imams. At first glance even that may strike us as being inflammatory. But the imams had always cautioned their followers about foolish acts of bravado and advised instead that they practice dissimulation (taqiyah) when it came to their beliefs and actions. Thus, the authorities had no compelling reason to intervene and with the exception of the seventh imam Musa al-Kazim, who was erroneously linked to an insurrection against their rule, they generally left the 'Alids of al-Husayn's line to their own devices. Moreover, as the last of the imams was in an extended state of deep occultation, and as no substantive political upheaval could be begin without him, the Imamis, now in their twelfth generation, had no direction to act against the regime and because of that could hardly be seen as an immediate threat to established order. The Husaynids who followed the course of Ja'far al-Sadiq had, for the most part, found that safe space they always sought, a situation the Sunnite regime could easily tolerate, however repugnant they found Shi'ite views known to them.

There were, nevertheless, Shi'ite groups that threatened the stability of the Abbasid state. We have already made mention of the radical proto-Shi'ite sects that emerged in Umayyad times and continued to mutate in some form or other after the Abbasid ascension. However, these sectarians were, at best, restricted to the margins of the ummah and could be dealt with minimal effort as they lacked broad appeal among the widely dispersed Muslim faithful. The descendants of 'Ali's son al-Hasan were another matter altogether. Unlike their Fatimid cousins who generally assumed a low profile since the martyrdom of al-Husayn, the Hasanids sought to boldly challenge the ruling regime, invariably without success. Beginning with their failed rebellion against al-Mansur, they awaited the opportunity to settle accounts with their unworthy Hashimite cousins. Truth be told, the Hasanids were themselves latecomers at rejecting unwanted authority by force of arms. Their record of open opposition against the Umayyads was hardly distinguished, surely no more distinguished than that of the Abbasids. The main concern of the family during the Umayyad interregnum seems to have been a dispute with their Husaynid cousins over the right to control the 'Alid family endowments, an extended and acrimonious affair that deserves greater consideration than it has received. In any case, Shi'ite revolts against the new regime were few and far between until the latter part of the ninth century C.E., and especially the century to follow when a breakaway branch of the Husaynid line served to inspire a widespread revolt that extended from North Africa to parts of al-Sham and even Iraq. In the next chapter, we will see how this revolutionary movement resulted in a Fatimid counter-caliphate of political resilience, economic strength, and cultural vibrancy.

The seeds of that later Shi'ite "revolution" were planted in the early years of Abbasid rule; at issue was the succession of Ja'far al-Sadiq within the Imami community. Most of the community recognized his son Musa al-Kazim as the seventh imam, and with that the expected continuation of a passive response to unwanted authority championed by Ja'far. But others opted for another son, Isma'il, and thus became known as the Isma'ilis. The Isma'ilis contended that, contrary to conventional wisdom, this Isma'il did not die before his father (that would have made succession impossible); rather Ja'far had chosen him imam and announced his death as a ruse designed to protect him from potential enemies. As would the twelfth imam, Isma'il entered into a state of what turned out to be extended occultation and would, so it was said, emerge someday as the Mahdi. A second group maintained that Isma'il had indeed predeceased his father but Ja'far then designated the former's son Muhammad to be the rightful imam. One ought to be extremely skeptical of these accounts; as both alleged factions of Isma'il's line seem to disappear from history until the middle of the ninth century when a unified Isma'ili movement makes it appearance and sets into motion events that would shake the foundations of the Sunni Abbasid regime in the following generation. That challenge will be discussed in a later chapter along with other 'Alid splinter groups that made their appearance from time to time and in different regions of the Islamic realm. The complex views and methods of the Isma'ilis are our immediate concern here, especially when compared with those of an ongoing Abbasid propaganda.

Abbasid apologists were extraordinarily sophisticated in promoting the cause of their patrons. They employed a wide variety of rhetorical strategies, all of which were designed to trap audiences into considering the Abbasid line regardless of the views they brought to the texts they read, the oral presentations they heard, and the political theater they observed. The promotion of Abbasid propaganda became an elaborate game that capitalized on the inventiveness of the regime's apologists while at the same time exploiting the audience's curiosity. In effect, the propagandists challenged their targeted audience to piece together the thrust of the Abbasid argument from scattered references to persons, events, and declarations deftly strewn within the propaganda tracts and performances. It was as though they were being asked to assemble the disparate parts of an intricate puzzle. The apologists assumed that having done that, the audience would be reluctant to give up the triumph of having fit together all the pieces, and with that, they would be more inclined to accept, or at the least consider, the pro-regime message. As the less-sophisticated targets of Abbasid propaganda required a simpler form of communication—an easier puzzle, so to speak—the dynastic apologists used different messages and techniques of presentation simultaneously. Offered in multiple versions, the Abbasid message could be easily absorbed by all manner of Muslims. In each and every instance, the ultimate point was abundantly clear. The Abbasid case was carefully defined according to claims to rule based on a transfer of authority from one discernible figure to another. Despite occasional challengers from within the ruling family, the line of succession was clearly drawn. There was no secret about who would claim leadership of the ummah; the days of a mysterious unnamed "chosen one" ended with the emergence of the dynasty. There was nothing hidden about the Abbasid leadership.

The Isma'ilis utilized similar rhetorical strategies in spreading their propaganda. Their revolutionary movement was also modeled on the clandestine apparatus utilized by the Abbasids as they prepared to take power, and the manner in which they disseminated their views in secret borrowed as well from the Abbasid revolutionaries of old. Even the vocabulary and slogans invoked by the 'Alids had a familiar ring. We are not surprised that the Fatimid insurgency and the Abbasid revolution share much in common as mirror images of one another. Both movements were designed to reflect a still-earlier history, that of the Prophet Muhammad and his mission to spread Islam in Arabia. There could be no valid claim to leading the contemporaneous ummah without links to the Prophet's life and times. But in articulating their case, the Isma'ilis, unlike the Abbasids, tended to wax philosophical—and beyond that, mystical. Their philosophical positions were highly technical and not easily understood by their average follower. The Isma'ilis drew a distinction between the exoteric or outward manifestation of religion and its inner or esoteric manifestations—in Arabic between what is *zahir* and what is *batin*. To truly understand the eternal immutable truth of Islam that was contained in esoteric doctrine, one had to be skilled in its interpretation (*ta'wil*). Having pierced the mysteries of inner religion, Isma'ili apologists were able to construct a framework for broadly conceptualizing all of (monotheist) religious history, although only learned initiates were likely to grasp the true complexity of Isma'ili thought.

As articulated by Isma'ili scholars, history has undergone successive phases, each of which witnessed the emergence of major prophetic figure. Beginning with the biblical Adam, there were Noah, Abraham, Moses, Jesus, and then the last of God's messengers, Muhammad. Many followers of these prophets might have grasped the outward meaning of the message but only special interpreters were privy to the inner meaning of their words and only the imams could carry on fully the roles previously assigned by God to his prophets. Over the years, the methods of interpretation employed by the Isma'ilis grew more and more complex as their scholars embraced the neoplatonist philosophy of the Hellenistic world. One had to be well grounded in neoplatonism to grasp the full weight of Isma'ili doctrine. The embrace of Hellenistic thought (the technical details do not concern us) led to notions quite unfamiliar to Muslims of the original ummah. Accordingly, Muhammad, 'Ali, and the imams are all said to have been conceived through a light created by God before the creation of the material world; the very same light created out of a single word uttered by the Almighty was then used to shape all of creation. Not only were Muhammad, 'Ali, and the imams created of this light, but then God spoke another word which became a spirit that combined with the sacred light and then settled within the bodies of the future Shi'ite imams thus giving them unique knowledge and license to interpret God's wishes above and beyond what is revealed in the Qur'an and demonstrated through the living actions of the Prophet. These and similar ideas were heavy stuff indeed for the average Muslim. The vast majority of Shi'ites who accepted the line of Isma'il and laid the groundwork for the revolts of the ninth century and the establishment of a widespread Fatimid dynasty the following century had little if any understanding of the intellectual foundations of what would become complex Isma'ili doctrine. Nor did it really matter to the success of the 'Alids in challenging the Sunnite world. There were, as we shall see, other factors that stimulated broad interest in the Shi'ites, pragmatic concerns that made their political agenda attractive to certain elements of the ummah.

The Sunnites were well aware of the "exaggerated" ideas (*ghulu*) embraced by Shi'ites, particularly by the more radical sects; such ideas allowed the authorities to declare these partisans of 'Ali tainted Muslims. In many quarters, particularly in Saudi Arabia, Shi'ites are regarded even today as nonbelievers (*kafir*, pl. kafirun). And so, as the Sunnites considered the Shi'ite world from time to time, they not only saw the more radical groups as a potential threat to existing political order; there was something alien about how they championed the cause of 'Ali's family, a sense of strangeness that demanded further suspicion of their Hashimite cousins and their partisans. How did occultation and the expected return of a hidden imam, or death as an ophthalmic illusion, or the transmigration of souls, or the call for bizarre social behavior that conflicted with accepted norms of society, or transcendent lights entering corporeal bodies, or, above all, declaring that 'Ali ibn Abi Talib and other 'Alids had been divinely ordained, albeit without the gift of prophecy, become part and parcel of an Islam whose religious ideals and practices were so crystal clear in the age of the Prophet?

Surely such alien concepts and behavior had to be imported from an individual and world foreign to the early Muslims and their immediate environment in west Arabia. Sunnites identified the culprit as 'Abdallah ibn Saba', reportedly a Jewish convert to Islam who hailed from Yemen and had a strong influence on 'Ali. Following 'Ali's death, 'Abdallah and his followers the Saba'iyah propagated the strange ideas and practices that seeped into the world of the Shi'ite Islam. The alleged Jewish roots of Shi'ism (though not proven by modern research) were more than enough to tarnish the more exuberant followers of 'Ali and his progeny. When in the ninth century one Hamdan Qaramat initiated a widespread and lengthy Isma'ili revolt against the Abbasids, the chroniclers reporting the events of the times would occasionally refer to the rebels as al-Yahud, the generic and pejorative label to designate Jews. The Abbasid apologists did not wish to imply that the Qarmatians were in fact Jews but the alleged links between bizarre if not heretical Shi'ite doctrine and a Jewish convert who strongly influenced 'Ali and his followers was sufficiently damning. The linking of Shi'ites to Jews continues in certain Sunnite circles even today.

Whatever course the two major Shi'ite camps followed—that held true as well for various groups that splintered off from mainstream Shi'ism—they were incapable of mounting a threat that would bring down the Abbasid dynasty once and for all. Even when reduced to ruling a truncated empire and with less real authority than before, the house of Abbas continued to enjoy the de facto recognition of most Muslims. One may presuppose the lingering support for the very existence of the Abbasid polity derived at least in part from the foundations of the regime established by its most able founders, those who transformed a revolutionary movement into a polity of true imperial dimensions. The salient features of that story are revealed in the pages that follow.

Centralizing Power: The Rise of a Universal Islamic Empire

More surprising than the Abbasids' ability to co-opt the revolution that brought down the house of Umayyah and beat back the challenge of their more illustrious 'Alid cousins was the manner in which the second Abbasid caliph, Abu Ja'far al-Mansur, established the foundations of a dynastic order whose rule was formally recognized from Central Asia in the east to the most distant reaches of North Africa in the west. One could easily make the case that al-Mansur was the architect who shaped Abbasid rule and with that laid the foundations of a more universal and cosmopolitan Islamic community than ever existed before. Indeed, one might wish to argue that the caliph and his progeny were instrumental in laying the groundwork for so much of what we now recognize as medieval Islamic civilization. How is it then that the rather nondescript older brother of al-Saffah, a figure who played no significant role before or immediately after the outbreak of the general revolt against the Umayyads, took command of the family and established the foundations of a dynastic order that would keep the Abbasid house on a more or less even keel despite internal and external stresses and strains?

With the formal recognition of al-Saffah's caliphate, the politics of the Abbasid family was exposed to public view for the first time. Numerous relatives, all more or less the same age, took command of the ummah, a task for which they had prepared for several decades. Among the inner circle of the Abbasids were several of the new caliph's paternal uncles ('umumah), his nephew 'Isa ibn Musa, and his elder brother Abu Ja'far. Once in the open, the caliph's kin were dispatched to take control of the functioning government bureaucracy as well as various Khurasani regiments that had entered Iraq. In these rapidly changing times, the caliph's brother Abu Ja'far seems to have played the least consequential role of all the former conspirators. Of all the family members, he alone was dispatched to make an appearance in the failed rebellion of the 'Alid 'Abdallah ibn Mu'awiyah, a likely indication that he was considered dispensable to the Abbasid revolt in the making. In any case, Abu Ja'far's appearance in the 'Alid disaster was at best perfunctory, a harbinger of the truncated role he later played at the outset of Abbasid rule. Unlike his uncle 'Abdallah ibn 'Ali or his nephew 'Isa ibn Musa, the future caliph al-Mansur had no significant part in the subsequent military campaigns against the Umayyads, nor was he awarded, as were his other uncles, responsibility for governing a particular region. His most significant assignment was that of negotiating agreements for his brother, at times in bad faith, however much this duplicity served the new dynasty's interests.

The death of al-Saffah revealed the family that had meticulously planned their rise to power and that for so long exercised a sense of discipline was capable of being wracked by inner dissension. The expected successor of al-Saffah was his uncle 'Abdallah ibn 'Ali, the appointed governor of Syria, who commanded not only the Khurasani troops that had initiated the revolt but also the Arab tribal regiments that had defected from the Umayyads. One could also have expected 'Abdallah to be supported by his brothers, four of whom were also very prominent; perhaps even his great-nephew 'Isa ibn Musa, who like him was a successful field commander. Indeed, 'Abdallah claimed the right to succeed al-Saffah had been guaranteed him from the outset of Abbasid rule, if not earlier. One recalls that as their revolution began to unfold, the leader of the family, Ibrahim al-Imam, died suddenly. Faced with this unexpected crisis, the family circle drew up the line of succession. The group responsible for this decision included Abu al-'Abbas, four paternal uncles including 'Abdallah, and 'Isa ibn Musa, but not Abu Ja'far, an indication that although he was Abu al-'Abbas's elder brother, he received no consideration to succeed Ibrahim. No wonder then that the eleventh hour decision by al-Saffah to choose his brother to be the next commander of the faithful was greeted with defiance.

Abu Ja'far may have had a nondescript career until that point, but he proved to be a quintessential manipulator of men and situations. He had a particular talent for ferreting out conspiracies and for conspiring

against others himself. With many of the old revolutionaries disposed of
largely through the efforts of Abu Muslim, the Khurasan army looked to
its paymaster for guidance. The new caliph, aware of Abu Mulim's importance, used him to drive a wedge between the Khurasani forces under his
uncle's command and the old Umayyad contingents that formed the rest
of 'Abdallah's army. With his forces divided and some brothers and his
great-nephew 'Isa unwilling to support him in an expanded civil war,
'Abdallah was unable to marshal sufficient strength to carry the day. Upon
his defeat, he was placed under house arrest and lived out the rest of his life
confined but at peace. Even as he was restricted to his riverside domicile in a
fashionable area of Baghdad, his advice was sought, at least one occasion, by
al-Mansur. The caliph showed great wisdom in trying to keep the family
united behind him. The other paternal uncles were given provincial
governorships, but none that would have given them a base from which
to challenge their nephew or his successors.

In the line of succession drawn up by al-Saffah, 'Isa ibn Musa was
made Abu Ja'far's heir apparent and thus had no quarrel with the new
caliph, at least not at that moment. Later, he would be replaced in favor
of the caliph's own son Muhammad (al-Mahdi) and then removed
altogether from the line of succession. From that moment on, only the
offspring of the Mansurid branch of the family were considered worthy
of being caliphs of the realm. The pattern of dynastic succession established by the Umayyads had been taken a step further. Over time, relatives from other branches of the house were marginalized. They were
given great honors but increasingly the day-to-day workings of the
government were carried out by a professional class of bureaucrats linked
directly to their sovereign and patron, the commander of the faithful.

Abu Muslim, although he supported the caliph against his uncle and
was no doubt a client of the ruling house, proved in the end too independent to be reliable, and certainly too close to the army. With relations
strained between himself and the caliph, Abu Muslim was reportedly
lured to a social function with a guarantee of safety, and while he traveled
with a sizeable entourage of armed retainers in case of unexpected developments, he suddenly found himself separated from his guard, at which
point al-Mansur had him killed. With that, al-Mansur's path to rule was
well on its way to being secured. The army, the very backbone of the
regime, could have been a problem as the caliph, unlike Abu Muslim,
never had an ongoing connection with the military. Recognizing the
situation, al-Mansur secured the loyalty of the army through a variety of
pragmatic measures including generous bonuses paid to the field

commanders. Simply buying off the army was, however, a prescription for disaster waiting to happen at a later moment. As we shall note later, the Abbasids, and particularly al-Mansur, had a clear vision of how the military had to be transformed into a professional fighting force that suffered from none of the independence and divisiveness that characterized the Arab tribal armies of the past. The transformation of the army is a story of mixed success that will be told shortly; our present concern is with the formation of the government bureaucracy, particularly the introduction of large numbers of non-Arab clients as functionaries of the regime. From the outset, the Abbasids set about transforming the Arab kingdom of the Umayyads into a more universal Islamic empire.

Governing the New Ummah: The Universal Character of the Abbasid Ruling Institution

The development of early Abbasid governance reflects not only the interplay of complex forces within the ruling family and army, but also relations between the new rulers and a burgeoning bureaucracy staffed by large numbers of individuals designated as *mawali* "clients"; these were individuals, most often non-Arabs linked to the caliph by personal ties of fealty. Our sources reveal that al-Mansur was the first of the dynasty to institutionalize on a grand scale the use of mawali in the provincial administration and other critical areas, a practice then continued by successive caliphs of his line. Concurrent with this development was an intended and perceptible decline in the number and status of pure-bred and freeborn Arabs serving the regime. The general use of trusted clients to perform delicate missions was, needless to say, well known among past Arab tribal sheikhs and rulers. What is striking is the way the in which Abbasid clientage is linked to the decline of Arab leadership and privilege. We would assume the caliph recognized the preeminence of freeborn noble Arabs within the highest circles of Umayyad government as reflections of that regime's structural weakness and preferred instead non-Arab agents tied exclusively to his house.

Rather than rely on persons with well-established affiliations to tribal and other political units of importance, the kind of extensive political circles that could command their allegiance and give them strength to subvert their ruler's intentions, the Abbasids seemed to have followed a course set out by the Prophet Muhammad, whose greatest supporters, other than the original Muslims who emigrated from Mecca to Medina, were disenfranchised Arabs whose sole political affiliation of importance was their personal relationship to the Prophet himself. The ummah had become the equivalent of their tribe with religion really replacing blood ties; with that, the theoretical foundations of a universal ummah had become a reality.

Proximity of the mawali to the levers of power was not lost on various members of the Abbasid family; especially those relatives who were not part of the Mansurid circle. 'Abd al-Samad ibn 'Ali, the only one of al-Mansur's paternal uncles to throw in with the rebellious 'Abdallah, was nevertheless granted a pardon as well as the opportunity to serve several caliphs of the line in a number of honorific but not politically significant positions. He was anything but pleased at the influence of the clients serving the Mansurids and reportedly complained to al-Mansur's successor, al-Mahdi, that the ruling house was filled with excessive love for its clients, and this intimacy with them might cause the Khurasan army and their commanders to waver in their allegiance to the regime. The caliph replied that his clients deserved to be treated with trust (a subtle riposte referring to his great-uncle's role in contesting al-Mansur's caliphate). He went on to say that he could rub knees with a *mawla* one moment and then have him groom his animal the next (a rather degrading act) Clients were satisfied with this kind of relationship, unlike certain members of the ruling family and the army who would consider themselves beyond such menial tasks and would instead draw attention to the prestige of their fathers' or their own past service to the Abbasid cause.

That this paternal uncle should have been the center of such a complaint against the extensive use of clients is only too fitting. The long-lived 'Abd al-Samad eventually witnessed the political machinations of no less than five caliphs, all of whom compromised the 'umumah and their noble offspring, favoring instead their own progeny with the support of their loyal clients, many of whom were former slaves, converts, and/or non-Arabs in origins. One always has to suspect that accounts of this sort can be marked by considerable literary shaping—such is the nature of medieval Arabic historiography. But such accounts can also be revealing, as woven into the legendary fabric of the stories are often the strands of historic circumstances. Even if one were to weave a tradition out of wholly new cloth, it is doubtful one could improve on this account which conceptualizes with great insight, one of the central problems of early Abbasid society: the complex relationship between the various elements of the ruling house and its instruments of rule.

Why would the caliphs often prefer the pleasure and service of their clients to some of their own blood kin? Above all, why did they feel free to entrust their mawali with matters of the most delicate nature? One might understand why the caliphs held 'Abd al-Samad at arm's length; he had been rebellious at the outset of Mansurid rule and was mildly disrespectful to them thereafter, but what of all the other relatives? Did not ties of blood outweigh ties of clientage? Had Arab tribal sensibilities sunk so low within a few decades? It is instructive that the mawali are described by al-Mahdi as not above grooming the caliph's animal. The metaphor, whether intentional or not, is well taken; the Arabic word for grooming and training animals became in time identical with that of training political constituencies to be obedient, namely *siyasah*, "the art of politics." The caliph's remark thus illustrates the clients represented a class of public and personal servants brought into government and courtly circles because the complex machinery of state in the post-revolutionary period required functionaries of unquestioned loyalty, individuals and small family groups who tied their future to the caliph by personal bonds. Some circles within the ruling family might well harbor ambitions of their own, and if given the opportunity to set their hands on the real levers of power could challenge the decisions of the caliphs if not even their right to rule. There is little if any evidence that the Mansurids faced any such family challenges after the abortive revolt of al-Mansur's uncle, but, given al-Mansur's conspiratorial outlook, an outlook honed on his own duplicitous activities, it makes sense that he began to rely so heavily on a class of servants who owed him their exclusive loyalty. How did all that work and what if any was the legal basis for the institution of clientage?

The Arabic legal sources of the Middle Ages contain extended discussions of clientage. However, formal definitions derived from the legal literature alone are not likely to be very informative in helping us describe, let alone define, Abbasid governance. The enormity of the Abbasid ruling institution suggests that the rules that governed behavior within the house of Abbas had a dynamic of their own—a code of political conduct that could circumvent the ordinary limits imposed by law and social convention. The manner in which clientage actually functioned with the ruling family was likely to be very different from descriptions of clientage in the law books, which, in any case, were set in writing after the events in question. How then does one speak authoritatively about the function of clientage and the role of clients within the government of the ummah? There is, to be sure, the testimony of the Arabic chroniclers and belletrists who surveyed the condition of the times. But medieval Arabic historiography generally did not attempt to define social institutions or even preserve the material necessary for modern scholars to reconstruct these institutions in detail. Instead, writers preferred to view the course of human events in narratives almost exclusively weighted by biographical considerations. Even then, their focus was highly selective; historians of the times tended to limit themselves to the grandees of Islamic society omitting thereby hundreds of individuals of lesser rank whose careers appear at first glance significant and thus of considerable interest to modern scholars. Some of the most important people among the mawali remain shadowy figures woven into threadbare historical accounts.

What is clear is that the institution of clientage, as expressed by the Arabic root *w-l-y*, is pre-Islamic in some of its forms and was likely to have been exceedingly complicated in the Islamic Middle Ages. Given the types of association described by the medieval lawyers, the mawali of whom the caliph's great-uncle spoke could have been tied to the ruling house by a complex series of relationships rather than a single all-embracing formula. That is, the law, as it was elucidated, allowed for patron-client relations that covered kinsmen of sorts, freemen entering into voluntary agreement with a powerful patron, and men long freed as well as recently freed slaves owing allegiance to their former master. Who were these clients of the caliphs and how was their status defined?

A survey of the historical sources strongly suggests that those clients who served in the upper echelons of the government and in courtly circles during the early Abbasid caliphate were recruited largely from freedmen rather than the freeborn. Looked at from a different perspective, they were not typical freeborn Arab tribesmen who signed agreements with more powerful or equally powerful parties for purposes of mutual support, usually a form of military alliance. The clients of the Abbasid house were usually converts, or the offspring of non-Arab converts, and/or slaves manumitted by the dynasts themselves. The freedman generally enjoyed the same legal rights as the freeborn, but unlike the latter whose clientage was both flexible and terminable, he and his male descendants were attached by clientage to the family of his master-manumitter in perpetuity. He is described as a passive member of the kin to whom he is attached, and is considered by most legal scholars as markedly inferior with regard to social standing.

When the most powerful of all the caliph Harun al-Rashid's clients, a man who had been suckled by the same wet nurse as the caliph, a figure who had been raised almost as the caliph's brother and had been allowed a marriage of convenience with the caliph's favorite sister so that al-Rashid could enjoy their company simultaneously without setting tongues wagging, when so prominent a figure went too far as faux husband and actually impregnated the royal princess, not once but several times, all that proximity to the caliph came to naught. According to the chroniclers the caliph came down savagely against Ja'far and the rest of his relatives, all of whom had been and were then trusted servants of the Abbasid house. The actual details of this alleged sequence of events will probably never be known, at least not to the satisfaction of Western scholars. It is clear, however, that medieval Muslims understood the point of the story. Certainly, no client attached to the ruling family ever got that close to the caliph or commanded as much power as did the Barmakid, but there were discernible limits to Ja'far's influence. Even the most important of the mawali had to be satisfied with the power that accrued to them as confidants of the commanders of the faithful and careful not to overstep the bounds that separated them from their patron/master-manumitter and the latter's blood relatives. In sum, the mawla has to be understood as a figure entirely dependent on a patron whose position in the relationship was clearly preeminent.

Needless to say, the sense of dependency generated by this form of clientage could be very useful to the house of Abbas, particularly in the aftermath of the Umayyad collapse. The Umayyads also made use of clients; certainly of individuals inherited from a pre-Islamic past. For decades their administration was staffed with large numbers of Byzantine and Sasanian functionaries. It took the better part of half a century before Arabic became the language of the government bureaucracy. One can only assume the vast majority of the civil servants inherited from the defeated regimes continued in place even if they did not convert to the new faith. No doubt, many found their fortunes tied to Umayyad patrons. The collapse of Umayyad rule could therefore have given rise to variations of hitherto accepted forms of client-patron relations. One can well imagine public servants and manumitted slaves, whose once ironclad ties to their administrators and/or master-manumitters were shattered by the change of dynasty, now entered into the service of the Abbasid house as de facto freemen, unlike the manumitted slaves of their Abbasid patrons. Be that as it may, any distinction between freemen voluntarily seeking Abbasid patrons and slaves manumitted by the latter is likely to have been more apparent than real. The mawali long removed from slavery as well as the slaves set free by the Abbasids were equally dependent on their patron. Regardless of his personal status as defined by the law generally recognized, the freeman who entered into the service of the Abbasids as a client would have found his ties to his patron neither flexible nor terminable, as was true of free Arabs in times gone by. Confronted by reality, he could no more leave the caliph on his own volition than a soldier of the mafia voluntarily abandons his mafioso family by invoking his constitutional rights.

What remains to be researched and written about in detail are the subtle relationships that must have existed among and within the different client families. Such a study would require teasing an enormous amount of hard information from the widest variety of literary sources; the equivalent of searching for needles in haystacks. Whether such a project is in fact doable remains to be seen, but it is surely worth considering. Be that as it may, we can still draw some broad conclusions about clientage and state and society under the early Abbasids. Legal definitions notwithstanding, the term "client" could be applied to servants of the caliph's household, individual generals of the freeborn army, the royal executioner, and powerful viziers and secretaries, who in addition to running the daily affairs of the Abbasid state, tutored the young princes of the house in the conduct of governance. Some important clients later became confidential advisors to the young and highborn once the latter assumed significant roles within the state apparatus including the caliphate.

All the aforementioned positions were open to highly placed clients because they had no recognizable constituencies of their own. Whatever powers accrued to a mawla and/or his family were not derived from nor were they transferable to his social class as a whole. The clients did not form a powerful guild; they were not equivalent to a tribe and did not constitute a social unit tied by blood but rather by commitment to public service. The system was well suited to the conspiratorial outlook of the Abbasid rulers for the individual client or even the client's family could be more easily isolated from the fulcrum of power than a member of the ruling house or some other recognizable political structure with transferable assets. At best, the loyal and talented mawla could pave the way for other talented and loyal members of his family to establish highly advantageous sinecures within the corridors of power. The forces that guarded the caliph and his household (*haras*) and his security police (*shurtah*) were entrusted to several generations of families whose service went back to the Abbasid revolution. These mini-constituencies were, however, always susceptible to unexpected developments within the ruling house. The client realistically assessing his circumstances understood only too well the limits of his political power and promoted his career with that in mind. The well-advised and prudent mawla always aligned his ambitions with the particular needs of his patron. With the extensive use of clients, the Abbasid regime, though ruled by noble Arabs drawn from the house of the Prophet, created a more universal ruling institution that favored modest men of talent to fatuous or dangerously ambitious aristocrats of high birth. Social mobility for the mawla did not extend, however, to acquiring even indirect control of the ummah. The clients of the house were always subjected to the whims of their patrons; their room for maneuver in the best of cases was always limited.

From Tribes to Professional Armies: The Changing Shape of the Military

As did the government bureaucracy, the professional army of the Abbasid state came to include various ethnic groups from diverse regional backgrounds and social strata. The first fifty years or so of Abbasid rule saw the evolution of a professional fighting force based largely on the revolutionary army from Khurasan. Contrary to earlier assumptions of a grassroots uprising among the indigenous Iranians—a point of view that has been revived as of late, largely by native Iranians imbued with nationalist fervor—the backbone of the Abbasid military was an Arab army that had been sent to the region not long before the outbreak of the revolution. These Arab units identified themselves according to their blood lines, a sensibility that gave rise to the damaging effects of tribal xenophobia. As a result, the Umayyad governor of the province was seemingly unable to unite them for common purpose, thus making them a worthy target for Abbasid propagandists operating in the vast regions of Khurasan.

Another component of the early Abbasid army was the descendants of the old Arab warriors who left Iraq in different waves to campaign and then settle in the eastern provinces. Transplanted into the villages of Khurasan's many regions, they too retained their tribal identification, but intermarriage and assimilation to Iranian ways eroded their tribal sensibilities even before the outbreak of the revolution. They even seem to have lost the capacity to speak pure Arabic, resorting instead to a hybrid language much corrupted by Persian called "the language of Khurasan." When the formal structure of the army was first established during the revolution, the settlers received their service pay according to a military roll in which they were inscribed according to village rather than tribe, in part an indication that allegiance to blood kin was subsumed within a sense of local and regional loyalty. In all likelihood, they retained some martial skills but could not to be relied upon as soldiers of the first rank, for unlike the Arab tribal army in Khurasan, they had for some time ceased to function as cohesive military units who maintained their fighting trim in the field. Nevertheless, the old settlers produced a disproportionately high number of commanders and political agents. No doubt, that was because these individuals committed themselves to the Abbasid cause during the clandestine phase of the revolt and could be relied upon to carry out the wishes of the family. The final element of the army that came to be known as the "people of Khurasan (*ahl Khurasan*)" was the local mawali. Their contributions to the military campaigns were negligible, although some assumed positions of importance within the political apparatus and the financial administration of the nascent Abbasid fighting force.

As the Abbasid army evolved, it took a rather different course from the Islamic armies of the past, be they regular fighting forces, tribal auxiliaries, irregular volunteers, local militia, or a combination of all the above. Despite its varied Arab tribal components, the Abbasid army rapidly developed a distinctive Khurasanian identity that competed with other forms of affiliation thereby paving the way to establish a truly professional military, the kind of army that might be compared with the Syrian contingents commanded by Mu'awiyah ibn Abi Sufyan when he was governor of that province and later when he became caliph. Readers will recall the Syrian army, though tribal in origins, had long been accustomed to taking commands from a centralized authority. A blueprint for the formation of an army totally responsive to the Abbasid commander of the faithful is articulated in a remarkable treatise addressed to the caliph al-Mansur. The author, Ibn al-Muqaffa', was a well-known litterateur and public servant of the time. A late convert to Islam, Ibn al-Muqaffa' attached himself to the Umayyad ruling establishment in Iran and then with the change of regime prudently shifted his allegiance, becoming a client of the house of Abbas, first of the caliph's parental uncles and then of al-Mansur himself. Unfortunately for Ibn al-Muqaffa', his earlier association with the paternal uncles together with a delicate assignment for the caliph which went awry left him open to intrigue at court. As a mere client without support, he fell from grace and was put to death, but not before giving al-Mansur some unsolicited advice on how to rule.

Included among his many recommendations was a plan for winning the hearts and minds of the Khurasan army, half of which remained in Iraq, the province from which they were originally dispatched to the east. The author regards the qualities of the Khurasanis as unmatched by any Islamic fighting force. According to him, their devotion to the caliph defies imagination (or, better put, gives rise to flights of fancy). Indeed, there are officers among them who actually believe that if the caliph ordered mountains to move, they would move; and if he ordered them to turn their backs to the Ka'bah during prayer, they would do so. Perhaps, the author means to suggest this seeming license against natural order and religious law appealed to these Khurasani officers because they were imbued with the messianic fervor of the times and the radical views that it fostered (see the previous chapter). An army capable of such bizarre thinking is, however, a mixed blessing and therefore requires strict control, lest the caliph appear, as Ibn al-Muqaffa' put it, "like the rider of a lion who terrifies all who see him, but is himself the most terrified of all." A proper religious education is prescribed for all men in the ranks who are capable of assuming leadership roles, the presumption being they will then follow the caliph as orthodox Muslims and not extremists given to familiar radical views.

Although written in the general style of a universal literature that offers broad advice to princes, this work lists concrete proposals to lay the solid foundations of Abbasid rule based on the uncompromising loyalty of the army. The basic thesis is that all the institutions of government whether temporal or religious should be subordinated to the direct control of the caliph. Implicit in this notion is the marriage of religion to political authority. Whether intended or not, this represents a plea to return to the pristine ummah of the Prophet when all institutions of rule were directly linked to Muhammad's authority and Muhammad's authority came directly from God. Although the caliph could not declare himself in any way a prophet, he could certainly declare himself the analogue to his kinsman, the founder of the original ummah. Were the caliph to stress his religious authority and take direct control of the military, the troops would follow him blindly (as the early Muslims allegedly followed the Prophet).

Our author proscribes drawing up a manual of conduct with which to indoctrinate the military forces, and offers advice as to how the army should be kept at arm's length from any activities that might corrupt and break its morale. For example, they should not be given responsibility for the collection of taxes (as that would make them less dependent on and less grateful to the central government for their regular service pay and food allotments). Lest we forget, for most fighting men military service in the formative centuries of Islam was never quite a noble calling that was sufficiently rewarding in and of itself. Muhammad's warriors who set off on an extended campaign to conquer Mecca for the Islamic faith were keenly aware at all times of particular needs that were not of a spiritual nature. The Abbasid army, even subjected to intensive religious and political propaganda, could hardly have consisted of holy warriors who were impervious to temporal concerns. They understood only too well the value of regularly scheduled service pay and food allotments, and fully appreciated a payroll that took into consideration fluctuating prices that might erode their purchasing power. The author's practical strategy seems clear. Pay heed to the physical needs of the military because an army relieved of responsibility for its own sustenance becomes increasingly dependent on its provider; the mouth filled with nourishment is more likely to be muted in criticism.

The operative force of this program was zealously carried out by the Abbasids, at least as regards the all-important question of the payroll and food allotments. At the outset, the long string of Khurasani military successes and the booty obtained together with regular service pay probably did more to bind the army to the ruling regime than any ideological indoctrination by Abbasid agents. In the end, the favors bestowed upon the army and its commanders after the regime was in power were likely to have been more decisive in winning their support than any claims by the caliph of religious authority or any system of religious education that might have been implemented among the officer corps and then filtered down to the men in the ranks. Whether Ibn al-Muqaffa''s suggestions had any direct impact on the caliph is a moot point. There is no question that al-Mansur and the Abbasids that followed him were keenly aware of the need for a highly professional fighting force displaying absolute loyalty to the regime.

What of the army's identity? How did the newly formed imperial force conceive of itself? Related to that, was its esprit de corps linked in any discernible way to a conscious Abbasid policy to shatter any residual loyalties to tribe? Beginning in 762, the main regiments of the Khurasan army in Iraq were quartered in a new Abbasid capital being built at Baghdad, a magnificent project of urban planning that will be described shortly. By taking up residence in Iraq, the Arab tribesmen in Khurasan had returned to their place of origins. The military encampments, established by the caliph al-Mansur, were situated at first in al-Harbiyah, a vast army camp north of the so-called Round City, the administrative center the caliph was building on the west bank of the river Tigris. Some ten years later, half the regiments in al-Harbiyah were assigned to a new caliphal complex that was going up on the opposite shore for al-Mansur's son and heir apparent Muhammad al-Mahdi. What is of particular interest is the organizational pattern of the earliest military encampments on the West Side.

Our sources make it clear that the cantonments were arranged to house units according to geographical areas in Khurasan where they had been stationed a short time before. It is remarkable that among the many references to Baghdad's military cantonments in the topographical literature, that is, the literature which describes in great detail the various locations of the city, there is not a single reference to a specific area of tribal settlement. Scholars have assumed that the Khurasani regiments of the Abbasid revolutionary army were originally registered according to two distinct rolls: the old settlers according to geographical origins, usually villages, and the main units, the disaffected Arab standing armies, according to tribal affiliation. The emerging pattern of military settlement at the new capital would seem to indicate the Abbasids were intent on destroying the tribal structure of their most skilled forces within the first decade or so of the revolution, perhaps even before they settled them at Baghdad. To be sure, the Abbasids continued to employ Arab tribesmen, but not as part of the regular imperial army stationed in Baghdad. Those tribesmen, all without links to the revolution, were part of the provincial forces. How long it took the tribal armies of Khurasan to fully assimilate their new regional identities and overcome thereby any lingering traces of tribal xenophobia is not entirely clear. What evidence there is suggests the process was more or less complete within a decade of the completion of al-Mansur's administrative center, certainly by the time of his grandson Harun al-Rashid (r. 786–809). The first Baghdad army was later joined by other forces recruited in the eastern provinces, so that by the beginning of the ninth century, the imperial army stationed at the capital, a force reportedly numbered in the tens of thousands, all identified with the generation of Khurasani warriors that brought the Abbasids to power, albeit under a new label.

Sometime in the reign of Harun al-Rashid, the Khurasani forces in the capital assumed a new identity; they became the *abna'*, literally "the sons." Often the term is affixed with *al-dawlah* and/or *al-da'wah*, meaning "the sons (of the revolution)" and/or "the sons of the (Abbasid cause)" or "(propaganda)." In either case, the reference links with evident pride the contemporaneous army in Baghdad to the service their fathers performed on behalf of the ruling house at its moment of inception. The ninth-century court figure al-Jahiz has the *banawi* (singular of abna') proclaim the root (*'asl*) of his own lineage is Khurasan, the region from which the Abbasid revolution and propaganda burst forth to bring about a new age. The banawi then reminds us that if Khurasan is the root, then Baghdad is its branch (*far*) and is therefore to be called the Khurasan of Iraq. Taking all these tidbits into consideration, it seems abundantly clear the Arab identity of the original tribal army in Khurasan had eroded within no more than a generation, probably even sooner. In that respect at least the professional army and the functioning bureaucracy of the Abbasids shared something in common. Arab privilege had given way as the new regime shaped a more universal and cosmopolitan state and society. Concurrent with this significant shift was the manner in which the Abbasids opted to defy Arab tribal inclinations to anarchy and created a highly centralized system of authority, something their predecessors sought from time to time but never managed to carry out. The quintessential symbol of the highly centralized Abbasid state was the great capital built by al-Mansur at the confluence of the Tigris and the Sarat Canal.

The Formation of the Imperial Center

Much has been written about the foundation of Baghdad and the magnificent architecture of al-Mansur's Round City. Although nothing remains of the original structure, and nothing is likely to be retrieved through archeological discovery—the present Iraqi capital is built over the medieval site—scholars have been able to reconstruct its basic design. At first, they relied exclusively on detailed descriptions found in medieval literary sources; following that, they compared the literary material with the actual remains of Islamic and non-Islamic monuments in Iraq and western Iran. Different plans have been suggested by a number of scholars, but all recognize the basic shape and size of the administrative center (a perfectly round structure divided into perfectly symmetrical quadrants encompassing some 450 hectares, or about five square English miles). Moreover, the same scholars, whether those engaged in texts or archeologists and architectural historians, all place great emphasis on how the medieval architects and engineers made use of axial planning and exquisite symmetry. That said, there has been considerable disagreement as to how the Round City functioned in relation to the larger urban setting and, more important for our discussion, what it represented as a symbol of Abbasid rule.

Some modern interpretations of the Round City and its function may be described as fanciful, at best. The attempt to link the Abbasid regime to a new Iranian empire in Islamic garb, an old idea that has been resurrected from time to time, has led some modern scholars to imagine that in choosing his plan for the city, al-Mansur was attempting to emulate the Sasanian khusraw. Admittedly, the Iranian emperor's own capital Ctesiphon had been situated downstream along the Tigris but a few miles away, and the caliph initially sought to salvage some material from the ruins of the emperor's palace to reuse in building the Round City, but there probably was little left standing at Ctesiphon to serve as a specific model for his own administrative center. Charles Wendell, undeterred by the absence of a specific prototype from the most recent Iranian past, goes so far as to argue that the origins of al-Mansur's city are deeply rooted in a far more ancient history, not the world of the Sasanians at Ctesiphon but a unified Indo-Iranian world that existed before the great migrations of the second millennium B.C.E. (a population movement that brought the precursors of the Sasanian rulers to the Near East). Thus, in the course of time, cosmic symbols and the images of a world eventually held in common by Hindus, Buddhists, and Zoroastrians was translated into the curious architectural arrangement of the great Abbasid capital. Wendell goes on to maintain that the Round City is certainly a schematic representation of the world of the Sasanian monarchs. To sum up Wendell's learned article, al-Mansur deliberately chose the plan of the Round City so that he might present himself as the legitimate heir to the great emperors of the past, especially those of the Banu Sasan. Arguing on behalf of this viewpoint, one can certainly say that perhaps no caliph before al-Mansur so intensely felt the need to establish his legitimacy. Allowing for that need, the images of Iranian sovereignty supposedly conveyed by the Round City would have been suited to the perceived needs of its Arab-Muslim founder.

But why should al-Mansur have linked his legitimacy to pre-Islamic conceptions of rule and how they were represented symbolically? What we have here is an argument that depends on the following propositions: Iranians from Khurasan brought the Abbasids to power; to stay in power the caliph had to appeal to their Iranian sensitivities; hence the need to promote himself as the heir to great Iranian rulers of the past and win the continued favor of his Khurasani supporters. The Round City was the visual symbol of Sasanian rule reborn, but a rule that embraced Islam rather than the Zoroastrian faith of the khusraw. There is no reason to deny a lingering interest in pre-Islamic conceptions and realia, but the argument for consciously imitating a Sasanian style of rule does not stand up to the historical facts now known and discussed earlier. The Round City was designed expressly for an Arab caliph brought to power largely by Arab tribal armies led by Arab generals embracing an ideology that called for the return to the pristine Islamic ummah that originated in the Arabian Peninsula. The legitimacy of al-Mansur's rule, as indeed with all the Abbasid caliphs, rested on demonstrating they were the analogues of the Prophet and the community they ruled was the Prophet's ummah reborn.

There is, in short, no way of directly tying the architectural arrangement of the Round City to cosmic symbols emanating from the world of Hindus, Buddhists, or even Zoroastrians, the rulers of Iraq immediately before the Islamic conquest. Even if one were grudgingly to admit the existence of a vague connection between the Abbasids and a remote eastern world in which the monarch was the symbolic presence on earth of some divine being, and the realm of the monarch was in some way designed in the image of the cosmos, it would hardly imply a recognition, let alone acceptance, of all the cultural baggage from pre-Islamic times. Moreover, if there were a deliberate cultural borrowing of things Iranian or even Buddhist as has been suggested, it should be possible to isolate at least one statement where the Abbasids themselves acknowledge that to be the case. There ought to be a point of entry into the argument of eastern influence where the modern historian feels on safe ground; but there is none. There is no unambiguous text that would lead us to believe al-Mansur was deliberately emulating the Sasanian emperor when he established the Round City as the quintessential symbol of his regime. Quite the opposite, there are a number of accounts that clearly indicate the caliph wanted to distance himself from radical notions and behavior that suggested possible Iranian origins. Al-Mansur took pains to draw a line between himself from the more radical proto-Shi'ite groups whose Islamic beliefs suggested a religious syncretism of sorts. When forced by circumstances he took up arms against them.

In the end, one has to ask, who among the subjects whose loyalty he coveted was likely to be impressed by representations derived from Iranian cosmology or by conscious efforts to link the commander of the Muslim faithful with the Zoroastrian emperors of the Banu Sasan, Iranian rulers whose armies had been crushed by the Muslims? Leaving some small and marginal groups aside, what Muslim would have favored resurrecting the image of an unbelieving dynasty whose vast realm had been dismembered, thus ending a thousand years of continuous Iranian rule? Or, seen from the perspective of the Abbasid caliphs, why should they have wished to be hailed as successors to non-Muslims who disappeared along with their realm a hundred and twenty-five years earlier? Did they really feel compelled to make concessions to the former subjects of the unbelievers?

The most likely breeding ground for a challenge to the caliph's authority was among the 'Alids and their sympathizers. There was, in addition, the more remote possibility of a pretender who might raise messianic expectations among the defeated followers of the Umayyads, mostly in the regions of Syria. Here, among these political groups, the Abbasid caliph could find individuals he could fear. But as did the Abbasids, the 'Alids did not propose themselves as heirs to the great khusraw, but of the Prophet Muhammad. Indeed, the right to rule based on the authority of the Prophet and thus derived from the earliest Islamic experience was the only ideological position the Abbasid caliph consciously understood and promoted on his own behalf and that of his kin. Furthermore, this was the only ideological position understood by the potential allies of those would-be rebels who would contest his claims to rule: the vestigial contingents of the Syrian tribal armies, the local populace of Iraq who favored the 'Alids, and particularly the imperial army recruited in Khurasan who, having defected from the Umayyads, might find reason to defect once again. The Khurasani fighters, also of Arab origins, may have assimilated to Iranian ways, but their identity was entirely rooted in the history of Islam, and their role in the revolution could only be comprehended in Islamic terms. The notion that al-Mansur built the Round City with the full intention of becoming a Muslim khusraw with all the symbolic trappings of an Iranian monarch begs for palpable evidence.

Nor does the perfectly round shape of the caliph's city necessarily imply a conscious link to some ancient cosmology that made al-Mansur's grand edifice the unsurpassable incarnation of an ancient tradition, that of the king in his cosmic city, an argument advanced with considerable flair, but precious little evidence by the art historian H. P. L'Orange. Muslims may have found the symmetrical arrangement of the Round City remarkable, or as one observer put it: as if poured into a mold and cast. But such words of praise were for the exquisite architectural plan and not because it reminded the faithful, even the recent converts, as it did L'Orange, of a king in physical surroundings that made him "the Axis and Pole of the World," "The King of the Four Quadrants of the World," and were that not enough to offend Muslim sensibilities, "The King of the Universe." The art historian's interpretive leap based on the shape of the Round City and its symmetrically arranged quadrants asks readers familiar with the history of the times to suspend all belief in what our sources tell us about the Abbasids and their regime. If Wendell stretches the evidence to claim al-Mansur successor to the Sasanian emperor, L'Orange takes us into the world of smoke and mirrors.

This not to say that al-Mansur did not appreciate the political significance of monumental architecture, or that he was oblivious to the symbolic transfer of power. There was, however, no need for him, or for modern scholars, to propose vague prototypes for the Round City that go back to an ancient past. There were all too many examples from more recent events that were firmly implanted in the consciousness of all Muslims, al-Mansur among them. The Round City was protected by massive iron gates, four of which were taken from Wasit, the great Umayyad capital in Iraq established by the province's celebrated governor al-Hajjaj ibn Yusuf; another gate was taken from Kufah where another powerful Umayyad governor, Khalid al-Qasri, had it built and installed; one reportedly stemmed from Pharaonic times, another had been built for King Solomon's residence at al-Zandaward. Pharaoh and Solomon are mentioned in the Qur'an and in the vast literature that commented on Muslim scripture. The powerful Umayyad governors were legendary figures in their own right. In the medieval Near East, the transfer of gates from one city to another may have had practical significance, as did the salvage and reuse of all sorts of architectural members from ruined buildings, but it was also an act that signified the transfer of authority from one ruler and his city to another. There can be little doubt that al-Mansur's Round City was meant to legitimize the Abbasid regime visually, but not as the inheritor of the Sasanian monarch's authority or world view. Rather the caliph presented the Abbasids as the family that put an end to the Umayyads and restored the Hashimites to their rightful place as commanders of the faithful.

That still leaves us to explain why the caliph chose to build a perfectly symmetrical round structure. There were, to be sure, the remains of round settlements from Sasanian and earlier times in Iraq and western Iran. It is conceivable that at some point al-Mansur was made aware of these structures, less likely that he actually visited the sites. One can argue the advantages of a round fortification for purposes of defense as have architectural historians—a rounded wall is less susceptible to damage from ballistas, the primitive artillery of the time. Nevertheless, no such reason is given in our sources. The only explanation for the round shape of al-Mansur's city takes us in a rather different direction, albeit a direction of enormous significance for understanding still another aspect of the Abbasid revolution, one which should be linked to the development of the government bureaucracy and imperial army. A medieval Muslim authority explaining the unusual shape of the Round City indicates that the caliph built the city as he did because a circular structure has advantages over one which is square (or rectangular), because if the monarch were to be in the center of a square structure, some parts would be closer to him than others, whereas if he were to be in the center of a round structure, all (the outer parts) would be equidistant from him. By all accounts, the caliph's palace was situated at the very center of the circle. Geometry aside, there is a profound truth expressed here, namely al-Mansur's perceived need for a highly centralized form of government with himself at the center of rule.

Mu'awiyah ibn Abi Sufyan, the first of the Umayyad caliphs and no mean politician in his own right, ruled as if he were a tribal sheikh, skillfully deflecting the grievances of his enemies and would-be enemies, always careful to play the game with Arab sensitivities in mind and according to tribal conventions. Hence, he ruled by guile and persuasion. Only when forced did he exercise license to inflict severe punishment, as he knew the limitations of authority that accrued to the standing caliphs of the realm. However, paying lip service to the Arab's distrust of imposed authority proved in the end the undoing of the house of Umayyah as the tribal armies of the state broke ranks in unsettled times and followed their own interests. Al-Mansur surely recognized the structural imbalances of the Umayyad regime and sought a different model of governance. Having assimilated lessons painfully absorbed by his predecessors in the unruly garrison towns of Iraq and elsewhere, al-Mansur offered no concessions to Arab tribalism in creating his urban environment. The development of the new Abbasid capital, including its suburban areas, was intended as the antithesis of anarchical sentiment and the haphazard growth that characterized the likes of the early military settlements at Basrah and Kufah. In particular, the Round City, was designed to symbolize stability and order by featuring a monumental architecture that encased the ruler, his courtly entourage, a highly centralized bureaucracy, and 4,000 troops to protect the city from attack.

Western historians originally thought the Round City contained a highly diverse population and an economic infrastructure able to provide the entire range of services to sustain all who settled within its walls. Put somewhat differently, they imagined it to be a fully integrated urban center. In Arabic, al-Mansur's edifice was referred to as a *madinah*, a term commonly used in the modern language to denote city. But in classical Arabic madinah also meant a place from which the rule of law emanates, that is, a center of administration. More recent studies reveal the Round City was in fact not a city at all but a glorified palace complex of such immense size that it was larger than any city ever built in central Iraq with

the exception of Ctesiphon. The Round City consisted of massive fortification walls and protective gates that enclosed two concentric rings, each
hermetically sealed off from the other by an intricate network of protective gateways and arcades. The outer ring, the first security zone, housed
the caliph's trusted clients, the functionaries that staffed the government
agencies and 4,000 troops responsible for overall security. The inner ring,
the second security zone, housed the offices of government, the public
kitchen, and the apartments of the caliph's younger children. Passing
through the four guarded arcades that divided the city into symmetrical
segments, one reached the zone of maximum security, the open inner
court of the structure. There at the very center of this immaculately
planned edifice was the golden domed palace and adjoining mosque of
the caliph as well as quarters for the personnel entrusted to safeguard his
person.

There were no markets in the original Round City; nor were there any
settlements of the local populace. Services were to be provided by merchants and artisans from al-Karkh, the great market suburb separated
from the Round City by the lower arm of the Sarat Canal to the south.
Directly north of the Round City in the suburb called al-Harbiyah were
the cantonments of the imperial army, a force that numbered in the tens
of thousands. Like the Round City, al-Harbiyah, which was bounded by
the upper arm of the Sarat to the west and by the Tigris to the east, was
a restricted zone, although given the size of the military force and their
families, some distributive outlets were allowed there. They were called
in Arabic *suwayqat* or "little market shops" that provided essential com-
modities. Along the Tigris shore, which formed the east reaches of this
restricted sector of Baghdad, were the palaces of the caliph's older children
and the notables of the Abbasid house. In effect, the palace complex of
the Round City and the areas immediately beyond it formed an island
cut off from the general populace by the upper and lower Sarat and the
Tigris. A more illustrative example of concentrating imperial power
would be hard to find in the Islamic Middle Ages.

Al-Mansur's choice of this location reveals the caliph's grand design of
centralizing power. Arabic chroniclers have the caliph himself acknowledging that he chose the site because it connected the two great river
systems of Mesopotamia, the Tigris and the Euphrates by way of the
Sarat, a man-made canal that allowed for the traffic of large boats.
Located in the geographic center of Iraq, it also straddled all the major
overland routes connecting east and west, but, above all, it was in the
province that was the very center of the empire's major geographic

components: the vast territories to the east that gave rise to the revolution, and greater Syria and Egypt to the west. It is no small wonder proud Baghdadis referred to their city as the "navel of the universe." Greater Baghdad thus represented an imperial style of rule that radiated from the caliph's centrally located palace outward. Surmounting the walls of each of the four major gateways of the Round City was a domed chamber in which the caliph held audiences and surveyed his domains beyond. The gates were named for the cities and regions they faced: The Kufah Gate, the Basrah Gate, The Damascus Gate, and the Khurasan Gate. It was as though the caliph sitting in these domed audience chambers, clearly meant to be an extension of his domed palace in the inner court, looked out at his domains and could imagine himself and the house of Abbas at the center of a polity that controlled those cities and regions beyond. No doubt, he would have felt a great sense of contentment, both personal and for the house of Abbas. However, in the end the exquisite design of the imperial capital as well as that of the government agencies and army was too intricate to survive the weight of impending historical realities. Al-Mansur's grandiose and overly ornate sense of government undermined not only the meticulous plan of the capital but that of the Abbasid polity itself. The center of Abbasid rule could not hold the disparate parts of empire together. Within decades, the structural imbalances of the Abbasid capital and state precipitated the incipient decline of their universal empire.

10

Emerging Cracks within the Universal Islamic Empire

At its height, greater Baghdad represented the largest and most populated city ever seen either in the ancient or medieval Near East. We can say with absolute certainty it covered some thirty square miles, a land surface one-third larger than Manhattan Island, which, some New Yorkers will recall, was once whimsically advertised as "Baghdad on the Hudson [River]." At its zenith shortly after World War II, Manhattan was home to some two million inhabitants, and, like today, it served as the cultural, industrial, and administrative center of New York City, as well as a hub of world finance. To be sure, it is equally if not more appropriate to link the Abbasid capital to a comparable medieval city. Baghdad was eleven times larger than the original walled city of Byzantium (Constantinople) when the Byzantine capital had a population conservatively estimated at one hundred fifty thousand. When the Byzantine city was enclosed by a second retaining wall, the total area was still one-fourth as large as the land surface of Baghdad; the population of the double-walled city has been estimated by one authority at some 360,000. Others speak of one million inhabitants, although without much if any justification.

Unlike the land surface of Baghdad, which is based on medieval surveys conducted by the ruling authorities, the population of the Abbasid city is more difficult to estimate. Medieval authors usually relied on multipliers such as the consumption of foodstuffs, the number of bathhouses and bathhouse attendants, licensed doctors, and the like. One author, using a variety of multipliers, including the volume of soap consumed at the city's baths, claimed that by his overly conservative estimate, Baghdad's population was 96 million, a figure that certainly invites skepticism, whether speaking about the hygiene of the natives or their true numbers. One thing we know for sure; by all indications the West Side (over 60 percent) of the city became so heavily populated that new construction was restricted there. There is reason to believe the same was eventually true of the city neighborhoods on the opposite shore— hence a picture of vast urban sprawl reminiscent of a modern metropolis. Indeed, for legal purposes greater Baghdad in the early Middle Ages actually comprised several cities within a broad metropolitan area, much like New York and London today with their system of autonomous boroughs; areas not ordinarily referred to by the locals as "the city" but nevertheless subject to a central municipal authority. With the data at our disposal, it would not be unrealistic to suggest that greater Baghdad was home to between two hundred thousand (a very conservative estimate) and six hundred thousand people, perhaps as many as one million.

The rapid growth of the city population quickly compromised al-Mansur's plan to create an enclosed administrative center and palace residence with large armed forces situated in isolated military camps nearby. Ideally, the government sector would be close enough to be supplied with all means of basic services from the private sector, but at arm's length from the caliph's presence and that of his bureaucracy and standing army. Security within the Round City had already broken down within the caliph's lifetime, and various adjustments had to be made to the intricate architectural arrangement. In similar fashion, the exclusivity of the military camps broke down as the need for services and supplies called for more accessible and larger market areas. Eventually al-Mansur moved to a new palace along the Tigris shore, the first of three other palaces or palace complexes in the city that came to be occupied by subsequent caliphs who, as did al-Mansur, configured private and public space with an eye to security. Separating the private and public sectors became, however, increasingly difficult. Because the city and its new economic opportunities had become a magnet for the surrounding rural population and peoples from areas still further removed, distances between hitherto discrete sectors became more and more narrow; in certain areas they collapsed altogether. With land becoming more and more scarce, public officials, including members of the ruling family, took advantage of rising real estate prices and subdivided their property, leasing it out to rent-paying merchants and artisans. The two contingencies al-Mansur had not anticipated were rapid growth that placed great demands on land to settle and develop for commercial purposes and, linked to that, the part of human nature which gives rise to excessive greed.

When the Abbasids built a second capital at Samarra some sixty miles upstream from Baghdad in 836 C.E., the old capital, given its advantageous location astride the major inland waterways and overland routes, continued to function as the economic hub of the regime. During the more than fifty years in which both urban centers thrived, the hinterland of the twin cities, the so-called Diyala Plains, took on the characteristics of a dwarf whose truncated rural body was surmounted by a massive urban head. Of the sixteen thousand or so built-up hectares in the Diyala Plains (one hectare equals two square kilometers), some 13,500–14,000 hectares were taken up by Baghdad and Samarra. Clearly, these great urban centers, the likes of which had never graced the Near East before, did not live off the immediate hinterland and its shrinking agricultural base. In Sasanian times, 308 agricultural villages helped support an urban infrastructure of cities and towns that amounted to less than 3,000 hectares, including the imperial center of Ctesiphon (540 ha.). In Islamic times only 234 villages supported an urban infrastructure of approximately 15,500 hectares. Clearly Baghdad and then Baghdad and Samarra were in a manner of speaking artificial entities that thrived from the immense wealth of an empire that extended from North Africa in the west to central Asia in the east.

But the highly centralized regime, conceived of by the early Abbasids to control the excesses of Arab tribalism, served to weaken the government's hold on the periphery of the empire, then increasingly on regions closer to Iraq whose tax revenues sustained the state, and ultimately within the capital city itself. Given the enormity of the empire they governed with authority so highly concentrated in the capital, the Abbasids could never reconcile the universal Islamic ummah, that idealized community transcending geography and ruled by a single proper successor to the Prophet (in this case the Abbasid caliph), with the pragmatic need to retain the absolute loyalty and of course tax revenues of the ummah's varied parts by formally ceding decisive authority, if not indeed autonomy, to rulers of distant regions and diverse populations.

Unable to obtain real legitimacy for themselves and the peoples and territories they ruled, petty dynasts in those distant regions gave formal recognition to the authority of the caliph, as expected of them. But, often as not, they formulated policies independent of and sometimes opposed to weak if not impotent caliphs in Baghdad. Slowly but surely the center of Islamic rule gave way as had the periphery before. Samarra was essentially abandoned after less than sixty years. The extensive building activity there, particularly by the caliph Ja'far al-Mutawakkil (r. 847–861), virtually bankrupted the state; his policies and odd behavior fueled his assassination and weakened the caliphate dramatically. Sixty miles downstream, the Round City, the quintessential symbol of the Abbasid regime and its highly centralized mode of governance, was already obsolescent by the mid-tenth century and on its way to becoming a ruin. Over the ensuing centuries, the first Abbasid capital, once a heavily congested city with a continuous line of occupation running the length and width of the entire urban area, was reduced to a series of shrunken neighborhoods at some distance from one another. Still, it remained a vibrant city and the symbol of Abbasid rule until the Mongol invasion of 1258 effectively ended the longest-lived ruling dynasty in the history of Islam and reduced the once proud capital to a provincial city. It remained a provincial city until the emergence of the modern Iraqi nation-state and the imposition of central authority within that state's artificial borders.

Structural Imbalances in the Islamic Ummah: The Lingering Problem of Succession

Contested geographical space on the periphery of the Abbasid Empire was paralleled by contested political space within the ruling family itself. The problem of succession that had plagued the early caliphate and then the house of Umayyah remained unresolved under the Abbasids. In an earlier chapter we noted the first Umayyad caliph, Mu'awiyah ibn Abi Sufyan, introduced the notion of dynastic succession, a concept both alien and grating to Arab tribal sensibilities. As a rule, Arab tribal leaders participated in open elections, a sort of participatory democracy whose outcome could not always be guaranteed. While the participants were called upon to close ranks once a final consensus had emerged, the choice of a new leader could and did lead to the alienation of individuals and factions. As did the Umayyads, the Abbasids sought to rationalize the mechanism by which each caliph would be succeeded. The point was to eliminate political paralysis during the interregnum, and, above all, to forgo a contested succession that might lead to civil war, as was the case during the early caliphate, during the Umayyad regime, and then again when al-Mansur succeeded his brother only to be challenged by his uncle 'Abdallah ibn 'Ali. In order to create an orderly succession that could be sustained in perpetuity, the Abbasid caliph devised a scheme to eliminate all the other branches of the Banu Abbas and restrict rule to his progeny and his progeny alone.

The first step was for al-Mansur to reverse the current order of succession in which his nephew 'Isa ibn Musa was the declared heir-apparent, followed by his own son Muhammad, the future caliph al-Mahdi. At a humiliating public ceremony attended by all the Hashimite notables (those who formally took the oath of allegiance to the caliph and his intended successors on behalf of the entire ummah), 'Isa found himself seated to the left of the caliph while al-Mansur's teenage son sat to the right, the reverse of what might have been expected given the existing line of succession. The notables then approached and one by one they first kissed the hand of al-Mansur, then that of al-Mahdi, and following this they shook hands with 'Isa ibn Musa, a well-orchestrated ceremony of great symbolic importance. The postscript to this account told by the Arabic chronicler reveals that the order of succession was then officially reversed. As 'Isa ibn Musa was roughly the same age as al-Mansur, in effect he had little chance of outliving the caliph's son and assuming the mantle of the Prophet. Conspiratorial by nature, al-Mansur took no chances and later had 'Isa removed from the line of succession altogether. The latter then retired from public life having received as compensation a certain peace of mind and a more than adequate yearly income.

Despite all the efforts to promote a universal outlook and remove the debilitating effects of Arab tribalism, the Abbasids remained an Arab family that shared traditional Arab values. This complicated al-Mansur's plans for orderly succession among his progeny as the number of male offspring that might claim rule for themselves was generally not limited to a single son. In accord with tribal custom, future caliphs generally took as their initial wives first cousins (preferably the daughters of paternal uncles). Barring that, they married prestigious women within the extended family or clan, an effort to preserve all-important blood lines. But as these noble women could be barren, or suffer the death of their infant children, or have the child survive only to die while very young, or, worse yet, give birth only to females, the fathers took on other wives and, given the wealth of the caliphs, took females from a constantly shifting harem of concubines. The latter often provided the caliphs with their firstborn male offspring and heirs apparent. Virtually every Abbasid caliph following al-Mansur was the son of a concubine; al-Mansur himself was the offspring of a Bedouin woman. At times, a caliph would find particular favor with a son much to the disappointment of the mothers of his other offspring. As some women of the caliph's household were not above promoting their own children and becoming enmeshed in court intrigue, there was potential for serious internal conflict. This was evident at the time of al-Mahdi's succession.

The caliph's heir apparent was his son Musa al-Hadi, the son of the beautiful and politically adroit Khayzuran, a former slave. Our sources indicate that al-Mahdi had a change of mind and was on his way to see al-Hadi with the intention of forcing him to relinquish his rights in favor of another of Khayzuran's sons, the younger Harun al-Rashid. It is indicative of Khayzuran's influence, if not other unknown factors, that her two sons were the clear heirs apparent and not any male offspring that might have been born to the noble wife chosen for the caliph, his first cousin Raytah, the daughter of al-Mansur's younger brother, the former caliph al-Saffah. One might question whether or not al-Mahdi actually intended to replace al-Hadi with Harun, the favored younger son of his beloved Khayzuran. The account has all the trappings of a back-projection designed to legitimize Harun's ultimate rise to power after a bitter dispute that involved many leading figures of the Abbasid government and court. In any case, al-Mahdi's sudden and untimely death while en route to see al-Hadi, left the door open to the latter assuming the role of commander of the faithful, an event that caused some initial rioting in the capital but no open conflict of any consequence. Shortly thereafter the new caliph al-Hadi sought to remove his brother from the line of succession preferring his own son as did al-Mansur in a previous generation. After Harun resisted stepping aside, the caliph had him placed under house-arrest.

Khayzuran's favorite was not without considerable support. His mother could be neutralized by al-Hadi, but the influential Barmakid family was another matter. True, they were mere clients of the Abbasid caliphs, but as a family whose influence penetrated deeply into the government, they could back another of the caliph's sons without compromising their loyalty to the regime as a whole. As noted in the previous chapter, the Barmakid Ja'far, whose father Yahya was perhaps the most influential of all al-Mahdi's clients, was unusually close to Harun. Since both Ja'far and Harun reportedly suckled the breasts of the same wet nurse and at the same time, one might refer to them as milk brothers. The two boys grew up in each other's presence from infancy. Harun so enjoyed Ja'far's company, when he later became caliph, he arranged for his client to enter into the infamous mock marriage with his sister 'Abbasah, a princess of the ruling house. In that way, he could entertain both of them without any hint of impropriety. More to the point, Ja'far's father had been Harun's mentor and introduced to him to leading military commanders as he took him along on major military campaigns against the Byzantines. Yahya was extremely influential and commanded considerable support throughout the government. In short, the intervention of the Barmakids on behalf of Harun had the potential for occasioning still another civil war. Not surprisingly, the new caliph attempted to limit his mother's influence and reportedly imprisoned the powerful Yahya. Still, Harun, confined to his domicile, remained unwilling to bend to the caliph's wishes. He insisted on continuing as heir apparent to the standing caliph.

Fortunately for Harun, his supporters, and the Abbasid regime as a whole, al-Hadi died within the first year of his rule before matters came to a head. The issue of succession was then resolved by making Harun commander of the faithful with the regnal title al-Rashid. Al-Hadi's death at a young age gave rise to theories of a conspiracy. One version held that he was smothered, allegedly by a slave girl when the two were alone (highly unlikely); another indicates poisoning (also unlikely). In both these cases, we are dealing with a single terse account that raises our suspicion that al-Hadi's alleged murder is a figment of a historian's imagination. No member of the Abbasid house had ever gone so far as to murder another; even the rebel 'Abdallah ibn 'Ali was allowed to live out his life confined to his residence. Nor would any Abbasid ruler declare licit the blood of his close relatives in the future. In all likelihood, we are dealing here with a well-known literary device of medieval Arabic historiography: a natural death is transformed into a brilliantly conceived political murder that leaves no clear forensic evidence and hence no accusations of foul play that could carry any legal weight. The circumstances of the time certainly invited a flight of such literary fancy to titillate the reader's imagination.

There were many individuals who stood to gain by the caliph's demise: his mother whose stock had fallen, the Barmakids, whose leader Yahya was in prison, the various clients and retainers that had been attached to Harun, and of course Harun himself. Be that as it may, there is reason to believe that the caliph died of nothing more sinister than internal bleeding caused by a stomach ulcer or something to that effect. Other sources describe him as being indisposed and then increasingly ill and in pain over an extended period of time; so much so he could not meet with the military commanders to secure their support in deposing his brother. Under the circumstances, the army's leaders, fearing the caliph's death, or at worst his being too incapacitated to rule, were reluctant to bind themselves to him. They thought it prudent to hedge their bets and let matters run their course. Upon al-Hadi's death they fell in line behind Harun.

Arabic litterateurs, followed by Western romantics, have pictured the reign of Harun al-Rashid as a golden age, the high-water mark of Islamic civilization and political influence. But the fabled caliph of *The Thousand and One Nights* and other fanciful tales obscures the real story of Harun's caliphate. To be sure, the realm was filled with men of culture and learning and by all outward appearances the center of the empire prospered. The commander of the faithful also waged war vigorously against the Christian enemy who had turned increasingly bold. At the end of his reign, Harun al-Rashid was readying an enormous military base on the Byzantine frontier. Once completed, it was to serve as a platform to launch a major, perhaps even decisive, offensive against the Byzantine heartland. All of this spoke of a vigorous dynasty displaying self-confidence.

The situation within the outlying domains of the Abbasid Empire and even the capital itself presents us with a rather different picture. Despite the grandeur attributed to the caliph and the resplendent image of the capital city, he never developed an administrative center of his own there as did his grandfather and father before him. There was nothing comparable to Madinat al-Salam, the magnificent Round City, nor was there anything like the palace complex of al-Rusafah inhabited by al-Mahdi, or perhaps even 'Isabadh, the pleasure palace at the outskirts of the capital briefly occupied by his late brother. On the contrary, he appears to have grown restive and disenchanted with Baghdad, preferring to pass his later years at another palace complex which he built adjacent to the city of al-Raqqah in the northern province of al-Jazirah, a place closer to borders that separated the Muslims from their Byzantine enemies. The new complex called al-Rafiqah was reportedly modeled after the Round City and was to have served a similar function; it was close enough to the markets of al-Raqqah to be supplied with basic services but sufficiently distant for the caliph to live in complete security. The ruins of al-Rafiqah's walls, which can be seen today, bear clear similarities to the city of al-Mansur portrayed in our literary sources, although, unlike Madinat al-Salam, the shape of al-Rafiqah is that of a horseshoe and not a perfect circle. The new palace complex was for a while the unofficial seat of the realm. At the time of his death (809), he was building the giant military base at Tawanah along the Byzantine frontier itself. We have the impression that he planned to settle there, if only temporarily, while launching a decisive campaign against the long-standing Christian foe.

The seeming wanderlust of the caliph may have run much deeper than his alleged disaffection with Baghdad and a pressing concern with

Muslim-Byzantine relations. He appears to have understood only too well the inherent contradictions of an overly centralized and overly extended Abbasid regime. As did his father, perhaps even more so, the caliph relied heavily on the imperial army commanders, based largely in Iraq and Khurasan, and his trusted clients, none more trusted than the Barmakids who had risen to unprecedented ranks in the administration of the state, including service as political commissars with various fighting units. Even after their mysterious fall from grace seventeen years after the beginning of his reign, members of the extended Barmakid family continued to serve the caliph as did a vast array of other clients. But that concentration of power at court and the great military cantonments of Baghdad and Khurasan could not prevent Abbasid rule from fraying at the edges of the empire and regions still closer to Iraq.

The distant Yemen was in revolt for nine years until it was finally pacified in 804. To the west, Harun al-Rashid was beset by unease in Egypt, where the provincial administration, far removed from the capital, could not react quickly or adequately to unfolding events. The populace chafed at the heavy taxes levied on them to underwrite military campaigns in a still more distant western North Africa, the area known in Arabic as Ifriqiyah. Once order was restored in Egypt by a trusted general sent from Baghdad, matters got out of hand in the lands of the Islamic west. The semi-independent petty dynasty of the Aghlabids was established in North Africa (800–909) in return for which Harun al-Rashid's caliphate continued to receive formal obeisance and some forty thousand dinars annually, hardly an imposing sum. At the very edge of the Abode of Islam, the Iberian Peninsula, which had been conquered in 711 when the Umayyads ruled the Islamic world, reverted back to the deposed dynasty as early as 755. One could claim, and rightfully so, that Muslim Spain represented the outer fringes of the orbit of Islam and was always different in so many respects from the more centrally located provinces, in sum, a case all to itself. The Abbasids with their initial concerns about setting their house in order never expended any effort to retain the land beyond the Straits of Gibraltar. And so the early loss of a province separated from the rest of the Islamic world by the Mediterranean was not a reflection of the relative strength of the newly established dynasty in Iraq. However, during Harun al-Rashid's reign, the central authorities were hard pressed to maintain order much closer to their base of power, a seeming indication of incipient decline.

In Syria, Arab tribes with residual memories of the Umayyad regime and beset by tribal xenophobia were in conflict with one another, which destabilized, thereby, the regions they coinhabited. Initially, the caliph's governors refused to intervene, viewing the tribal strife as a purely local dispute that did not require their intervention. A second look at the situation might lead modern historians to interpret the governors' reactions rather differently. One could imagine they felt they had no mandate to act, or thought they lacked a clear mandate from the central authorities to sort out the situation. The administration of the state had grown too top heavy to allow for a rapid response to developments even in nearby Syria. In the end, the uprisings were quelled when the caliph sent his personal representative, his trusted client Ja'far the Barmakid, to take command of the situation. The same held true for distant areas to the east, where the 'Alid Yahya ibn 'Abdallah al-Mahd revolted, and in western Iran, where the Kharijites began successive rebellions that were crushed, but not without some difficulty. Even in Khurasan, the cradle of the revolution that brought the Abbasids to power, Harun al-Rashid paid the price for governors unable to act resolutely—and when they did, their excessive zeal only served to enflame passions even further. The most successful representatives of the government there, as elsewhere, were clients of the caliph sent from Baghdad.

One is then left to wonder whether the caliph's move to al-Rafiqah was not merely his distaste for Baghdad, or to be closer to the Byzantine enemy, or to establish a formal presence in order to pacify and win the firm allegiance of a broad region away from the capital. It may well have been part of a grander concept that he slowly came to envision, that of decentralizing the Abbasid state by forming strong regional constituencies that could more efficiently manage pressing local concerns and conflicts that were in evidence in so many places from the farthest reaches of the west in North Africa to provinces far to the north and east. Put simply, the caliph may have come to the conclusion that the empire was simply too vast to be ruled from a single location and as if it were a single unified religious community. The prevailing notion of a transcendent ummah was severely challenged by the reality of an overextended Islamic empire, burdened as it was by its geographical vastness and by a highly centralized authority concentrated in Baghdad.

There were other potential benefits to the decentralization of the empire. The major provinces, whose administration would be decoupled to some extent from the capital in Iraq, could serve as a brake against ill-conceived policies emanating from the city and insure an orderly succession within the ruling family. This might have been seen as particularly important at a time when the outer edges of the empire, and even provinces as central as

Egypt, Syria, and Khurasan, were beset by one crisis after another. It is difficult to imagine that in these troubling circumstances Harun al-Rashid was not aware there was no margin for the kind of disputed succession that had greeted his grandfather's investiture or his own accession to the caliphate. Perhaps that is why toward the end of his rule he granted three of his sons, each designated in the line of succession, the administration of a major province. In such fashion, the caliph who followed Harun al-Rashid would have great difficulty tampering with the established line. His heir apparent Muhammad al-Amin, born to a Hashimite mother and hence of noble birth on both sides of the family, was given the capital, Iraq, and Syria to administer, certainly an advantageous situation. The second in line 'Abdallah al-Ma'mun, the eldest of Harun al-Rashid's sons, born to a slave but raised by Zubaydah, the granddaughter of al-Mansur and noble wife of Harun, was given the immensely rich province of Khurasan and its large standing army. The third, al-Qasim, was assigned Egypt and the west. In theory, the new caliph al-Amin should he have decided to replace the other heirs apparent with his own son would not have had the wherewithal to carry out this plan, because al-Ma'mun as governor of Khurasan had sufficient power to block him, and had al-Ma'mun joined forces with his brother in Egypt, they would have had the ability to bring an end to the caliph's rule. If we have understood Harun al-Rashid's intentions correctly, we would have to declare the plan was both well conceived and elegant, but as with so many elegant schemes of the ruling regime, in the end it came to naught.

Despite the checks and balances built into Harun al-Rashid's plan, al-Amin, once in power, followed an old ploy, and sought to substitute the name of his infant son for that of the new heir-apparent in the line of succession. In this case, al-Amin's impetuous behavior would lead to personal disaster and enormous damage to the Banu Abbas and the empire as a whole. As governor of Khurasan, al-Ma'mun had been provided with both the human and physical resources to deny his brother. Neither seems to have wanted armed conflict, and so negotiations were opened between the brothers, but they led nowhere. It is not clear to what extent the caliph and his brother actually controlled events at the time. The decentralization of power meant that each of Harun al-Rashid's sons, surrounded as he was by mentors in government, usually drawn from the ranks of the caliph's clients, and by military officers drawn form the standing army where the future caliph's were stationed, was influenced by their advice. Some of these advisors had been attached to the princes of the house since the latter were young boys.

This was a pattern that had emerged early in the regime. Al-Mahdi was made governor of Khurasan by his father when he had hardly reached his majority, if that. In effect, the province was ruled by the caliph's regent, but the opportunity was there for the boy to be tutored in the art of political administration as well as become acquainted with key army personnel. When al-Mahdi made his way to Baghdad to replace 'Isa ibn Musa in the line of succession, he was accompanied by a vast retinue from the province he ruled in name. Needless to say, all his handlers had a vested interest in seeing him the next caliph, as their self-interest was tied to his fortunes. In that respect, Harun al-Rashid's decision to decentralize the empire was stood on its head for it created competing circles whose futures were tied to and expressed through the ambitions of the princes they served. Indeed, leading clients acted as provocateurs in an effort to promote the position of their youthful patrons and thereby enhance their own political and personal gain. Shadow governments had been formed to serve the young Abbasid princes, and the once reliable army created by al-Mansur out of the Arab tribesmen in Khurasan became a vested interest group available to the highest bidder with prerequisite credentials to rule.

In time, civil war erupted and, as had happened at the outset of Abbasid revolution, a Khurasan-based army once again invaded Iraq. After some stirring victories, al-Ma'mun's generals surrounded the reigning caliph in his capital. After an extended siege, al-Amin was prepared to surrender to his brother, but not to the generals of the opposing army. No doubt, he understood that al-Ma'mun was likely to do what his predecessors did before him; the strong likelihood was that, at worst, the deposed caliph would be placed under house arrest for the better part of his life. He was, however, caught trying to escape the city and was killed and then brutally mutilated by the troops who apprehended him. When the severed head of al-Amin was presented to his brother in Khurasan, he let out a cry of true anguish; he had not only lost a brother, but the manner in which the war was conducted and had come to an end was likely to alienate the populace of Baghdad.

It would be a mistake to think the civil war was a conflict driven by ideology as was the Abbasid rise to power. At the time of the Abbasid revolution the objective was to end the usurper regime of the house of Umayyah and to restore the clan of Hashim to its proper place at the head of the ummah. At issue was a fundamental question: Who had the right to represent the community of the faithful? Put somewhat differently, how could the ummah tolerate caliphs without proper credentials to rule as successors to the Prophet? No such question drove the conflict between the brothers. Both were Hashimites, Abbasids, Mansurids, and sons of Harun al-Rashid who were considered by him and the Hashimite notables worthy of a place in the line of succession. Hence, both al-Amin and al-Ma'mun were legitimate candidates to command the faithful. The differences between them were those of more narrowly defined politics stimulated by the self-interest of their intimate advisors.

Nor should one exaggerate the ethnic differences between the Baghdad army of al-Amin and the Khurasanis who fought on behalf of his brother. Although situated in Baghdad and the eastern provinces respectively, the forces of al-Amin and al-Ma'mun were both of Khurasani origins and were both part of the professional army that served the regime. The generals on both sides were well known to each other, much like those who commanded the Union and Confederate forces in the great American civil war or the Indian and Pakistani armies during the short but bloody conflict over Bangladesh. Many on both sides of the civil war were the spiritual if not direct descendants of the earlier Khurasani forces that brought the Abbasids to power.

Readers will recall that after restoring the Hashimites to rule, major elements of the first Abbasid army, the so-called *ahl Khurasan* or "people of Khurasan" were situated in the military suburbs of Baghdad. Their cantonments reflected the diverse eastern districts where they had been billeted under the Umayyads. They were inscribed in the first Abbasid military roll according to these villages and towns. In that sense they retained their local Khurasani identities even as they served the caliph in Iraq. Two generations later, apparently in the reign of Harun al-Rashid, they assumed a unique identity of their own as the abna', the "sons (of the revolution, or the sons the Abbasid call or propaganda)." But they did not deny their origins. To the contrary, as they put it, or at least as they were said to have put it, their branch may have been in Baghdad and Iraq, but their roots were in Khurasan. The sons of the revolution are portrayed as having been particularly proud of the role played by their fathers and grandfathers in establishing the Abbasid regime.

As half the original Khurasan army remained in the east after the revolution, those elements of al-Ma'mun's forces descended from the original ahl-Khurasan could have made similar claims about the role of their ancestors. Some of the abna' who had been sent to campaign in the east actually joined forces with al-Ma'mun and the descendants of the original Abbasid army. One of his two field commanders, Harthamah ibn A'yan, was a banawi. In fact, they and the new recruits from beyond the Oxus (perhaps the main contingents of al-Ma'mun's army) identified their cause as a "second (Abbasid) calling," a slogan that spoke to a glorious revolutionary past and was intended to be predictive of an equally glorious future. If Baghdadis supporting al-Amin had any distinctive claim, it was their claim they were "born in the court of their rulers" and not their Khurasani or revolutionary roots. And so, when examined closely, this civil war was not a war over ideology or ethnic pride; it was a conflict created in the crucible of family politics at a time when the structural imbalances of the regime could no longer be ignored or overcome. Decentralizing the empire did not lead to autonomous regions that carried the stamp of their own legitimacy but to courtly retinues and army contingents who saw their own interests (that is, political influence and the distribution of military pay and bonuses) best served by promoting the cause of the Abbasid princes who demanded their loyalty. Perhaps the most telling comment on this state of affairs was that of one of the military commanders who fought in the Abbasid civil war. He rued the day the war ended, as never in his memory had a conflict been so beneficial to opposing armies, made rich in this case by extensive military bonuses.

The Fallout from the Civil War

The brutal killing of al-Amin and the devastation of certain areas of the capital left the supporters of the deposed caliph in a less than conciliatory mood. They no doubt suspected that the victory of the pretender would enhance the Khurasanis who supported him at their expense and that of their city, which was in need of being rebuilt. The nature of the heavy fighting within Baghdad is reflected in the boasts attributed to the abna'. They are described as expert in close combat, the kind of fighting—and one might add personal bravery—to have engaged the enemy in confined places such as the entrances to defensive moats and the approaches to the city bridges. The abna' speak of bloody death for all who oppose them at the breaches in protective walls and in narrow lanes. They fight at night as well as in daytime and kill openly in the markets and roads. We have in these and other comments a picture of the grim battle for Baghdad where the defensive lines of al-Amin's forces were established around the natural barriers protecting the Round City, the last bastion of the beleaguered al-Amin and his weary supporters.

After the fall of Baghdad, the abna' remained a potentially volatile element with considerable military skill and still in possession of their weapons. The new authority in the city continued to pay their military salaries, no doubt to buy their acquiescence and because a force was needed to keep order in the chaos that could have ensued well after al-Amin's fall. The abna' could boast: "All of Baghdad is ours. It is quiet when we are quiet and in turmoil when we are in turmoil." Although beholden to the new government for their position, the abna' were anything but fully committed to the new regime. It would be some years before al-Ma'mun would set foot in Baghdad; even then he spent most of his reign in Khurasan. The city of the realm was ruled by the caliph's handpicked governor, the brother of his vizier, although it remained for official purposes the capital of the Abbasid realm until al-Ma'mun's successor moved the center of Abbasid administration to Samarra.

Al-Ma'mun's politics followed those of his most able predecessors. He established a coterie of clients that attended to the government and appointed army commanders whose families had long served the house of Abbas. But the simmering revolts that confronted Harun al-Rashid continued and required greater and greater effort to control. With the caliph in Khurasan and attention diverted to various rebellions, the long-dormant partisans of 'Ali took up arms in their traditional strongholds Kufah and Basrah, as well as in Yemen. As always, their rebellion was crushed, but this time it required considerable effort. Then, in an unprecedented move, al-Ma'mun seemingly sought a reconciliation with the 'Alids and established as heir apparent in 816, not a brother (as designated by Harun al-Rashid), nor any other descendant of al-Mansur, nor even someone from the extended house of Abbas. He chose instead 'Ali, the son of Musa al-Kazim and the brother of two recent 'Alid rebels. Following that, the display of the Abbasid color black was replaced displaced by 'Alid green, a symbolic gesture that spoke volumes to those who supported the house of the caliph's forefathers.

The new heir apparent bore the title *al-Rida* (*min al Muhammad*), "the chosen one (from the family of Muhammad)," a regnal title that conjures up memories of the "chosen one from the [Prophet's] house," whose cause was espoused by the revolutionary armies carrying the black banners of the Abbasids. The choice of successor, which was reportedly promoted by the caliph's vizier, his client Ja'far ibn Sahl, invites great speculation. Why should the caliph have reversed the policy of every one of his predecessors and allowed an 'Alid the opportunity to rule the ummah when not even the non-Mansurid line of the Abbasid house had license to do so in the past? What could be gained by such a concession? At first glance, one might think reconciliation with the 'Alids might have made their family and supporters backers of a regime that was increasingly beleaguered at the periphery of their empire. To be sure, a major 'Alid revolt had taken place recently in the heart of the realm. However, the rebels seemingly lacked the residual strength to offer a serious challenge in the very near future. Nor can we simply say that the caliph was a naïf susceptible to the pleadings of his vizier and mentor Ja'far ibn Sahl, admittedly the most powerful figure in the government bureaucracy. Like many of his predecessors who commanded the faithful, al-Ma'mun was very much his own man once he became fully established in power. There is something inexplicable about this remarkable turn of events. Given the caliph's learned pursuits and unusually deep knowledge of the Islamic sciences, one is tempted to speculate that there might have been a religious or intellectual rationale to al-Ma'mun's decision, but that is mere speculation on our part. The mystery of 'Ali al-Rida has been with us for nearly 1,200 years; no doubt it will continue to invite speculation for many years to come.

Whatever the caliph and his vizier had in mind, the decision to choose an 'Alid successor caused a major rift among the supporters of the dynasty, especially in Baghdad where elements of the populace joined some leading members of the ruling house in deposing the standing caliph and replaced him with his uncle Ibrahim, a son of Muhammad al-Mahdi. With that, they attempted to keep the Mansurid line intact. One should not conclude, however, that all the Abbasids and their supporters approved of the decision to proclaim the lesser-known Ibrahim successor to a line of distinguished Abbasid rulers, or that there was unanimous enthusiasm to take up arms on behalf of the usurper. One might have thought the rebels would have chosen al-Ma'mun's brother al-Qasim, the third heir apparent in Harun al-Rashid's line of succession. Having been governor of Egypt and territories further west, al-Qasim commanded considerable power and was a far more likely choice to replace the deposed commander of the faithful, but al-Qasim remained loyal to his brother. Even within the capital and its environs there was support for al-Ma'mun, not only from the governor of Iraq—that was to be expected as he was the vizier's brother—but surprisingly enough among various commanders of the abna' who a short time earlier had defended the city against al-Ma'mun's Khurasani army. No doubt, the loyalists had a realistic vision of the likely outcome of the struggle that was unfolding.

By 819, the rebellion had been crushed as various rebel commanders joined forces with the standing caliph and his superior armies. The caliph then marched into the city he had forsaken and was to abandon again in favor of his beloved Khurasan. The path to his success was sealed by a convergence of two events that arguably remain no less mysterious than his choice of an ʿAlid successor. In 818, Jaʿfar ibn Sahl was murdered in his bath by members of the caliph's guard; following that, the caliph, stunned at the loss of his client and longtime mentor, had the assassins executed. Such dramatic deaths generally give rise to conspiracy theories in the medieval Arabic chronicles. It did not take much imagination to see that the fortuitous death of the vizier, allegedly the architect of the policy favoring an ʿAlid succession, left the caliph able to shift the onus for that ill-timed decision onto the dead public servant; the execution of those responsible for assassinating the vizier was intended to indicate that the caliph played no role in an act that conveniently served his purpose. His hands were shown to be clean on both counts.

More important yet was the concurrent death of ʿAli al-Rida, which gave rise to even more fanciful interpretations than the murder of the caliph's right hand. Some said the ʿAlid grew ill and expired after having been fed a poisoned pomegranate by an aide of al-Maʾmun; another tradition maintains that the caliph himself offered his heir apparent pomegranate juice liberally sprinkled with a deadly substance. As we have already seen from the account of the Prophet's victory dinner at Khaybar and the death of ʿAli's alleged heir Muhammad ibn al-Hanafiyah, political assassination by use of poison is a well-known literary trope. When there is no forensic evidence to declare the deliberate taking of a life, it is always easy to claim death by poison or strangulation, effective means of murder which leave no telltale marks of foul play. In any case, with these two principal players gone, only Ibrahim the usurper had to be accounted for. As a rule, the early Abbasids did not do away with those who broke ranks within the family but instead kept them from any levers of power or placed them under house arrest for a period of time as was the case with rebellious uncles of al-Mansur. Ibrahim was, by all accounts, a fairly innocuous figure, more given to the refined arts than to politics; and so after a period of comfortable containment, he was allowed to return to poetry and the like, his brief misadventure notwithstanding.

The Creation of Slave Regiments: An Attempt at Correcting Structural Imbalances in the Imperial Army

The war between the brothers and the rebellion in the name of Ibrahim ibn al-Mahdi underscored the fragile nature of the imperial army's loyalty, a sign of a crack in the universal Islamic empire and a clue to the incipient decline of the regime. Al-Ma'mun's two victories resolved only the issue of who was to be commander of the faithful. The Baghdadis remained, despite two defeats on the field of battle, fully entrenched in their political and military sinecures; such was the power emanating from the capital city. However much the Abbasid grip on the periphery of the empire was beginning to loosen and even if the caliph now ruled—unofficially—from Khurasan, Baghdadis could still claim their city to be the economic hub of the realm. Al-Ma'mun did not find the vitality of the city enchanting. He twice returned to the more familiar and friendly surroundings of Khurasan for fear he would never be able to command the full loyalty and affection of the imperial center. Ibn al-Muqaffa's advice to al-Mansur regarding the creation of a fighting force fully dedicated to the Abbasid ruler simply did not account for the corrosive effect of unforeseen political contingency and self-interest anymore so than did the intricately designed urban planning for the government sector at Baghdad. The Abbasid government described in the previous chapter might be compared to a bicycle whose wheels were compromised by loosened spokes that gave way one at a time. The rider could continue to ride the bicycle by exerting greater effort at lower speeds but inevitably the absence of a full complement of strong spokes weakened the wheels making this means of transportation inoperable.

Having discovered that the imperial army, whether stationed in Baghdad or Khurasan, was fully capable of acting in its own interest, particularly when loyalties could become fluid, the Abbasid caliphs, especially al-Ma'mun and his successor, his brother Muhammad al-Mu'tasim, looked for new forces to prop up the regime. This did not mean disbanding the tens of thousands of warriors already in service; any such move would have resulted in a massive rebellion that would have invited civil conflict among competing elements within the Abbasid family where the likes of another Ibrahim ibn al-Mahdi might be co-opted to step forward and proclaim himself commander of the faithful. Rather, the two caliphs, especially al-Mu'tasim, sought to augment the existing forces with an infusion of new regiments recruited from the Islamic West (Maghrabis); groups from beyond the Jaxartes (Shashis); and various Iranians from Transoxiana, that is, the farthest eastern reaches of Khurasan. The further subjugation of lands beyond the river Oxus in al-Ma'mun's reign also brought significant numbers of Turkish slaves to the center of the Islamic empire, a trend that gave rise to the regular acquisition of such slaves by al-Mu'tasim who used them to form an elite regiment within the larger imperial army. In addition to the considerable number of individual slaves purchased directly from the east, the caliph also acquired a number of Turks, who already belonged to various Abbasid notables. Included in this second group of slaves were persons who were soon to become the commanders of the newly formed Turkish units as well as confidantes of the caliph and other caliphs to follow.

The servile Turks were not recruited exclusively to serve as the caliph's praetorians—for that, he had his trusted household guard and security police. Given their considerable fighting skills, especially as mounted archers, the Turks soon became individual fighting units supplementing, but not replacing, the other regiments of the imperial army. As were the servile Turks, many of the new fighting men were recruited from the distant provinces of the east—what is today Central Asia. The result of mixing these newer forces with the freemen of the old imperial army was a fighting force of considerable ethnic diversity which, at first glance, spoke of an even more universal empire. One notes in this respect the attempt of the contemporaneous essayist al-Jahiz, a client of the Turkish vizier al-Fath ibn Khaqan, to demonstrate a common bond, even as regards blood, among all the diverse elements of the Abbasid army. One suspects the hired pen of the Turkish official is as disingenuous as he is ingenious in pleading his case. In other writings, he is only too happy to express racist views. Be that as it may, as a matter of course, the addition of the new units from the east made for increased friction between the different elements of the imperial forces.

Although a regular regiment within the army, the Turkish contingents quickly became the most important single unit in providing the Samarra-based caliphs with a sense of overall security. In addition to their fighting prowess—pregnant women were said to miscarry at the sight of the fearsome Turkish warriors—what most attracted al-Mu'tasim to the newly formed Turkish contingents was their servile status. The Turks are frequently referred to as mawali, which in our previous discussion generally meant "clients." As regards the Turks, the term would seem to reflect a general as opposed to technical legal meaning. To refer to the Turks as mawali did not suggest that the Turkish officers and men under their command were attached to the caliph by well-defined ties of clientage similar to those which bound to the Abbasid sovereigns slaves and manumitted slaves (also called mawali) within the their household and the civilian bureaucracy. But the designation mawali for the Turks did imply that their loyalty to the ruling house and the person of the commander of the faithful transcended any other loyalties. Indeed, what other loyalties could they have cultivated, brought as they were in servile status from lands far removed from Iraq? In effect, they became the caliph's personal contingents within the broader framework of the imperial forces; that is, they were in effect his mawali. As long as the caliph inspired the confidence of the Turks as with the politically astute al-Mu'tasim, the bonds between the commander of the faithful and his newly acquired privileged regiment remained secure. To be a slave or manumitted slave of the caliph was a mark of distinction and was often perceived by others as a source of considerable influence. It is true that slavery coincided with the very origins of Islam and had deep roots in the pre-Islamic cultures of the Near East; all the leading Muslims possessed slaves, including the Prophet himself. But the *mamluk* or military slave institution did not blossom until the reign of al-Mu'tasim (833–842) when it first served as a central factor in the formation of Islamic military society.

One might view the conception of forces tied exclusively to the commander of the faithful as the logical outgrowth of earlier efforts to professionalize the army along the lines suggested by Ibn al-Muqaffa' to the Abbasid caliph al-Mansur, whom readers will recall was in many respects the caliph most responsible for shaping the institutions and nature of early Abbasid rule. However, unlike the free regiments billeted in Baghdad and Khurasan who could and did exercise a measure of independence in politically charged situations, such as the choice of various commanders to follow Harun against his brother al-Hadi or of the Khurasan army to declare itself for al-Ma'mun rather than follow the command of al-Amin, the reigning commander of the faithful situated in Baghdad, the servile Turks were presumed to be nothing less than the personal forces of the caliph and were thus entirely dependent on his patronage. In a society largely governed by informal structures and dependent on ties of personal loyalty and leadership rather than the formalized politics of universally recognized government institutions, the advantages of the Turkish regiments and, more generally, of certain forms of slavery would have appeared self-evident. When the populace of Baghdad rioted against the presence of Turkish horsemen galloping through the crowded streets of the city, al-Mu'tasim was fully disposed to move his new regiments and the seat of government to another location, an endeavor that led to the creation of Samarra, that sprawling city sixty miles north of Baghdad.

As at Baghdad, the imperial army at Samarra was billeted in quarters separate from those of the general populace. But that separation would not suffice for the Turks and other servile units from beyond the Oxus.

The caliph placed them in areas that were essentially walled off, not only from the general populace, but also the other military contingents. The elaborate system of walls and private entrances was intended to keep the Turks out of harms way presumably so as not to repeat their experience in Baghdad. A hippodrome was also constructed to allow them to gallop their horses without trampling others under foot. Some scholars believed the hippodrome to be a race course, but it is more likely that the cloverleaf shaped structure served as a training ground for cavalry combat at which the Turks excelled above all others. And yet, the enforced separation of the Turks was not enough for al-Mu'tasim; he sought not only the physical isolation of his prized forces of mawali, but a seemingly strange and unprecedented social isolation as well. He forbade the Turks to take wives from the existing pool of available women. Rather, he paired them exclusively with handpicked women of servile status. The Turks were not permitted to divorce the wives chosen for them. These women were considered so valuable by the caliph they were inscribed, as were the men, on the military roll and received a permanent monthly allotment.

What could have prompted so unusual an arrangement? Perhaps the answer lies with the exception to the rule. Only when these women had produced male offspring, thus providing more slaves to stock the servile regiments, were the Turks permitted to seek women of their choice, for the purchase of individual slaves to serve in the Turkish regiments was likely to have been very expensive. The same was no doubt true of waging continuous war to restore the fighting units to full strength with new men taken captive in distant campaigns against the nonbelievers. Breeding a fighting force locally was an idea that might have appealed to the caliph's plans for the future. Whether or not these attempts at social engineering were maintained over a period of time cannot be ascertained. Nor do we have any inkling of the number of prospective troops that might have been born to the women selected. Neither the physical isolation nor the social isolation of the Turks is likely to have survived the rapid growth of the city. By all accounts, Samarra suffered the same fate as Baghdad. Over time, the meticulous plans outlined by al-Mu'tasim fell victim to urban sprawl. It is then very possible that the Turks became better acquainted with the broader society of the city and realm. Nevertheless, the mamluk or slave institution remained powerful in influencing the course of politics throughout the remaining decades of the formative period of medieval Islamic civilization; it played an even more significant role in the Islamic polities of later times when mamluks beyond the Abbasid realm established dynastic polities of their own.

Looking back at the first Islamic century, we see an army of independent Arab tribal forces loosely united by religious ties and prospects of conquest and material gain. Such an army was difficult to discipline and had to be manipulated by rulers and commanders familiar with traditional Arab culture. In the end, the central authorities and their representatives failed to curb Arab tribalism, and ultimately the "Arab Kingdom" of the Umayyads collapsed because of the manner in which it privileged tribal prerogatives rather than create a professional army and more universal Islamic society. In contrast, the first Abbasid century also began with an army of independent Arab tribal forces, albeit forces whose identity had been reshaped by years of active duty in Khurasan and later in Baghdad, giving rise thereby to an army bound by ties of loyalty to the ruling house. Six decades of Abbasid rule ended with still further changes in the composition of the military: a slave corps of Turks taken prisoner in Transoxiana augmented by men born to slave women specifically chosen to replenish the Turkish regiments. These regiments were part and parcel of a collection of warriors consisting of the old imperial armies and new recruits from other regions far removed from Baghdad and Samarra. By the end of al-Mu'tasim's reign, the Abbasid military represented a highly diverse organization whose loyalty to the commander of the faithful was conditioned by the exigencies of the moment, the caliph's claims to rule over the universal ummah notwithstanding.

In time, even the servile Turks learned how to promote their own interests when they deemed it necessary. Their loyalty to a strong ruler such as al-Mu'tasim was unquestioned; the same could not be said for all those who followed him, particularly when the troublesome question of succession surfaced as it often did and the Turks were asked to choose sides. Unlike the caliph's clients in government service, collectively the Turks represented a formidable force that could make and break the commanders of the faithful. Attempts to keep the army united behind each and every reigning caliph could and did fail in different moments of crisis. That is, the internal dissension within the ruling house of Abbas that surfaced as a result of contested successions and family intrigue created opportunities for self-aggrandizement that challenged the loyalty of the one institution capable of keeping any regime in power: the imperial army, most particularly the Turkish officers who were closer to the caliph than the generals of the other regiments and whose absolute loyalty was counted upon. When the Turkish generals deliberately murdered the caliph al-Mutawakkil in 861 a dangerous line had been crossed.

One may think of al-Mutawakkil, however mercurial in temperament and impolitic in behavior, as the last of the truly powerful Abbasid caliphs. Never again would an Abbasid sovereign demand and receive from the armies of the realm the type of allegiance routinely expected by the likes of al-Mansur, al-Mahdi, al-Rashid, al-Muʿtasim, and even al-Mutawakkil before he allowed his reign to come unhinged. The direct intrusion of the military in court politics simply eroded the trust that had previously existed between the commander of the faithful and his leading generals. How and why did this come to pass? We have no evidence to give proper explanation, but we suspect the princes of the Mansurid line destined for future rule no longer cut their political teeth in powerful provinces under the personal tutelage of the existing caliph's trusted clients, the kind of political tutoring that allowed the future caliphs to win the confidence of the administrative and military apparatus they would rely on when at the helm of the state. The military, which had become increasingly powerful at court at the expense of the civilian officials, were less inclined to manage the subtleties of the complex politics of the ruling family and the family itself lacked the accumulated political wisdom to avoid the pitfalls of potentially disputed successions.

Al-Mutawakkil's murder marked the first time an Abbasid commander of the faithful had been assassinated as part of a deliberate plot hatched by military officers; with that an undeclared rule had been broken. In short order, chaos ensued. With only a thin veneer of caliphal authority in evidence, conditions in the realm deteriorated. The army that had been the backbone of the Abbasid state had been reduced to warring factions and subgroups within factions. The esprit de corps among elite units began to unravel. Leading commanders behaved as if they were mafia dons rather loyal clients of the commander of the faithful. The troops whose loyalty the generals commanded at times reflected bands of fighting men rather than the traditional formations: a thousand professional soldiers each for the front rear and flanks of a major fighting unit. The caliphs, who until al-Mutawakkil's death had been treated with at least deference by their military clients, became subjects of abuse and targets of assassination; heirs apparent were similarly dealt with. The Turks had come to realize that although they remained technically the clients of the caliphs, they were in effect capable of bending them to their will. To make matters worse, civil war nearly broke out once again; this time between the partisans of Baghdad and those of Samarra. The conflict was only resolved when all the parties concerned helped themselves to the public treasury; the leading rebels were given estates with rich tax revenues; and the unpopular standing caliph who was partially responsible for precipitating the crisis abdicated in favor of the relative he had initially displaced as commander of the faithful. In the 870s and following the return of the caliphate to Baghdad in 892, central authority was restored to some extent. However, that was not due to the prestige of the standing caliph, nor because of the prestige of the institution he represented, but to the successful maneuverings of the vice regent al-Muwaffaq, an extraordinarily able administrator capable of commanding the respect of the bureaucracy and army alike. One cannot exaggerate what al-Muwaffaq was able to accomplish given the hand he was forced to play, but in the end the fortunes of the once-proud universal Islamic empire had changed dramatically and were never fully reversed. Measured against the reputation and strength of the Abbasid caliphate in the eighth century, the respect for the dynastic order of the Banu Abbas had diminished along with the size and power of their realm. By the fifth decade of the tenth century, the politics of old had come to an end. The formative period of Islamic governance was replaced by a new order that marked the onset of what might be described as the intermediate period of medieval Islamic civilization.

11

The Changing Political Climate: Heralding the End of the Formative Period of Medieval Islam

The hundred years or so between the succession of Harun al-Rashid and the caliphate's return to Baghdad witnessed both great cultural achievement and incipient political decline. On the one hand, Arabic, having taken root among non-Arabs, became widespread throughout the realm and gave rise to an efflorescence of magnificent literary production. This was true of belles lettres, historical writing, descriptive geography, religious scholarship, and scientific and philosophical works. Men of court and of commerce alike underwrote the efforts of literary figures and of learned scholars in a wide variety of intellectual endeavors ranging from preserving the wisdom of the Greeks and other ancient peoples to what became known among Muslims as the Islamic sciences. Various caliphs gathered about them a coterie of poets and court singers, whom they rewarded regally for their literary and artistic efforts. Some noted figures became the caliphs' boon companions, spending considerable time with them in their private chambers. Other rulers, al-Ma'mun the most noted among them, were themselves men of considerable learning, or at the least displayed a measure of intellectual pretension, a tribute to the value assigned to scholarship in varied disciplines and to the literary arts.

Even among the Turks, described by medieval Arabic authors as course and uncouth louts (a reflection of the distant and austere climes from which they came) one finds a figure such as al-Fath ibn Khaqan. While serving as vizier in the court at Samarra, this well-bred and cultured Turk was benefactor to the likes of al-Jahiz, arguably the greatest Arabic litterateur of his time, if not all the Middle Ages. One might go so far as to claim that while he remained in office, al-Fath was the significant arbiter of cultural taste in the second Abbasid capital. Admittedly, al-Fath was not the average Turk. He was raised at court from childhood, given a formidable education, and spent his career in public service; that is to say, in contrast to most of the leading Turks, he was destined for notoriety as a cultured public official rather than a commander of military forces.

At Baghdad, the pace at which grand public buildings were erected may have slackened dramatically during the period in question. We have noted earlier how Harun al-Rashid became disenchanted with the city; how al-Ma'mun preferred Marw in Khurasan to the official capital in Baghdad; and how al-Mu'tasim moved the seat of the realm to Samarra. But the hundred years in which Baghdad experienced a sense of official neglect did not mark the end of monumental building efforts throughout the realm, particularly at the new capital Samarra. Before it was abandoned by the Abbasid caliphs, Samarra was the site of an unprecedented building campaign that produced monuments that could very well have rivaled the so-called Wonders of the World, the fabled edifices that captured the imagination of the modern West, when it went about imagining the glories of an exotic more ancient East. Unlike the Colossus of Rhodes, the Lighthouse of Alexandria, the Hanging Gardens of Babylon, and similar monuments that remain only as memories of great and distant civilizations, the fairly rapid abandonment of Samarra left many of its magnificent palaces and the grand mosques intact—ruins to be sure, but still fully visible *in situ*, like the Pyramids and temples of Egypt and the Great Wall of China, "wonders" that still bedazzle onlookers.

The design and dimensions of the structures at Samarra truly excite the imagination. Take, for example, the grand mosque with its tall and graceful minaret modeled after the ancient ziggurat towers of Mesopotamia, those unusual structures with serpentine staircases. That, in this one and only case, a pagan tower thousands of years old should have inspired a minaret from which Muslim monotheists were called to prayer represents an ironic cultural turn. How and why the caliph and his architects decided on the so-called Malwiyah or "Serpantine [Minaret]" still calls for an explanation. What can be said is that the minaret, which rises to the height of a modern multistory building, requires an adjective beyond imposing. The same can said for the mosque itself. As a means of comparison, the largest athletic structure in the United States is currently is a university football stadium with a standard playing field of 360×150 feet and a seating capacity in surrounding stands of approximately 110,000. The mosque at Samarra, even without the walled outer court in which it was situated, was three times the size of that modern playing field and no doubt was visited by tens and tens of thousands of worshippers at the required Friday prayers. The ruins of the contemporaneous palaces bear similar testimony to the grand scale of the building activity of the time and the attempt to give visual expression to the greatness of a polity of truly imperial claims, albeit diminished imperial capabilities. The grandeur of Samarra when the empire had already undergone incipient decline serves to indicate the delusions that afflict rulers at times of profound historical change.

Measured by intellectual activity and monumental architecture alone, one would have to conclude the hundred years between the ascension of Harun and the return of the caliphate to Baghdad was a period of unprecedented achievement. And indeed it was, but only if one discounts the disruptive internal politics of the times, the loss of control in distant provinces (to be discussed shortly), and, related to the latter, the manner in which the Abbasid empire was less and less able to bear up under the weight of increased expenditures at the center while receiving diminished taxes from the periphery. As the caliphs at Samarra were building on a grand scale, petty dynasts, situated well beyond Iraq, though nominally loyal to the caliphs, operated somewhat independently of the central authorities and withheld tax revenues for their own personal use. One writer observed the oath of allegiance may have been rendered to the caliph in the Friday sermon (*khutbah*), but the taxes (*kharaj*) were retained by the local governor. That last turn of events was bound to have a more lasting effect on the political course of an empire beginning to fray at the edges than building on a grand scale to preserve the image of its ruler.

What caused the caliph Ja'far al-Mutawakkil to virtually bankrupt the realm by creating a city within the general area of Samarra known after him as al-Ja'fariyah? After building his own city, a prideful al-Mutawakkil reportedly claimed: "Now I know I am [really] a ruler because I've built myself an administrative center in which I'll dwell." The comment was no doubt a reference to the degrading circumstances to which al-Mutawakkil had been subjected years earlier when his elder brother, the standing caliph al-Wathiq, sought to deny him his proper place in the line of succession. As did several earlier caliphs, al-Wathiq refused to honor the established heir-apparent so that he might favor his own son, a beardless youth who had not yet reached his majority and who, because of his slight stature, seemingly disappeared when cloaked with the robes of the commander of the faithful immediately after the caliph's unexpected death. In the end, the mawali who served in the highest echelon of the government and Turkish commanders of note, took stock of the situation, recognized the absurdity of following the late caliph's dictates and resurrected the fortunes of the discredited brother who then became the caliph al-Mutawakkil. Like so many of his predecessors whose claims to rule were initially disputed or called into question, Ja'far al-Mutawakkil seemingly compensated for that initial lack of recognition by encasing himself in monumental architecture; witness al-Mansur's Round City of Baghdad; al-Mahdi's palace complex at al-Rusafah; al-Rashid's capital at al-Rafiqah; and al-Mu'tasim's decision to leave the potentially rebellious Baghdadis to build an administrative center of his own in Samarra.

What staggers the imagination are the costs of what may be called al-Mutawakkil's folly, a series of palaces, mosques, access roads, and canals reportedly erected and dug at a cost in excess of 275 million dirhams, and that only for the buildings, roads, and canals reported. One could speculate that when one factors in all the construction work initiated by the caliph, the sum total could easily have risen another fifty to seventy-five million silver coins, and that does not include an administrative center he began to build near Damascus for reasons yet unexplained. Adding up the costs of the construction undertaken by al-Mutawakkil at Samarra, the geographer Yaqut informs us that none of the other rulers at Samarra built on so grand a scale and spent so much of the public treasury. The question before us is what such expenditures, if accurately reported, mean in relation to the larger expenses and revenues of the empire. What effect did such seeming profligacy have on the political and economic health of the Abbasid realm?

The Financial State of the Abbasid Realm

Sources of the time produce three lists of tax revenue for the Abbasid state in the ninth century. The first, reportedly for the reign of al-Ma'mun, indicates that the annual land tax in medieval Iraq generated (cash) revenues of some 28 million dirhams, that is, somewhat less than al-Mutawakkil spent on his personal residence alone. The total tax revenue of the entire Abbasid realm is given at 332 million dirhams (cash), roughly equal to the estimated sum spent by al-Mutawakkil on all his building enterprises. Perhaps more revealing yet are the figures reported by Qudamah ibn Ja'far, as he was an expert in taxation. He gives the yearly tax in Iraq (probably for the reign of al-Mu'tasim) at 130 million dirhams, but that includes kind as well as cash. The revenues from the empire as a whole are 388 million dirhams, cash and kind, an indication that the taxes shipped to the central treasury from provinces outside Iraq had begun to fall, presumably because petty dynasts withheld tax revenues for their own purposes. Khurasan, which accounted for cash revenues slightly greater than Iraq in the reign of al-Ma'mun, now produced cash and kind that was that was approximately one-third of the Abbasid heartland—a dramatic drop, especially when one considers that al-Ma'mun ruled from Khurasan virtually throughout his reign and could have been expected to retain a large share of the taxes from that province rather than forward it to his governor in the capital Baghdad.

The third list, that of Ibn Khurradadhbih (b. ca. 820 C.E.), a learned public official, probably reflects conditions in the latter half of the century when he was attached to the government bureaucracy at Samarra. In his account, the cash and kind are given as falling to 78 million in Iraq and 300 million altogether. When are thus left with the impression that al-Mutawakkil's building projects alone may have exceeded the tax revenues of the entire empire for a given year. How can we massage these figures so they become meaningful for responsible scholars and not mere bits of information that are at best only suggestive of economic conditions? Allowing for the fluctuating value of the silver dirham—canonically set at 1:10 to the gold dinar—it would appear that al-Mutawakkil's building projects cost 200 times as much as al-Mansur expended on the magnificent Round City at Baghdad, a structure which included the caliph's palace and the great Friday mosque adjoining it.

Let us not forget that Baghdad was the economic hub of the empire because of its most advantageous, indeed unique, position astride the major land and water routes. It thus generated revenues because of its commercial importance, much like New York and London, the great financial capitals of modern times. Samarra, lacking such natural advantages, could only have served as a drain on the resources of the Iraqi hinterland and the empire as a whole much like Brasilia and Islamabad, centers of government built *ex nihilo* by modern rulers seeking visual manifestations of greatness at the expense of effective planning. To what extent was the local economy able to offset the enormous costs of urban development, particularly when the new capital city was dependent for sustenance of all sorts on a slowly shrinking imperial environment?

A decade or so after the completion of al-Mansur's grand edifice, the yearly rents and taxes from the markets at Baghdad reportedly yielded 12 million dirhams. Put somewhat differently, the ruling authority recouped approximately three times its initial investment in palace and mosque construction with a single year's revenue from the local economy; and that did not include the taxes of the agricultural zone established by al-Mansur on the outskirts of the government complex. In al-Muʿtasim's time, the total revenues derived from taxes and rental properties in Samarra amounted to ten million dirhams plus a reported 400,000 dinars (or four million dirhams according to the canonical rate of 1:10 for gold and silver coinage) from agricultural investment on the other side of the Tigris. In his son al-Mutawakkil's reign that would have represented 1/40 the costs of the caliph's elaborate building projects. Allowing for new commercial zones that were developed in the city proper by al-Muʿtasim's successors al-Wathiq and al-Mutawakkil, the revenue from commercial establishments would no doubt have risen above the fourteen or so million dirhams that entered the caliph's treasury, but even if the yearly taxes and rents doubled, it would only have represented one-twentieth the cost of al-Mutawakkil's lavish building campaign. The caliph's personal residence alone would have cost 30 percent more than the yearly commercial revenue from a city almost equal in size to Baghdad.

All these and similar data, however sketchy and inferential at best, seem to indicate that the Abbasids were less and less able to cope with the hemorrhaging of the state treasury and the fall of the dirham in relation to the gold standard dinar. A thirteenth-century author reports that in the time of al-Mutawakkil, the dirham was pegged to the dinar at 1:25. Medieval authors describe the shortfall at Samarra by comparing it to the earlier mismanagement of state funds by the Barmakids, the trusted client family who personally served the Abbasid caliphs, especially Harun al-Rashid. For his habitual free sending, the most important of al-Rashid's Barmakids, Jaʿfar ibn Khalid reportedly paid with his life; other members of the family saw their personal fortunes confiscated. In similar fashion, al-Wathiq and especially al-Mutawakkil sought to stem the fiscal bleeding of the state treasury by expropriating the money and possessions of a wide range of wealthy bureaucrats, who as clients of the

caliph and therefore entirely dependent on his patronage were in no position to resist. Many of the public officials kept estates and warehouses in
Baghdad, no doubt because the economic climate was more conducive to
investment in the old capital, but also because they could conceal the
extent to which they had become wealthy and thus guard against the
confiscation of their accumulated riches.

The savage treatment of key officials, which included incarceration,
also tended to weaken the very agencies that kept the state afloat. In a
comic aside a medieval author, well informed of developments in
Samarra, reports that al-Mutawakkil had to release two noted public
officials whom he had imprisoned, as there were no experts left to run
the bureaus of taxation and estates. The accusations against clients
for embezzling funds, whether true or invented, amounted to the pot
calling the kettle black. Rather than halt or at least scale back construction
in a time of declining revenues, the caliph deliberately expropriated
monies to offset costs, and in doing so damaged the bureaucracy that
managed the state, as well as tearing asunder the implicit understandings
between patron and client that represented one of the pillars of Abbasid
rule. His threat to deal harshly with leading Turkish officers undermined
the other prop of the regime, its military forces.

Some modern historians suggest the intermittent confiscations at
Samarra (and also Baghdad) were an attempt to curtail the growing power
of those Turkish commanders who were most closely linked to important
individuals within the state bureaucracy. But the victims also included
individuals who do not seem to have been overly involved, if at all, with
politics at court. Many of the public officials were Christians, raising
the possibility they were brutally treated as part of a general campaign
reportedly launched by the caliph against the dhimmis or protected
monotheist minorities.

Although al-Mutawakkil's invoking Islamic legislation against the
minorities was said to have been universally applied, the Christians are
clearly singled out in our sources. Among the various measures allegedly
taken against the dhimmis was the confiscation of one in every ten residences, a figure of great magnitude, as the Christians still represented a
significant percentage of Iraq's population well into the ninth century
C.E. If the confiscation of these properties is correctly reported, allowing
even for considerable exaggeration in the number of residences taken by
the state, the resort to discriminatory legislation, which was rarely
invoked, and, more often than not, indifferently applied by Muslim
authorities, may be more a question of the caliph's depleted treasuries

than his religious intolerance. Describing al-Mutawakkil's actions against the protected minorities, the court poet 'Ali ibn Jahm reportedly recited:

> The [distinctive] yellow badges [that mark the dhimmi] divide
> Between the righteous [Muslims] and the errant [nonbelievers]
> Why should the wise care if the errant [dhimmis] increase?
> There will be all the more loot [for the caliph's taking].

The Loss of the Periphery

Whatever interpretation one wishes to give the aforementioned confiscations, they are undoubtedly linked to an economic reality that extended well beyond political squabbles at the Abbasid court in Samarra or even the massive building campaigns. The vast and wealthy province of Khurasan, the breeding ground of the Abbasid revolution and historically a principal source of revenue and manpower, had been administered since 820s by the Tahirids, the family of al-Ma'mun's great general Tahir ibn al-Husayn. Although formally subjects of the caliph, the Tahirids, themselves native Khurasanis, or at least of Khurasani descent, became in fact the rulers of all the provinces east of Iraq including distant areas from which the regime had brought large numbers of captives to serve in the slave regiments of the imperial army. So powerful had the Tahirids become, they withheld tax revenues for their own purposes and went so far as to omit any mention of the caliph's name in the Friday sermon, a symbolic gesture of their relaxed ties to the central authorities to whom they still paid tribute. Moreover, they administered the older capital when the caliphs moved to Samarra. One would assume their behavior in Iraq was more properly respectful of the caliph and the native Baghdadis who no doubt still remembered the role played by Tahir in the war between the brothers.

A proper history of the Tahirid petty dynasts (821–873) has yet to be written, and so we cannot determine the effect they had on the overall economy of the Abbasid realm. However, it does not take much imagination to conclude based on the available evidence, especially the revenue lists previously cited, that the central authorities never recovered the lost revenue emanating from the east. Nor is it likely that the Abbasids fully recovered that source of funds after the Tahirids were replaced by a series of other petty dynasts beginning in the last quarter of the ninth century. Whatever taxes might have found their way back to Baghdad after the caliphate was restored to the older capital in 892 could hardly have matched the previous levels in the heyday of the universal empire. Although the house of Abbas continued to rule for another four hundred years or so, they were never able to reestablish firm control over the vitally important eastern territories as one petty dynasty supplanted another, all at the expense of the regime in Baghdad. Beginning in 868, similar developments took hold in the near west, as Egypt became nominally independent under its Turkish military governor Ahmad ibn Tulun, founder of the so-called Tulunid dynasty (868–905), a regime that remained firmly fixed within the Abbasid constellation but often acted in its own on interests until the Abbasids reasserted their rule. Only a few decades later, the Abbasids saw their authority compromised once again under the Ikhshidids (935–969), Turks who formed a petty dynasty like that of the Tulunids. As had happened earlier in North Africa, the Abbasids were unable to regain full control of provinces they once commanded with some measure of authority.

With Abbasid rule essentially limited to Iraq and Syria, the only area left for large-scale combat was the lengthy frontier with the Byzantines and that of the provinces to the northwest. The Byzantine frontier, which featured continuing conflict with the nonbelievers, had long been a place to dispatch independent-minded troops, stouthearted but unruly individuals and groups who might cause problems for the central authorities. The frontier dividing the Muslim world from that of the Christian enemy also served as a magnet for Muslim fighters of all sorts who were prepared to offer their lives for the faith. Over the centuries it had given rise to a distinctive culture that tended to attract militant Muslims and breed a militant Islamic society. More often than not, the Muslims held the upper hand along the frontier, but, in its weakened state, the caliphate of the late ninth and especially the tenth century suffered losses of territory and treasure as a resurgent Christian enemy pressed its advantage.

As regards the northeast, ceding control of the frontier to petty dynasts is likely to have created serious problems. We have already noted the decline of revenues from regions once directly controlled by the central authorities. The Samarra caliphs were also dependent on captives from distant campaigns against nonbelievers to staff the ranks of their slave corps. With state revenues declining and access to booty and slaves, usually obtained from Central Asia, more and more limited because of the rise of local dynasts, the caliphs had difficulty in regenerating the servile regiments maintaining the standing imperial army. It was as though the situation that emerged after the rapid Arab conquest of the seventh century had slowed was reenacted two centuries later. Large standing armies that did not earn their keep in combat and/or expand the territorial and hence tax base of the Islamic center were not cost-effective instruments of rule.

The Baghdad and Samarra regiments were assuredly more responsive to firm leadership than were the anarchical Arab tribesmen of the early caliphate, but the extraordinary profligacy of the caliphs and the loss of booty and military bonuses that accompany constant and successful warfare created economic circumstances that tested the patience of even loyal troops. Accurate figures are difficult if not impossible to come by, but it would appear that military salaries ('ata') remained relatively stable over generations. In the absence of booty and bonuses, the only hedge against inflation was to increase the monthly allotments of food and other necessities (rizq) for the armed forces and their dependants. But that could be difficult in times of shortages or general economic decline. Time and again, our sources relate that merely meeting the military payroll was a problem in the ninth century. One would not be surprised if the early decades of the following century revealed the same. The failure to provide routine service pay at the proscribed time led to undermining not only the authority of the caliph but that of his military commanders as well. It is perhaps no accident that some semblance of order was restored during the last two decades of Abbasid rule at Samarra, that is, during the "regency" of al-Muwaffaq, a son of al-Mutawakkil who was caliph of the realm in all but name. Al-Muwaffaq was an extremely capable administrator and a decisive leader, but his success in consolidating what was left of Abbasid rule was advanced, ironically enough, by a dangerous insurrection of marsh Arabs and black servile laborers (Zanj). Given the unusually difficult terrain of Iraq's southern marshes, the campaign against the rebels demanded the full energies of an imperial army that had become relatively inactive. It took two decades of constant fighting to finally put an end the so-called revolt of the Zanj. Nevertheless, the die was cast. Even the defeat of the Zanj and the return of the caliphs to Baghdad in 892 could not postpone the further decline of Abbasid rule and the universal empire they had created.

The shrinking of the imperial center did not guarantee a long life for the newly created autonomous polities beyond. Having arrogated a place for themselves in the sun, the petty dynasts also became victims of the structural imbalances plaguing the Islamic polity from its very inception. Foremost among these imbalances was the absence of a clearly defined line of succession. From the time of the Prophet's death, it was determined that any commander chosen to lead the faithful had to be of Quraysh, the Prophet's tribe, and preferably the clan of Hashim, Muhammad's extended blood relatives. Following the ascent of the Abbasids, the choice of caliph was further restricted to a member of the Prophet's house. For the 'Alids this meant a direct descendant of the Prophet; the Abbasids, as noted previously, defined the Prophet's house so that it included, as well, the descendants of their progenitor, his paternal uncle al-'Abbas. The election of Muhammad's early successors was dictated by notables of the realm; with the ascent of dynastic orders, succession was determined within the inner circle of the ruling family. Although Muslims most often closed ranks once the choice was made, the decisions could be revised or unofficially negated by various factions within the ruling house or the larger Muslim polity.

When those factions perceived a fatal weakness in the ruling regime or when Muslim societies buckled under the stress of more cosmic strains (say, a failing economy), rebellious energies could be channeled toward open insurrection or some accommodation with the existing caliphs that allowed local rulers great license to conduct their own affairs. As regards open rebellion, formal marriages of convenience could, were, and indeed had to be arranged between disgruntled elements of society and notable figures with the requisite blood ties to replace the incumbent commander of the faithful. In the latter case, provincial rulers continued to recognize the suzerainty of the caliph but acted in a more or less autonomous fashion, with or without the caliph's formal permission. The preferred venue for open revolt was generally away from the prying eyes of the caliph's trusted security; the successful rebellions tended to be distant from the immediate reach of his most reliable military forces. But rebellions that did not invoke the name of an authentic would-be caliph, be they armed coups against established authority or local and regional governors merely taking license to withhold taxes from the central authorities or otherwise disobey direct commands, could not and did not withstand the test of time. The petty dynasts who managed to gain de facto control over slices of an overextended Abbasid realm simply lacked the credentials to perpetuate their hold on the territories they controlled. Historical circumstances may have given them temporary power to bend their subjects and the caliph alike, but as they were not members of the Prophet's house, they had no stamp of legitimacy that could sustain them in times of crisis.

Put somewhat differently: With the larger Islamic polity officially declared a religious community that transcended the boundaries of ethnicity, geography, and linguistic distinction, no regional polity headed by a provincial ruler could *formally* declare its independence—note the emphasis on *formal*. For official purposes, those who were nominally independent of the caliphs still had to recognize and be recognized by the titular head of the indivisible Islamic community. That said, endorsing the caliph, and being endorsed by him in turn, was hardly sufficient for independent-minded governors to establish dynasties of their own. The longevity of de facto ruling houses that first emerged in the ninth and early tenth centuries were sustained, by and large, by highly visible instruments of power. But once the power of the local or regional rulers to coerce dissipated, or once these rulers were threatened by a greater external power, no mechanism existed that allowed them to perpetuate their weakened states, as did the commanders of the faithful. The Abbasid caliphate was destined to endure even when the house of Abbas lost actual control of its realm because its stamp of legitimacy was deeply ingrained in the consciousness of Sunnite Muslims. A greatly weakened Abbasid caliph might not have been be able to rule as freely and confidently as did the likes of al-Mansur and his immediate successors. He might even have been a ruler in name only, but, if it was any consolation at all, no one other than a member of the Prophet's house could rule legitimately. Only the 'Alids, who were also blood relatives of the Prophet, had the credentials to formally depose the ruling order and establish a dynasty of their own—fortunately for the Banu Abbas, 'Alid politics during the heyday of Abbasid rule tended more toward accommodation than confrontation, especially when the 'Alids took stock of political realities. Their occasional armed rebellions always resulted in catastrophic failure. But once Abbasid rule contracted, and the caliph, at times with great difficulty, exercised real control only over Iraq and parts of Syria and Arabia, the partisans of 'Ali's descendants, the emergent Shi'ites, found considerable room for maneuver.

In the tenth century, an 'Alid dynasty, the Fatimids (909–1171), firmly established itself, at first in North Africa, and then in Egypt and parts of Syria. This was no petty dynasty paying lip service to Abbasid rule in return for unofficial regional independence, but a Hashimite rival of imperial pretensions and, beyond that, of imperial capabilities. The aim of the Fatimids was not to win the official approval of the Baghdad caliphs to pursue their regional ambitions but to replace the caliphate of old with dynasts of 'Ali's lineage. And so, two rival caliphates, each empowered by blood ties to claim legitimacy, existed concurrently for well over two hundred years. Seen in retrospect, the establishment of the rival Fatimid caliphate might be considered, with some justification, as marking an end to the formative period of medieval Islam, those early centuries in which the political and religious institutions of classical Islamic civilization were first shaped. Such as it was, the break with the past, if indeed we may label the tenth century a break, can most easily be seen in the world of politics. The transcendent Islamic *ummah* was always an idealized rather than real community, and while it remained and still remains a compelling ideal for the Muslim faithful, it could not in and of itself serve as the foundation of a single universal empire. The imperial order of the Abbasids, an Islamic polity that had at one time extended from North Africa to eastern Iran and the lands beyond, had become too fragmented to ever be reshaped as a whole, nor would the competing empire of the Fatimids take its place. Formed originally in North Africa and then extended to Egypt and parts of the Fertile Crescent and Arabia, the first 'Alid dynasty would fall victim to circumstances similar to those that undermined the authority of their Hashimite rivals, particularly internecine conflict within the ruling house.

It is curious, but not surprising, that the intensive efforts of the Fatimids to win the allegiance of the Islamic world closely mirrored that of the Abbasid revolutionaries who overthrew the Umayyad usurpers. As did their Hashimite cousins, the Fatimids employed propagandists called *du'at* and grounded their propaganda in images of an earlier and more idyllic age when the Prophet himself commanded a unified Muslim community. Like the Abbasids, they also constructed great monuments, built an administrative capital (al-Qahirah, or as it is known in the West, Cairo) adjacent to an already existing commercial center (the old Islamic foundation Fustat), and laid the groundwork for large-scale commerce and trade with a relaxed style of rule that encouraged the possibility of developing a true civil society. But no Islamic regime of the Middle Ages, or even in modern times, could resist the temptation of imposing coercive measures when additional revenues were needed in times of perceived economic or political unrest. Shortsighted policies based on immediate needs thus undermined the future welfare of Islamic societies at large. Despite many successes, the 'Alid resurgence could not sustain its truly impressive gains. The partisans of 'Ali's descendants could never apply the coup de grace to the house of Abbas and unify the lands of Islam as the Abbasids had in the glory days of the caliphs al-Mansur and al-Mahdi.

In time, the Fatimid state, a polity of extraordinary cultural and political vitality, would fall victim to the same stresses and strains as befell their Abbasid cousins, but with more damaging consequences. After more than two centuries of Fatimid rule, the fabled Saladin, a Kurd of Sunnite origins, overthrew the last of the 'Alid rulers and declared his allegiance to the emasculated Abbasid caliphs in Baghdad. As did all the petty dynasts before him, his recognition of the Abbasid branch of the Prophet's house did not prevent him from consolidating the vast territories of a state he ruled independently of the commanders of the faithful. Although they retained their status as the titular heads of a universal Islamic community that had in fact been rendered into disparate parts, the Abbasid caliphs had become largely irrelevant as regards exercising political control. Ironically, that very irrelevance enabled the Abbasid caliphs to remain in theory the leaders of the universal ummah; weakness became the key to the longevity of their regime. Unlike the Abbasids, the Fatimids could not survive their decline, for Saladin's shift to Sunnite Islam meant the once powerful 'Alid dynasts had no legitimate place in the ruling order, not even a ceremonial role as commanders of the faithful.

The Ayyubids, Saladin's dynasty (1169–1250), were in turn replaced by the Mamluks, a powerful sultanate or ruling authority led by former Turkish slaves whose power, like that of the Ayyubids, was based largely in Egypt and Syria (1250–1517). The Mamluk sultanate lasted until the Turkish Ottoman Empire conquered vast stretches of the Abode of Islam, including what had been in earlier times the Abbasid heartland of Iraq. The emergence of the Ottomans resurrected the universal Islamic empire, one that would in time extend deeply into Europe as well as the Near East and North Africa. Only in Iran and points east did the Ottomans face rival polities that successfully resisted their advances. During the five centuries in which they ruled, the Ottomans did more than control a vast territorial expanse; they were not a petty dynasty writ large, so to speak. Eventually proclaiming themselves caliphs as well as sultans, the Ottoman rulers appropriated a legitimacy hitherto reserved for the true family of the Prophet and reconciled, at least in theory, the problem of who had the authority to rule the ummah. With that, still another decisive period had begun in the long history of the Islamic world, one that is recognized as distinctive by all historians of the Islamic Near East.

In the last chapter, we noted al-Jahiz's ninth-century epistle on the virtues of the Turks. The author's bold attempt to link the Turks to the Arabs and the Prophet's family was undoubtedly regarded by learned readers of his time for what it was: clever intellectual musings and linguistic pyrotechnics to please his Turkish patron, the vizier al-Fath ibn Khaqan. In sum, the work commissioned by the vizier was an extraordinarily clever piece of writing but nothing more. Ottoman claims to the caliphate, which persisted as did their regime for some four hundred years, were taken more seriously in light of the great power the ruling house was able to wield for so long a period of time. Even during the incipient decline of the Ottoman regime in the nineteenth century, local rulers who were nominally independent of the Ottoman Porte, or even contested the central authorities in Istanbul for territory beyond their local or regional domains, formally recognized the legitimacy of Ottoman rule. In effect, they were the modern equivalent of the powerful petty dynasts who could not disavow the concept of a universal ummah led by legitimate successor to the Prophet. In the end, Turks, forging the modern Turkish nation, and not the subjects of the empire, formally abolished the Ottoman dynasty in 1924 and along with it the sultanate and caliphate. The transcendent ummah remains nevertheless an idea of powerful emotive force among many Muslims today. Some strident followers of the faith even call for the restoration of a Sunnite caliphate, albeit without reference to a particular person to assume the role of commander of the faithful.

Epilogue: The End of the Universal Islamic Empire in Baghdad

We have already noted that by the tenth century, the eastern borders of what had been the universal Abbasid Empire were controlled by a series of relatively short-lived petty dynasties. All the while the empire of the Banu Abbas continued to be celebrated in the dynastic heartland and the east as if the non-'Alid branch of the Prophet's house actually ruled a transcendent Islamic community. But that impression would undergo a subtle change that was to represent a turning point in the history of the Abbasid state. In the tenth century Iranian peoples from regions of the Caspian Sea, the area called by the Arabic geographers Daylam, began a massive movement into western and central Iran. The causes of this movement from a peripheral region that had been nominally independent of Abbasid control into areas closer to the Abbasid center have yet to be ascertained. What is clear is that by 936, the Daylamites were able to establish dominion over a vast swathe of territory including the provinces of Fars, Khuzistan, Kirman, and Jibal. But unlike the Abbasids (and also Fatimids) who nearly always sought a highly centralized authority with which to rule under the direction of a single commander of the faithful, three sons of a Daylamite military commander named Buwayh divided the conquered provinces they controlled among themselves and respected each other's authority, thus beginning a dynasty known as the Buwayhids or Buyids that would last for 230 years (932–1062). One is tempted to say they came to the same insight, though in all likelihood quite inadvertently, as did Harun al-Rashid. The reference is to when the caliph divided a still powerful Abbasid realm among his three sons, a move Harun designed in order to decentralize an unwieldy empire and establish truly legitimate regional polities, each under a strong and universally recognized leadership. At least, that is our understanding of Harun al-Rashid's policy.

In 945, the Buyids entered Baghdad and took effective control of the Abbasid state, a situation that was continue for 110 years before the Saljuq Turks replaced the house of Buwayh in Iraq. If one had to seek a dramatic watershed in the fortunes of the Banu Abbas, an event from which they would never recover, and a date which might serve to mark the end of the formative period of medieval Islamic politics, Ahmad ibn Buwayh's entry into what had been at one time the political fulcrum of a vast and universal empire, ought to be seriously considered. What is particularly interesting is how and why the Buyids, who had Shi'ite leanings, conducted themselves with regard to the Abbasid caliph and his family, longtime rivals of the Hashimite branch they themselves favored. Why not turn to the Fatimids or form alliances with the Qarmatians, Isma'ili elements in the nearby provinces of Iran who had links with the Fatimids? Acting in what they likely perceived as their best interest, a long line of Buyid rulers recognized the symbolic authority of the politically impotent Abbasid caliphs, although they gave them no room to exercise any means of political independence. In such fashion the Buyids retained their own independence vis-à-vis potential Shi'ite rivals. An old and infirm dog was certainly less of a nuisance or threat than vigorous young lions.

The Buyid rulers of Baghdad were not above taking regnal titles as did the caliphs; and so they were called the likes of 'Adud al-Dawlah, which signified at the same time "the support, or [right] arm of the dynasty." They may not have declared themselves "commanders of the faithful (*amir al-mu'minin*)," a title reserved for the caliphs, but they assumed the role of "supreme commander" or "commander of the commanders (*amir al-umara'*)." The Buyids who ruled in the caliph's name could and did build magnificent palaces of their own as the Abbasids had. The emir 'Adud al-Dawlah is said to have spent considerable time studying the caliphal enceinte in the capital in an attempt to emulate the physical surroundings of the Abbasid sovereign, and in the end built his own magnificent Dar al-Mamlakah in Baghdad. He also married into the caliph's family, taking as his bride the caliph's daughter. But at the moment of his greatest triumph, and in full public view, the real ruler of Baghdad and all of Iraq was asked in accordance with protocol to kiss the ground before acknowledging his sovereign the caliph. At first, 'Adud al-Dawlah was inclined to refuse, or so we are told. In truth, he had the power to depose the caliph if he wished; indeed, he might have been able to dispose of him altogether. But taking stock of the situation, the Buyid emir yielded, as he was a political animal who fully grasped the consequences of expected political behavior. The caliph could always be manipulated behind the scenes to suit Buyid interests; there was no need to tamper with society's expectations in public, crass behavior that might play badly in the streets and cause unwanted disturbances. A litterateur writing of court ceremonials described the event and declared 'Adud al-Dawlah as a man of true *adab* or "culture," that is to say, an individual who in this case had a fine command of the nuances of political etiquette.

Even so partisan a Shi'ite as the historian Ibn Tabataba could appreciate the complex irony of the situation that existed between an Abbasid caliph that commanded no formidable army and petty dynasts who could crush him in an instant, if it were only a matter of exercising raw power. In citing the opponents of the Abbasid regime after it had turned impotent, he draws attention to the Shi'ite Buyid 'Adud al-Dawlah (949–983); the Sunnite Saljuq Turk Tughril Bak (1038–1063) who replaced the Buyids as master of Baghdad in 1055; and the Iranian Khwarizm Shah 'Ala' al-Din (1200–1220) who took control of the Abbasid capital ca. 1200. All of the above dominated the city as the caliph seemed powerless. However, the question of who holds power and how power is held can be exceedingly subtle, as the author points out in a passage that shows grudging admiration for the manner in which his unworthy cousins from the house of the Prophet managed to beguile the Islamic world into recognizing theirs instead of 'Alid claims to the mantel of Muhammad: "All this [tribulation] and yet Abbasid rule continued. No dynasty was powerful enough to put an end to their rule and obliterate the traces of their existence. On the contrary, each of the aforementioned rulers [of those dynasties] would assemble and lead large armies before arriving at Baghdad. And when he arrived, he would seek an audience with the [Abbasid] caliph; and when admitted to the caliph's presence, he would kiss the ground before him. His utmost wish was that the caliph would grant him to some [honorific] position, and present him with a standard and a robe of honor [which would give visual expression to his own legitimacy before the public]. When the caliph did that, the ruler would kiss the ground before him and would walk astride the caliph's stirrup, the latter's saddle cloth tucked under his arm."

One detects a certain wistfulness in the Shi'ite's declaration of events. He seems to ask, how is that God could have allowed his undeserving cousins to command the stage of history after power had deserted them, while the legitimate claims of his noble and deserving 'Alid family went unheeded. That such symbolic appearances before the caliphs were still important centuries after the founding of the dynasty and the loosening, and then dissipation, of caliphal control is perhaps a tribute to the firmness and skill with which al-Mansur and his early successors laid the foundations of their regime. At the earliest stages of the regime, perhaps even before it came to power, the Banu Abbas came to the realization that divisive ethnic loyalties and demands for regional independence should not be allowed to compromise the powers of the emergent dynasty. Concessions to groups bearing other loyalties would have served only to recreate the conditions that afflicted the early caliphate and the house of Umayyah. What was initially required was a polity based on the intensive concentration of power and the cultivation of new attitudes that would create for all public elements, a vested interest in the orderly process of government. The manner in which the Abbasids created the requisite institutions for establishing a universal empire that could command the allegiance of its widespread and diverse constituencies has been treated earlier in this book, as were the limitations of these policies. What interests us at present are the attempts of the Banu Abbas to give visual expression to the new order.

As no Muslim rulers had done before them, the Abbasid commanders of the faithful surrounded themselves with symbolic trappings of authority. So dazzling and highly stylized were these visual manifestations of Abbasid rule that it was difficult, even when the caliphate declined, for many subjects to distinguish between form and substance. A sense of community had been created and had taken hold even as the shifting realities of power changed the political landscape in the years of caliphal decline. The most humble subject of the regime as well as the most learned political theorist understood only too well that a sense of community and a recognized communal leader was preferable to a state of anarchy. The caliph may have been without real power but the symbolic presence of the caliphate as an institution gave the populace reason to believe their world, however troubled from time to time, would be marked by a sense of continuity that provided hope for the immediate and distant future. The petty dynasts, who lacked credentials to claim the caliphate itself, understood only too well that to tamper openly with the expectations of the populace was to invite their own downfall, and so they along with the caliph performed their assigned roles until the Mongols conquered Baghdad in 1258.

Because they were not Muslims, the Mongols did not fully appreciate the delicate balance that had been achieved between the Abbasid sovereigns and the powerful men that controlled them. When Hulaku, the son of Genghis Khan, considered executing the Abbasid ruler in Baghdad thus signifying the end of the caliphate and the dynasty, he was warned by elements of the local populace to desist. For an act of such magnitude might very well tamper with the cosmic order of the universe. The end of the caliphate might cause the sun to be veiled, the rains might cease to fall, and the earth might fail to give rise to all vegetation. It is reported that Hulaku was initially persuaded by the dire prediction of events to come. Whether or not the Mongol actually experienced any sense of doubt is very much beside the point. Until the tragic moment that was about to unfold, the presence of a caliph, no matter how chosen or how legitimate, had long been recognized as a prerequisite for established order. In the end, the caliph was brutally tortured and put to death. As it turned out, the sun continued to shine, the rains continued to fall, and the earth continued to yield its bounty. If that were not enough, the Mongols eventually converted to Islam and established a vast empire that extended from Iraq through Iran and beyond. Their advance was halted in Syria by the Mamluks, and they would later lose Iraq to the Ottoman Turks. But they retained their lands in Iran and areas further to the east. The Mongols, contrary to their reputation as barbarians, actually proved to be highly tolerant, not only of Islam but of all religions including Judaism and Christianity—at least they looked favorably on the other monotheist faiths before their conversion to Islam. Moreover, they established an elaborate court of their own and became great patrons of the arts and letters. The one blemish they could not expunge from their record was ending the Abbasid caliphate in Baghdad. Although some future Abbasid caliphs were installed for appearance's sake in Egypt, the final act of a remarkable story had been written. If 945 did not mark an end to the formative period of the Islamic Middle Ages as we have suggested, 1258 could be considered such a turning point, certainly as the regards the political landscape. Between them, the Mongols and their heirs—the great dynasties of Iran—and the Ottoman Turks who at one time held sway over extraordinarily vast domains, put an end to the primacy of the Arabic speaking peoples in the Fertile Crescent, Egypt, and points further west. By the seventeenth century, if not before, Istanbul, at the crossroads of Europe and Asia Minor, and the great cities of an Iranian domain that extended into Central Asia became the new fulcrum of the Islamic world.

PART III

RELIGIOUS SCHOLARSHIP AND PIETY

12

The Qur'an and Its Commentators

All Islamic religious writing touches base at one point or another with the public utterances of the Prophet Muhammad, the last authentic revelations received by the final and most perfect messenger of God. Even historical and belletristic works dealing with subject matter not of a strictly religious nature draw reference to God's word. Throughout the Middle Ages and beyond, rulers and common folk alike were inclined to cite the Qur'an when considering their actions in temporal as well as religious settings. Drawing attention to the message sent by God to Muhammad was commonplace in framing understandings of this world and the world to come, in expressing deep feelings, in justifying actions, and in establishing relations with non-Muslims. Most important, it was also one of the foundations of Islamic law. In virtually all respects, it was much like the Hebrew Bible for Jews and the Old and New Testament for Christians.

We speak of the Qur'an as Muslim scripture, but in Muhammad's lifetime and the first generation or so of his followers the Qur'an was not yet formed as we have it now, a book between two covers with a fixed text and established structure. Precisely when the Prophet's individual revelations were transfixed into a final organized written text, thus becoming Muslim scripture, is a point of contention. But even before the existence of a formal text, the message of the Qur'an was a dominant fact in the life of the nascent Muslim community. It supplied the early believers with liturgical matter for their prayer services and other communal gatherings; it provided material for the spiritual observances and meditations of individuals; the power of its language and ideas helped to persuade skeptics and to win new converts; it set the tone for relations with Jews and Christians; and perhaps, above all, it established principles, laws, and rulings regarding many urgent issues.

Before the Quran

It appears that at first these materials circulated widely in oral form, beginning in Arabia and then wherever the early Muslims went. However, these oral materials were also committed to writing in a desultory fashion. Fragments of these texts reflecting different circumstances were assembled until at some point they became redacted, or, as the Arabic sources say, "collected," into the fixed text of the Qur'an. This redaction had enormous consequences for Muslim theology, jurisprudence, and religious life in general. We should be aware, however, by the time that the Qur'anic message became fixed in the authoritative versions that have been preserved over a millennium and more, it had already spread widely and would then continue to do so, with or without the support of the fixed, redacted text. For even though Muslims have always venerated the written Word, the Qur'an and its message have also, to borrow a phrase from the Arabic historical narratives about the collection of the Qur'an, constantly inhabited "the hearts of men." Accordingly, it may be useful for us to keep in mind a distinction between Muslim scripture, that is, the redacted, promulgated text of the Qur'an, and the Word in the sense of a divine Qur'anic message that many Muslims have literally memorized, and that most Muslims have carried around with them wherever they have gone throughout their lives. This includes the many believers who cannot read, or at best are able to pronounce the written Arabic text without formal knowledge of the language.

The central place of the Qur'an in Muslim spiritual and social life can help us to understand any number of historical issues, of which a good example is the long-term spread and expansion of Islam. This expansion of a religion and religious community, though occasioned by a rapid and decisive conquest and perpetuated by a Muslim ruling establishment, must have been driven at least in part by a willingness to accept the Prophet's message and the general authority of those who applied it to changing circumstances. Although, as a rule, Muslims usually did not compel or even actively encourage the local populations to convert to Islam, over the long term most of these local populations accepted the new faith for a complex variety of reasons.

Clearly, one key to understanding the eventual conversion of so many people and groups to Islam is the very nature of the Qur'anic message.

Not only did this message have a powerful rhetorical appeal, it had an internal logic and structure that spoke directly to people in many environments, first to Arab tribesmen in early seventh-century Arabia and then to varied communities far beyond. Even those Arabs and non-Arabs who were attracted to Islam by concerns of a more worldly nature came to recognize the power of the Qur'an's language and the force of its message. By contrast, it is somewhat more difficult to perceive why the redactors of the book between the covers chose to structure it as they did. The written text before us presents interpreters, past and present, with numerous problems regarding the meaning of specific words and passages, as well as the broader message of its many disjointed narratives.

Later on, we shall outline some of the interpretive approaches to the Qur'an in both traditional Muslim and modern Western scholarship. For now it may be useful to think, in a preliminary way, of two broad avenues of approach. The first of these is what we find most often, in both Muslim and non-Muslim (especially Western) environments: identifying passages in the Qur'an and setting them in their context. Not surprisingly, this context consists mainly of the life of Muhammad and the history of the earliest Muslim community. However, it also turns out that despite various attempts, it is quite difficult to contextualize the Qur'an solely on the basis of the text. Some of these difficulties have already been referred to in our survey of Muhammad and the rise of Islam. As a result, scholars who have set out to perform this work of contextualization have always needed to make use of a later and more extensive Arabic/Islamic literary tradition that included biographical and historical works, collections of traditions relating to the life of the Prophet, tracts that are subsumed under the Arabic label *adab* or belles lettres, and above all, a vast and ongoing literature known in Arabic as *tafsir*, that is, Qur'an commentary and exegesis.

For traditional Muslim scholarship, the basic goal of contextualizing the Qur'an and recovering elements of the Prophet's life has been to achieve a more profound and detailed understanding of God's will and the obligations that it imposes on Muslims. In modern Western scholarship, on the other hand, the goal of contextualizing the Qur'an has generally been to establish a more correct or "scientific" narrative of the life of Muhammad and the origins of Islam. To a remarkable extent, however, all these scholars and interpreters (traditional and modern, Muslim and non-Muslim) have shared this broad approach, together with traditional methods and techniques. One simply cannot do Qur'an scholarship without having mastered the material of its numerous commentaries, supra-commentaries, and related texts—a vast body of literary production that over many centuries has both informed the interpretation of Muslim scripture and has been informed by it.

Although they fully recognize the importance of events taking place in real time, those scholars who embrace the second approach to the Qur'an are often less concerned with the concrete circumstances of Muhammad's life and times. Accordingly, they sometimes shy away from establishing or confirming a sequential narrative of events—a difficult, indeed impossible, task under any circumstances. Instead, they search the Qur'anic material for patterns and structures that reflect or constitute coherent doctrines, sources of motivation, and world views. The goal here is to discover the inner logic of the Qur'anic message. Although this approach may not greatly improve our understanding of the concrete circumstances of the rise of Islam, it can help us to answer some of the questions we have posted: Just what was it in the Qur'anic message that people found so appealing? How and why did this message reverberate through so many lands and populations?

2nd way to interpret Qur'an

Each of these broad approaches has its strengths and its drawbacks, be it for the modern orientalists seeking to recover the origins of Islam or devout believers, past and present, emphasizing the importance of the text for Muslim belief and observance. In any case, it is important to keep in mind that the Qur'an has always been, both in Muslim dogma and in the general understanding of Muslims, literally the Word of God transmitted to the world through His quintessential and last messenger, the Prophet Muhammad. As such it represents the most complete, direct, and final message that humanity has received from its Creator. The Qur'an, although fixed in time and place for humankind, is nevertheless the first source for the divine law of Islam that has evolved over time as an eternal guide for Muslim perceptions and behaviors.

The Transmission of the Qur'an

Like other scriptures in other religious traditions, the Qur'an that is available to us in the form of a book was the result of an extended process. Muslim scholarship calls this "the collecting of the Qur'an." We only know about this process by relying on a wide variety of later Muslim writings, especially Qur'anic exegesis and commentary. We also have specialized works devoted to the collection of the Qur'an, tomes that were produced when the Qur'anic sciences had grown into an important and sophisticated discipline within that wide body of learning that constituted the so-called religious sciences of the Islamic world. During Muhammad's prophetic career, the revelations that he received were disseminated mainly through oral communication. This is not surprising for a society, like that of western Arabia, where literacy was not likely to have been widespread and where it is not clear to what extent the system for writing Arabic was well-developed. Throughout history, such oral presentations have also been the accepted means by which those who claimed the gift of prophecy have communicated with their audiences. However, there are indications that Muhammad dictated at least some revelations to several trusted scribes, including, it is said, Zayd ibn Thabit, his close associate. Muhammad may well have wished to establish an authoritative text during his own lifetime, but if this is so, the evidence for it is, to say the least, sparse. Barring the unlikely discovery of Qur'an fragments of the first generation of Muslims, the issues surrounding the growth and transmission of Muslim scripture will remain at best clouded.

After Muhammad's death, we are told that the first caliph, Abu Bakr, in an effort to establish a text of the Qur'an, assigned the task to this same Zayd ibn Thabit. Zayd found and assembled fragments written down on all sorts of material including shoulder-blades of camels, stumps and branches of palm trees, papyrus, bits of cloth, stones, and as we have already seen, verses located "in the hearts of men." In this way, we are told, a unified text found its way into writing, but then, strangely enough, it was said to have been set aside for a good twenty years. The project was renewed when 'Uthman was caliph. Once again, Zayd ibn Thabit was assigned to the task, this time with a committee of notables. How they used the previous written version (if in fact it existed) is not clear. But one way or another, at least according to the most commonly held Muslim view, the committee produced an authoritative text of the Qur'an. This text, which we know as the 'Uthmanic recension, forms the basis of the Qur'an that we now have. From his capital in Medina, 'Uthman reportedly sent copies of this text to the most important garrison cities of the Islamic empire.

Unfortunately for modern scholars, none of these first Qur'an manuscripts have survived. Nevertheless, we can surmise some things about them. First, they were supposedly written in the dialect of the Hijaz (the area of western Arabia which includes Mecca and Medina). This dialect had its own characteristics, of course, which led to some odd spellings. (Here we have an explanation for some of the spelling rules that still make life difficult for students of Arabic.) Second, the 'Uthmanic Qur'an was written in what we sometimes call the "defective script" of early Arabic writing: "defective" not only because it gave few indications of vowels (long or short), but also because its indication of consonants was highly ambiguous, with a single character often indicating one of several possible consonantal sounds. One can imagine by way of comparison a text written in English without dotting the *I* or crossing the *T*, and also without vowels to guide readers. In fact, what the 'Uthmanic text provided was a ductus, or set of simple letter shapes, which in this case represented a series of consonants (or possible consonants). Most subsequent Muslim scholars considered this ductus authoritative. And in any case, for people who already knew the text by heart, none of this presented any difficulties. However, since the text was destined to be the object of careful, literary transmission in the future, the way was now open for endless variants and disagreements as to how Muslim scripture should be read and understood. In the following generations, Muslim scholars invented ways to indicate consonants (when these were ambiguous), short and long vowels, diphthongs, pauses, and so on. However, all these signs were merely superimposed onto the letter shapes of the 'Uthmanic Qur'an, which remained (at least in theory) immutable and unchanged.

We are told that each of the copies distributed by 'Uthman was bound in the form of a codex (*mushaf*) or written manuscript. We are also told that when these codices arrived, they had a mixed reception. In the Iraqi garrison town of Kufah, an old companion of the Prophet, 'Abdallah ibn Mas'ud, opposed the newly promulgated text and upheld the superiority of a text that he had in his possession. Here we have the beginning of the long history of "readings" (*qira'at*). It seems there were local traditions of reading the Qur'an as well as in Medina, the first capital of the Islamic empire. As we do not have these early manuscripts of the Qur'an, with their "local" readings, we must derive our information entirely from a variety of later literary works and some papyrus fragments. It is therefore extremely likely that many different ways of reading the Qur'anic text existed simultaneously, including the ones associated with Ibn Mas'ud, at least in the form in which we know about them from our later sources. Muslims believe that however different, these readings derive in essence from the fixed consonantal letter shapes already established by the 'Uthmanic recension. Be that as it may, it seems reasonably clear that in the first decades and even centuries of Islam, there was considerable variety and latitude as regards reading scripture. With time, however, there seems to have been pressure to conform to a more standard reading. This does not mean that variants were simply outlawed: after all, who was to decide which was *the* correct reading? It was rather that control was exerted over when and where readings could be recited, and how they could be used in scriptural exegesis. This process culminated in the work, in the early tenth century C.E., of the Iraqi scholar Ibn Mujahid and the emergence of seven acceptable systems of variant readings, each of them associated with respected scholarly authorities.

Afterward, other scholars found other systems of readings to be acceptable, and so the "seven readings" became expanded to "ten readings," and then fourteen and more. In this way the matter of readings became systematized, though not greatly simplified. We now use one of the aforementioned seven readings adopted in the printed edition of Muslim scripture that appeared in Egypt in 1923. That text has become authoritative throughout the Islamic world although the sequence of particular verses varies slightly in different printed editions. Modern Western scholars citing the Qur'an follow the authoritative text usually giving both verse numbers, one in either in brackets or parentheses. Richard Bell's translation into English, first published in 1937, attempted to reconstruct Muslim scripture by adding parallel columns which rearranged the order of particular verses and even fragments of verses. His ambitious project provides much food for thought but, to put it gently, has elicited considerable skepticism among his Western peers, let alone the Muslim faithful.

The early authoritative versions of the Qur'an were initially written on all sorts of materials including parchment, vellum, papyrus, mosaic, and stone. When paper arrived in the Near East, beginning in the ninth century C.E., it served this purpose as well. We have already seen that the Qur'an stands apart from the rest of the early Islamic literary tradition in Arabic in that we have surviving examples of Muslim scripture before 800 C.E.—other early literary texts are preserved in manuscripts whose colophons and scripts date them to later times, indicating that the earliest texts were displaced by later copies and/or preserved in part by later authors. However, there are no surviving manuscripts or inscriptions of the Qur'an from the generation of Muhammad and his immediate followers. The earliest example is in the Dome of the Rock in Jerusalem, built by the caliph 'Abd al-Malik in the early 690s. And here there is a difference (of detail, not substance) between the verses cited in this inscription and the supposedly "fixed" text of the 'Uthmanic recension, an indication that the final version had not been established at that point of Islamic history. At any rate, from 'Abd al-Malik's reign onward, Qur'anic manuscripts and inscriptions become common in the Islamic world.

Presentation and Style

The Qur'an's structure

We have mentioned in our previous discussion of scripture and historiography (see Part One) that the Qur'an does not have the form of a single, sequential narrative. It is organized into 114 surahs, a term that may roughly be translated as "segment" or "chapter." Most scholars hold that surah is derived from Hebrew *shurah* meaning a "row" and by extension "a line of writing" though not "a verse of scripture," which in that language would be signified by *pasuq*. Bell, who sees Muslim scripture in close relation to eastern Christianity, looks to the learned language of the eastern Christians and prefers a Syriac cognate *surtha*, but admits that philologically that is difficult to maintain because, in this case, the consonants of the Arabic and Syriac words are not interchangeable as they are in Hebrew. As regards the origins of the word "surah," cultural borrowing from Hebrew or Syriac was not and is not now a concern of traditional Muslim scholars. The same holds true for the Arabic word for Qur'anic verse "ayah" which has been linked to Hebrew *oth* "letter" and, for Bell, Syriac *atha*. While both etymologies are possible, they are anything but certain. There is a clear difference between a letter of the alphabet and an entire verse. One has to be wary indeed before assigning cultural borrowing with absolute certainty when the evidence is problematic.

The order of the surahs

The first surah, "The Opening" (*al-Fatihah*), is a sublime prayer that is familiar to all Muslims. The remaining surahs are arranged (roughly) in order of descending length. That is, the second surah is the longest (with 286 verses, many of them quite long); the third is the next-to-longest (with 200 verses); and so on, until we arrive at the last surahs, which are quite short (only six brief verses in 114). However, this principle of descending length does not apply strictly each time. It has been suggested by Abraham Geiger, the nineteenth century German scholar whose earliest work was devoted to Jewish influences on Muhammad, that this system of ordering the surahs might have been based on the manner in which Jews had an earlier time arranged the so-called "orders" of the Mishna, a Jewish law code dating back to the third century C.E. Such a claim is, to say the least, also highly problematic. The arrangement of the Qur'an remains open to other suggestions.

Each surah has a name, a superscription assigned to it very early in the transmission of the text. These names may derive from a surah's overall content, or from a particular episode or reference. Thus, the first surah is called "The Opening" or "Beginning." The second is known as "The Cow" because at one point it tells the story of Moses, the Israelites, and what Jewish scripture describes as the incident of the Golden Calf (or heifer) but the Qur'an describes as a cow. It is fairly common for tradition to preserve more than one name for a surah (such as the ninth, known as "Repentance" or "Acquittal"). In any case, these names are the way in which the surahs have been known over the centuries. It is only recently that a system of numbered chapter and verses has come into use, and this has still not completely displaced the old system. Traditional Muslims still refer to the chapters by name although the printed editions of the Qur'an and most of the traditional Qur'an commentaries number the verses and some also number the surahs.

Each surah, with one exception, begins with the invocatory formula "in the name of the merciful, forgiving God" (known technically as the *basmallah*). In several surahs, we find next a brief series of Arabic letters situated between the invocation and the text of the surah itself. These letters, sometimes referred to as "mysterious letters," remain a mystery despite various theories proposed to explain them. No doubt the most attractive explanations come from numerological and mystical imaginings and serve as a segue to Qur'anic exegesis and commentary that we will discuss briefly below. The content of a surah cannot be predicted from its place in the overall sequence, and often not even from its name. In general, a long surah is likely to cover several different topics, while a short surah may be devoted to only one. The most basic tool that traditional exegesis has applied to this problem has been the division of the surahs into the categories of "Meccan" and "Medinan." This refers, of course, to placing the surahs, that is, the moment they were revealed, within the chronology of Muhammad's prophetic career, which is neatly divided by the Hijrah, the "emigration" from Mecca to Medina.

Often this division seems persuasive. Many so-named Meccan surahs have eschatological fervor, describing the terrible events surrounding the end of days leading up to the Day Judgment, an early theme of Muhammad's message to the polytheists of his native Mecca. The Medinan surahs tend more toward legal and doctrinal phraseology, disputation with adversaries, and so on, a reflection of Muhammad's concerns when he established his *ummah* and became, as W. Montgomery Watt put it, statesmen as well as Prophet. However, this system also presents problems. First of all, the earliest Qur'an does not make this division for us, so once again we have to rely on later scholarly tradition to tell us which surah belongs to which period. And here the tradition is far from unanimous, presenting many contradictory views. As we have mentioned previously in our description of the Qur'an as a historical source, this division into two large categories supposes that each surah is in fact a coherent unit and was, so to speak, revealed all at once. Yet a close look at many of the surahs shows that this is often not so. Indeed, traditional Muslim exegesis recognized that different passages within a single surah could have been revealed at different times of the Prophet's career.

Qur'an's prose —

Most of the Qur'an was delivered in a kind of rhymed prose (*saj'*), in which a series of sentences or periods all have similar, rhymed endings. A particular rhyme will often apply to a piece of text that forms a unit, both in its subject matter and its rhetoric; a change in the rhyme may indicate (though it does not have to indicate) that a change in subject matter has taken place as well. In any case, the outstanding characteristic of the Qur'an, from the point of view of language and rhetoric, is its overwhelming eloquence. This eloquence has become a theological dogma: for Muslims, the Qur'an is, as a matter of principle and by definition, the most beautiful speech; its grammar and rhetoric set the standard for the Arabic language as a whole. Similarly, Arabic is declared most eloquent of all languages. Lest we believe these Muslim declarations concerning their scripture is simply a matter of dogma imposed by the guardians of the Muslim faith, countless Muslims—Arabic-speakers above all—have been moved to contemplation and ecstasy upon hearing the Qur'an recited. This is self-evident even in our own time and in many places. Even those non-Arab speakers or those who can pronounce the vocalized letters but cannot understand the text are profoundly moved by the recitation of it. Most recently, Western audiences have been introduced by their media to schools where scores of young Muslim boys are trained to read and recite Muslim scripture in rhythmic chanting, although they may know nothing or little of Arabic language and grammar. The system is not entirely unfamiliar to Orthodox Jews whose earliest introduction to Jewish learning was to acquire the Hebrew alphabet and move from there to learning how to recite prayers without knowing their content, a first step to gradual stages of more advanced learning.

The perspective of the Qur'an —

It is the universally held belief of Muslims that the Qur'an is literally the Word of God communicated to humankind with the Prophet Muhammad serving as transmitter or vessel. Throughout the Qur'an, God addresses either the Messenger or some other audience, employing the first-person singular or plural and often switching abruptly from one of these to the other. But there are many other passages in the Qur'an where God is not so obviously the speaker: prayers, disputations, narratives of events long past, references to current events, and so on. Many of these passages begin with the word "Say!" (*qul*). This has the effect, of course, of making God the author of the words.

Interpreting Scripture: The Emergence of Qur'an Commentary (Tafsir)

Qur'an interpretation began before the book between the covers emerged; the Prophet himself is sometimes credited with some of this work. Several Muslims of the first generations labored long and hard establishing the foundations of Qur'anic exegesis and commentary; these include the Prophet's cousin, the industrious and learned Ibn 'Abbas. Unfortunately, we do not possess any actual texts from the earliest generation of exegetes and commentators; rather their observations are preserved in later works that contain long chains of transmission in which individual accounts are traced back to the original exegete. What follows is an outline of some of the main issues of concern for interpreters of the Qur'an as well as some of the main streams of interpretation.

One of the prime concerns for exegetes and commentators has been to relate Qur'anic verses to the history of the early community and the life of Muhammad. In the early centuries of Islam this was also a concern for the genre of literature devoted to the biography of the Prophet, of which the most famous example is the previously discussed eighth century C.E. book compiled by Ibn Ishaq and preserved by Ibn Hisham (d. ca. 830). Although the biography in our possession has all the features of a straight-forward historical narrative, it often serves to describe the circumstances in which many individual verses first came to Muhammad, and at times does so for entire sequences of verses, so that embedded within the stories is often a commentary on these verses, albeit a commentary that can be so subtle it can escape the grasp of those unaccustomed to the close readings of texts. Most Qur'an commentary is, however, structured rather differently. All the standard commentaries, that is, works that are technically tafsir, are arranged according to surah with appropriate comments following each verse. The most comprehensive commentaries, like that of the ninth–tenth century polymath Muhammad ibn Jarir al-Tabari, can take up multiple volumes and have a set order. Each verse or rather elements within the verse is discussed with regard to philological and grammatical problems arising from the text. The linguistic discussion is followed by an attempt to contextualize the verse so as to give it broad meaning in relation to the life and times of the Prophet. Thus, it can be put to use for didactic purposes, a guide so to speak for all Muslims in all generations. In that fashion, the Muslim Qur'an commentaries resemble the Jewish use of legendary material to explicate biblical verses (midrash) but with a significant difference. The Muslim commentators were apparently the first monotheists to explicate in sequential segments and verses rather than tell a story in which occasional verses were interpolated. Medieval Jewish exegetes would later write commentaries on the Hebrew Bible imitating this Arabic model.

In time, the flourishing discipline of Qur'an commentary came to enjoy high prestige within the so-called Islamic religious sciences. Biography and more general historical works were considered disciplines of decidedly lesser importance. And so as Muslim scholars arrived at the interface between scripture and narrative with regard to the life and times of the Prophet, they tended increasingly to privilege scripture. We see this in the popularity and respectability of an exegetical subgenre called "the circumstances of revelation (*asbab al-nuzul*)." Here it became possible, so Muslims claimed, to identify precisely when any particular verse was revealed to Muhammad, according to place and time. But again, it was the Qur'an and its commentaries and not what we describe as historical works that dictated this subgenre's structure and format, although its debt and more directly that of classical Muslim commentaries on scripture can be traced back to the wide variety of literary sources that we label, for lack of a better term, Islamic historical works.

We have always to ask ourselves to what extent tafsir preserves echoes of how the earliest generation of Muslims understood the Qur'anic message, and, related to that, to what extent did they invent a past that filled in gaps presented by the highly allusive and elusive style of Muhammad's public utterances. Even less-critical modern readers of this medieval literature have been inclined on occasion to throw out the baby with the bath water, holding that tafsir in its varied forms tells us more about then-current Muslim understandings of scripture and what it relates about the life and times of Muhammad than it does about the views of the Prophet's contemporaries. From this perspective, the later commentaries tell us virtually nothing about how the first generation of Muslims received and understood the Prophet's message. While there is every reason to express great skepticism of Qur'an commentary when it serves to explain the origins of Islam, we believe that claiming the tafsir's historical materials are entirely the invention of later times to be a rather harsh judgment. The allusions to events past and present in Muslim scripture must have been understood by Muhammad's contemporaries, otherwise their foundational text would have held no meaning for them whatsoever.

Surely some echoes of that understanding could have been retained by the next generation and then preserved in the later literature. That reservation aside, only the most naïve reader would take all of Qur'an commentary to be an actual reflection of how Muhammad's contemporaries perceived his message.⌡

The early centuries of Qur'anic exegesis reached a culmination with the aforementioned Muhammad ibn Jarir al-Tabari, a native of Iran who settled in Baghdad and died there in 923 C.E. His monumental work *Jami' al-Bayan* provides a summa for the entire discipline. In it we can see the main concerns that animate the work of Tabari and many of his predecessors. Typically, he and the other major classical commentators devote considerable time and attention to issues of Arabic grammar and rhetoric. This is often necessary, because, as we noted, the text of the Qur'an contains many obscure words, difficult grammatical constructions, and so on. Quite naturally, the sciences of grammar and rhetoric as they evolved in the Islamic Middle Ages became closely allied to the study of the Qur'an. One challenge that arises is how to find proof-texts for difficult words and constructions in the Qur'an and in texts other than the Qur'an, especially as all of Islamic literary output postdated Muslim scripture. For the medieval exegetes, the solution was to look to pre-Islamic Arabic poetry, a rather ironic solution at that, since these poems, which predated Muhammad's revelations, were generally devoid of any monotheist message. No doubt, this poetry remained in vogue after the rise of Islam because it titillated the imagination and aesthetic sensibilities of the Arabs.

Precise understanding of the revelations was no mere academic concern. Many verses of the Qur'an have legal and juridical content that is reflective of the times and continued to have legal importance as the Qur'an is the first source for knowledge of the divine law (see the following chapter). Accordingly, medieval Muslims maintained that a fully qualified interpreter of the Qur'an needed to be deeply learned in Islamic law and its subdisciplines as was Tabari. Although not presently considered a founder of one of the major schools of Islamic law, he was one of Islam's greatest jurists; much of his commentary (like that of his predecessors) consists of juridical analysis. However, the main purpose of his analysis is to understand the Qur'an, not the systematic construction of Islamic jurisprudence. Over time, however, the two disciplines grew together, as in the subgenre of Qur'anic explication (which emerged mainly after Tabari's time) called "the prescriptions of the Qur'an (*ahkam al-Qur'an*)." Here we find detailed interpretation of verses of

Muslim scripture that have juridical content. These verses are compared with one another, considered in their historical context, and weighed for their juridical implications and consequences. All of tafsir was, to be sure, a highly technical discipline with many subdisciplines. But the Qur'an also contains broad moral messages that were directed to the Arabs of the Prophet's time, messages that can be more easily extrapolated from the text and arranged thematically by readers exploring the Holy Text.

The Major Themes of Muslim Scripture

How to read the Qur'an

Any search for the patterns and structures of Muslim scripture and, to the extent possible, the inner logic of the Qur'an's message requires a shift in reading the text as a possible reflection of historic moments to concentrating on its broad series of messages. The quickest way for us to orient ourselves to this task is to consider the contents of the Qur'an under a series of thematic headings. By focusing on the themes of Muslim scripture, scholars provide themselves with a safer point of entry into reading the holy text. As we have observed in our discussion of Arabic historiography and the origins of Islam as well as our chapter on the Qur'an and its interpreters, the modern reader who turns to the Qur'an in order to understand developments in Mecca and Medina in the early seventh century will experience frustration, since the text does not actually tell that story in detail, and what echoes of that history are preserved are not presented in chronological order. Because the contextually minded reader requires some semblance of chronology, he or she will have no choice but to turn to sources outside the Qur'an itself, and as has been noted in these pages time and again, those later sources can be exceedingly problematic. Be that as it may, traditional Muslims of the Middle Ages and modern times are less bothered by these concerns for historiography even when they fully comprehend the inherent difficulties.

For the reader who follows a thematic approach, the ordering of the Qur'an represents less of an obstacle to understanding. After all, it is perfectly possible to read that text in whatever order one likes, while identifying certain themes and searching for Qur'anic passages that address these themes. For this purpose it is also appropriate and effective to make use of modern research tools such as the index, the concordance, and searchable databases. Lest we appear overly smug, the attentive reader has to allow that some general themes extrapolated from Muslim scripture can show evidence in various passages of marked differences in outlook and content because attitudes toward religious observance, beliefs, and peoples, and even a basic outlook on life, changed over the Prophet's lifetime. Medieval commentators understood these shifts only too well when they introduced the principle of abrogation to their reading of scripture—that is, they maintained that, where the text seemed to contradict itself, the later revelations took precedence over the earlier. That being the case, we are still left with the conundrum of relying on chronology. Nor can we recover and analyze every theme in the Qur'an with equal certitude as Muslim scripture deals in greater detail with certain themes than with others. These reservations aside, the thematic approach can be revealing and instructive for Muslim and non-Muslim readers alike.

What follows is a sample of some of the broad themes that can be found in the Qur'an. To be sure, the list is utterly incomplete, since some areas (such as wealth, almsgiving, and warfare) receive our attention, while others that must have been equally important to the early Muslim community (such as prayer, inheritance, and marriage) are hardly dealt with. With space limited, it seemed more useful to try to develop a few themes somewhat fully, rather than to summarize everything of interest in a few words. Modern reference works, especially the new and highly informative *Encyclopedia of the Qur'an* (E. J. Brill, Leiden) can help the reader to fill gaps quickly and accurately with cutting edge scholarship. In any case, the themes of the Qur'an and the methods by which we analyze them are endlessly rich. As it is, the themes discussed here are presented with little regard to where they appear in the Qur'anic text (be it the beginning, middle, or end). They are also presented with little regard to how they relate to the life of Muhammad and the history of the earliest Muslim community, since this can only be discovered, and then with no real certainty, by employing the difficult contextual approach spoken of earlier.

Recalcitrant Civilizations

Among the themes of interest in Muslim scripture is that of obdurate peoples whose failure to conform to God's expectations leads to their extinction, a theme also prominent in the Bible and biblical lore. That should come as no surprise as the Qur'an contains narratives and characters that also appear in the Jewish and Christian scriptures, not in identical versions but generally similar. There are also stories that are not biblical but hearken back to a remote Arabian past. There are clear thematic links among all these stories, what we may call recurring scenarios, one of which may be summarized as follows: Sometime long ago, a people lived in flourishing circumstances but then went astray. They may have been indulging their tendency toward heathenism, or else perverting or ignoring a monotheism that they already possessed. One way or another, they incurred divine wrath for their ingratitude and arrogance. God offered them a last chance and sent to warn them a man who was charged to act as their specifically designated messenger or prophet. This messenger, who was most often a member of the very group he was sent to warn, offered his people a chance to repent while spelling out the dire consequences of their failure to do so. However, because they rejected both the messenger and the message, they suffered the inevitable consequences. They perished and disappeared; the desolate traces of their dwelling places are reported as still being visible and familiar to the audience—indeed references to ruined habitations, found throughout the Qur'an, are also a well-known image of pre-Islamic Arabic poetry.

An eloquent example is the story of the Thamud of ancient Arabia and their messenger Salih, a tale that occurs in several different versions. Here we draw attention to Surah 54:23–31:

> The [people of] Thamud rejected the warners, calling them liars, [23] and said: "Are we to follow a man, a solitary man from among ourselves? If we do that, surely we shall be in error and out of our minds! [24] Is the Message sent only to him from among all of us? No, he is a brazen liar." [25]

Their negative responses to God's chosen messenger is clearly unacceptable And so Muslim scripture, speaking through God, warns that by rejecting the Prophet Salih, and thus Allah Himself, the recalcitrant Thamud face impending disaster:

> Tomorrow they will know who is the [real] brazen liar. [26] For We will send the she-camel as a trial for them. So keep watch, [Salih,] and remain patient. [27] And inform them that the water is to be divided between them [Thamud and the camel], with each [of the two] having its right to drink in turn [from water brought forward] [28] But they [the Thamud] summoned their companion; and he stretched out [his hand] and

hamstrung [the Camel so it could not partake of the water]. [29] How [great then] was My punishment and My warning! [30] [In consequence] We sent against them a single [devastating] roar after which they became like the dried stubble [with which] one encloses cattle in their pens. [31]

Some nations will not vanish, but generations of their people will pay the price for not heeding the Lord's message, delivered in each historic occasion by a specific messenger chosen by Him. These are narratives of God's prophets or messengers bridging epochs of time and several religious and/ or ethnic communities, that is, didactic tales of the past intended to serve as lessons for the present and future. This chain of prophets and prophecy, linking different nations and lands, forms another overarching theme of the Qur'an. As in the story of the Bible, Noah's generation is destroyed by The Flood, save those creatures whom God allows to survive so as to reconstitute humankind. In similar fashion, Moses is constantly admonishing the Israelites for their indiscretions, but they refuse to listen—a theme frequently employed in the Qur'an and subsequent Muslim polemics against the Jews who denied Muhammad. Other figures in this chain of messengers include well-known figures from the Old and New Testaments and the vast postbiblical literature that informs Jewish and Christian scripture. Among the protagonists we find figures such as Abraham, Joseph, Saul, David, Solomon, Moses, and Jesus, all of whom are given Arabic names and considered prophets even when some are described in the Bible as patriarchs and mere kings. Some of these biblical persons receive more attention than others in the accounts of the Qur'an. Not surprisingly, Abraham, the first monotheist, and Moses, a great lawgiver, as was Muhammad, are the most prominent of the Israelites.

The final and culminating figure in the long chain of legitimate monotheist messengers is the greatest of them all, the Arabian prophet in the Qur'anic age who faces the same sort of opposition from his contemporaries that Salih once faced in his confrontation with Thamud, and that the biblical prophets faced with some of their obdurate brethren. The sequence of messengers leading up to Muhammad who will bring God's prophecy to a close is one of the most ubiquitous themes of Muslim scripture and gives logic to Muslim claims vis-à-vis contemporaneous Jews and Christians who reject the authenticity of Muhammad's mission.

The Origins of Monotheism in Arabia

This linking of biblical figures together with Arabian messengers such as Salih, and also Hud , Shu'ayb, and ultimately Muhammad, leads us to the distinctively Qur'anic theme of granting monotheist credentials to the Arabs. To make this abundantly clear, Abraham, the father of Ishmael, his eldest son who will be the progenitor of the Northern Arabs and a direct ancestor of Muhammad and his tribe, is given a place in the history of Arabia. It is Abraham who establishes the Ka'bah of Mecca as sacred ground. As later Muslim writers point out, that was long before the Jews built their temple in Jerusalem. Monotheism has been practiced in the past by Jews and Christians and perhaps by others as well. However, none of these peoples have a monopoly over it, especially since the Arabs, who lived recently in barbaric ignorance (Surahs 3:154, 5:50, 33:33, 48:26), are now becoming fully qualified monotheists once again. God's word is no longer revealed in foreign languages, but rather "in clear Arabic" (16:103). This brings us to a famous question of Qur'anic interpretation: The phrase *nabi ummi* (7:147–148) has generally been thought to mean "illiterate prophet," hence emphasizing Muhammad's miraculous ability to bring forth a book, a clear sign of his appointed mission. There is no doubt that *ummi* came to mean illiterate, but that is a secondary meaning of the word derived from the later interpretation of the verses rather than how it was originally understood. Philologically, *ummi* is linked to "mother" (*umm*) and by extension "people" (*ummah*). Thus, according to another interpretation that has been proposed by modern scholars, nabi ummi would have meant something more like "prophet of all the Arabs," a people who are currently living in an age of barbaric ignorance. The argument over the meaning of this Qur'anic term will certainly continue. In any case, there is no doubt that the monotheist credentials of the Arabs were greatly enhanced by the idea, expressed often in the Qur'an (and also in the *Sirah* and other extra-Qur'anic sources) that Arabian monotheism is actually old and venerable, having been part of the regional landscape before the onset of the Age of Ignorance.

Abraham, the monotheist of old, made his way to the Hijaz (in western Arabia), where he founded the Meccan sanctuary together with his son Ishmael. Ishmael and his offspring maintained the sanctuary, but with the passage of time the Arabs fell into polytheistic ways. Nonetheless, the memory of the original monotheism never died completely. The message of the Arabian prophet (Muhammad) is thus nothing new, but rather the restoration of an ancient and true faith of his and all the Arabs' ancestors. Although the Qur'an mentions Muhammad by name no more than four or five times, it contains over 200 references to "the Messenger," and somewhat fewer references to "the Prophet." What seems to matter is not the man's name, and perhaps not even his individual characteristics, but rather his role in the establishment (or rather, restoration) of monotheism and the confrontation with monotheism's adversaries. From here we proceed to the absolutely central issue of Muhammad's world view.

The unicity of God and His omnipotence are starting points for any monotheist discussion of the universe. In that respect, the Qur'an like the Hebrew Bible insists at all times on God's uniqueness and oneness. God has created everything in the cosmos, He is aware of everything that happens, and He is present everywhere. He is unique unto Himself; His power is both immanent and transcendent. With that humankind owes gratitude to the Creator. Life on this earth is assuredly a fine and beautiful thing. We humans, however, lack the strength and competence to benefit from it, or even to survive, by ourselves. Instead we depend completely on God, who creates the good things of the earth and makes them available to us, regularly and predictably. God is not required to do any of this, and in fact he has no need of us at all: "Oh you people! You are the ones in need of God; but God is the one who is free of want, and worthy of praise" (Surah 35:15). Similarly: "God is the one free of want, while you are the needy" (47:38). We receive God's bounty through natural processes, as the rain quickens the fields, the plants and animals provide us with sustenance, the sea and the land allow us to travel through the world's open spaces, while the sun and stars tell us where to go and how to keep time. It is interesting to see that we are expected to deduce both the existence and the beneficence of God from the marvelous way in which His creation is organized. These are his signs made manifest for us to comprehend.

Characterist[ics] of Allah. [handwritten margin note]

Human Responsibility and Divine Judgment

Life is thus a gift that God has bestowed gratuitously, and which humans are unable to reciprocate, at first glance a strange notion among the Arabs who emphasize reciprocity as an integral value of their society. This inability to reciprocate has grave consequences. Having received a gift for which one is unable to reciprocate requires, at the very least, a show of proper gratitude. Gratitude in this case means obedience to God. Nonetheless, most humans remain ungrateful; and "ungratefulness" (*kufr*), constitutes the most basic, widespread, and baleful sin in the Qur'an, the functional opposite of "belief." The word "kufr" also came to signify apostasy. But even unbelievers can make their way back into the fold before the Last Judgment that will precede resurrection and afterlife, one of the most powerful themes of Muhammad's message, a theme characteristic as well in the older monotheist faiths: Judaism and Christianity. In many surahs, especially the ones traditionally thought to have been revealed in the earlier Meccan period of Muhammad's prophetical career, the terrors of the Last Day and the afterlife are a primary theme vividly and powerfully portrayed as in Surah 81:1–14.

When the sun shall be darkened, [1]
When the stars shall be thrown down, [2]
When the mountains shall be set moving, [3]
When the pregnant camels shall be neglected, [4]
When the savage beasts shall be mustered, [5]
When the seas shall be set boiling, [6]
When the souls shall be coupled, [7]
When the buried infant shall be asked [8]
For what sin she was slain, [9]
When the scrolls shall be unrolled, [10]
When heaven shall be stripped off, [11]
When Hell shall be set blazing, [12]
When Paradise shall be brought nigh, [13]
Then shall a soul know what it has produced. [14]

This catastrophe accompanies the Last Judgment, when everyone is consigned to Hell or Paradise. The scenario is familiar from other monotheist religions, of course. What is especially striking about the Qur'anic eschatology is its great sense of immediacy: it seems that these terrible events are expected to erupt at any moment. Accordingly, some modern scholars have proposed that we look at the Qur'an as an eschatological text, a work dominated by this immediate expectation of the End of Days, an event brought on by a terrifying apocalypse. Understanding the Qur'an in this way, namely as a document that is in essence an expression of salvation history, remains a minority view, but, given the frequent references to the end of historical time in Muslim scripture that view leaves us with much to ponder.

Charitable Deeds and the Concept of Wealth

Muslim scripture also enjoins us to perform good deeds in our own times so as to prepare for us a better dossier on the Day of Judgment. Such deeds consist of alms-giving and generosity, the equivalent of the "acts of loving kindness" that the rabbis proscribed for all Jews and that are also obligatory for good Christians. Classical Islamic law insists on a distinction between voluntary giving to charity (*sadaqah*) and the poor-rate, an involuntary tax (*zakat*). Although both these terms are found in Muslim scripture, the distinction between them seems to matter less in the Qur'an than it does in later Islamic law. At times they seem almost interchangeable so that the use of one word or the other in a particular context may not be so important in and of itself. What is important is the Qur'an's emphasis on the voluntary nature of the believers' contributions:

> Those who slander and ridicule the believers who freely give of themselves to perform acts of charity, together with those who find nothing to give save the fruits of their own labor: God will turn their ridicule against them, and theirs will be a grievous punishment. (Surah 9:79)

Feeding the poor is an identifying trait of the believer, an act that makes a person one of the "Companions of the Right Hand" (Surah: 90:18). A person who denies the Day of Judgment is identical to one who rejects the orphan and does not urge feeding the poor (107:3). Damnation is in store for whoever does not believe in God "and does not urge the feeding of the misfortunate" (69:34). Refusal to feed the poor goes hand in hand with inordinate love of wealth: "Nay, it is you who do not honor the orphans, and do not encourage the feeding of the poor, and who devour inheritance avidly, and who love wealth inordinately" (89:17–20). The righteous are those who "give food, though it is dear to them, to the poor, the orphan and the prisoner" (76:8).

To give sustenance to the poor is also a way of expiating a sin (Surah 5:89, 95) and of retracting an oath (58:4). However, the most familiar setting for purification is regular almsgiving: "Take alms (sadaqah) from their possessions so as to cleanse and purify them with and pray on their behalf" (9:103). A vaguely similar principle is applied in Jewish law where funds that were at one time consecrated for the holy Temple (*hekdesh*) could be consecrated, now that the Temple lay in ruins, for alleviating the distress of the needy through an act of *zedaqah* (Hebrew zedaqah is the equivalent of Arabic sadaqah). Note also that both classical Arabic lexicography and modern philology have associated the Qur'anic word "zakat," the involuntary poor tax, with the root *z-k-y*, which has to do with "purifying." In other words, zakat is that which purifies wealth: if we wish to keep our property, we must abandon a portion of it. As with *s-d-q*, the Arabic root *z-k-y* is linked to purity in other Semitic languages, suggesting conceptual links between the Qur'anic concepts of charity and those of Judaism.

Consistent with what we have just seen, wealth is permissible and even desirable, as it can be put to good purpose, but possessing wealth can also have a corrupting influence. Muslim scripture makes this abundantly clear. To begin with, God is *ghani*, which means both "wealthy" and "able to dispense with" something He has no need of—His creation and the world (Surahs 29:6, 35:15, 39:7). Human beings, however, need at least some of the goods of this world, which can only come from God. God combines His wealth with mercy (6:133), providing humans with property to satisfy their needs (53:48), expressed on Arabic by the term *rizq*. This divine beneficence is also called in Arabic *fadl*, which is usually translated as "grace," but often means something more like "surplus." So if you fear poverty, God will make you wealthy out of His fadl (9:28); for example those who lack the means for getting married should wait chastely for God's fadl (24:33). One thus discerns that God's gifts are related to the sustenance He provides. There is, however, a marked difference between sustenance and the accumulation of wealth that is not applied to those who are needy.

God's generosity contrasts with the hoarding, greed, and vengefulness of certain people (Surahs 9:73–74, 10:58). In the days of old, the Israelites rejected the appointment of Saul as king over them because they didn't consider him rich enough (2:247). The people of Midian asked Shu'ayb (identified in Muslim commentaries as Jethro, Moses's father-in-law, no doubt because the biblical Jethro came from Midian) if his religion would require them "to cease doing whatever we like with our property" (11:87). The dazzling splendor that God permitted to Pharaoh and his chiefs caused them to mislead people away from God's path (10:88). In Muhammad's time, the unbelievers spend their wealth the same way (8:36). Acquisition of wealth is repeatedly paired together with having numerous children. The polytheists consider acquiring wealth for its own sake and being blessed with numerous [male] children to sustain organic and extended families signs of good fortune. They do not, however, attribute this good fortune to God's intervention in their world.

Some verses speak of arrogance and the arrogant, rather than of wealth and the wealthy. Like the New Testament (Mark 10:25, Matthew 19:24, Luke 18:25), the Qur'an speaks of a camel passing through the eye of a needle, but here the object of comparison is not the wealthy man seeking entrance to heaven, but rather "those who reject Our [i.e. God's manifest] signs and consider them with arrogance" (Surah 7:40). More often, however, arrogance, hoarding, and avarice all go together (see 57:23–24, and 4:36–48: "God does not love the arrogant and vainglorious . . . or those who are stingy and who hide the benefits that God has bestowed on them . . . or those who spend of their substance so as to be conspicuous before others."). Every time someone sent by God to give warning appears before the people to whom he has been dispatched, its well-off members say, "We do not believe. . . . We have more in wealth and children, and we cannot be punished." (34:34–35) Of course they are proved wrong, and in the afterlife, the saved call down to the damned: "Of what profit to you were your hoarding and arrogant ways?" (7:48; see also 14:21, 40:47). Avarice, with its implicit claim to self-sufficiency (92:11), thus comes at the cost of one's soul (47:38), and to be saved from the "covetousness of one's soul" is to achieve true "prosperity" (64:15). Similarly, greed is a form of ingratitude: the creature God created and to whom He granted abundant goods and sons, and whose life He made comfortable, is now greedy for more (74:11–15). Man, though created for toil and struggle, still boasts, "I have squandered abundant wealth." (90:4–6)

Despite all its dangers for us, we can purify our wealth by giving it away without any thought for favors in return (Surah 92:18–19). However, we should not mar our acts of charity with reminders of our generosity or with unkind remarks (2:264). In this way, our wealth may come to resemble God's original gift to mankind. This reciprocity between God and the (human) donor becomes clear when we are called upon to help meritorious slaves: "give them some of God's wealth which He has given you" (24:33). Wealth becomes even more of an aid to salvation when it has not only been "purified," but also spent "in the path of God" (2:261–265, see the section on Salvation in this chapter), which is to say, in support of warfare. Repeatedly, the believers are enjoined to struggle with their possessions and their persons. God has purchased the possessions and persons of the believers in return for Paradise (9:111). Here, through war and conquest, material wealth becomes a positive value: "He made you heirs of the lands, houses and goods [of the People of the Book], and of a land which you did not frequent previously" (33:27)—no doubt originally a reference to the forceful acquisition of the lands of the leading Jewish tribes of Medina. Wealth and property thus constitute a coherent and, it may be argued, highly original set of themes in the Qur'an. A summary of these views in Surah 7:36–38 makes it clear that if people believe and do the right things, if they are generous and openhanded, and if they remember that this life is mere play and frivolity, then God will allow them to keep their worldly property after all.

The Qur'an recognizes that goods must circulate in society—but always according to certain principles. We see this in a passage about *riba,* "increase" or "profit," which in a more fully developed later Islamic law means "usury." In the Qur'an, riba seems to hover between the economies of commerce and gift giving: "The riba that you give, so that it may increase the wealth of people, does not increase with God. But the zakat (alms) that you give out of a desire for the countenance of God: those are the ones whose [wealth] is doubled" (30:39). This verse contrasts some kind of bad circulation of goods (riba) with some kind of good circulation (zakat). Encountering this verse, the medieval exegetes are nearly united in saying that riba here means a gift that a man gives to another man, in the hope that he will receive a greater gift in return. Some identified this expected exchange, no doubt correctly, with a practice of gift giving that took place in Arabia before Islam when tribesman sought to establish relations through individual or mutual exchanges of property.

The concept of riba (Hebrew *ribit*) is found several times in the Hebrew Bible where it is understood as usury, although with different gradations of meaning. We should not be surprised that sentiment against gift giving for the advantage of the giver and worse yet as usury should be found in tribal societies, or societies with residual tribal sensibilities like those of the Arabs and the ancient Israelites. In kinship groups, the stress is on collective responsibility as the conditions of life can be harsh and suddenly punishing owing to unforeseen events, particularly in the more marginal environments in which tribal groups were often situated. In a moment, an individual blessed with riches can become poor: the loss of capital because of a caravan gone astray or attacked by enemies; the loss of a flock that provides all means of sustenance by illness or natural predators; the unexpected death of kin who provide the labor necessary for survival; all these possibilities can be and were experienced by tribesmen living on the margins.

When in distress, kinfolk are obliged to alleviate the suffering or distress of their blood relatives and associates. It may be necessary to give them temporary use of animals with which to rebuild diminished or depleted flocks or provide them with shelter and clothing to protect them from the elements. Such may be considered a loan to be repaid, but to demand interest for such a loan is considered against the accepted values of society, hence the prohibition against usury or the expectation of advantage for gift giving to the misfortunate. When tribal societies engaged in more complex economic activities (international trade) or when blood lines became more diffuse as a result of an enlarged polity— which happened to both the ancient Israelites and the Islamic ummah— adjustments had to be made to balance profit with risk in commercial adventures and different forms of social services had to be institutionalized for the unfortunate victims of circumstance, hence changes in the interpretation of riba/ribit in later formulations of Islamic and Jewish law. Remarkable, however, is the staying power of the notion of collective responsibility and its links to charitable acts in Judaism and Islam, even in larger Jewish and Muslim societies no longer exclusively linked by ties of blood and other forms of tribal affiliation.

Circulation of goods may also be linked to other concerns, namely the public treasury, which in Arabic was known as *mal Allah* "the wealth of God," for example Surah 59:7:

> That which God has bestowed on His Messenger from the people of the towns is for God and His Messenger, and for him who is close [to the Messenger], for the orphans, for the poor, and for the traveler, lest it become something that circulates among the rich among you.

This verse is probably the clearest statement in the Qur'an regarding the proper circulation of goods. Medieval Muslim commentaries provide three explanations. First, the verse may be referring to the Prophet alone. This interpretation is based on the narrative of a particular moment of a particular event: Muhammad came into possession of certain goods that had formerly belonged to Jewish clans, the Qurayzah and Qaynuqa', and in this verse he was instructed by God on how to dispose of those goods. Linked to that, the second interpretation holds, quite plausibly, that the passage consists of instructions regarding the broader division of the spoils of war. These spoils are to be divided entirely among the named categories: God [the public treasury], the Messenger, relatives, orphans, poor, and travelers [who happened upon the dwelling places of the Muslims]. The third interpretation is that the verse refers to the revenue accruing to the central treasury of the Islamic state from the taxes paid by the protected non-Muslims living under Islamic rule, the *ahl al-dhimmah.* All in all, what emerges from a reading of these surahs is a clearly defined Qur'anic notion of the circulation of goods: these must go from top down, from rich to less fortunate, and not from the rich to the more fortunate. The movement of these goods was, however, also connected to the distribution of spoils, and thus to fighting and warfare.

Warfare

Frequent references are found in the Qur'an concerning the imperative for war and the manner in which it is to be conducted. These passages have, as of late, become a matter of interest and considerable discussion, the result of a resurgence of Muslim militancy and frequent reference to "jihad" as "holy war" in the media. In the few places where the word "jihad" itself occurs in the Qur'an, it apparently refers not specifically to warfare, but rather to "disputation" and efforts made for the sake of God and in His cause, which needless to say, is often coded language for combat. How to understand jihad in these verses needs to be determined by contextual analysis, never an easy task. Similarly, in the approximately forty instances of other Arabic words deriving from the Arabic root *j-h-d*, which denotes "effort," or "striving," the Qur'an calls for devotion to God, righteous conduct, dedication, and, indeed, sacrifice of oneself ("striving with one's person and one's wealth" for the sake of God). Such an attitude may, as a matter of course also involve physical combat, but in most of these cases this is not obvious or seemingly intended. Yet fighting and warfare do constitute a major theme in the Qur'an. These activities are most often described there with a vocabulary derived from Arabic roots other than *j-h-d*: these roots include *q-t-l* "fighting, killing," and *h-r-b* "fighting, making war." The passages relating to warfare include exhortations to take up arms, commands to fight or to desist from fighting, the distribution of military duties and of exemptions from these duties, rulings on the distribution of spoils of war and the treatment of noncombatants and prisoners of war, and other matters.

Discussing warfare and jihad as themes of Muslim scripture presents us with a number of problems, as it is clearly more difficult in these cases to separate the larger thematic message from the context in which it is presented. We face what seem to be, from a thematic point of view, a number of contradictions. More precisely, a number of discrete themes relating to warfare appear in the Qur'an which are not, at first glance, easy to reconcile without resorting to a tortured discussion of the historical circumstances that might have given rise to the apparent contradictions These include: (1) Injunctions to self-restraint and patience (*sabr*) in propagating the faith, inflicting punishment only in accordance with injuries already suffered, as in Surah 16:125–128: "Call thou to the way of thy Lord with wisdom and good admonition, and dispute with them [your adversaries] in the better way. . . . And if you chastise, chastise even as you have been chastised . . . And be patient." (2) Permission to engage in defensive war. "Permission [to fight] is granted to those against whom war has been made, because they have been wronged" (22:39–41). (3) Permission to wage offensive war, but within certain limits, especially during the "sacred months" and "sacred mosque" (a time and a place where war is not allowed nor was allowed even on the eve of Islam), unless the enemy is the first to violate these limits (2:194, 2:217). (4) Lifting some or all of these restrictions, as in the famous "sword verse": "But when the sacred months have passed, then kill and capture the infidels wherever you find them. Lie in wait for them making use of every strategy" (9:5). Similarly: "Fighting has been prescribed for you though you may dislike it" (2:216), a verse positioned immediately before a reference to fighting during the sacred month.

Of particular interest are the verses devoted to conflict with Jews and Christians. The text at times calls for (1) Patience with the "People of the Book," and reconciliation and peacemaking: "if they incline to peace, then incline to it also, and trust in God." (Surah 8:61) (2) Loss of this patience is accompanied by the requirement to subdue the Jews and Christians. The classic example is known as the other "sword verse" or the "*jizyah* verse," a highly problematic text that has given rise to considerable and contradictory commentary among scholars medieval and modern, most especially what is meant by "humbling the Jews and Christians," a verse that has been interpreted as ranging from mere insult to physical abuse. The full verse states: "Fight those who believe not in God and the Last Day and do not forbid what God and His Messenger have forbidden—such men who do not practice the true religion [even] those who have been given the Book—until they pay the tribute (jizyah) [the special poll tax levied against Jews and Christians] out of hand and have been humbled" (9:29).

As noted above, it happens often enough that a theme within the Qur'an contains several subthemes that tend in different directions. It is also fairly common to find indications and instructions on a particular matter that seem, at least at first glance, to be contradictory. Nowhere else, however, is there such a long and bewildering array of options as we find here regarding warfare and jihad. To resolve these differences, scholars, Muslim as well as non-Muslim, have always had to consider the historical context. The task of linking the revelations on warfare to events allegedly from the time of the Prophet has been undertaken not only by writers of medieval historical narratives, but also, and above all, by Muslim jurists seeking to discover the divine law. After all, what are Muslims actually supposed to do in their confrontations with members of other religious communities, something that occurred throughout the course of the Middle Ages and beyond? Where did the subsequent generations of Muslims find the context to illuminate verses commanding

Muslims to behave albeit without the explicit instruction of how and in what circumstances to carry out God's commands.

Scholars who have entered this debate in search of instruction or, as in the case of non-Muslim orientalists, to achieve a better understanding of Muslim views at the time of the Prophet have found that all the afore-mentioned subthemes of Muslim scripture can be connected to narratives in the medieval Muslim biographies of Muhammad and other extant post-Qur'anic sources. To be sure, as we have so often observed, these sources, all written, or if you prefer, redacted, after the Prophet's lifetime, at best contain dim memories and tendentiously driven interpretations of what actually happened during the course of Muhammad's revelations. Still, in this way, scholars managed to determine, at least to their satis-faction, the chronological order of events that gave rise to Muhammad's public pronouncements concerning other religious communities. For many of the Muslim jurists, the next move was to apply the aforemen-tioned juridical theory of abrogation to the general themes of how and why to conduct war. Briefly put, Muslims came to hold that whenever a new revelation came to Muhammad, it canceled or abrogated any revelations that he might have received previously on the same topic. Thus many (though not all) Muslim jurists dealing with the seeming con-tradictions of scripture as regards combat and other religious commun-ities came to adopt a rather hard-line approach. In any case, the matter was complicated, and the Qur'anic data were only a part of the evolution of the doctrine and practice of jihad against the nonbelievers and more generally of warfare.

The Qur'an and Other Scriptures

An obvious concern for both medieval and modern readers was and continues to be the relationship of the Qur'an to other scriptures. In many passages, Muhammad's revelations seem to have an oral character: they are meant to be recited out loud, as the meaning and etymology of the word "Qur'an" imply—the root of *q-r-'* in Arabic means both "to recite" and "to read." Many other passages, however, emphasize the notion of a divinely established scripture in the form of a book. This emphasis on the written book, as opposed to the spoken word, leads to many issues and con-siderations. Among Muslims, many of these are loftily metaphysical and theological. There emerged the belief that beyond and behind the Qur'an and the earlier revealed scriptures on earth there is a heavenly prototype, the *lawh mahfuz*, the "eternal, unchanging word." Muslim scholars also have had to consider that other scriptures, most notably those of the Jews and Christians, were already known to most people living in the Near East at the time of the rise of Islam. This leads in turn to one of the most complicated and fascinating thematic areas within the Qur'an.

[Marginalia: Central to Islamic identity]

We may recall that in the Qur'an, there is a sequence of prophets reaching back from the earliest history of monotheism, down to what, in Qur'anic terms, is the age of Muhammad, the last and most perfect of God's messengers. We may further recall the close relation between God's prophets and their revealed scriptures and the mutual sustaining of these two in the Qur'an, *sirah*, and other genres of medieval Muslim writing. There is then, from the Muslim point of view, the idea of a sequence of God-given scriptures parallel to the sequence of God-sent prophets. The divine word came previously to the Jews, in the form of Torah, and then to the Christians, in the form of the Gospel; now the believers (or, as they become generally known at a later, post-Qur'anic time, the Muslims) have their revealed book, the Qur'an. The Qur'an is its most authentic expression of these revealed works and Muhammad the most authentic messenger of the divine word. And so Muhammad takes precedence over all previous prophets sent by God and Islam has priority over Judaism, Christianity, and other rivals. All that was predicted in the earlier revelations sent by God to the long line of prophets sent by God who preceded the messenger from the Arabs of Quraysh. All that was predicted in the earlier monotheist revelations and was relayed to the monotheist peoples by their own prophets. The Qur'an is thus obliged to inform us why the other monotheists reject the last of God's prophets. The accusation, made in the Qur'an as well as in extra-Qur'anic Arabic sources, is that other monotheists (the Jews in particular) were careless in their handling and transmission of the scripture that had been entrusted to them, or worse yet, they deliberately distorted it, thus helping to explain the discrepancies between their scriptures and the Qur'an, and the differences between their beliefs and practices and those of the Muslims.

Muslim scripture devotes considerable attention to Jesus and Christianity, thus forming the basis of Muslim attitudes toward the second monotheist faith. The complex figure of Jesus can be considered not only as an example of the larger theme of "prophets," but as a theme all on his own. This is because the arguments over Jesus that we see in the Qur'an point to an encounter with Christianity, which at the time of the rise of Islam was the dominant religion in the Near East. Jesus the son of Mary (in Arabic 'Isa ibn Maryam) is known also in the Qur'an as "the Messiah" (*al-massih*), where the term is more a name than a title. His story, as told in Muslim scripture, extends back to before his birth to Mary, "the chosen above all women" (Surah 3:45), and to Zachariah and John (beginning of Surah 19). The miracle of the virgin birth is related, much as in Christian tradition, except that in good Qur'anic fashion, the ultimate lesson here is the omnipotence of God: "Even so, God said, God creates what He will. When he decrees a thing, he does but say to it 'Be,' and it is" (3:42, 19:16–40). Jesus appears as a prophet within the Qur'anic sequence of prophets (19:41–60), where his role is similar to that of the others. However, he also has characteristics that are his alone. He is confirmed [in his calling] with the Holy Spirit" (2:253, 5:[108] 110). He speaks from the cradle (5:113 and 19 throughout), receives the Gospel (5:27) and has Apostles (3:252, 5:111–112, 61:14). At his request, God sends down a miraculous "table out of heaven" (5:115–118). Jesus breathes life into a clay bird (3:49, 5:113), he "heals the blind and the leper," and resurrects the dead. He has special teachings and special merits, especially those of tenderness and mercy (57:27). At the same time, like all Qur'anic prophets, he is an exemplar of obedience.

The crucifixion of Jesus is reported, but in one passage (Surāh 4:157) it is claimed that it was only a false likeness of him that died on the cross. This must be seen as part of a larger set of Qur'anic polemics against Christian teachings and practices. "He [God] does not beget nor is he begotten." (Surah 112:3) "And they say, 'The All-Merciful has taken unto Himself a son.' You have indeed advanced something hideous!" (19:88–89) "And say not 'three'" (4:171) "The Messiah, son of Mary, was only a messenger; messengers before him passed away; his mother was a just woman; they both ate food [an indication of his corporeal being]" (5:75 [76]) "And monasticism they [the Christians] invented. We did not prescribe it for them—[they did this] only seeking the good pleasure of God; but they observed it not as it should be observed" (57:27). All these verses were prominently mentioned in medieval Muslim polemics against Christianity.

Salvation

In this seventh-century world of competing and conflicting monotheisms, much is at stake in the choice of community. But, as far as the Qur'an is concerned, persons making that choice have not necessarily solved their problem once and for all time. From the perspective of Muslim scripture, one has to ask if membership in the community guarantees salvation. Scholars have usually dealt with this question by referring to the historical context of the Qur'an, which refers to "hypocrites," internal dissension, and so on. These references are to those who for the sake of convenience accept Islam but not in their hearts and, as a result are portrayed—at least by the medieval Arabic chroniclers—as attempting to subvert Muhammad's mission. But if we insist on a thematic rather than historical approach, we can readily find indications of answers to this question as articulated in scripture and relate it to the theme of salvation. The Qur'an speaks of hypocrites, but of course only God knows what is in anyone's heart and mind, and God will determine the fate of each individual. The emphasis here is on "individual," since each soul is ultimately responsible only for itself. But if the individual does not know his or her fate, even after making the correct choice of community, he or she still has a possibility and a duty that are entirely Qur'anic and Islamic, namely that of "striving" in the service of God, or, as the slightly later, post-Qur'anic doctrine would express it, jihad. We see this in an argument concerning the most tepid of all believers, the nomadic Bedouin (Surah 49:14–15):

> The nomadic Arabs say, "we believe." Do not say you believe; rather say, "we Submit"; for belief has not yet entered your hearts. If you obey God and His Messenger, He will not diminish anything of your works. God is all-forgiving, all-Compassionate. [14] The believers are those who believe in God and His Messenger, and have not doubted, and have struggled (*wa-jahadu*) with their possessions and their persons in the path of God; those are the truthful ones. [15]

The Qur'an is rich in imagery concerning the ultimate consequences that may derive from one's earthly actions on the Day of Judgment. It contrasts the glories and pleasures of Paradise with the Hellfire below. But a full description of these matters as well as many other thematic elements of Muslim scripture are beyond the scope of this enquiry, which has been essentially limited to themes that inform the other segments of our work.

The Formation of Islamic Law and Legal Tradition

A full exposition of Islamic law is well beyond our mandate, which is to produce a book accessible not only to Islamicists but also to readers broadly interested in medieval Islamic civilization. As it is, our treatment of law and legal institutions takes the form of a rather complex and lengthy discussion divided among two interlocked chapters: one treats the issues surrounding the formation of the law; the second the legal schools that established its juridical principles. Our point of departure is to reexamine a familiar series of questions long debated by scholars, this time from a comparative view that calls to attention Jewish as well as Muslim perspectives.

Every legal system based on an immutable holy scripture that is fixed in time and space must make adjustments to historical realities far removed from the cultural milieu where God's word was last revealed. This represented a particular problem for the oldest and youngest of the monotheist faith communities, as both Jews and Muslims attempted not only to establish the ideological boundaries of their faith but also to regulate the behavior of the faithful throughout their daily lives amidst shifting social and economic environments and invasive cultural values. The problem is already evident within scripture itself. As to the law, there are any number of contradictions within both Jewish scripture and the Qur'an. As we have seen in the previous chapter and elsewhere in this book, contradictions in Muslim scripture apparently resulted from conditions that evolved within the Prophet Muhammad's lifetime; the Hebrew Bible's different pronouncements of the law reflect a text comprised of diverse literary traditions sewn together and committed to writing over centuries marked by distinct changes in outlook and behavior. At least that is the view adopted by modern biblical scholarship on the five books of Moses, known to Jews as the Torah.

For believing Jews, the core of Jewish tradition was the law given to the ancient Israelites at Mount Sinai and the pronouncements of Moses, their first prophet and lawgiver. All these laws were described in detail and placed within a particular historical setting described in the Hebrew Bible. There were, to be sure, many prophets to follow Moses, but their task was to uphold the ideals of the community rather than to legislate for it. The law of Moses, or as it would later be known "the written law," was already set in stone (so to speak). As regards Muslims, the Qur'an was at the core of their beliefs and the supreme guide to their behavior past and present. Like the Hebrew prophet Moses, with whom he is often compared in Islamic tradition, Muhammad was not only a vessel for revealing God's word, he was also, in effect, a lawgiver.

As were Jews, Muslims relying only on scripture were faced with pre-scribed behavior that did not fully account for changing conditions over time and space. Again, like the Jews, they were forced to exercise considerable ingenuity to develop new laws that were not explicitly mentioned in sacred scripture but which nevertheless carried the authenticity to force their compliance among believers. Legitimizing this later legislation was no small problem because both Jews and Muslims declared a given point of history at which prophecy had come to an end. Jews employed a rather pithy expression to point out that after the destruction of the Second Temple in the first century C.E., the long dormant gift of prophecy was left to fools, mutes, and small children—that is to say, to all intents and purposes, prophecy had ended for all time and God had ceased to directly reveal his intentions to future lawgivers. Muslims were less charitable to fools, mutes, and even small children; for them revelation terminated in seventh-century Arabia with the death of Muhammad, the "Lord and Seal of the Prophets."

The Jewish response to the dilemma of laws that were fixed chronologically and spatially was to declare that in fact two sets of laws had been revealed simultaneously at Mount Sinai: the written law delivered by Moses to the ancient Israelites and an "oral law" which reflected the teachings of subsequent generations. Accordingly, both laws were handed down without interruption to a long chain of authoritative transmitters:

Moses to Joshua, who was of the generation of Israelites following those who experienced the Exodus from Egypt; Joshua to the elders (of the tribes); the elders to the (early) prophets; the early prophets to the later prophets Haggai, Malachi, and Zechariah; and the latter to the men of the Great Assembly, the progenitors of rabbinic Judaism, that system of beliefs and institutions that regulated Jewish life until the onset of modern times and continues to do so for believers even today. To insure there might be no misunderstanding concerning the oral law, the rabbis maintained that God spoke in a clear voice and in no less than seventy languages. Still doubts remained that any such transmission could be without flaws, and so it was declared that not only the ancient Israelites received the oral law in the desert of Sinai, but also the souls of all the future Jews which hovered overhead. These souls, the reservoir of God's original commands, waited for the moment at which they would be united with the corporeal bodies of those yet to be born.

Such intellectual gymnastics were recognized for what they were—and by the very rabbis who utilized them for their own purposes. One might even say they gently mocked their own tendentious enterprise that gave almost equal weight to the laws of Moses and those of their invention. Muslims were faced with similar problems and employed similar responses. According to Muslim tradition, Muhammad was confronted by a puzzled believer from an area distant from Medina. The Muslim wished to know how he and his community could ascertain that a particular statement attributed to the Prophet was indeed an accurate recollection of the Prophet's words. Muhammad replied that he should first consult the Qur'an. If that statement is found therein, then it is most assuredly God's word revealed through him (meaning that it is obligatory for the questioner and his community to accept as true). However, if it is not found in the Qur'an, the alleged statement of the Prophet should be examined to see if it is of benefit for the general welfare of the Muslims; and if that it so, the statement which had been attributed to the Prophet should be regarded as his word, whether or not he had in fact uttered it. The tradition is, as we shall point out, part of a larger debate on the various ways medieval Muslims adjusted the law and its interpretation to changing times and conditions.

Shari'ah, *the Nature of Islamic Law*

The most usual way to refer to Islamic law in Arabic and other Islamic languages is with the term *shari'ah*, which literally means "way" or "path." For Muslims both today and in the Middle Ages it meant divine law as a whole, including both its theory and application. But what does it mean to speak of divine law that is all comprehensive?

For believing Muslims, law has ultimately only one true source, one true lawgiver, namely Almighty God who resides in the Heavens and whose manifest will is self-evident in the intricate nature of the universe. Only God issues laws, commandments, statutes, prohibitions, and the like. Kings, emperors, governors, councils, assembles of notables, modern parliaments and "the people" all lack the authority and legitimacy to do so. As we have seen, even prophets such as Moses, the great lawgiver of the ancient Israelites or Muhammad, the greatest prophet and lawgiver of all, do not act as independent legislators, but only as direct transmitters of divine law. Similarly, caliphs may not issue or enact laws, at least not according to the theory of Islamic law that evolved. Some caliphs did try to legislate; the point here is that according to strict legal theory, this was not their legitimate function. Since the role of lawmaker is denied to the caliphs, then it must also be denied to high officials who derive their authority from them, such as viziers, emirs (governors or commanders), and sultans. Nor does expertise in the divine law in and of itself qualify a person to act as legislator. This applies even to the greatest jurists and interpreters of the shari'ah, let alone experts in other fields, whether they have received their training in practical matters such as bureaucratic administration, or in religious disciplines such as theology, or in that branch of scholarship known among medieval Muslims as the "philosophical sciences."

Just as God is the sole source of the Law, He is ultimately the only legitimate ruler. The Qur'an proclaims that God has "sovereignty (*mulk*) over the heavens, the earth, and all that lies between them" (Surah 58:18–19). Accordingly, any person who holds authority and power in the world does so only at God's pleasure. As a result, all rulers in the world who do not derive their authority from God can never achieve legitimacy—this applies, by definition, to all rulers outside the world of Islam. These rulers are nothing more than usurpers and tyrants, even if they belong to well-established dynasties and rule over extensive realms. And just as God is the only legitimate ruler, the only legitimate polity or state is the Islamic ummah, the universal community of all the Muslim faithful.

Since God is the sole lawgiver and sovereign, those who set out to examine the nature of jurisprudence and law face several fundamental tasks. First of all, they must discover the divine law. God has communicated directly with humans on several occasions, most recently and definitively in the Qur'an. However, it may then turn out that we still need further data in order to comprehend the divine law in its entirety. Locating such sources of the divine law (in addition to the Qur'an) and evaluating them properly can be an arduously difficult task. Once we have determined what the law is, we need to understand it correctly and to interpret it. Finally, we need to apply the law, which means the administration of justice with all its procedures, bureaucracies, courts, prisons, judges, witnesses, police, and so on.

In a legal system where everything derives from a single, supreme source, one might expect things to be arranged hieratically and rigidly, but this turns out not to be so. The shari'ah is relatively informal. If one comes across an Islamic law book from the classical period—by now quite a few of these have been translated into English—and opens it anywhere at random, the reader is likely to be struck by the rather conversational tone; at times, it may be downright chatty. Of course this is not always so, since legal texts are often quite technical and always show enormous respect for their subject matter; sometimes they are written in a rather clipped legal language similar in certain respects to Jewish legal texts and as a result can be rather opaque to the novice reader, even one who has a firm command of classical Arabic. In any case, entering this world of shari'ah puts one in the center of an extensive and ongoing conversation. Who participates in this conversation? Within a particular legal text, the author will, of course, be addressing his peers, approving what some of them have said, and arguing against others. All these peers are experts in the law, and our author is likely to know a great deal about them; not only their lectures and books, but also with whom they have studied, where they have lived and traveled, their dealings with other scholars, their political and religious leanings, their reputation for honesty, and so on. Often a legal scholar will engage in a technical discussion on a point of law with a colleague at the other end of the Islamic world. It is equally common to engage legal authorities of past generations. In other words, the juridical conversation embraces an Islamic world, densely networked both in space and in time.

Another characteristic of this conversation among jurists is its inclusiveness. Not surprisingly, polemical arguments take place frequently, and these can involve much acrimony. But no matter how fierce these arguments become, they still tend to take place between adversaries who agree on admitting one another into the larger scholarly fraternity. No matter how heated the argument may be, the adversaries still recognize each other as members of their scholarly community and as accredited experts in the divine law. To be sure, all jurists and juridical schools do draw a line, beyond which they no longer recognize an adversary's legitimacy or credentials. But to a remarkable extent, they extend this line to include as many participants as possible. Still another characteristic of the divine law is its comprehensive subject-matter. Islamic law covers areas that first-year law students in our modern world contend with, such as penal law, contracts, and torts, although it considers these matters under headings and categories that are applicable to the conditions of an Islamic environment. The shari'ah devotes careful attention to family law, including marriage, divorce, inheritance, the treatment of household slaves, setting them free, and so on. It also covers matters of religious observance, including ritual purity, prayer, fasting, pilgrimage and alms-giving, in addition to many areas that are less well known. It deals unflinchingly with earthy, intimate matters (detailed references to sexual activities, the emission of various bodily fluids and their relationship to ritual purity, and so on), as well as abstruse, theological considerations. Nor is the law for Muslims alone. For it covers as well relations between the faithful and non-Muslims, be they protected minorities or unbelievers yet to be conquered. Accordingly, we can say that the shari'ah is nothing less than a comprehensive system that applies to all aspects of a Muslim's life on earth, as well as to aspects of life in the hereafter, a matter taken quite seriously by believing Muslims.

Shari'ah

Law and the State

In the modern world of the West, the study and practice of law are closely tied to the activities of government. For example, in the United States, Congress, a body of legislators elected by the public, passes a bill and the President, the supreme elected official, signs it into law; from this point onward, enforcement of this new law, like the administration of justice in general, is a function of government. For the premodern Islamic world, that is, before European legal codes and procedures were introduced in Islamic countries, the law did not work quite in this way. We have already observed the theoretical limitations placed on temporal rulers by an evolving Islamic law. The Muslim legal establishment did have a relationship to government, but it was often an uneasy one that produced tensions between the two. We can see this in the reluctance of many jurists to serve the state when they were offered positions within the legal system, judgeships in particular, as they knew only too well how they might be pressured to rule against their better judgment. No less than the great Abu Hanifah, the founder of one of the recognized schools of Islamic law (see the next chapter) rejected the pleas of the caliph al-Mansur to be the chief judicial authority (*qadi*) in the newly established Abbasid capital in Baghdad, preferring instead to supervise the construction of bricks used in making the caliph's great administrative center. Unlike Abu Hanifah, who remained steadfast in refusing the caliph, many honorable legal scholars wound up accepting judgeships after making a show of reluctance. They did so fully realizing that as the government's appointee they could be subjected to pressure to rule in favor of the caliph or his administrators, and if they chose to stand by their convictions when much was at stake politically for the commander of the faithful, they could not only be displaced from office, but physically abused as well. There are sufficient reports to indicate that was indeed the case. Nevertheless, administrators, indeed the caliph himself, realized they were to be judged by not only by their constituents but by a higher authority. In deference to their supreme belief in God and the power invested in them to carry out God's will, they frequently sought and when necessary manufactured legal support for the actions they took.

In the end, the shari'ah developed apart from the Islamic State, although it settled into what at times was an uneasy coexistence with it. This coexistence between the religious establishment responsible for defining the law and the temporal authority that enforced it worked in part because much of Islamic law has a theoretical and at times even unworldly character that generally did not disturb the ruling authorities who appointed the judges. As regards the law, the major concern of the temporal authorities was that judges did not interfere in matters of state. In effect, the legal establishment and the state enjoyed—if that is the proper word—a symbiotic relationship in which the state allowed its judges a more or less free hand in religious rulings in such areas that did not directly interfere with the politics of the realm. As both the religious authorities and the government preferred authoritarian and even despotic rule to anarchy—the latter might unravel the threads that held the ummah together—they were able to negotiate the difficult situations that might arise. The state recognized the official religious establishment as having primacy in matters of a Godly nature, and the religious establishment in turn generally argued on behalf of subservience to the state.

An Overview of Classical Islamic Law

Seeking a comparative perspective, it might be profitable to compare Islamic law with that of the Jews. Because Jewish law has an especially close resemblance to Islamic law in so many ways, one can argue, as have learned Jewish orientalists of past generations, that elements of the Jewish legal system, presumably transmitted by Jewish scholars who converted to Islam, had a profound influence on how their new religious compatriots conceived of divine law. In any event, the Jewish concept of *halakhah* is similar to the Islamic concept of shari'ah, and in fact both these terms literally mean "path" or "way." In Jewish law we find God as the sole lawgiver; among rabbis, there was an exhaustive search for the "sources of the law," and, as in the medieval Islamic world, there was an animated conversation among experts in law, extending over many centuries and throughout many regions. We also find among Jews a legal system that regulates virtually all aspects of daily life and extended life cycles while maintaining a certain distance from the authorities that rule the community, either the independent rulers of an independent Jewish polity, or the appointed intermediaries who represented the Jewish community to the political powers following the Roman wars of the first two centuries C.E. Moreover, we find many common practices beginning, as we have seen, as early as the lifetime of the Prophet.

This introduction brings us to the point of attempting to establish a brief outline of Islamic law and of the ways in which it interacted with medieval and premodern Islamic societies. Given the constraints of size and taking into consideration the broad audience for whom this book was written, a sketchy and incomplete outline has disadvantages. Islamic law is a complex and subtle system, with many interlocking parts. Even more importantly, it has always been a living system, constantly evolving with changing contingencies, a fact often distorted by misinformed modern media commentary in the Western world, but not by trained Islamicists of the Western academy. What makes constructing an outline of Islamic law especially problematic, however, is that the early stages of its development, meaning the emergence of Islamic law during the first three or so centuries of Islam, are often the most difficult for us to recapture. As with the early history of the Islamic community and state, there are major controversies among modern scholars over the transmission of the available data (both oral and written), the reliability of this information, and how we should interpret the materials at our disposal.

It is reasonably clear that by around the turn of the tenth century C.E., Islamic law had evolved greatly, both as regards juridical theory and in its relation to the everyday world of Islamic society. For lack of a better expression, we might think of Islamic law as having reached maturity.

Changes would continue, to be sure, but by this time many of the outstanding characteristics and structures of Islamic law were already set in place. Accordingly, the outline that we present of Islamic law in the Near East pertains to the situation in the tenth century C.E. and the centuries immediately following. This static "snapshot" of an Islamic law, already basically formed, may help us move backward to better understand the more controversial origins and early development of Islamic law. Admittedly, there is always the possibility of reading contemporaneous situations into a past where they did not apply; as we have seen, that is a danger for envisioning virtually every aspect of the formation of classical Islamic civilization, be it the world of politics or religious institutions. In attempting to envision the formative centuries of Islam, we are obliged to examine some of the approaches to these issues and some of the controversies that have swirled around them.

To begin with, Islamic law may be subsumed under two discrete headings, or, if you prefer, divisions. One of these is substantive law, which amounts to the law's interface with the everyday world. What does the law oblige people to do, or make them think they should do? What does it require or impose regarding particular issues and areas of experience? This substantive law is known in Arabic as *furu'*, "branches." As in any legal system, substantive law is vast and cannot be done justice with a few representative examples.

The other heading or division of the law is jurisprudence, known in Arabic as *fiqh*, which means literally "understanding." Jurisprudence is a metascience, a methodology in the strict sense of the term. That is, it involves the study of the structure of the law and of the hermeneutic or interpretive principles that underlie this structure. It does not involve the study of any of the law's particular manifestations, which belong under the heading of substantive law. The investigations and literary products of Islamic jurisprudence are often referred to in Arabic with the term *usul al-fiqh*, "the sources [literally the roots] of jurisprudence"; these roots (*usul*) are contrasted conceptually to the branches of substantive law. Before looking at some basic aspects of jurisprudence and the sources of the law, we are obliged to ask who performed this work. Generally speaking, jurisprudence was the domain of specially trained experts, the jurist or jurisprudent (*faqih*) or more generally, the "learned individual" (*'alim*). How could a young person become a faqih? In the first four centuries of Islam, there were no institutions that bore much resemblance to our modern universities and law schools, with their formal and often standard curricula, common degrees and so on.

Even with the emergence of the madrasah, an academy of learning similar in certain but not all respects to the yeshiva and beit midrash, institutions of advanced Jewish learning at the time, Islamic legal education remained, by modern standards, rather informal. Unlike the Jewish yeshiva of medieval Islamic lands, the madrasah had no judicial function, but like the yeshiva and unlike those modern madrasahs where young boys memorize the Qur'an, sometimes without knowledge of Arabic, the medieval madrasah organized the study of the law according to rigorous standards. A young student needed to show individual initiative, traveling to wherever the best teachers resided, attending their lectures (in their homes or in the mosques) and absorbing their teachings. Above all, he needed to learn and apply the strict techniques and rules that governed the transmission of religious and legal knowledge. After years (many of them on the road), a student might begin to acquire a reputation as an authority on a certain subject or subjects. Then he might begin to give lectures of his own, and to publish books, two achievements that were very closely related to one another.

Because there were no formal degrees, nothing counted in this world of legal education and scholarship so much as one's personal reputation for learning and probity. Accordingly, it became necessary for people to know a great deal about the many jurists, lawyers, and teachers who were active at any given moment as well as those who had been active in the past. To satisfy this need, diligent authors compiled a diverse body of literature that we often refer to as "biographical dictionaries." These were books that contained entries on hundreds or even thousands of law scholars giving details about their training, character, teachings, scholarly affiliations, and political and religious allegiances. Biographical dictionaries were also composed on members of other groups and professions, such as poets and physicians; however, the longest and most detailed were devoted to the men of law. The great biographical dictionaries often were arranged according to different generations of notables or more often according to scholars who achieved prominence in a particular geographical center of learning although in any number of cases they were not born there. There is even a case where the entries on particular notables are arranged in the form of death notices for given years. There is in short much variety in these works. The great biographical dictionary of the Khatib al-Baghdadi (d. 1071 C.E.), the so-called *History (ta'rikh) of Baghdad* contains more than 8,000 entries, the overwhelming majority of them scholars, but also of other notables. The published edition of the work, which appeared in Cairo in 1931, comprises fourteen volumes, each containing around 450 pages, some 6,300 pages in all including indices. Some entries are limited to a few lines, giving the scholar's full genealogy and some scant details of his life. Others relate whom he studied with and the men who studied with him. Sometimes, these entries inform us of significant networks of jurisprudents and scholars of Islamic tradition. As a matter of course, the great scholars were treated to more extensive biographical entries that ran into several pages and that contained all sort of tidbits of personal information. A technical vocabulary emerged to describe the subjects of these biographical entries, ranging from "highly reliable," "trustworthy," and "a model for emulation," all the way down to "arch-liar," "fiend," and "an enemy of God." In that way, one had a better sense of where to turn for a more favorable reading of the law and/or of Islamic tradition.

This world of juridical learning was, in every sense, a dense network that extended across large reaches of space and time and it existed, to a surprising extent, independently of the networks of government and state. Only the general consensus of the jurisprudents could grant an individual the reputation of being truly learned and maintain him in the scholarly fraternity they comprised. The patronage of caliphs, governors, or viziers was often viewed with suspicion, as was the support of wealthy, private individuals. At the same time, however, the networks of legal scholarship and government did converge at certain points, the most important of which was the position of qadi, the Islamic judge. This was basically a government job, paid for out of public funds and integrated into a legal bureaucracy. The main point, however, is that one could only become a qadi by rising within the extra-governmental networks of scholarship in jurisprudence and other related fields. In other words, the extensive training and sound reputation that a person needed (at least in theory) to qualify as a judge were all acquired independently of the governmental bureaucracy within which that job was actually performed.

The Sources of Law

Like their counterparts in other legal systems, Islamic jurists faced the task of discovering the law, which for them meant detecting, understanding and interpreting the will of the sole, Divine Legislator. Not surprisingly, they disagreed among themselves, often quite severely. However, their arguments and disagreements revolved around a limited number of sources of law. All Muslim jurists agreed that the first source of Islamic law, the primary text of the divine legislation, is the Qur'an. Muslims have always maintained that as a point of theological dogma and an article of personal belief the words of the Qur'an are of divine origin, and have been delivered to humanity through the agency of the Prophet Muhammad. Furthermore, the Qur'an contains much material that is well suited to constructing a legal system in the real world. Many of its verses are devoted to topics that are of immediate concern to jurists and lawyers. In particular, the surahs that traditional exegesis identified as coming from the Medinan period of the Prophet's career contain prescriptions and proscriptions, many of them detailed, and often using a rather technical, we could even say legalistic language.

On the other hand, it would be difficult to construct (or more properly, to discover) a complete edifice of law on the basis of the Qur'an alone—there have been groups within Islam who have maintained that this is possible and necessary, but the position turns out to be quite difficult to advocate. To begin with, the Holy Book is limited in its length. Many of its verses that contain legal or juridical material are general in character; these verses provide basic principles for religious ritual, family and commercial law, and many other areas, but they do not provide all the details that lawyers need for their briefs and arguments and that judges need for their verdicts and sentences. Furthermore, it happens fairly often that the Qur'an gives differing instructions regarding a single matter, in different passages or verses. For instance, inheritance is discussed chiefly in two long passages which seem, at least at first glance, to establish different systems for transmitting property across generations. Relations with non-Muslim communities and the conduct of war and peace present a similar problem as we have seen in the previous chapter.

Faced with questions of this kind regarding the Qur'an as a source of the divine law, the jurists had two basic options available to them. One was harmonization. This could involve saying that a certain passage of the Qur'an presents the underlying principle, and that other passages that touch upon the same area offer particular applications or cases. Harmonization could also consist of reconciling the contents of two or more different (and apparently conflicting) Qur'anic passages into a single system, without privileging any one of these passages over the other(s). The other option, which has been mentioned several times in earlier chapters, may be described as that of abrogation. If different verses of the Qur'an offer instructions or principles that seem to conflict with one another, it is because the Qur'an came into this world through a prolonged process of revelation:

its contents are inextricably linked to different moments in the life of the Prophet and to the history of the earliest Muslim community.

God's later instructions to Muhammad are seen as superseding or, more technically, abrogating the earlier ones; what matters is not precisely where these verses fall within the 114 surahs of the Qur'an, but rather the time of their revelation and their place within the overall chronology of Muhammad's career. As far as the lawyers and jurists were concerned, this method could yield useful results. Beyond harmonization and abrogation, it is difficult to think of a third option. One could hardly admit the Qur'an contains clear contradictions as this would violate basic theological principles regarding the oneness of God and the finality of His Word. But no matter which option they chose, the Muslim jurists needed to engage in interpretation of the Qur'an. Only in this way could they hope to discover the divine will, whether regarding a general principle or area of the law, or as applied to a particular case. Thus the jurists had no choice but to have recourse to other sources of information that did not derive directly from the sacred text. For those jurists who opted for harmonization, this meant finding some intellectual ground upon which the differing Qur'an passages and verses could be reconciled. For those who opted for abrogation, it meant referring to historical narratives that the Qur'an, by itself, did not provide. Either way, the process of discovering the divine law made it necessary for the jurists to consult sources beyond the Qur'an itself.

There is wide, though not universal, agreement among Muslims regarding a second source of the law, known as the *sunnah*. Before Islam, this old Arabic word meant "ancestral custom": the venerable, time-tested, correct way of doing things. Under Islam, sunnah retained this meaning, but now in a more precise sense it came to mean the example that has been dictated by predecessors in the faith, the Prophet Muhammad first and foremost among them. Indeed, the concept of sunnah has often been understood to mean no more and no less than the example that the Prophet Muhammad set for his community through his words and deeds, and in many contexts it is correct to translate the term precisely that way. However, in some periods of legal history and among certain groups of Muslims, the concept of sunnah extended more widely, so as to include other persons associated with Muhammad, whether these were his biological descendants, his companions, the broad community around him, or others.

Muhammad's prophetic career spanned some twenty-two years, and apparently there were people around him who were eager to observe and record everything about him. Nonetheless, medieval Muslims asked themselves how one knows precisely what Muhammad said and did.

After all, it is possible that at some time, Muhammad may have indicated a juridical principle, or given the solution to a legal problem, but that the people around him afterward forgot what he said, or misunderstood him, or disagreed as to what he said or did. There was no single, authoritative text that recorded all these prophetical sayings and deeds because the only authoritative text dating from this time was the first source of the divine law, the Qur'an.

The solution to this dilemma lies in the hadith, an important concept sometimes referred to in English as tradition, or, more specifically, the traditions concerning Muhammad. In this context, we may briefly define hadith as reports of authoritative sayings and deeds that have been attributed to the Prophet or to those around him, or to respected persons of the following generations. What happened, we are told, is that on some occasion, Muhammad did or said something that afterward proved to be important from a juridical, theological, political, or ethical point of view. Someone from among his family, friends, or entourage observed this event, and retained it in his or her memory. Afterward, this person transmitted this tidbit of information (which we can already call a hadith) to others, who then transmitted it to others in turn. In this way, through a process of oral transmission, a great number of prophetical sayings and deeds entered into circulation throughout the Islamic world. Meanwhile, at some point, probably quite early on, people took notes as they heard these reports, and before long, books began to circulate that put the reports into the form of written texts. In this way, the hadith or tradition emerged as a major genre of Arabic literature. Nonetheless, orality remained the outstanding characteristic of passing on this information. The only way that an individual tradition or hadith could ever be considered to have been transmitted properly was person to person, with books or notes serving only to aid the memory, and according to rules and techniques that grew more and more stringent and formal as the generations went by.

The first thing to keep in mind here is that the sunnah and hadith, though obviously linked, are not the same thing. The sunnah is, in effect, a body of law, though not a law code, which governs all aspects of human behavior. It was demonstrated to mankind through the inspired, infallible actions and sayings of the Prophet Muhammad (and possibly also of certain other persons) and then circulated within the Muslim community through a long process of oral communication. It is a kind of oral law, standing next to the written law that is provided by the Qur'an. In this and other ways, the Islamic sunnah has much in common with the oral law of the Jews, which found its way into writing in a somewhat similar fashion. Like the written law of the Qur'an, the oral law of the sunnah cannot, in theory, contain any internal contradictions. The reason in both cases is the same: since God is the legislator, His law must ultimately be perfect and without contradictions.

The hadith, on the other hand, refers to the actual material that we have at our disposal, the oral reports that have been written down and put into circulation in the world. We may think of it as the vehicle for our knowledge of the sunnah. More precisely, the hadith is important and necessary because it provides the only possible way of discovering what the sunnah dictates or requires regarding any particular point. In and of itself, however, the hadith is no more than a collection of sayings. The problem here is one of authentication: does a particular report, or tradition, or hadith, tell us what Muhammad actually did or said on a certain occasion, and does it, therefore, inform us accurately about the sunnah regarding this particular matter? Very early on, Muslim jurists recognized that false hadith reports could be, and, indeed, were being manufactured and put into circulation for a variety of reasons. In dealing with hadith, there was at first no controlled or promulgated text, such as we find in the 'Uthmanic recension of the Qur'an (see chapter 12), only thousands upon thousands of generally pithy statements. As hadith reports found their way into writing (especially from around 800 C.E. onward), many books were produced in what soon emerged as a major branch of Arabic literature. These books came to contain literally hundreds of thousands of individual traditions. A few of these books became famous and revered, as they reportedly had screened out the spurious hadith thus leaving readers confident they had a safe point of entry to the sunnah of the Prophet. This was especially true of the two collections known as *Sahih* "sound" or "true" works that were produced in the later ninth century C.E. by two preeminent scholars: al-Bukhari and Muslim ibn al-Hajjaj.

In formal terms, a hadith or tradition has two main parts: the *isnad* or "support" that lists, in order, the persons who have transmitted the report, usually going back to the time of the Prophet and indeed to the Prophet himself. Then there is the *matn*, the "body" of the report, which is usually rather short, often only a few words, or at most a few lines. In the vast collections of legal hadith, the individual traditions pertaining to a particular statement of the Prophet may vary only very slightly, the differences between them being largely word order—the meaning of the text remained, however, unchanged. Countless hadith are in fact identical or virtually identical as regards the matn; but they are preceded by different transmitters making up the isnad which suggests the authenticity of the report. The hadith scholars employed a number of technical terms to indicate the reception of the tradition from one transmitter to another. These Arabic terms, although seemingly marked by differences of nuance, are all generally translated into English as "[scholar x] related (or received) on the authority of [scholar y]." Muslim writers sometimes employed an abbreviated form of these terms and modern Western scholars have followed suit using diacritics, usually an extended straight line or the print symbol >. The following is a representative example of isnad and matn, in this instance a hadith dealing with the subject of jihad.

> 'Abd al-Razzaq > Ma'mar [ibn Rashid] > [Ibn Shihab] al-Zuhri > Ibn al-Musayyab > Abu Hurayrah, who said: The Messenger of God, may God's blessings and peace be upon him, said: "The person who fights in the path of God—and God knows best who [truly] fights in His path— is like one who stands fasting [in late-night vigil]. God has pledged to whoever fights in His path that He will keep His promise with him and will cause him to enter Paradise; or He will bring [the fighter] back safe and sound with the reward he has gained, or else with spoils [of war]."

The topic of an individual tradition may be a precise point of legal or theological doctrine, or else an argument of a more general, ethical character (like the one just quoted here). Either way, the hadith, if it is considered authentic, provides a basis for knowledge of the sunnah, the example of the Prophet. It does not, however, constitute the sunnah in and of itself.

These first two sources of the law, the Qur'an and the sunnah of the Prophet, constitute what we might call the raw material of the Muslim law, divine legislation as it has been communicated to the world through Muslim scripture and the inspired example of the Prophet. By contrast, the remaining sources of the law are almost entirely functions of human agency and effort. They are, for the most part, intellectual tools, methods and approaches toward Islamic jurisprudence. Furthermore, these remaining "sources of the law" were matters of constant controversy among Muslim legal scholars. Once they took shape, the different juridical schools recognized different sources as valid; they disagreed with one another over the meaning of certain sources and how they were to be applied. The juridical schools also tended to list these sources in accordance with their own priorities and views. The numbering that we assign to these sources of law should not be seen as significant in any way.

The third source of the Law that we bring up here is known as "opinion" (*ra'y*). As the word itself seems to indicate, this activity was often viewed with suspicion. How can one regard opinion as definitive truth? However, there were many jurists, most notably in the early period of Islamic law, who maintained that a person who has attained the highest level of legal and juridical knowledge and who has mastered the techniques of legal reasoning and argumentation is entitled to pronounce upon difficult cases, following the dictates of his own reason. Of course, wherever the Qur'an offers a clear solution to a problem, there is no need for such an exercise of opinion. Regarding the sunnah, however, there was considerable disagreement, especially in the first centuries of Islam, over precisely what ra'y meant and how it must be approached in theory and used in practice. Accordingly, there was considerable room for the so-called "practitioners of opinion" (*ashab al-ra'y*), who had a major role in the development of Islamic law, as we will see shortly.

A fourth source, or to be more accurate, hermeneutic tool for determining divine law, is "analogy" (*qiyas*). This is what lawyers and judges in the modern world actually seem to be doing much of the time: whenever a new, problematic case arises, they look to past precedent in search of an underlying principle that governs both the old familiar problem or case (where the solution is already known), and also the new troublesome one. If they discover an underlying common principle (and usually they do), they can apply it to the new problem and thus arrive at a solution. This activity is, of course, closely related to the previous one (ra'y), since the exercise of "opinion" or "reason" in law often involves arguing by analogy and seeking common ground between old cases and new.

Another, fifth source of the law takes us in a different direction. This is known as "consensus" (*ijma'*). The idea here is that if the entire community of Islam comes to agree on a practice or principle, then this practice or principle must be correct; it must be considered as divine legislation, even if it is not part of the sunnah and is not found in the Qur'an. The principle of ijma' is expressed in a well-known hadith, in which Muhammad says, "My community will never agree on an error." Who or what defines "the community" here? The answer, in brief, is that the views that count are those of the learned jurisprudents who have competence in these matters. Other members of the community, the great majority in fact, are not given license to show any initiative in this area. Here, as elsewhere, the jurisprudents assume the role of the community's representatives. Furthermore, both the community as a whole and its learned representatives extend well beyond any particular generation or time. In other words, if consensus has been achieved regarding a particular question, it is the result of generations of accumulated practice and agreement. Accordingly, legal consensus is, by its nature, an intensely conservative principle. If a group (even a very large group) decides to reverse its position on a matter that has already been determined through consensus, it will find itself accused of "innovation" (bid'ah), a word that also came to be associated with "heresy," hence universally considered to be condemnable by medieval Muslims.

6th source of Islamic law

Still another juridical consideration that comes up in discussions of the sources of the law, and which we may list here as a sixth source, is what we may call considerations of public or common weal, in Arabic often referred to as *istihsan* and other related terms. When a jurist seeks an answer to a difficult question, he may be guided by what he sees as the long-term interests of the community as a whole, especially when these do not conflict with a principle or practice of the Qur'an or sunnah.

7th source of Islamic law

A final, seventh source of the law (here we are not following the most conventional order) is "independent effort" (*ijtihad*). This source has much in common with "opinion" and in many contexts these two (ijtihad and ra'y) amount to different expressions of the same idea. Invoking ijtihad calls for great emphasis on the institutional structures of the legal world and on the rigorous requirements that jurists face with regard to the material of substantive law and the theory of jurisprudence. But the basic idea is similar: a jurist who has mastered his discipline and who enjoys a high reputation for the breadth of his erudition and his capacity for discernment may apply his own reasoning, at least to difficult and unprecedented situations where the Qur'an and the sunnah do not provide a clear answer.

The concept of ijtihad has been much discussed in modern times because of a continuing controversy regarding classical Islamic law. The idea has been expressed—again, largely in modern times—that during the first centuries when Islamic law took shape, jurists had a great deal of latitude for developing original theories and ideas. By roughly the tenth century c.e., most legal problems had already been solved as the dividing lines among the major schools of juridical thought had been more or less established. Accordingly, the prevailing attitude became one of following the masters of one's particular juridical school, without engaging in the independent exercise of legal or juridical judgment. In this way, the "gates" of ijtihad became closed. Again, this is largely a modern argument, undertaken as jurists in Muslim countries have sought to reopen the gates and reinterpret classical Islamic law in such a way as to make it the basis for legal systems in the modern world. Meanwhile, other modern scholars have shown that in historical reality, the so-called gates of ijtihad did not close, neither around the beginning of the tenth century nor at any other time.

The Formation of Different Schools of Islamic Law

By the beginning of the tenth century C.E., approximately the starting point of the classical Islamic law sketched here, the environment of legal interpretation and substantive law had become dominated by a variety of groups and schools. This is not strange or unusual in itself, but two characteristics of this environment stand out. First, most of these groups and schools did not have a monopoly on political relations with the powers that be, and for the most part they did not seek such a monopoly. As we have already mentioned, they preferred to coexist with the temporal authorities that ruled the Islamic state while maintaining a certain measure of distance. Second, these groups and schools acknowledged and even respected each other, even as they disagreed over questions of substantive law and juridical methodology.

This brings us to one of the most basic and characteristic concepts of classical Islamic law. This is the *madhhab*, derived from an Arabic verb meaning "pursue a course." At times this term was applied to various kinds of groups. It could refer to people who followed a certain teaching, whether in theology, law, artistic production, or just about any other area. In the world of law, however, madhhab took on a more technical sense, that of a school of law, using the concept of a school in its broadest meaning, that of a school of thought. The establishment of madhhabs, understood in this way, became an institutional phenomenon within the evolving world of Sunnite Islam. By or soon after the tenth century C.E., virtually all Sunnite Muslims belonged to one or another of the juridical schools. The number of these schools varied at first, but in the course of the tenth century it became stabilized at four, a number which then remained fixed until modern times. These four are known as the Hanafite, Malikite, Shafi'ite, and Hanbalite schools. Each is named after a figure regarded as its founder. These were, in chronological order: Abu Hanifah (d. 767), who came originally from eastern Iran and spent most of his working career in Iraq; Malik ibn Anas (d. 795), who spent his life in Medina, in western Arabia; al-Shafi'i (d. 820), who lived in Iraq and then in Egypt; and finally the Iraqi Ahmad ibn Hanbal (d. 854). Several other great jurists were also considered to have been the founders of madhhabs, but in the long run their schools did not survive. By the end of the tenth century, there was general agreement that these four schools constituted the entire Sunnite legal universe.

Although we translate *madhhab* as "school of law," by modern standards these were informal, even amorphous groupings. As previously noted, there were no formally organized law schools that organized the curriculum and the granting of credentials. None had permanent councils, directors, or other aspects of institutionalized leadership. Instead, there were the wide networks of learning and teaching that we have already described. Students who sought legal and juridical training would gravitate toward teachers of their own school; they would acquire expertise in that school's teachings, and perhaps eventually set themselves up as teachers in their own right, always within that same madhhab. Nevertheless, they could and also did frequent the lectures of teachers from the other schools of law. Beyond these educational networks, the schools of law were vitally important in the everyday life of the Sunnite majority, because they provided the only way in which the shari'ah could actually be administered. An ordinary individual who lived in Baghdad and who belonged to the Hanafite madhhab would pray, give alms, marry, inherit, conclude business contracts, and so on, all according to Hanafite law. If he entered into a commercial dispute with a business partner, he would bring his suit before a Hanafite judge because it is likely that his Muslim business partner would also have subscribed to Hanifite law. Indeed, although Abu Hanifah himself refused to serve as qadi in Baghdad, for generations his students and student's students were the chief magistrates (*qadi al-qudat*) of the city and the Hanafite teachings took root there. As the city was the economic hub of a far-flung empire, the Hanafite rulings, which were flexible as regards commercial matters, made Hanafite legal scholars a decided asset for the caliphs and others residing there. To be sure, there were bound to be legal disputes between individuals who owed allegiance to different schools; in such cases there were procedures to resolve the issue to the satisfaction of both parties.

We speak here not only of various scholars who carried on the legal tradition of the major schools, but of the broad Muslim population that identified with a particular madhhab. Most often, one was simply born into it: you were a Malikite because your parents were Malikites. Broadly speaking, the schools of law had a geographical distribution, which shifted somewhat in the earlier centuries of Islam and then became fixed. For instance, Central Asia and Khurasan tended to favor the Hanafites. Iraq was mixed (after all, it was the original homeland of three of the four schools of law). Malikism came to prevail in Muslim North Africa and Spain. Egypt had a mixture of all the madhhabs, though Shafi'ism did particularly well there over the long term. Syria was also mixed, but Hanbalism flourished there, somewhat unusually, since this school of law generally had fewer adherents than the other three. It was not geographical identity that defined and united a madhhab, however. Adherence was a matter of personal status: you carried it with you wherever you went. Accordingly, the fourteenth-century North African jurist Ibn Battutah, in the course of his travels across much of Asia and Africa, earned his keep and more along the way by taking employment as a judge of the Malikite school (qualified candidates for this position became scarcer and scarcer as one journeyed further to the east). But what defined a madhhab above all was loyalty to a body of teachings associated with the eponymous founder (Abu Hanifah, Malik, al-Shafi'i, or Ibn Hanbal). It is unlikely that during their lives these four men actually thought that they were founding juridical schools. However, their students and followers carried on their work after them, and as the generations went by, each school of law developed its distinctive doctrines and approaches both to substantive law and to jurisprudence.

With regard to substantive law, the differences among the four madhhabs were, on the whole, not severe. The religious rites and observances of Islam remained substantially the same among them all, as did the basic structures and doctrines of commercial, family, and most other areas of law. Where the schools of law parted company was in their juridical methodology. Each of the four had a distinctive approach to the "sources of the law" that we have outlined. Each of them put more emphasis on some of these sources and less on others. They also defined and interpreted the sources of the law in different ways. The positions of the schools on these matters were complex, of course, and they evolved over time. The Hanafites followed their founder, Abu Hanifah, in favoring the use of juridical "opinion" or "independent reasoning." The Malikites, who had their origin in Medina, claimed a distinctive understanding of the sunnah: sunnah for them could, of course, derive from the Prophet's actions and words, but if a certain doctrine or practice had prevailed in Medina over the generations, it had legitimacy, because Medina had been the home of the Prophet and his Companions, and the capital of the Islamic ummah during the reign of the first four caliphs. The Shafi'ite school, whose founder was one of the greatest jurists in the history of Islam, devoted much subtle thought to the problem of reconciling the prophetical sunnah with the Qur'an. The Hanbalite school, like its founder, adhered to the first two sources of the Law, maintaining that once one discovered what the Qur'an and sunnah have to say about a matter, one must adhere to the ruling derived from that knowledge without confusing the issue by interjecting independent reasoning. Sources of the law favored by the Hanafites, such as "opinion" and "analogy," were thus suspect for the Hanbalites from the outset.

Although the schools of law remained largely marginal to the structures of the Islamic government and state, where a majority of Muslims belonged to a particular madhhab (as was the case of Malikism in North Africa and Spain), or where the governing class had loyalty to a madhhab (as in the case of Hanafism in Khurasan and the East), that madhhab inevitably found itself enmeshed to some extent in politics. However, it was not until the thirteenth century, in the Mamluk Sultanate of Egypt and Syria, that the classical schools of law became more or less systematically integrated into the structures of the State, with all four of them represented in court ceremonial as well as on payrolls, but even then, this integration was far from complete.

Our discussion of the madhhabs has been limited to the world of the Sunnites, which held the allegiance of the Muslim majority, but there were other branches of the universal ummah. Because of limited space, we can only discuss the most important of these, the Shi'ites, who over time developed their own distinctive system of law. The Shi'ites were themselves divided into various groupings and subsects, and their legal universe became complex and ramified, much like that of the Sunnites. Since most Shi'ites belonged (and still belong) to the Twelver or Imami persuasion, we are inclined to base our all-too-brief discussion on them. As was true of three of the four Sunnite schools of law, the legal doctrines of the Imami Shi'ites originated in Iraq. In the case of the Shi'ites, the spawning grounds were the cities of Kufah and Basrah. Possibly for this reason, the substantive law of the Imamis or Twelvers was not very different that of the Hanafites and, to a lesser extent, of the Shafi'ites and Hanbalites. Shi'ite law did differ from Sunnite law on some well-known points, such as a different way of calling the faithful to prayer, a more favored situation for women in matters of inheritance, and allowing a form of "temporary marriage" (*mut'ah*), which Sunnite lawyers tended to find abhorrent. However, the real difference was in juridical methodology. As we noted in our earlier discussion of sectarian politics within the ummah, the Shi'ites believed that 'Ali was the only Muslim truly worthy of being caliph and legitimate heir to the Prophet's authority. After him, a series of his direct descendants had been his heirs to that authority, even though they did not hold power in the temporal world of Muslim politics. All told, there were twelve legitimate heirs to the Prophet, beginning with 'Ali and ending with Muhammad al-Mahdi, who disappeared in Samarra in 873. As imams, literally "leaders," they were much like the Prophet in that they received some means of divine inspiration, together with special knowledge of the law. Accordingly, Imami Shi'ite law books based their rulings and principles upon precedents set by the imams, as well as by the Prophet. In the eyes of Sunnite jurists, this was unacceptable. So, for instance, while a Hanafite jurist might recognize the legitimacy of the rulings of a Malikite jurist, he would be less likely to recognize the rulings of an Imami Shi'ite jurist, even though this jurist's substantive law was, on the whole, closer to his own than that of the Malikite. There have been efforts throughout the history of Sunnite law to recognize the Imami Shi'ites as a kind of fifth madhhab (sometimes referred to as the "Ja'fari" madhhab, after the imam Ja'far al-Sadiq). In the long run, however, these attempts have failed, and relations between Sunnite and Shi'ite jurists were marked by suspicion in the Middle Ages and are so marked until this very day.

Imami Shi'ite jurisprudence, like Imami Shi'ism in general, is focused on the imams, the line descended from 'Ali who held special knowledge and authority from God and who should have held (but were denied) supreme authority and power among the faithful. Because on substantive matters of law, the Shi'ites so often followed what might be described as standard religious practices, the areas of difference that existed between them and the Sunnites did not raise the hackles of Sunnite rulers. The political implications of the role of the imams in pronouncing law was another matter altogether, especially as the Abbasid dynasts never arrogated for themselves the kind of religious authority claimed by the disgruntled descendants of 'Ali. At best, the Abbasid caliphs contented themselves with regnal titles that invoked a special relationship between them and God. How, then, did the Abbasid rulers of the ummah deal with questions relating to Shi'ite law and legal authority? First and foremost, they rejected all Shi'ite claims that the imams inherited the Prophet's political authority, let alone his unique status as lawgiver directed by God. Still, the world was not so clearly divided between temporal and religious spheres. If, during the murky development of early Islam, the Umayyad and early 'Abbasid caliphs actually did not think of themselves as lawgivers as Muhammad had been a lawgiver, they certainly were cognizant of their responsibilities to set into motion laws that would maintain public order and see to it that the existing law was exercised in a manner consistent with the wishes of God and his deceased Prophet.

Soon after the Abbasid revolution, one of the caliph al-Mansur's courtiers, the gifted Ibn al-Muqaffa' (see Part Two), suggested he establish a uniform, centralized judicial system throughout his domains, reserving thereby ultimate control over the judiciary for himself. Perhaps if al-Mansur had followed this advice, or better put, been able to follow this advice, the course of Islamic law, certainly the development of Islamic legal institutions, might very well have taken a different direction from the one it did. For, several generations later, the authority of the Caliphs to intervene directly in religious matters became a major issue in the series of events that we know as the *mihnah*, or "inquisition," a rather unusual chapter of medieval Islamic history that began in the first part of the ninth century C.E. and lasted through most of the 830s and 840s (see the following chapter). At issue was the intervention of the caliphs into a series of theological disputes on such matters as whether the Qur'an was created or uncreated, not at first glance the kind of abstract issue that would have exacerbated the sensibilities of politically driven rulers the likes of al-Mansur and his immediate successors. Their concerns were with heretics who deviated from Muslim practices and those who challenged their political authority. In the end, the caliphs abandoned the theological position they had chosen to support and withdrew from the fray; one suspects more from flagging interest in intellectual matters and public resentment than doctrinal conviction. The upshot of all this was that the ability of the caliphs to pronounce upon matters of religious doctrine became constricted, apparently even more than previously. Thus by the mid-ninth century (if not before), jurists of what would be known later as the Sunnite schools of law agreed that in principle the caliphs must refrain from declaring religious law, and beyond that not even interpret or pronounce upon the law. These functions belonged only to the qualified jurisprudents living and working on the margins of the Islamic government and state.

What then was the role of the commander of the faithful as articulated by the Sunnite jurists? The question is controversial, all the more so as it evolved over time. We should therefore be cautious about making dramatic statements for a particular period. and, of course, we should even be more cautious about how theoretical pronouncements actually bound the hands of temporal rulers to act in the political sphere. In general, it may be correct (at least in Sunnite theory) to view the caliph as an enforcer of the law. He could exert a degree of administrative supervision over the legal bureaucracy. More importantly, he controlled the agencies of repression: the armed forces, including a unit known as the shurtah, which was first formed as a security force tied directly to the caliph and then evolved into something like an urban police force. However, the real gist of the matter, for the Sunnite jurists, was that the caliph's mandate consisted of allowing the free practice of the religion of Islam within territories under his control, of protecting Islamic territories from invasion by hostile outsiders, and, where possible, of expanding the territory under Islamic control through raids and invasions of non-Muslim territory. (These last two points belong to the doctrine of jihad, which is an important part of Islamic law.)

As we have seen all too often in the world of medieval Islam, legal theory and the realities of daily life diverged at times from one another, and rulers and administrators tended to operate independently of the shari'ah in several areas. One of these areas was what we now call penal law, especially in cases of homicide. In the shari'ah, murder cases are basically construed as occasions for private retaliation, a residual sentiment of the tribal society from which Islam evolved. While the victim's kin and heirs are encouraged to accept payment (blood money) in lieu of strict vengeance, they still have a right to seek redress against the murderer and his kin. We can easily imagine how such a system emerged from early seventh-century Arabia, but in an imperial urban center such as ninth-century Baghdad, it amounted to a great anachronism. To establish order, any government needs to limit mayhem, and to exert some degree of monopoly over the exercise of violence. As a practical matter, murder cases tended to be adjudicated outside the shari'ah courts. This also happened in certain other areas, especially anything that pertained to political loyalty, as infractions and uprisings against the ruling dynasty provided the rulers and their commanders with an occasion for making a show of force. The defeat and capture of political "rebels" (many labeled for convenience as religious "heretics") were often followed by gruesome public executions, in which the already dead victim was drawn and quartered (actually halved), and then hung from public monuments for all to see, the quintessential demonstration of the authority of the state.

Thus in certain areas—especially what we in the modern Western world call penal and constitutional law—the shari'ah was restricted to theoretical discussion; the application of the law fell outside the purview of the religious authorities and was left to the government. In many other areas, however, the shari'ah was consistently applied by the shari'ah courts. These included religious ritual and observance, the many areas of law relating to personal status, and commerce. Seen as a whole, this legal system is noteworthy for its dual character. Caliphs, governors, and other rulers even held their own courts, which lay to a large extent outside the boundaries of the shari'ah. We do not know a great deal about the inner workings of these institutions. In particular, we do not know to what extent they administered shari'ah law, and to what extent their officers were trained in jurisprudence. It is likely that these factors varied in different places and times. At any rate, one of the functions of these courts was administrative, regulating the affairs of the governmental bureaucracies. In keeping with their name, *mazalim*, "[courts of] redress," they reviewed the cases of at least some of the petitioners who arrived at the palace seeking relief from wrongs. For this reason, the mazalim have sometimes been described as courts of appeal, but this cannot be accurate. It may well be that on occasion, rulers and high officials used the mazalim to overrule decisions of regular shari'ah courts. But since these rulers and officials controlled the armed forces, they could simply do whatever they liked on individual occasions. The mazalim, which must have grown out of the universal practice of a ruler's hearing petitions from his subjects, had an ad hoc character and a weak or questionable connection to the mainstream courts. Meanwhile, Islamic law in general never had a system of judicial appeal and review.

Like most premodern legal systems, Islamic law recognized only real persons. That is, only individual persons could hold rights and exercise claims. Collective entities or fictitious legal persons did not exist. Accordingly, there was no way to bring suit against, say, "the city of Damascus," or some public official. Collectivities such as guilds (a later development in Islam), regiments of the army, or madhhabs similarly had no legal personality, no existence in law. This issue becomes especially interesting in the case of the caliph, governor, or sultan: if he oppresses his subjects, or suffers wrong from them, can he sue or be sued like anyone else? Does the ruler's office bring him immunity? Some jurists dealt with such questions in treatises on the caliphate and imamate; some articulate the circumstances when even caliphs may be removed, but, as we have seen, the discussion was largely theoretical in nature as the religious authorities preferred authoritarian rule to anarchy and, in any case, society at large, even if united in opposition to the caliph himself, lacked the means to contend with the forces of repression at his disposal or that of his handlers.

Only God can make claims on all of humanity as well as the natural world. Some of these claims on humans may be understood in a general, ethical way: for instance, we may fulfill some of our obligations to God by giving alms to the poor. In a more specific way, however, Islamic jurisprudence identified in the Qur'an a series of crimes that it construed as crimes committed against God. These crimes, known as "limits" (*hudud*), were unlawful sexual intercourse, making a false accusation of unlawful intercourse, drinking intoxicating beverages, theft, and highway robbery. The medieval jurists viewed these crimes as infringing on God's rights or claims (*haqq Allah*), but they recognized that rights of humans (*haqq adami*) were also at issue. Punishment for these crimes was severe, consisting either of death by stoning, crucifixion, or the sword; cutting off hands or feet; or flogging and the like. Incarceration was rare; the prisons were usually reserved for political enemies and their inmates did not survive there for long periods of time.

It is important to note, in any case, that this picture of classical Islamic law does not apply so broadly in the current Islamic world. The emergence of the modern nation-state and the introduction of Western legal institutions, partly chosen by Muslim rulers and partly the result of colonial encroachment, together with the emasculation of the traditional Sunnite schools of law have created dramatic changes that have caused much concern among Muslim revivalists. That is, however, a subject well beyond this chapter and certainly beyond the scope of this book, which is devoted to medieval Islamic civilization.

The Origins and Early Development of Islamic Law

As historians, we are interested in detailing more closely the evolution of what finally emerged as a coherent system of Islamic law. Looking back in time to consider the origins and early development of that law, some questions seem especially urgent. Why was there not a unified system for administering the law after the Arab conquest that saw the expansion of the ummah over a vast territorial expanse and the embrace of converts from highly diverse backgrounds and societies? How could so much diversity grow out of the alleged unity of the early ummah? In particular, how can we explain the existence and the role of the various schools of Islamic law? What prevented the eventual development of a single legal institution and approach to the law?

We can only give a brief outline of some of the most important views and controversies dealt with by current scholars. A likely point of entry into the origins and development of Islamic law has always been the response of traditional Muslim historiography and jurisprudence to the questions posed above. The traditional view might be summed up as follows: The original Islamic ummah was indeed closely united. As time went by, the original unity began to unravel, first during the civil wars of the early period, and then later in the gradual decline and then emasculation of the universal caliphate, a process that began in earnest in the ninth century and was, for all intents and purposes, completed in the tenth. The religious community of the Muslims managed to survive and even to flourish, despite all the political crises. But from the outset of the Islamic expansion, there was a lack of communication between diverse and scattered Muslim societies. Thus, when people later set about to work on such difficult issues as juridical method, they entered into conversation with whoever happened to be nearby, and with people with whom they were already affiliated. Despite all their travels, the world in which Muslims lived was simply too large to allow for a completely unified conversation on these matters. Instead, they worked through networks of learning and scholarship that took form through several generations. In these ways, the plurality and diversity of the madhhabs and the decentralized character of Islamic law as a whole are consequences of the community's dispersal over great expanses of space, the passage of time, and the unhappy political history of the caliphate and the petty dynasties that challenged its authority. One should point out this is a picture of what came to be called the Sunnite world; as we have seen, Shi'ites had a world view of their own and even a widespread caliphate that lasted more than two centuries.

This traditional Muslim view has much to recommend it, but Western scholarship has opted for a rather different series of explanations. The first thing to understand about these alternative views of the growth of Islamic law is that they are inextricably linked to an old argument over the authenticity of the hadith. All scholars, traditional and modern, Muslim and Western, agree that in the hadith (or at any rate, in Sunnite hadith) we often find a particular doctrine enunciated in one tradition and then contradicted outright or in part in another. We often find a hadith that says "A" and another hadith that says "not A," or even "B." Since a normative principle is likely to be at stake, and since that principle may well determine substantive law, listeners or readers of hadith, especially if they hold positions of responsibility, such as a judgeship, must choose between the conflicting traditions, and must state the reasons and methods that have brought them to their choice.

Well over a century ago, Ignaz Goldziher, who brought to his Islamic researches a vast knowledge of Jewish law and its tendentiously driven traditions, published a lengthy essay on the hadith that became one of the most influential pieces in all of orientalist scholarship. Muslim scholars had always said openly that some hadith were the result of falsification and forgery. Goldziher went further and claimed that even though the hadith purports to derive directly from the early seventh-century environment of the Prophet and his inner circle, it actually has its origins in the lively quarrels over doctrinal, legal, and social issues that took place during the eighth and ninth centuries. It is thus all or mostly forged. If some individual traditions have a core of historical truth, the substance of this truth remains beyond our capacity to recover.

Two generations later, the German scholar Joseph Schacht went further, in building a counterintuitive theory of the origins of Islamic law. Schacht began by saying that in the years that immediately followed the Islamic conquest of the Near East, Islamic law arose in basically regional contexts. Some legal activity did take place in the political hub of an evolving Islamic empire, which was at first in Umayyad Syria, but the bulk of it happened elsewhere, Kufah and Basrah in Iraq in particular, but also in Medina (the ummah's original political and intellectual center). In these places there arose what Schacht called the early, regional "ancient schools" of law. These "schools" (not to be confused with the madhhabs that we know from a later time) functioned largely on their own, maintaining only loose connections with one another. They derived their substantive law from a variety of sources. In his meticulous search through the Arabic legal materials known at the time—Schacht's pathbreaking *The Origins of Muhammadan Jurisprudence* appeared in 1950 (Oxford)—he discovered what he said was old Arabian customary law, to be sure, but also elements of Roman, Jewish, and other systems of law. All these foreign elements and the residual pre-Islamic customary law of particular places and regions thus became part and parcel of the evolving law of the Muslim faithful.

To some extent, these Arabic traditions also incorporated laws generated by the Umayyad rulers, governors, and judges; this applied especially to the so-called Syrian school, which was based in Damascus, the Umayyad capital, and which happens to be the school about which we now know the least, as so much about the Umayyads has been effaced from the pages of written history by their triumphant enemies. The jurisprudence of all these early schools was anything but fully developed. They circulated legal maxims and formulae, based on the authority of important figures within the regional schools, or even, in some cases, on the authority of the school itself as a whole.

As time went by, the regional schools became more concerned with integrating the teachings of the Qur'an into their legal doctrines. Note that for Schacht, the Qur'an enters the picture, for the most part, only at this relatively late stage. At the same time, the jurists increasingly recognized a need for consistency and conformity. This led the regional schools to become more aware of one another and to enter into competition for primacy. And as they competed with one another, they began to deploy the hadith as one of their chief weapons. In particular, they began to circulate their old legal maxims and formulae—which they used to attribute to important jurists in their own local schools—in the form of hadith that derived from no less than the Prophet. As they did this, they quickly discovered that a hadith traced back to the Prophet could trump all others. The hadith, and especially the prophetical hadith, then quickly became a growth industry and the vehicle of countless arguments. In Schacht's view, the sunnah is basically a back-projection, an attributing to the Prophet Muhammad of an enormous body of substantive law that had actually been generated by other means, a good deal of it pre-Islamic.

At this point, the regional schools began to resemble each other much more than before. They all had bodies of substantive law that they had developed over many decades; but now they were concerned to attribute all of this material to the sources of the law that we have described earlier in this chapter, Qur'an, sunnah, and, to varying degrees, opinion and so on. As they argued more and more with one another, the schools began to lose their regional character. In these arguments, which were very much of a jurisprudential character, certain important figures emerged beginning in the eighth century C.E. in the main centers of legal thought. These were men, such as Abu Hanifah in Iraq and Malik in Arabia, who carried on the work of the older regional centers where they had lived and worked, maintaining and developing its body of substantive law. At the same time, they developed distinctive theories and methods of jurisprudence. Legal theory, in this case the hermeneutic or interpretive principles by which to understand the substantive aspects of law had now emerged as a discipline of learning. Perhaps the old masters themselves did not get very far with refining the principles by which law might be interpreted, but their devoted followers took up the task with great energy after them. In this way, the old regional school gave way to the new madhhab. In particular, the school of Medina turned into the Malikite madhhab, and the school of Kufah (or part of it) became the Hanafite madhhab.

According to Schacht and many other modern specialists, the real hero of this drama of early Muslim jurisprudence was the great al-Shafi'i, the founding figure of the madhhab that is named after him. Al-Shafi'i formulated a comprehensive theory of Islamic law, in which he indicated a highly sophisticated method for integrating the example of the Prophet together with the Word of God (the Qur'an). Al-Shafi'i thought that it was possible to arrive at a knowledge of the authentic sunnah by weeding out the forgeries among the hadith—which were already numerous in his lifetime—and thus to identify the true, sound hadiths that form the basis of our knowledge of the example of the Prophet.

Eleven and a half centuries later, Joseph Schacht found himself differing from al-Shafi'i, despite his admiration for the great medieval jurist. Schacht thought that no hadith could be proved to date from before roughly the year 100 of the Hijrah (718–719 C.E.). To be sure there is much more to Schacht's theory than these brief comments reveal. Like Goldziher, who wrote of the hadith in the previous century, Schacht was a man of prodigious learning and a meticulous scholar. A fuller examination of his views is likely to take the general reader into murky areas of arcane scholarship. Suffice it to say, for over half a century, much of the argument in the West over the origins of Islamic law has been an argument over the work of Joseph Schacht.

Nonetheless, Schacht's work, together with Goldziher's, is somewhat less favored nowadays than it used to be. A few scholars have mounted fierce attacks against it, while others have developed more measured critiques, accepting the concept of the sunnah and hadith as back-projections, but claiming that some sources actually may reflect conditions that existed at the time of the Prophet, particularly as regards religious law and custom. As more and more texts of hadith and early Islamic law have become available, scholars have analyzed these materials, correlating the isnad (the supporting chain of authority for each hadith) together with the matn (the text of the hadith itself) in more painstaking and systematic ways than Schacht had done or perhaps even would have been able to do in his day. As a result of this work, we can perceive, often in rich detail, the activities of transmission of learning and production of written texts in early periods, sometimes before the turn of the first Islamic century, the date that Schacht declared to be the true birth hour for a systematized Islamic law.

We also have detailed studies of legal activity in individual locales—what Schacht would have called "ancient schools"—in much richer detail than we did previously, including centers of legal activity (such as Mecca) that Schacht had barely touched upon. On the other hand, some recent scholars, although a clear minority, have expressed even more skepticism than Schacht did himself over the reliability of this early juridical literature, claiming that the juridical works attributed to such early masters as Malik, Abu Yusuf al-Ansari (a founder of the Hanafite school), and al-Shafi'i do not reliably represent their work. And so, the debate on the origins and development of Islamic law continues in the learned academies of the West. As a result of this debate, we have acquired a richer knowledge of the workings and contexts of early Islamic law.

If we agree with Goldziher and Schacht in their broad conclusions, namely that the hadith is largely a back-projection to legitimize later legal practices and also political claims, we may then say—as regards the controversies that raged over many issues—that the hadith, read with a critical eye, allows us to pinpoint some of the elements in those controversies and even to discern the general outline of how the controversies proceeded over time. Even if one were to allow for some modification of their views and concede that the hadith may contain some echoes of a real past, we would still be hard pressed to claim accurate insight into much that happened as regards the law before the second Islamic century, and certainly not during the lifetime of the Prophet himself. On the other hand, if we follow the "traditional" Muslim view of the matter, as formulated (in considerable part by al-Shafi'i) around the turn of the ninth century, then we may say that yes, there are contradictions in and among these traditions, as Muslim scholars have always freely conceded; the task that lies before the community of believers is to separate the true from the false, the sound from the forged. No matter how difficult this task may be, it will always be possible to derive the sound core of Muslim tradition, which will convey what is necessary to know about the norms that God has imposed upon His community through the agency of His Prophet.

Finally, we may mention Christopher Melchert's contribution to this argument over the madhhabs that appeared in 1997. In his enormously learned book, Melchert takes Schacht's hypothesis concerning the regional schools of law as a starting point. However, he does not put much emphasis on the bodies of law that these schools developed, whether independently or in concert with one another. Nor does he concentrate on the question of the hadith and its authenticity, which has continued to preoccupy many modern scholars. Instead, Melchert highlights the intellectual and jurisprudential controversy that dominated juridical conversation in early Islam for many decades and, indeed, centuries. On one side of this controversy, we find people who advocated the use of reason and opinion in their legal and jurisprudential activity. These were the intellectual forebears of the later Hanafite school. On the other side, we find traditionalists, people who said that the divine law is already available, in the form of Qur'an and/or sunnah, and that the jurist's task is to discover that law and to apply it, without further ado; these were the forebears of the later Hanbalite school. Melchert portrays the madhhabs as emerging slowly from this prolonged, complex argument. At the same time, Muslim jurisprudents faced similar problems everywhere and had similar tools ("sources of the law") available to them. Especially after the four "classical" schools of law had become established, they tended in many ways to converge in their ways of handling these problems. Melchert's approach to the formation of the madhhabs has many merits, including its deep immersion in the primary texts and its linking of local events with the broader intellectual issues that preoccupied Muslim lawyers and jurisprudents at the time. It is clear that much is left to be done. Undoubtedly, the discovery of new sources, particularly texts situated in earlier times, will help clarify the development of Islamic law and legal institutions. What is less sure, is the possibility that many texts will in fact be discovered, if at all.

Islamic Theology and Popular Religion

On the whole, the promulgation of theology, "the science of divine things," was anything but an intellectually detached process that had little bearing on Muslim society. At several important historical junctures, particularly during the formative period of Islamic civilization, theology and theologians were at or near the center of political as well as intellectual developments, which could—and, at times, did—give rise to controversies of all sorts. The theologians—by nature a contentious lot—often argued among themselves. As theology evolved, there were also long-term conflicts between theological and other circles who viewed the theologians with suspicion and even contempt, whether on political or intellectual grounds. Still others came to reject the dry and overly intellectual fare of an emerging systematic theology in favor of a more popular religion based on joy and love of God expressed through ascetic and/or mystical beliefs and behavior. In sum, the efforts of Muslim theologians were part and parcel of spirited intellectual, political, and social activity.

Note the words that classical Arabic uses for "theology" and "theologian" are respectively "*kalam*" (literally, "word, discourse") and *mutakallim* (plural: "*mutakallimun*," "one who discourses or argues"), suggesting in the latter case a tendency to dispute other views. Indeed, in an entirely different context, the term "mutakallim" seemingly applied, not to professional theologians, but to various propagandists dispatched by the nascent Abbasid regime in order to explain and promote its ideological line to diverse audiences. Our concern in this chapter is more or less confined to practitioners of formal theology, namely, the study of divinity and religious doctrine, and the intellectual and political climate in which they and their craft evolved.

It would be entirely misleading to think that theology's role was designed for extensive public debate. Theologians clearly engaged in intellectual contemplation of a highly complex and broad nature that was well beyond the grasp of the average Muslim. We need to bear in mind that over the centuries, Islamic theology became closely tied to the study of law. As a result, those calling themselves theologians generally received formidable training in the science of jurisprudence, which involved of necessity extensive familiarity with other branches of the religious sciences previously discussed, and related to that a thorough understanding of Arabic grammar to create a precise technical vocabulary. The links between theology and law can help us understand certain lawyer-like habits of the mutakallimun and the argumentative character of kalam as a whole. In short, the development of Islamic theology was of a dual nature: a response to the politics of the moment and also to intellectual concerns that broadly reflected questions about God and the human condition.

What are the origins of what may be broadly described as theological reflection in a rapidly evolving Islamic civilization? When Muslims took their religion with them beyond Arabia into the old urban centers of the Near East, they entered a world where theology (as well as philosophy and science) was a well-established pursuit, especially among the Christian majority of the population. How this foreign ancient learning affected the nascent enterprise of Islamic theology is difficult to answer as we lack direct evidence. Still, whatever they may or may not have acquired from their monotheist neighbors, the first Muslim theologians had an earlier and distinctive starting point of their own in the Qur'an. Questions of a broad theological nature were already evident at the outset of the Prophet's mission. We have already seen in an earlier chapter that Muslim scripture did not take the form of a systematic creed or code. However, we can abstract from it a set of principles and themes that amount, in a general way, to a "Qur'anic theology" or, perhaps better put, "theological reflection."

Like Islamic theology in general, Qur'anic theological reflection begins with the principle of God's uniqueness and unicity. The Qur'an rejects any plurality of deities and excludes the idea of henotheism, fairly common in pre-Islamic Arabia and some other ancient Near Eastern societies, whereby a single supreme god was thought to preside over a pantheon of lesser local deities. Instead, God (Allah) is sole Creator and Master of the universe. This universe does include what we might now call "supernatural" beings such as angels and jinn, but these share no power with God; they are merely agents of his grand design. Angels may engage in intercession (*shafa'ah*) with God on behalf of humans. Generally speaking, the Qur'an is at best ambiguous as regards shafa'ah; that is, God may allow such interventions, but only when He sees fit. In any case, it is God who renders the final decision. As we have seen, the Qur'an describes an omnipresent and immanent God closer to you than the veins of your own neck. He is self-sufficient and has no need whatsoever of creation, including humankind and all its works, but as God has created the universe and all within it, humankind is obliged to seek guidance when negotiating daily life and making sense of the surrounding world.

For those who are able to see and to draw correct conclusions—or we might say, for rational observers and thinkers—the world contains proof both of God's existence and of His beneficence. The proper responses of humans to all this ought to be gratitude, but often humans fail this test. There is, however, no concept of original sin in the Qur'an; true monotheism, the right religion, has always been available for those wishing to be among the believers, and indeed has already been accepted in advance by all generations of humankind in a primordial compact (Surah 7:127). Over time, people may have fallen sway to bad habits or evil behavior, but there have been many attempts at restoring the most ancient and true faith. The most recent and thorough of these attempts is taking place during the mission of the Prophet Muhammad and the establishment of a community in Arabia devoted completely to God's Law.

The Qur'an assumes that humans are rational and responsible, so much so that God has appointed man (beginning with Adam) as His "deputy (*khalifah*) over the earth" (Surah 2:30). Furthermore, "each soul acquires [merit or punishment] only for itself, and no bearer of burdens must bear the burden of another." (Surah 6:164) Temptation (*fitnah*) exists, often taking the form of wealth and children (Surah 8:28). But guidance is available, and salvation can be achieved. How then does membership in the community guarantee salvation? This is a difficult question, but on one point Muslim scripture seems quite clear: the previous monotheist communities, while they were on the right path in some respects, strayed because of their lack of cohesion and unity. This especially applies to the Christians, known for endless sectarian quarreling.

The new community of the believers or Muslims, by contrast, has solidarity and unity, with its members standing "in battle array like a tightly-constructed building." (Surah 61:4) These are some of the main themes of what we are calling "Qur'anic theology."

Early Muslim theology was born not only from the perspectives of the Qur'an, but also from the historical circumstances of the rise and early expansion of Islam. On the one hand, the amazing successes of the Muslim armies provided confirmation and encouragement for all the believers. But on the other, the unity of the believers came into question very early on. Readers will recall internal disagreements and resentments simmered until they erupted, in 656 C.E., with the murder of the third caliph, 'Uthman, at the hands of full-fledged members of the community. After this shocking event came the civil war, known to historical tradition as the first fitnah (here the Arabic word means "sedition" or better "civil strife"). The two parties to the conflict, led by 'Ali and Mu'awiyah, never resolved the underlying issues that gave rise to their quarrel, even when the war itself came to an end in 661. More interesting from a theological perspective is the emergence of a third party to the dispute, originally supporters of 'Ali who bolted his camp (Kharijites) rather than accept arbitration of the dispute between the standing caliph and his adversary, Mu'awiyah, the governor of Syria. The newly formed Kharijite movement took the shocking approach of declaring the other two parties—that is, the vast majority of the Muslims—to be unbelievers. Accordingly, the more extreme Kharijites gave themselves extensive license to challenge established authority and to kill and plunder, which they proceeded to do periodically over large areas of the Islamic world throughout the ensuing centuries. Many Kharijites were, however, given to a more pacific sentiment and were thus regarded as a group in good standing within the universal Islamic community despite their theological views.

In the aforementioned political crisis of the early Islamic community, Muslims disagreed with one another violently, but unlike the Kharijites who declared all their opponents guilty of disbelief, the other parties agonized over the problem of whether their adversaries, who had the blood of innocent Muslims on their hand, actually remained believers. This problem was especially acute in the case of supreme leaders. For instance, 'Ali's followers were likely to consider 'Uthman guilty of misdeeds, and hence there was a valid reason for removing him as commander of the faithful, even if that meant killing him. Were the murdered leader of the faithful indeed guilty as charged, his kinsman Mu'awiyah had no formal recourse to avenge him because 'Uthman's successor 'Ali made no attempt to be bring those who spilled the caliph's blood to justice. Keep in mind, the failure of 'Ali to hold the regicides accountable was the basis for Mu'awiyah arbitrarily having himself declared caliph, while 'Ali still retained the title. Following that the 'Alids accused Mu'awiyah and his descendants, the Umayyad caliphs, of turning their backs on Islam, a widespread but historically incorrect accusation.

Whatever negative judgment one may wish to render about the Umayyads and their politics, they remained fervent Muslims. Not surprisingly, the partisans of 'Uthman and the Umayyads leveled criticisms against 'Ali and the 'Alids. The marked divisions within the Abode of Islam only grew worse with the passage of time, and, as subsequent civil strife came and went, the establishment of sectarian groups, including many minor groups, became an established fact. All this division and strife seemed to make a mockery of the Qur'an's embrace of an idealized and universal community of believers living and acting in unity and solidarity. As the concept of the idealized ummah could never be compromised, Muslims had to grapple with understanding and explaining the course of events as part of God's will, hence the emergence of theologians and the need for formal, or, if you prefer, systematic theology.

Reflective Muslims were force to ask: What is the status of a believer who commits a grave sin (*kabirah*)? Does he still have a chance at salvation? If we capture him in battle, do we give him the same options as a captured non-Muslim? And what should we do if we find ourselves ruled by a caliph or a provincial governor who is guilty of such a grave sin? Questions of this sort combined readily with others that arose from the conversion of newcomers: How closely should we examine the new converts, both for their religious knowledge and their moral character? Should we exclude them if we find them wanting in either of these areas? Are we at fault if we judge them incorrectly? Meanwhile, as the Umayyad dynasty ruled, further questions arose. The Umayyad caliphs faced rebellions on many fronts, and some of them conducted trials and executions of individuals whom they accused of heresy and false belief. The most famous of these was Ghaylan al-Dimashqi, executed during the reign of Hisham (724–743). Ghaylan seems to have held that since individuals are (as the Qur'an says) responsible for their actions, they have no need for a caliph, or a "deputy of God," as the Umayyads were wont to describe themselves. We may argue now over whether we should consider Ghaylan and these other judicial victims as "heretics" or "rebels," but this question did not arise at the time. In any case, our information about these trials is sparse. It does appear, however, that the Umayyad caliphs, with timely help from some jurists, presented themselves in these trials as the ultimate arbiters in matters of proper belief. The Umayyads also used their power over the court, the bureaucracy, and the mosques to portray their rule as the expression of God's will. After all, they emerged as victors in the first two civil wars in the 650s and 680s, and they ruled over an extensive empire. They noted the Qur'an repeatedly declares God is all-powerful and all-knowing. If God had preferred for 'Ali to continue ruling or for anyone other than an Umayyad to lead the faithful following Mu'awiyah's accession, He surely would have allowed that to happen; but He did not.

By pointing to the omnipotence and omniscience of God as arguments in favor of their rule, the Umayyads opened up the problem of divine predestination and human free will, that Pandora's Box of all monotheisms. Are men free to act or are their actions predetermined by the omnipotent God in heaven? Opinion was divided on the issue. Some people, apparently including the Umayyad rulers, held that since God has power over everything and advance knowledge of all outcomes, our sense of exercising free choice and free will is mere illusion. Needless to say, that position was intended to validate the current state of affairs. Such a view might have appealed to certain tribesmen who still embraced the fatalism of the desert Arabs. Other Muslims maintained the opposite, namely that we do exercise self-determination or free will; only in this way is it possible for God's judgment on us to be just, or even meaningful. Each side assembled numerous quotes from the Qur'an in favor of its position.

The most famous Umayyad-era text that we have relating to this controversy is ascribed to al-Hasan al-Basri (d. 728), a famous scholar and ascetic. This text takes the form of an epistle addressed to the caliph 'Abd al-Malik (r. 685–705). God, says al-Hasan, is not a capricious tyrant. He never would have sent his messengers (i.e., prophets) to people, thereby offering them a chance at salvation, if He had actually intended for them to end up in Hellfire. Similarly, it is unthinkable that God would have meant to punish these people in all eternity for not obeying him, when He never gave them the option of doing so. Al-Hasan's defense of the free will is remarkably eloquent. However, there has been controversy around the authenticity of this text, and it may well turn out to be the product of a later time, projected back onto this early period to serve as a criticism of Umayyad claims—we have seen this well-documented tendency in many so-called genres of Muslim writing.

This alleged epistle of al-Hasan al-Basri is rather rare among our sources for early Islamic theological reflection, in that it consists of a complete text, transmitted in what appears to be its original form. Most of our information for theological argument during the first Islamic century and the century that followed is fragmentary, amounting to snippets and quotes from early authors preserved in books composed at much later times. These later books mostly fall into two categories: first, heresiographies or doxographies, comprehensive works describing (and often condemning) a vast array of Islamic sects and their dogmatic beliefs; and second, collections of biographies of individuals associated with particular schools or sects. In this way, a good deal of information is available, but the modern researcher has much to do in order to find reliable information and evaluate it because many of the lesser-known sects, particularly those that skated on the margins of normative Islam, might well have been offshoots of still other groups, and in real terms indistinguishable from them. Moreover, there is also the question of when some sects appeared in real time, if at all. Beyond that, one is often unsure of the step-by-step evolution of certain creeds and dogmas. As regards all these early developments, modern scholars should resist explaining obscure groups and trends of thought by the still more obscure.

Theological Trends

The Umayyad era saw the emergence of several distinct theological trends. To begin with, people who favored al-Hasan al-Basri's view, the advocates of the free will, became known as the Qadarites (from the Arabic root *q-d-r* "to possess power" or "ability"). Proponents of the opposing point of view became known as the Jabarites or predestinarians (from the Arabic root *j-b-r* "to force" or "compel"). We might think that opponents of the Umayyads would embrace Qadarite views as such views tended to undermine Umayyad claims to rule—as noted, the dynasty saw their rule as an affirmation of God's will. Indeed, certain Qadarites were in league with various rebels against the regime; others, like al-Hasan al-Basri, who possessed non-worldly concerns, steered clear of any overt political involvement. Al-Hasan was more inclined to preserve public order and allow God to render a final judgment. Such a position concerning the politics of the times was reflected in the teachings of the Murji'ites, that is, "delayers or those who postpone [judgment]." This name derived from their teaching regarding the controversy between 'Ali and 'Uthman: they said that there was no way to know which of the two rivals had been right, and that decision should best be left to God. Oddly enough, this irenic position was not seen by the Murji'ites as conflicting with their general acceptance of predestination, but it forced them to inquire about the believing Muslim who has committed a grave sin. Such a person, they said, must be accepted as a member of the community. Faith, according to the Murji'ites, was constituted by belief, or by the profession of belief, and by knowledge, not by works. This position contrasted diametrically with that of the Kharijites, who maintained that the believer who sins is no believer at all, and thus that faith was constituted solely by one's actions.

Given their delicate balancing act as regards culpability for the civil war that brought the Umayyads to power, and more generally their nuanced approach to predetermined actions and the treatment of sinners, it might appear that the Murji'ites themselves espoused quietism, as did al-Hasan al-Basri, the Qadarite, but such was not the case. On several occasions they allied themselves with armed opponents of the Umayyad rulers, and they assumed a leading role on behalf of new, non-Arab converts to Islam who demanded equal treatment from the Arab authorities, especially along the eastern frontiers far removed from Arabia and the areas settled by Arab tribesmen immediately following the conquest. Their most famous member was said to have been none other than Abu Hanifah, the eponymous founder of the Hanafite school of law. Abu Hanifah and the early Murji'ites were generally described as predestinarians; beyond this, it is difficult to identify them with a coherent theological program. One reason for this may be that over time, "Murji'ite" became a term of abuse, applied by later Muslim writers to a variety of groups with widely diverging, indeed opposite, beliefs that included, in addition the pure Murji'ites, Qadarites, Jabarites, and even Kharijites. If nothing else, this juxtaposition of such diverse groups under a single label should warn us to be very cautious when relying, as we must, on later writings to reconstruct early theological tendencies in Islam. That said, it would appear the Murji'ites remained an important presence, especially in Iran and territories further east in Transoxania, the vast area that came under the control of advancing Islamic armies around the turn of the eighth century C.E. There, they reemerged combining their original beliefs, such as they were, with other, newer teachings that will be discussed below.

Like the political division of the Islamic world into competing camps of Sunnites and Shi'ites, the systemization of the various branches of Islamic scholarship (particularly kalam and fiqh) and the so-called Greek or foreign scholarship (notably philosophy and that which the ancients labeled science) was a later development, one that first emerges with official patronage during the ninth century. In contrast, early Muslim kalam represents the theological ruminations of various groups of individuals gathered in different locations and, by and large, without an institutional base. To put this in a perspective that might make better sense to modern readers, over the first two Islamic centuries, one does not, for the most part, find the equivalent of modern university departments who favor one method over another and hire accordingly. During the earliest stages of Islamic theology, the time frame that concerns us here at present, the speculation about God and the world was likely to have been a rather eclectic and loosely organized project.

Perhaps the first step to a systematic theology with institutional backing took place toward the end of the Umayyad era. What was to become a distinctive school began to emerge, one that dominated both the intellectual and political concerns of leading Muslims until at least the early tenth century C.E.. This school was known as that of the Mu'tazilites, "those who stand apart," a name that has never been fully explained. The preacher Wasil ibn 'Ata (d. 748) is often identified as the founding figure of the school, but in fact the Mu'tazilites were a loose conglomeration of scholars, teachers, and preachers, at least during the first century and a half of their activity. Despite considerable disagreement among themselves, the Mu'tazilites embraced several distinctive positions. They began with the familiar problem of the believer who sins. Here Wasil and the nascent Mu'tazilites adopted an intermediary position (*manzilah bayn al-manzilatayn*) between those held by the Murji'ites and Kharijites: the believing Muslim who commits a grave sin is indeed still a believer (as the Murji'ites maintained), but he is nonetheless guilty of sin, and unless he repents he is most liable to suffer eternal punishment. Thus, faith is constituted not only by adherence to the doctrines of Islam, but also by the performance of works. As the later Mu'tazilites put it, faith comes in the totality of acts of obedience to God.

The Mu'tazilites liked to call themselves "the people of divine justice and unity" (*ahl al-'adl wa-l-tawhid*), an epithet that defined them accurately to a remarkable extent. Regarding God's justice, they argued persuasively on behalf of human free will. To begin with, they would have us believe based on scripture and the exercise of our reason that God is just. From there the Mu'tazilites argued that it is impossible for God to commit injustice—the sort of injustice that would occur if, for example, He condemned to Hellfire a believing, pious Muslim who had performed only virtuous deeds during his or her lifetime. The unrepentant, believing sinner faces eternal punishment, like the unbeliever (though perhaps to a lesser extent), but this only makes sense if the sinner bears entire

responsibility for his or her acts. What stands out about this argument—
and what attracted the most fire from the Mu'tazilite opponents—is the
way in which it seems to constrain God. On the one hand because God
is just, He cannot behave unjustly. On the other, God knows all outcomes, including those occasioned by sin, before they happen; and yet
He allows humans free choice to produce sinful outcomes. Similarly,
although God is all-powerful, He cannot use His power to permit or to
impose situations of injustice, but injustice nevertheless occurs because
He does not intervene to prevent humans from acting inappropriately.
Clearly, we are presented with a seeming paradox, one that plagued
ancient, medieval, and modern thinkers when faced with harsh realities.

These teachings of the Mu'tazilites on divine justice are closely connected to their teachings on divine unity. Here the argument revolved
around the attributes (*sifat*) of God. For the Mu'tazilites these attributes
were the adjectives that appear in the Qur'an where it speaks of God as
"knowing," "powerful," "just," "living," and so on. One might think
these adjectives would have to apply to God in all eternity because there
never was a time when God was not powerful. (The situation may or
may not be different in the case of adjectives that describe discrete
actions, such as "generous," "merciful," and so on, as not everyone was
worthy of His generosity and the like.) Similarly, if God is "knowing,"
does it not follow that there must be divine knowledge? In other words,
do these adjectives ("powerful," "knowing," and so on) not correspond
to substantives that exist in and of themselves? And if that is so, is it
not the case that divine knowledge, power, and so on must have
always existed, making the listed divine attributes coeternal with God
Himself?

These lofty though perplexing notions, which can be put in the form
of queries, became a central topic of Muslim theology as a whole and were
also taken up by medieval philosophers for there is a seeming paradox in
this line of argument. To begin with, the Mu'tazilites pointed out that to
say that the divine attributes are coeternal with God is tantamount to
admitting the existence of a plurality of eternals, a violation of the basic
monotheist doctrine of the unity of God (*tawhid*). God, they said, does
not (cannot!) coexist in eternity with anything, including His own attributes. The Mu'tazilites then took the matter further, by taking a negative
view of the attributes. The way in this direction had already been indicated by Jahm b. Safwan (d. 746). Jahm was not one of the Mu'tazilites
(he was an outspoken predestinarian), but he had insisted on an absolute
distinction between God and everything else in the universe. God has no

dimensions and no qualities, and we cannot predicate anything of Him, beyond this absence of dimensions and qualities.

Some of the Mu'tazilites now went on to say that we know only of God's existence (that He is), and nothing of His essence (what He is). Yet we cannot avoid thinking of God as possessing sight, knowledge, and so on; God's acts originate in Him and extend to His creation. Beyond that we cannot go. Later on, Mu'tazilite thinkers such as al-Jubba'i (d. 912) proceeded to a compromise position between the extremes of out-and-out negation and affirmation of the substantive attributes of God. The adjectives that we apply to God ("powerful," "knowing"), they said, are not substances in themselves, but are rather the expression of a "state" (*hal*) of the essence of God. There is in God, for all eternity, a "fact-of-being powerful," a "fact-of-being knowing," and so on; without being "existents," these "states" are nevertheless onto-logically real. The function of these adjectives then was not to describe God but to infer that God could not be without knowledge, justice, and so on. All this may strike current day Westerners as a precious intellectual exercise; it was no doubt beyond the comprehension of the average Muslim, but it resonated deeply in intellectual and even political circles.

This question of the divine attributes was not only highly relevant to the controversy over free will, which continued to rage; it also figured in a newer controversy, which involved some of the theologians in high politics. This was the question of the divine word. God has communicated with humankind on several occasions, most notably in the Qur'an, which is for Muslims, as we already know, the word of God (*kalam Allah*). Everyone can see that on the one hand, the Qur'an is literally a book between two covers, composed and edited at certain moments in history, an artifact of this world. But on the other hand, the Qur'an was under-stood as telling us of the existence, in heaven, of an eternal prototype for itself (Surah 85:22). In other words, there exists (and has always existed?) a heavenly tablet, a communication from God that precedes (but also somehow includes) among other things the book between two covers that we have in our possession.

Quite obviously, God's word—and thus, the Qur'an—was like the divine attributes which were causing so much controversy among the the-ologians. Here the controversy culminated in the question: Is God's Word coeternal with God Himself? If the answer was "no," as the Mu'tazilites and certain other theologians maintained, then the Qur'an was, in their language, "created." In this view, the concept of the "Qur'an" and "God's Word" still included more than a mere book between two covers that we can hold in our hands, but it was nonetheless something less than God Himself. If the answer to the question was "yes" and the Qur'an was not created, then God's Word stood, in eternity, on an equal footing with Him.

It is striking to see how much this argument over the kalam (Arabic for "word") had in common with the argument over the logos (Greek for "word") that raged among Christians, especially in the eastern Roman Empire during the fourth century C.E. After all, the underlying issue was much the same. For both Christians and Muslims, God has intervened directly in the world at a critical moment in human history, with His communication taking the form of a son for Christians and a book transmitted by His Prophet for Muslims. Either way, theologians asked what this communication brought to the world from its place of origin. What did it mean for God's word to be made flesh as Christians believed, or what did it mean for that word to be diffused and published, both as a book and "in the hearts of men"?

The establishment of the Abbasid caliphate in Iraq, in the second half of the eighth century C.E., coincided with the emergence of theology as a distinctive discipline, leading to the rise of the early theological schools of the Murji'ites and Mu'tazilites. Under these circumstances, some theologians sought patronage in high places, including the caliphal court. In this quest they did especially well during the reign of al-Ma'mun (813–833). Al-Ma'mun was perhaps sui generis among the great caliphs of the Abbasid realm in so far as he was a man of considerable intellectual gifts, and beyond that substantive learning. He reportedly treasured hearing the disputations of theologians and jurists, which he fully understood. For whatever reason, toward the end of his life, al-Ma'mun entered into the theological controversy regarding the createdness or noncreatedness of the Qur'an, and made taking a position on this seemingly rarified debate an occasion for demonstrating and expanding his own authority, which had been established on the heels of the debilitating civil war that brought him to power.

The caliph did this by promulgating long decrees in which he expressed himself as the imam, not only in the ordinary sense of "leader of the Islamic community"—in this sense all the previous Abbasid caliphs laid claim to being imams—but in a loftier sense of an infallible discerner of religious truth and falsehood (a claim made by various descendants of 'Ali ibn Abi Talib who grudgingly paid formal homage to Abbasid rule). His views on the mind-boggling question at hand (the createdness of the Qur'an) coincided very broadly with those of the Mu'tazilites, but were not entirely identical to them—it is not the case (as one often reads) that al-Ma'mun granted official status to the teachings of the Mu'tazilites, although it is clear he favored them. What is undeniable is that al-Ma'mun declared himself the authority to dictate religious doctrine, and then tried to coerce people into assenting to his views. In earlier times, as we have seen, some of the Umayyad caliphs used to conduct trials and executions of rebels/heretics, and thus established themselves, to some degree, as arbiters of belief. The same was true of the early Abbasid caliphs, but the question in these cases generally involved a perceived religious syncretism on the part of the heretics, a falling away from the true faith rather than a judgment concerning a theological issue. No one, in any case, had ever done what al-Ma'mun attempted, nor with such a display of learning.

This audacious move triggered intense opposition. Many scholars took the opposite position regarding doctrine; they claimed that the Qur'an is uncreated, rather than created, as al-Ma'mun and the Mu'tazilites asserted. Leading the charge against the created Qur'an were scholars of the religious law, including the famous Ahmad ibn Hanbal. The showdown came in a dramatic series of events known afterward as the mihnah or "inquisition." Scholars and men of religion in the employ of the government—which meant, above all, judges—were subjected to a test of their beliefs. They were asked a series of questions, leading up to: "Is the Qur'an created or uncreated?" This question was posed under stressful circumstances that could include being forced to kneel on the executioner's mat with the axe looming over one's head. It took considerable courage to insist on the uncreated Qur'an. However, the confrontation was just getting underway when al-Ma'mun died suddenly, in 833. The mihnah continued under al-Ma'mun's successor, al-Mu'tasim. Its most famous moment came when Ahmad ibn Hanbal himself was brought to trial. Our sources disagree over the particulars of the event, but Ibn Hanbal's followers claimed that he held firm, enduring prison and lashes. Over the long term, the caliphs did not follow through. The mihnah was lifted in 848 when, unlike his predecessors, the caliph al-Mutawakkil did not embrace Mu'tazilism, nor did he advance philosophical and scientific learning. Ibn Hanbal thus emerged as the victor, and the doctrine of the created Qur'an did not prevail.

It is rather doubtful that the general public understood the nature of the debate as a theological problem. One of al-Mu'tasim's Turkish commanders witnessing the beating of a person who denied the Qur'an was created expressed curiosity as to why the man was being treated so harshly. When someone attempted to explain the theological background of debate between the caliph and those who opposed him, the Turk indicated that he knew nothing of these things and for him, to be a good Muslim it was sufficient to testify "There no God but God and Muhammad is his Messenger," the fundamental expression of faith by which one declared himself or herself a Muslim. The issue that agitated many scholars went well beyond whether Muslim scripture was created or otherwise. What was at stake was the assertion by al-Ma'mun and his successors of their right to distinguish between true and false doctrine. This, legal scholars said, was not the legitimate function of the caliph or imam. The question of how to define that function was left for future debates already noted. In the end the underlying issue of religious and political authority was decided in favor of the religious establishment. The scholars of law and religion ('ulama') would have the authority to determine religious doctrine and points of law, not the caliph. This does not imply the caliph was reduced to being a secular leader as current Western scholars might define secular. Rather it signifies that the caliph should be concerned with temporal affairs and leave religion to the religious establishment. What emerged eventually was an implicit understanding that the world of politics would be left exclusively to the caliph and those responsible for public order. Responsibility for the spiritual welfare of the faithful fell to the 'ulama'. In practical terms, the nature of the arrangement bought the cooperation of the religious authorities and those who followed them. They were enjoined to render unto Caesar that which was Caesar's while reserving interpretation of that which was God's for themselves.

Despite this defeat, the Mu'tazilites continued their scholarly efforts; they attracted students and maintained political connections in high places. Over time, however, they became marginalized, at least in the metropolitan province of Iraq. Certainly they did not have the popularity and respect enjoyed by the winning side in the debate, often known as the Traditionists or "people of the hadith" (ashab al-hadith). In these years (around the middle of the ninth century C.E.), the pursuit of hadith flourished; traditions were constantly recited to audiences of eager receptors in many venues and written down in books of ever-increasing size. The Traditionists' basic approach to juridical and theological problems was to refer to the sources, namely the Qur'an and the sunnah, that is, the way of the Prophet. If one could not find the solution in these sources, it meant either that one had not looked hard enough, or that such a solution was simply not forthcoming. The use of independent reasoning espoused by the Mu'tazilites fell victim to the authority of scripture and the established precedent derived from the sayings and deeds of the Prophet.

We can think of this conflict between Mu'tazilites and Traditionists as part of a larger confrontation between reason and tradition. Note the argument over reason versus tradition was at the core of the contentious development of Islamic jurisprudence at this very same time. However, we must bear in mind that the Mu'tazilites, like all mutakallimun, had endless respect and veneration for Muslim scripture (even created), and that most of them also respected the power of the sunnah (though not in a way that satisfied their Traditionist adversaries). Meanwhile the Traditionists, for their part, did not utterly reject the use of reason. However, the Mu'tazilites were truly dyed-in-the-wool rationalists, in that they insisted that certain truths, beginning with the existence of God, are accessible to us solely through the exercise of our mental faculties, and that it is reason that brings us, in the first instance, to revelation itself.

The quarrel between the Mu'tazilites and Traditionists proceeded, with each side sharpening its arguments and expanding its arsenal of texts. As the Mu'tazilites doggedly defended free will, the Traditionists argued unbendingly for predestination. For the Traditionists, after all, God's doings are beyond our knowing, except for what we know directly from the Qur'an and from the example of the Prophet as this knowledge has been handed down to us in secure, unbroken transmission across the intervening generations. Beyond these two (Qur'an and sunnah), we have no basis for inquiring into God's actions. Above all, we must not suppose that God "cannot" perform or allow an action, even if its outcome appears (to us) to be unjust.

We have seen that the Qur'an describes God with adjectives such as "powerful" and "wise." It also refers to God as having body parts: eyes, hands, sides, and so on. The Qur'an similarly (for instance, Surah 10:3) describes God as "seated on" or "standing over" a throne. The Mu'tazilites insisted on interpreting these passages figuratively; for them a reference to God's "eye" meant His knowledge, His "hand" meant His blessing, and so on. In Mu'tazilite thinking, God does not exist in any form or in any space that is within our capacity to imagine. Here, however, the Traditionists unflinchingly drank their own medicine; if the Qur'an says that God has eyes and sits on a throne, then that must be literally so.

This argument over the anthropomorphic expressions of the Qur'an which seemingly saddled God with human qualities was actually quite old, going back to some of the earliest interpretations of scripture and hadith texts of which we are aware. In some of those old texts, we find the following question: When Muhammad received divine revelations, and when he experienced his night journey and ascension to heaven (see Surah 17:1), was he vouchsafed the vision of God, or did he see only angelic beings, such as Gabriel? Modern Muslim opinion on this matter is overwhelmingly on the side of Muhammad having seen only Gabriel. During the early period of Islam, however, the other side had many advocates, who had some impressive evidence in their favor. At any rate, in these later debates of the theologians and traditionists, all these arguments (over anthropomorphism and the Prophet's vision or visions) now combined in one of the classic theological questions in all monotheist traditions: Will the blessed in Paradise be allowed to see their Lord?

Later Theological Trends

In some ways, Mu'tazilism continued to expand. In geographical terms, it had much success in Iran and Transoxania, where it flourished in combination with other teachings such as the old Murji'ism and the new Maturidism (see below). Mu'tazilism took root among thinkers of Twelver or Imami Shi'ism in the late ninth century and became a basic component of their thought from that time onward, a rather ironic turn of events as the Mu'tazilites had originally been favored by the Abbasid caliphs. Neither the Mu'tazilites nor their Traditionist opponents foresaw a new challenge, the origins of which was coterminous with the caliph al-Ma'mun's embrace of intellectual concerns, namely the rise, or, if you prefer, renewal of philosophy (*falsafah*) as an influential branch of intellectual enquiry. As the ideas of the Greek philosophers (basically some of Plato, most of Aristotle, and fragments of Plotinus) gradually became available through Arabic translations, the mutakallimun faced both an opportunity and a challenge. Some theologians used these translations to sharpen and to broaden their own inquiries. In particular, students of theology who worked carefully through the logical works of Aristotle found themselves in possession of a weapon of uncommon precision, which they could deploy in their disputations with devastating results. But on the other hand, the "new" philosophy could serve the purposes of people who wished to discredit kalam.

Quite early on, the Mu'tazilites had developed an account of the workings of the cosmos that showed much originality and ingenuity. Beginning with little or no knowledge of Democritus and Epicurus (the great atomist philosophers of ancient times), they constructed an atomistic theory, whereby the basic building-blocks of the universe consist of indivisible particles or atoms that combine and recombine into visible substances. As the Muʿtazilites elaborated this theory, they became preoccupied by exceedingly difficult problems regarding physical movement and change. Such a view of the universe—as materialist as one could imagine—seems like a strange choice for the underpinning of a system of theology. (Christian theology, by contrast, never took an interest in atomism.) But in fact, God remains right at the center of the atomistic system of the Muʿtazilites, as He busily micromanages the entire universe. Later, as the *Physics* and *Metaphysics* of Aristotle became available in Arabic, the Muʿtazilite atomistic theories lost much of their state-of-the-art status. The philosophers were able to move well beyond the theologians. We see this in the two greatest philosophers of the age, al-Farabi (d. 950) and Ibn Sina (or Avicenna, d. 1037), both of whom disapprovingly dismissed kalam, largely on the basis of its atomism.

It could be argued that this philosophical attack against kalam from the left, so to speak, was a preoccupation of intellectual elites, and of little concern to the majority of Muslims. The situation was different, however, in the ongoing attack "from the right," that of the Traditionists. Here the quarrel (roughly speaking, between reason and tradition) extended beyond theology into the domain of law and jurisprudence, which tended to directly affect all aspects and segments of Islamic society. The quarrel was so central, in fact, that a compromise was bound to emerge. And emerge it did, in the work of Abu-l-Hasan al-Ashʿari (d. 936). After spending most of his career as a member of the Muʿtazilite school, al-Ashʿari broke away and began to construct what amounts to a systematic synthesis of Muʿtazilite kalam together with the Traditionist teachings of Ahmad ibn Hanbal and others like him. Al-Ashʿari embraced the atomistic teachings of the Muʿtazilites and developed them further, but on the matter of the anthropomorphic expressions in the Qurʾan, he leaned toward the Traditionist view, rejecting the Muʿtazilite insistence on figurative interpretation of those expressions that shielded against compromising the unicity of God. Al-Ashʿari held if the Qurʾan states God has eyes and hands, then we must accept these statements as fact. If we find this matter beyond our comprehension, we must accept it all the same, as al-Ashʿari most famously said, *bi-la kayfa*, "without asking how or why." Regarding divine justice, al-Ashʿari once again abandoned the Muʿtazilite position, asserting that we cannot say that God is incapable of performing or allowing a certain action because (to our mind) this action would lead to an unjust outcome. Rather, said al-Ashʿari, actions are just or unjust precisely and only because God's Law has declared and made them so.

In the old debate over free will, however, al-Ash'ari did not side with the Traditionists who promoted predestination. The standard Mu'tazilite view was that God creates the capacity in man to perform his acts; once this has happened, man is master of his acts and has responsibility for them. Here al-Ash'ari advanced a line of argument that went back to the early ninth-century Mu'tazilite teacher Dirar b. 'Amr. Yes, God creates a human's acts (and not just his capacity for acts), just as the predestinarians say; however, humans also "acquire" their own acts in such a way that they share responsibility for them with God. In this way, God's omnipotence and justice are both preserved, together with man's responsibility for his actions. And so, the Muslims were able to confront a conundrum that has plagued all monotheists from most ancient times when they tried to reconcile the human condition without having to invoke a capricious diety. In effect, al-Ash'ari's view on predestination and free will mirrors Rabbi Akiba's dictum of the second century C.E., namely that God has planned all, but humans have the choice to act as they do. This "acquisition" of personal responsibility (*kasb, iktisab*) remained the keystone of thinking on this matter for the rapidly emerging Ash'arite school, and hence for much of an evolving Sunnite orthodoxy, for centuries to come.

In eastern Iran and Transoxania, another synthesis arose, in the work of al-Maturidi (d. 944). Al-Maturidi differed from al-Ash'ari on the divine attributes and put more emphasis on God as creator of man's acts, while trying to preserve human responsibility at the same time. But in their systematic structure, these two schools were rather similar on the whole. The brilliant success of Ash'arism and Maturidism, in the tenth and eleventh centuries, coincided with what we sometimes call the "Sunnite revival." In other words, Sunnism now became promulgated as an "orthodox" creed with a more precise, identifiable, and—most importantly— enforceable profile than it ever had before. One reason for this "Sunnite revival" in the central and eastern Islamic world was the triumph of Shi'ite movements in many places, including the new Isma'ili Shi'ite caliphate of the Fatimids in North Africa and Egypt. The new, more militant Sunnism was aided by the emergence of the madrasah as a Sunnite theological college attracting students from a wide variety of geographical locations, many of whom circulated far and wide after acquiring their credentials. They in turn attracted circles of followers in regions removed from the madrasahs in which they had studied. In such fashion, the views of al-Ash'ari and al-Maturidi became widely diffused through-out the Sunnite world.

Systematic theology, whose origins can be traced to the formative period of Islamic civilization, thus had an afterlife when it appeared to some contemporaneous observers as nearly doomed to extinction. Kalam was now integrated closely with jurisprudence, including the study of the hadith. It could also be integrated with philosophical studies if that were a theologian's inclination. The supreme example in Islam of a philosophi-cally minded theologian is the Iranian al-Ghazali (d. 1111), a member of the Ash'arite school. Toward the end of his life, as al-Ghazali leaned more and more toward the theological side, he published his *Tahafut al-falasifah*, "The Incoherence of the Philosophers," an attack against Ibn Sina (Avicenna) and the philosophical tradition in general. A century later, in Spain, the philosopher Ibn Rushd (Averroes) responded with a defense of Avicennan philosophy in his *Tahafut al-tahafut*, "The Incoher-ence of [Ghazali's] Incoherence." But this work went largely unnoticed in the Islamic world as a whole. In Ghazali's work and career, we see that theology finally found a secure place in Muslim orthodoxy, after many years of experimentation and adventure.

Popular Religion and Other Reactions to Islamic Theology

The dry and abstract fare of kalam was beyond the interest of most Muslims. Indeed many theologians held that exposure to the complexities of speculative theology might very well undermine basic beliefs, as the issues they discussed among themselves could confuse less sophisticated believers. Even among the faithful who commanded the intellectual assets to understand the arguments of the theologians, there were those who sought a more direct encounter with understanding God and their own place in the world. Eventually, this tendency gave rise to a full-blown mystical movement with numerous strands, which in its most rarified theosophical formulations could be as abstract as kalam if not more so. There was, however, a substantial difference between the two approaches to understanding the Almighty and the ways in which He made His will manifest. The world of the theologians was largely intellectual, that of the mystics was infused with all sorts of personal and group behavior, includ-ing rhythmic chants and physical exercises to overwhelm the senses and induce an intimate acquaintance with God.

Most assuredly, various forms of popular religion existed among Muslims before the learned faithful undertook the task of systematizing theology, and popular religion continued to develop not simply as a reaction to kalam but as a phenomenon of its own. It also developed long before Islamic mysticism emerged in full bloom with highly developed doctrines. What then were the origins of this popular religion? Here we may wish to put this popular religion in a different, broader perspective, which includes Muslim piety and asceticism as well as the highly structured forms of mysticism that followed. Did these forms of behavior originate in Arabia among the desert Arabs, perhaps even before the Prophet made his appearance, or were they grafted on to the earliest forms of Muslim beliefs and behavior after the Arab tribesmen came in contact with the diverse world beyond the frontiers that separated them and the conquered territories? Certainly Christians and Jews brought to the table a popular religion of their own, which included many if not virtually all the elements that came to be found in that of the Muslim faithful: the veneration of saintly individuals and the holy places where they visited, lived, or were buried; the practice of various forms of ascetic behavior; excessive displays of piety; mystical journeys in which one sought divine contact; and the like. Are we speaking then of two parallel phenomena: the development of Islamic intellectual institutions and approaches, especially in law and tradition; and that of popular religion, especially certain forms of asceticism, piety, and eventually a mystical tradition, all of which may well have been strongly influenced by direct or indirect exposure to the older monotheist faiths?

There is unfortunately little that we know for sure about the religious practices of the Arabs in western Arabia before they made steady contact with the world beyond. As we have noted in earlier discussions, there are no written sources, let alone documents from the period of the eve of Islam, or for that matter the lifetime of the Prophet, save of course for the Qur'an, which was collated and edited after his death. But the Qur'an, which tells us something about early Muslim beliefs and practices, has precious little to say about popular forms of religion, and even less as to whether there were mystical beliefs or practices of any sort among Muhammad's contemporaries. There is, to be sure, the vague reference of Muhammad's ascent to heaven, which has been dealt with before. But is quite a leap to go directly from there to Islamic mysticism of the ninth century and beyond, as does Fazlur Rahman in his survey *Islam*, a book we have discussed briefly in our Preface. The same is true with some other verses from the Qur'an cited by Rahman in his chapter on Sufi (that is mystical) doctrine and practice. Reading several of those passages of scripture one senses how the Prophet, speaking through

God, gives his audience a feeling for the moment of his first revelation. Such declarations are the common stuff of prophetic pronouncements, for example those of various biblical prophets, but with the possible exception of Ezekiel, the words and actions of the biblical prophets and their followers are a far cry from the beliefs and practices of later mystics. Generally speaking, there is a danger of confusing prophetic statements about revelatory moments with the kind of complex doctrines and practices that empowered ancient and medieval mystics throughout the Near East. However much the Qur'an was cited as a source for mystical inclinations, it does not serve as an authoritative guide to the development of early mysticism, let alone to the later development of the highly complex theosophical doctrine that instructed believers how to establish direct contact with the Divine Spirit. On the other hand, we do have a good deal of material from the biographies of the Prophet and the historical and belletristic works that touch upon his times, and these sources do contain tidbits of information on pietistic behavior; but as we have been compelled to say again and again, these accounts are the creations of later times and are filled with back-projections from those times. Still, there is reason to believe that literature, even when it is tendentiously driven, may contain echoes of historical reality, particularly in the historical as opposed to strictly legal traditions.

We have already observed the circumstances in which the Prophet received God's revelation via the angel Gabriel. Speaking to this event, our sources portray Muhammad as performing a pre-Islamic act of asceticism to prepare spiritually, it would seem for the pagan pilgrimage that took place yearly in his native Mecca, the holy sanctuary town controlled and administered by his tribe Quraysh. Accordingly, he withdrew to the hollowed valleys of the surrounding hills and remained there in total isolation before Gabriel came to him with God's word. The practice of preparing oneself spiritually among the Quraysh is described in this connection by the mid-eighth century Arab authors as *tahannuth*, but there is no clear explanation as to what that practice entailed. It is no doubt assumed that the reader understood the author's reference. By the late eighth or early ninth century the word is glossed with Arabic *tabarrur*. When asked the meaning of "tabarrur," writers indicate it is "tahannuth," clearly a circular explanation that betrays a lack of genuine understanding. There is surely no reason for inventing this confusion; it can only mean that we are dealing here with an old pre-Islamic custom that was already lost to an early generation of Muslims and remained opaque until a modern scholar, M. J. Kister, unraveled the mystery, albeit from other sources later than the time in which the event allegedly took place. In sum: the legitimization of the Prophet's mission, which Western scholars might ascribe to later Muslim authors, nevertheless contained an echo of pietistic behavior that existed in the life and times of Muhammad. There are other examples that might be cited to demonstrate that the Arabs had traditions of pietism and asceticism of their own. Still, there is no shortage of speculation as regards the religious beliefs and practices of the Hijazi Arabs on the eve of Islam and shortly thereafter.

For several generations, the noted Arabist and scholar of Judaica, S. D. Goitein (d. 1985), lectured his students at the Hebrew University on the origins of Islam, claiming that Muhammad was seriously influenced by a group of Jewish pietists who resided in Medina. In effect, they were his teachers of sorts, and through them the Prophet acquired his knowledge of Jewish lore and familiarity with local Jewish practices. There is ample and convincing evidence that there were Jews in Medina; that they were bound to influence the Prophet, whether or not they converted to Islam, is eminently plausible; but that they were a conduit for a form of Jewish pietism requires more evidence to say the least. As we know little about the religious practices of those Jews, it is rather difficult to assume they were in fact pietists, and more difficult yet to suggest they be compared, as Goitein did, with later Jewish pietist circles in Latin Europe, the Hasidei Ashkenaz of twelfth–thirteenth-century Germany. The origins of ascetic forms of behavior among Muslims thus remain a moot issue. Some scholars cast their net even wider in an attempt to link the development of Islam, even at its earliest stage, to movements and circles of which we know little first hand, and even less about their possible influence in Arabia. It is best, therefore, to begin on safer ground. What is clear is that by the eighth century a culture of piety and asceticism was already well established in the Islamic world, and this culture was informed and spread by popular preachers who combined the pre-Islamic and early Islamic past with all sorts of materials obtained from traditional Jewish and Christian lore, as well as Gnostic beliefs and practices well known among the Nestorian Christians inhabiting the lands of Islam—in the latter case, the very stuff from which mystical movements are created.

Pious Acts of Devotion

Among the most practiced expressions of popular religion were acts of devotion undertaken at the burial places of prominent Muslims, not always but often Muslims who had earned for themselves reputations for ascetic behavior. One notes in this connection the various accounts listed in the Khatib al-Baghdadi's eleventh-century history of Baghdad, to be more precise the chapter of the topographical introduction in which he writes of the cemeteries of the city where scholars and ascetics are buried. Because the Khatib is meticulous in listing his sources, we know the anecdotes he recounts are based on much earlier traditions going back to the ninth and certainly early tenth century. The following is a sample of the author's fare: We are told by the Khatib of a certain man who fled Baghdad because he feared he would be swallowed up along with its populace by the widespread corruption of the great Abbasid metropolis. He was then approached by a man who bore the signs of great devotion. The latter instructed him to return to the city and have no fear as its cemeteries contained the graves of four saints of God which served to protect the inhabitants against every misfortune: Ahmad ibn Hanbal [the great legal scholar and the ascetics], Ma'ruf al-Karkhi, Bishr al-Hafi, and Mansur ibn 'Ammar. Reassured, the man returned to Baghdad to visit their graves [as did many ascetics and pietists].

The Khatib reports that when Ahmad ibn Hanbal died, a man dreamt that he saw a lamp on each grave (at the Harb Gate cemetery). A voice called out to him in his reverie and told him that the all the graves were illuminated at the time of Ibn Hanbal's interment, for the tormented among them had now received compassion. Similarly, another man dreamt about a neighbor who died and was about to be buried with two shrouds as that had been the custom for those whose final resting place was the same cemetery as that of Bishr al-Hafi (a reformed criminal turned traditions scholar turned ascetic who preached poverty before dying ca. 840 C.E.). Pilgrims to the grave of Ma'ruf al-Karkhi (d. ca. 815) received their needs from God when they recited: "Say: He is Allah, One" (Surah 112:1) one hundred times. A person who visited the grave over seventy years was wont to say God dispelled the anxieties of every troubled person who visited there.

We learn from the traditions about Ahmad ibn Hanbal that the grave sites of figures other than well-known pietists were places that were visited by those seeking relief from misfortune. Nor were all the visitors ascetics. None other than the great theologian and legal scholar al-Shafi'i is quoted as saying he visited the grave of Abu Hanifah (the progenitor of the rival Hanafite school of law) every day to derive blessings from it, and when in need of something, he would go there, perform two genuflexions and ask God to satisfy that need—with that, God never disappointed him. On the east side of the city there was a place of prayer (*musalla*) that was used at the time of the festival—presumably celebrating the end of the fast of Ramadan. There was a grave there called the Grave of Vows from which people were said to derive blessings and have their wishes fulfilled. Reportedly, it was the grave of one of 'Ali ibn Abi Talib's descendants; the authorities are unsure as to which one. The account goes on to say that the Abbasid caliph wished to kill that 'Alid [without having the onus of spilling his blood], and so he prepared a trap into which the poor fellow fell and was buried alive (a variation of a well-known legend of how an earlier Abbasid caliph supposedly did away with his rebellious uncle, as well as an account that calls attention to the finer points of the law of homicide in Islam). In any case, the grave was visited regularly by those who faced difficult problems. The standard procedure was to make a devotional vow and perform two genuflexions. Upon fulfilling the vow, the visitor was granted relief by God. Among those said to have visited the grave was 'Adud al-Dawlah, the tenth-century Buyid emir and de facto ruler of Baghdad and Iraq who vowed to fill the chest of the tomb with no less than 10,000 silver coins of good quality, if only God relieved him of a pressing predicament. Needless to say, as told, the story ended well for the Buyid emir and also for the coffers of the shrine. There are most assuredly many other accounts of this sort and many other notable Muslims are mentioned in them, and that is only for Baghdad. So many other locations were visited by the pious in hope of relief, especially the sites of the Holy Land, which had a long pre-Islamic history of such visits.

What was it that gave rise to the veneration of so many sites, declared or at least considered sacred? One could understand the veneration of the great sanctuaries: the places in the holy cities of Arabia, Mecca and Medina; the Temple Mount of Jerusalem and the alleged graves of the biblical patriarchs that marked the landscape of the Holy Land. But why so many other sites as mentioned above? Such questions call for bold speculation. Can it be that the continuing breakdown of caliphal authority allowed for the creation of still more informal practices in a civilization that featured informal structures and associations even when centralized authority was most strong? The medieval Islamic world witnessed tensions between the state and the provinces, between the capitals of the provinces and regional and more local authority, and between different ethnic and religious groups. There were, in short, multiple loyalties that allowed individuals and groups to seek their own direction as long as it did not frontally assault the political sensitivities of the government or those of the religious authorities.

During the tenth century, certainly a time when the Abbasid caliphs ruled largely in name but not in fact, a remarkable process was evolving in the practice of Friday prayers. From the outset, Muslims were enjoined to pray daily wherever they might be, but on Fridays, they were enjoined to seek, wherever and whenever, the presence of other Muslims and gather at mosques specifically designated as Friday or congregational mosques (*masjid al-jami*'). There they listened to sermons declaring fealty to the caliph and his appointed local authority. The Friday mosque and prayer were not only a place and service to pay homage to God, but they were also institutions to demonstrate the legitimacy and authority of the state. In the formative centuries of Islam, what we refer to as the classical period, only towns and cities could lay claim to a masjid al-jami'. In fact, the congregational mosque and judicial authority went as a rule together and belonged to the legal criteria that distinguished city and town from village and other rural environments.

By law, and more particularly by practice, a town or city, though it might have many mosques for daily prayers, was limited to a single structure for Friday worship. In heavily populated rural areas where no large urban settlements were found or in suburban precincts of major cities far removed from the Friday mosque, social and perhaps even legal innovation was possible. In the great imperial and regional capitals, centers of large populations, an enormous strain was put on the capacity of the single great mosque to hold all those who sought to congregate. Considering the enormous size of some of these mosques, one can readily understand how the local population had outgrown the very concept of a single Friday mosque for any location that merited it. But, even then, the formal establishment of a Friday mosque did not rest with a local decision. As the law evolved, the more lenient Hanafite jurists allowed for additional mosques subject to caliphal approval; the Shafi'ites demanded as well a valid reason. Only in extraordinary circumstances did the authorities allow a second Friday mosque within a single town or city, but even here a legal fiction was necessary. For example, if a body of water separated one part of an urban settlement from another, the separated areas could be considered independent entities for the purposes of establishing a second mosque. During the classical period, greater Baghdad had no fewer than three such mosques because of its unique geographical configuration, separated as it was by the Tigris and a network of canals. And yet, there is a description of how worshippers seeking to pray at the great mosque of the Round City were arranged in rows that extended well beyond the structure and the enormous open court surrounding it. Indeed the worshippers were said to extend beyond the original Round City until the shore of the Tigris, the river that bisected greater Baghdad into eastern and western cities.

By the end of the tenth century there seems to be a proliferation of Friday mosques in many places that did not previously merit them, along with local shrines attached to smaller places of prayer and tomb structures and graves at cemeteries where devotional acts were performed, one has the impression with greater frequency than before. There were also as before numerous popular preachers who worked the streets and also attached themselves to small houses of worship, presumably not as the chosen agents of the state. All this coincided with the erosion of central authority and the emergence, even within urban settings, of quarters and neighborhoods as distinct social units with their own informal local governance. There was, in short, a growing expansion of what might be considered sacred space and along with it a presumed increase in popular religious practices. Admittedly, this linkage between a compromised central authority and a growth of popular religion is to a large extent conjecture, although based to be sure on gleanings from a wide variety of contemporaneous sources.

One could, of course, easily exaggerate the alleged expansion of a popular religion that had no doubt taken root early in the classical period of Islam; even more so of the concept of expanded sacred space. The fact that Baghdadis praying at the mosque of the Round City assembled beyond the structure and the area of the original Round City did not mean the total area of their assembly was considered sacred once the Friday worship had ended. We should be cautious lest we read too much into the sources at our disposal. Some scholars have a tendency not only to see through walls that do not exist, but to invent those walls in order to see through them. At a scholarly meeting a few years ago, a learned presenter wished to demonstrate that the Tigris was itself considered sacred space as he found a tradition claiming that the aforementioned ascetic Ma'ruf al-Karkhi never used the bridges spanning the river to cross over from his native al-Karkh on the west side to the eastern city. The assumption was that a man of such religious fervor could actually walk on water, or to be fair to the presenter, that Muslims inclined to extreme asceticism believed that he could. With that, the Tigris itself could be considered sacred space. There are times, however, when simple explanations are in order. Using the available bridges to cross the river from al-Karkh to the designated location on the opposite shore would have entailed walking several miles on both sides of the river. Ma'ruf simply did what any sensible person would have done under the circumstances; he opted for a shorter route by going the docks and taking the ferry or one of the many skiffs that were available for hire.

Sufism: The Development of Islamic Mysticism

The practice of a popular religion that embraced acts of pious devotion and asceticism had many strands. It was both personal, as in the cases mentioned above, and organized, initially among small groups of devotees and later in a large-scale and highly diverse movement that came to be broadly known as Sufism (in Arabic *tasawwuf*). There is a massive scholarly literature on both Sufi doctrine and the various groups of Sufi orders that evolved over the Middle Ages—and continue to evolve today. Arguably, the more interesting developments in Islamic mysticism come after the period of our concern: the first four Islamic centuries or formative period in Islam. From the fifth Islamic century onwards, one observes the evolution of an increasingly sophisticated Sufi doctrine, the establishment of more complex rituals, and the congregation of Sufis into larger orders. Such an order was often referred to in Arabic as *tariqah*, a group that assembled in special houses of religious devotion referred to by a number of names, most commonly a *khanqah* or "convent."

Regardless of the period to which one refers, the literature on Sufism seems to be growing exponentially. This growth is not surprising, given the broad interest in mysticism, not only among scholars of Islam and other religions, but among the general public as well. Virtually all the surveys of Islamic civilization, past and present, give their due to the development of Islamic mysticism, and there are by now a number of books devoted entirely to the subject that are geared to the inquisitive nonspecialist. There is a virtual smorgasbord of books and articles for the general reader to peruse; some scholarly, some decidedly less so. Among our intended audience, there are likely to be a number of readers who are already familiar with Sufism in varying degrees. Our intention is not to go over familiar ground but to place the early formation of Sufism within the wider context of devotional practice and general historical developments in religion and politics during the early centuries of Islam.

An obvious and hardly novel point of entry into early Islamic mysticism is a philological note about the Arabic term "Sufi." The most accepted and likely explanation is that the early adherents of tasawwuf wore plain garments made of coarse wool (*suf*) rather than adorned silk or cotton, a testament to their denial of the spiritual corruption of the material world. In that respect, they bore a similarity to various Christian Monks, some of whom embraced Gnostic, that is, mystical ideas, a comparison that did not escape contemporaneous Muslim critics of the early Sufis and, more generally, popular preachers who drew on Jewish, Christian, and even Zoroastrian and Buddhist themes to warn their listeners of dangerous enticements. As Sufi views developed, the core of Sufi belief became the imperative to seek a more intimate knowledge of God, not only by renouncing material pleasures, but through expressions of love of the Almighty, and by inducing a state of ecstasy that separated their spiritual souls from their worldly bodies. Initially small groups Sufis practiced ritual chants based on the repetition of God's name; later, musical instruments were employed to set the necessary mood; and finally various physical exercises were employed, perhaps the most well known to Western readers being the dance of the whirling dervishes. As the object of all this was to achieve knowledge of God, some modern scholars have conjectured the term "Sufi" was actually derived from Greek *sophos* "knowledge," but most authorities consider that source unlikely, along with other explanations based on fanciful Arabic etymologies.

Attempts to gain intimate knowledge, if not fusion with the Divine Being, could give rise to suspicion of heresy—at least from the perspective of more conventionally inclined religious authorities, the so-called orthodox figures who stressed that God by His very nature could be known only through the visual signs of his will made manifest in the universe. That unknowabilty of God (to coin a rather awkward but useful expression) was considered the foundation of true monotheism from the time of the ancient Israelites through the onset of Islam. Although not related to any discussion of Sufism, the commentary to the Qur'anic story of Solomon and the Queen of Sheba (Surah 27:15–44) is an illustration of how orthodox Muslims were repelled by claims that human beings could somehow obtain intimate knowledge of the Almighty. Veering far from scripture, the Muslim exegetes describe a particular moment in the game of wits between the God-fearing prophet Solomon and the sun worshipping Bilqis, the ruler of the Land of Sheba. When the prophet has finally convinced the queen to join the ranks of the believers, she, apparently in all innocence, asks the prophet to describe the essence of his God. Upon hearing this question which he could not answer (who indeed has such intimate knowledge of the Lord?), the world's wisest man by far, a person who commanded knowledge of supranatural as well as natural phenomena, fainted straight away and his retinue fled in terror. Such was the dread of even asking such a question of a believer, let alone assuming that any human being had the knowledge to provide the answer. In the end all turned out well; the angel Gabriel intervened and forced time backward. The queen forgot the question that occasioned the uproar and offered herself in submission to a God made knowable to her *only* by His miraculous intervention on behalf of her adversary, the prophet Solomon.

In the formative era of Islam, mystics, as well as ascetics who did not embrace mystical views and behavior, shared a great deal in common. Both movements—taking license to use that term in this case—rejected the excesses of more extreme groups, the so-called *ghulat*, those who trumpeted views like the transmigration of souls; attributed divinity to certain human beings, which was considered rank heresy; and outwardly practiced behavior that outraged all sensitive Muslims, such as the alleged communal sharing of women. More importantly, many of these extremist groups harbored revolutionary sentiments against established authority. As noted above, al-Hasan al-Basri was perhaps the most significant of the early figures identified with the denial of materiality and was extremely critical of the Umayyad governors of Iraq, castigating them in fiery sermons. But, significantly, he did not himself participate in open rebellion despite the invitation to do so, nor would he encourage others to follow a path of resistance to existing rule. The low political profile of the Sufis, together with their decision not to break with the basic tenets of Islamic law, allowed the authorities to give them room to evolve into a significant movement that captured the loyalty of many Muslims. The early accusation that the wearing of coarse woolen garments somehow mimicked the habit of Christian monks was no doubt of lesser concern as Sufism took root.

It would appear that, broadly speaking, Sufism had a particular appeal to elements of Muslim society that were less fortunate, those who were never wearers of silk or adorned garments and never experienced the pleasures of great abundance in the material world. We should be wary, however, of drawing a uniform profile of Sufis and Sufism, one that covers the earliest centuries of Islam until and beyond the emergence of large Sufi orders several centuries later. H. A. R. Gibb, in his survey *Mohammedanism*, asserts that the earliest Sufi leaders were drawn from the ranks of orthodox religious teachers. But, he then goes on to say that in the ninth century C.E. they were replaced by individuals who were not formally trained in religious scholarship. According to Gibb, this new leadership belonged to the lower-middle or artisan classes of towns and cities. With that, he argues that "certain implications of a social (and one might assume economic) character began to enter into what had been a hitherto exclusively—and still remained primarily—a religious movement." (p. 91) In that respect, the Sufis were the safe outlet for social discontent against conditions he argues were sanctioned by the official Sunnite religious leadership (which we might add was then first taking shape under the Abbasid caliphs).

According to Gibb, this placed the Sufis in competition with the more politically inclined Shi'ite movements who sought converts to their own cause from the same strata of Muslim society, albeit without appealing to the same ascetic sentiments. This is of course a possible reconstruction of developments in the ninth century, but given a lack of definitive evidence, one should be wary of drawing dramatic conclusions; the picture becomes more clear a hundred years later. For one, it appears, contrary to Gibb, that there were scholars trained in the religious sciences who turned to Sufism in the ninth century and that the movement, which seemingly appealed at the time to a less scholarly audience, nevertheless gave rise to an incipient literature that addressed intellectual as well as residual socioeconomic sensibilities. Still, Gibb was quite right to stress that economic and social discontent was most often expressed in the early Islamic Middle Ages by embracing a wide variety of religious views and associations. That was no doubt true of the rank and file Sufis as well as those Shi'ites who trumpeted the 'Alid cause but chose nevertheless to remain quiescent. There was some consolation in choosing this path. Despite their station, the disenfranchised elements of society were given the means to retain their dignity and claim the religious/moral high ground, that is, as long as they did not directly confront established authority. For the believers, that tendency to eschew the dangers of seeking political power in the present in favor of certain redemption in the future began with the early mission of the Prophet Muhammad, a precedent that could serve as an example for Muslims in future generations.

To be sure, when a figure such as the mystic Mansur al-Hallaj (d. 922) became fully embroiled in the politics of his time, he was accused of heresy, namely, seeking union with God. Because of that he was subsequently put to death. In the end, it could be argued he was more a victim of political intrigue than of religious doctrine and behavior. His accusers included a number of individuals who were sympathetic to Sufi views. For the most part, the Sufis were on relatively safe ground throughout the formative period of Islam, and even in the centuries beyond, because their teachings drew upon the Qur'an and the tradition of the Prophet, and their religious behavior, despite various eccentricities, was still firmly tied to Islamic law. The adherence to Muslim tradition, broadly defined, served as the religious equivalent of a Bedouin boundary marker that provided initial safe haven for all who entered.

As orthodox Islam began to solidify in the ninth century, Sufi doctrine drew distinctions between manifest or perceptible knowledge (*'ilm al-zahir*) and inner knowledge (*'ilm al-batin*). The former, practiced by the non-Sufis, was, to be sure, indispensible in that it sanctioned Islamic law and provided general guidelines for Muslim behavior based on the tradition of the Prophet. However, the more significant knowledge was that of the inner self, which brought one closer to God. In that sense, the Sufis could be considered orthodox Muslims, but on a higher spiritual plain. As with orthodox scholars, the literal text of the Qur'an did not provide the Sufis with enough ballast to keep their ideological ship afloat however much they cited and massaged specific verses, and so they turned to the tradition of the Prophet. Where the already existing body of hadith literature did not go far enough to suit their claims—which was often the case—the more learned Sufis made use of tools acquired from orthodox scholars, and, as did the latter, they became highly inventive in shaping an imagined past. Retroactively, the Prophet was made out to be one of them, the prototype of those Muslims who transcended, indeed denied, material pleasures and concentrated on developing a greater sense of moral righteousness by constant self-examination. By the tenth and eleventh centuries, the features of what one may term classical Sufism were already formed and circulated in a series of learned manuals or text books that enshrined Sufism as part of part of mainstream Islam, albeit an eclectic version that was distinct from traditional orthodoxy.

The quintessential figure in combining the ascetic inclinations of individual Sufis and truly substantive traditional learning was al-Ghazali, who represents the high point of Sufism in the classical age of Islam, although, given the time of his career, he forces us to extend somewhat the chronological parameters of our study. As we see it, the formative period of Islamic civilization is confined by and large to the first four Islamic centuries; al-Ghazali's conversion to Sufism took place toward the latter stages of the fifth century. Despite his humble origins, al-Ghazali could hardly be described as a member of the class of artisans, shopkeepers, and the like who were attracted to Sufism because it gave them a sense of personal dignity at a time when others better connected sought self-aggrandizement, and because their embrace of Sufism placed them in tightly knit religious groups that allowed them an honored space in which to overcome their modest learning and station in life. As indicated below, al-Ghazali was a great theologian and jurist and was familiar as well with the broad discourse of contemporaneous Muslim philosophy, which he seriously criticized. In short, he was very much at home with the orthodox establishment, as it happens, not only on intellectual grounds. He fully enjoyed the support of the eleventh-century Saljuqid minister Nizam al-Mulk, the great patron of learning who established the Nizamiyah college in Baghdad, an institution that attracted the leading intellectual figures of the age. There at the Nizamiyah, al-Ghazali lectured to hundreds of students, becoming thereby one of the leading men of learning in the official capital of the realm.

After suffering a breakdown of sorts, and having become disaffected with what he considered the corruption of the religious authorities (who were seduced by the very system of patronage that allowed him to thrive) he left his post at Baghdad and wandered about the Islamic world before embracing the life of a simple Sufi, spending much time in isolation and meditation. Shortly before his death he established a convent in Khurasan to instruct others in the Sufi path, while adhering strictly to Islamic law and tradition. Al-Ghazali's great Sufi work was his *Ihya' 'ulum al-din*, "The Revival of the Religious Sciences," a massive work divided into four major segments: dealing with (1) religious practice, (2) social customs or behavior, (3) vices leading to perdition, and (4) virtues leading to salvation. The remarkable feature of this magnum opus is its accessibility to the average literate Muslim as opposed to the more scholarly works of the learned theologians and jurists. Having digested the subject matter of the *Ihya'*, the Sufi of modest learning had at his disposal a veritable daily guide to the life of a dignified Muslim whose future path to Paradise was abundantly clear. The greatness of al-Ghazali was his ability to translate the arcane scholarship of the world in which he was raised into a system that had broad appeal among less learned Muslims seeking to fulfill their spiritual needs. Many other works, including those of a much more arcane nature, have been attributed to this great thinker, but scholars are anything but sure that they actually reflect al-Ghazali's thought and are not back projections to make it appear that he embraced the abstract Sufi theosophical doctrines and the systematization of Sufi thought that were to emerge after the classical period of medieval Islam. We refer in particular to the emergence of Sufi Neoplatonism with its reinforced emphasis on seeking intimate knowledge of God by passing through different stages of self-awareness, thus overcoming human rationality in search of a higher truth. That somewhat later Sufi doctrine and behavior, however important to the history of the movement, falls outside the scope of this enquiry.

The innovative nature of the Sufi movement beyond the time frame of our discussion is an indication of how Muslims continued to adapt to changing circumstances even after the classical period. We should always be aware how porous chronological boundaries can be when speaking of medieval Islam and how, as regards Islamic civilization of the Near East and North Africa, the very term "medieval" is, as we have observed, a label of convenience.

Appendix 1: Dynastic Orders

*Reigns of the Righteous Caliphs (*Rashidun*)*

Abu Bakr (632–634)
'Umar ibn al-Khattab (634–644)
'Uthman ibn 'Affan (644–656)
'Ali ibn Abi Talib (656–661)

The Umayyad Dynasty

Mu'awiyah ibn Abi Sufyan (661–680)
Yazid I (680–683)
Mu'awiyah II (683–684)
Marwan ibn al-Hakam (684–685)
'Abd al-Malik (685–705)
al-Walid I (705–715)
Sulayman (715–717)
'Umar ibn 'Abd al-'Aziz (717–720)
Yazid II (720–724)
Hisham (724–743)
al-Walid II (743)
Yazid III (744)
Ibrahim (744)
Marwan II (744–750)

The Abbasid Dynasts of the Eighth and Ninth Centuries C.E.

al-Saffah (750–754)
al-Mansur (754–775)
al-Mahdi (775–785)
al-Hadi (785–786)
al-Rashid (786–809)
al-Amin (809–813)
al-Ma'mun (813–833)
al-Mu'tasim (833–842)
al-Wathiq (842–847)
al-Mutawakkil (847–861)
al-Muntasir (861–862)
al- Musta'in (862–866)
al-Mu'tazz (866–869)
al-Muhtadi (869–870)
al-Mu'tamid (870–892)
al-Mu'tadid (892–902)

Appendix 2: Glossary of Technical Terms

ahl al-dhimmah: Minorities protected under Islam; applied to Jews and Christians who also are known as *ahl al-kitab*, the "People of the Book."

amir: English emir; military commander; governor of a province.

amir al-mu'minin: Commander of the believers, title as well of caliph.

Ansar: "Helpers," residents of Yathrib/Medina who embraced the Prophet and his faith in Medina.

'ata': Gift, stipend, or grant given to armed forces.

bay'ah: Oath of allegiance.

da'wah: Call or summons to join a cause.

dawlah: Turn of fortune; revolution; dynastic order.

dhimmah: Protection, especially applied to people with revealed scripture.

dhimmi: Person protected under dhimmah, especially Jews and Christians.

dinar: Gold coin, from Latin *denarius*.

dirham: Silver coin, from Greek *drachma*.

faqih: Jurist, jurisconsult.

fiqh: Jurisprudence, methodological study of law and its structures.

fitnah: Temptation, trial, inquisition, civil war.

fuqaha': Plural of faqih.

ghaybah: Occultation, condition of being hidden to view applied to the hidden Shi'ite imam.

ghulat: Groups of Muslims who allegedly embraced syncretistic religious beliefs during the seventh and eighth centuries C.E.

ghulu: Syncretistic beliefs which offended Orthodox Muslims and moderate Shi'ites.

hadith: Literary tradition, sayings and deeds attributed to the Prophet Muhammad and his companions, originally via oral testimony.

ijma': Consensus; in jurisprudence, consensus of the entire Muslim community.

ijtihad: In jurisprudence, independent legal reasoning.

imam: Leader of prayer, leader of a religious community, has special significance for Shi'ites who believe their imams are endowed with special authority.

Imamis: Shi'ites who follow a series of twelve imams from 'Ali ibn Abi Talib (d. 661 C.E.) to Muhammad al-Mahdi (d. 874?). Also known as the "Twelver" Shi'ites.

Isma'ilis: Shi'ites who follow a series of imams culminating in Muhammad ibn Isma'il ibn Ja'far (ca. eighth century); also known as "Sevener" Shi'ites. Emerged as a political force in the ninth century eventually establishing a far-flung dynastic order that challenged the Abbasid caliphate.

isnad: Chain of tradition in which the transmitters of hadith or historical texts are listed to verify the account's credibility.

jihad: Striving (for the faith), often meaning holy war.

jizyah: Poll tax levied on non-Muslims in the Abode of Islam.

kalam: Literally "word"; disputational theology.

katib: Secretary, equivalent of cabinet officer.

kharaj: Tax on land or its produce.

Kharijite: "Those who leave," in reference to dissident purists who left the camp of the caliph 'Ali during the first civil was (656–661). They subsequently became a major sectarian group that challenged established authority from time to time.

khutbah: Sermon, especially delivered at communal prayer on Fridays.

laqab: Nickname, regnal title.

madhhab: School or trend within Sunnite law. The four classical schools being Hanafite, Malikite, Shafi'ite, and Hanbalite, named after eighth- and ninth-century jurists considered to be their founders.

maghazi: Raids; as a literary genre, accounts of the Prophet and the early Muslims and their military campaigns.

al-Mahdi: The "rightly guided one" who will restore peace and justice on this earth. Used as a regnal title by various Abbasids and 'Alids.

mawla pl. *mawali*: Client, retainer, freedman, patron. Generally applied in Islamic times to Arabs or more specifically non-Arabs who attached themselves to Arab Muslim kinship groups.

mihnah: Test, inquisition, with particular reference to the test of belief in the createdness or non-createdness of the Qur'an.

muhajirun: Emigrants form Mecca who became part of the Muslim community first formed in Medina.

Murji'ites: An early school of theology that emerged in Umayyad times.

Mu'tazilites: Major school of theology prominent in ninth-century Baghdad and afterward in the eastern provinces and elsewhere. They were considered rationalists and opponents of those who embraced the sunnah or tradition of the Prophet to the exclusion of rational thought as a source of Islamic law.

Qadarites: Theologians, proponents of free will and opposed to predestination.

qadi: Islamic judge

qiyas: In jurisprudence, the use of analogy as a tool of legal reasoning.

ra'y: In jurisprudence, the use of independent reason in arriving at legal decisions.

riddah: Apostasy, reverting to one's former religion; describes the wars taking place in Arabia after the death of the Prophet in 632.

shari'ah: Literally, "the way" taken as meaning divine law as a whole.

shura: Originally tribal council formed to elect tribal leader, later applied to council that convened to select new caliph.

sirah: Literally, "the way" refers in general to the biographical literature on the Prophet, most specifically, the work of Ibn Ishaq (d. 767).

Sufism: Islamic mysticism, broadly defined.

sultan: Literally, "authority" or government in its broadest sense. Beginning with the Saljuqid arrival in Baghdad (1055), it denoted the formal title of the Saljuqid rulers.

sunnah: Normative behavior; among Muslims the example set by the way and deeds of the Prophet, one of the foundations of Islamic law.

tafsir: Qur'an commentary and exegesis.

'ulama' pl. of *'alim*: The community of learned men in the various disciplines of advanced learning.

wazir: English "vizier," the right hand of the caliph and usually head of the administration of the state.

Appendix 3: Chronology

Ca. 570	The birth of Muhammad, the Qurayshite from the clan of Hashim, in Mecca.
602–628	War between the Sasanians and Byzantines.
Ca. 610	Beginning of Muhammad's career as Prophet in Mecca.
622	The Hijrah, or emigration of the Prophet and his followers to Medina (Yathrib), the event that later marked the beginning of the Muslim calendar.
624–628	Intermittent warfare between the Muslims and Quraysh and their allies until the Truce of Hudaybiyah.
628	Muhammad subdues the Jews of Khaybar ending all Jewish political and military opposition to the Muslims.
630	The Meccans submit to Muhammad and convert to Islam.
632	Muhammad dies in Medina and is succeeded by Abu Bakr.
632–634	Abu Bakr conquers all of Arabia for Islam during the so-called wars against apostacy (*riddah*).
634–644	The conquest of Syria, Iraq, Egypt, and parts of Iran, and the emergence of the nascent Islamic state under the caliph ʿUmar ibn al-Khattab.
Ca. 653	The promulgation of an official text of the Qurʾan by ʿUthman ibn ʿAffan, the third caliph.
656	ʿAli is chosen caliph after the murder of ʿUthman, an event that triggers the first civil war (*fitnah*).
661	ʿAli is assassinated and his rival Muʿawiyah becomes caliph marking the beginning of the Umayyad dynasty and the end of Hashimite rule.
670	The beginning of the conquest of North Africa.

680	The martyrdom of al-Husayn, the son of 'Ali in an attempt to overthrow the Umayyads.
685–705	The caliph 'Abd al-Malik brings about the Arabization and Islamization of the government and begins a massive building campaign in Jerusalem during a civil war against a counter-caliphate of the old Muslims at Medina.
692	The Umayyads crush the last rebels in the civil war.
705–715	Muslim armies dispatched by the caliph al-Walid campaign in Central Asia.
711	The Muslims cross the Mediterranean and conquer the Iberian Peninsula.
717	Failure of the Muslims to capture Constantinople, allowing a conflict between the Muslims and Byzantines to continue for another 700 years or so.
724–743	An overextended Umayyad regime feels the pangs of incipient decline.
744–745	Civil war breaks out among different Umayyad factions and their tribal units.
747–750	The Abbasid Revolution destroys the ruling house of Umayyah and returns the Hashimites to the head of the *ummah*.
755	Al-Andalus (Islamic Spain) becomes independent of the Abbasid caliphate and is ruled by a surviving Umayyad prince.
762	The Abbasid caliph al-Mansur founds Baghdad as the capital of the realm.
786–809	The reign of Harun al-Rashid, regarded as the apogee of Abbasid rule.
800–909	The Aghlabids establish a semi-autonomous regime in North Africa while formally recognizing the Abbasid caliphate in Baghdad.
809–813	Al-Amin becomes caliph, an event that initiates civil war between him and his brother al-Ma'mun the governor of Khurasan.
813	Baghdad falls to al-Ma'mun's forces and al-Amin is killed in Egypt.
813–833	A learned al-Ma'mun promotes the study of ancient science and philosophy.
821–873	The emergence of the Tahirids, who become a petty dynasty in the east.
833	Al-Ma'mun becomes involved in theological dispute on the "createdness" or "uncreatedness" of the Qur'an introducing thereby the inquisition (*mihnah*).
833–842	Al-Mu'tasim succeeds his brother al-Ma'mun and the mihnah continues; on the political front, the new caliph introduces a Turkish forces and regiments from Transoxania into the imperial army while establishing a new capital of the realm at Samarra, some sixty miles from Baghdad.

837	Al-Mu'tasim moves his court and major elements of the army to a new capital at Samarra, some sixty miles from Baghdad.
847–861	Reign of al-Mutawakkil who succeeds his brother al-Wathiq (842–847). He ends the mihnah and undertakes a major building campaign in the capital, which creates a financial crisis in the regime.
861–870	The murder of al-Mutawakkil results in a decade of near anarchy and a weakening of the Abbasid caliphate.
869–883	Revolt of the Zanj in the swamplands of southern Iraq.
868–905	The Tulunids establish an autonomous petty dynasty in Egypt. The 'Alid Muhammad al-Mahdi, considered the twelfth imam, disappears in Samarra.
873–900	The Saffarids, another petty dynasty, gains control over Khurasan.
873	Radical Isma'ili Shi'ism spreads across the Islamic world.
892–902	The caliph al-Mu'tadid and his vice regent al-Muwaffaq restore the Caliphate's power and return the regime to the old capital Baghdad.
892–899	The Samanids take control of Khurasan and Transoxiana.
908–932	The reign of the Abbasid caliph al-Muqtadir and the decline once again of Abbasid rule.
909	Beginning of the Shi'ite Fatimid caliphate in North Africa.
922	Execution of the mystic Mansur al-Hallaj.
936	Death of the theologian al-Asha'ri.
941	Death of the theologian al-Maturidi.
945	The Buyid emir Mu'izz al-Dawlah becomes de facto ruler of Baghdad.
950	Death of the philosopher al-Farabi.
969	The Fatimids conquer Egypt and establish a widespread Shi'ite dynasty centered at their newly established capital al-Qahirah (Cairo).
977	Beginning of the Ghaznavid dynasty in the east.
996–1002	The reign of the Fatimid caliph al-Hakim and the persecution of Jews and Christians.
996–1030	The Ghaznavid ruler Mahmud raids and conquers northern India.
1037	The death of the philosopher Ibn Sina (Avicenna).
1040	The Saljuq Turks defeat the Ghaznavids and move across Iran.
1055	Tughril Bak, the Saljuqid, enters Baghdad and assumes the title sultan.
1171	The Sunnite Ayyubids end Fatimid rule.
1258	The Mongols conquer Baghdad, effectively ending the Abbasid caliphate.

Appendix 4: Illustrations

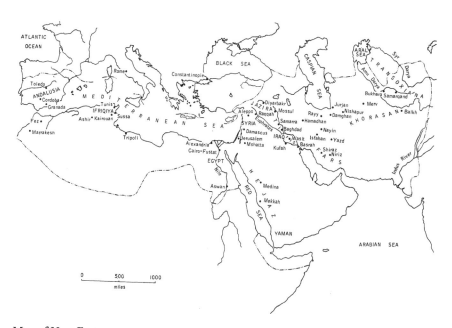

Map of Near East.

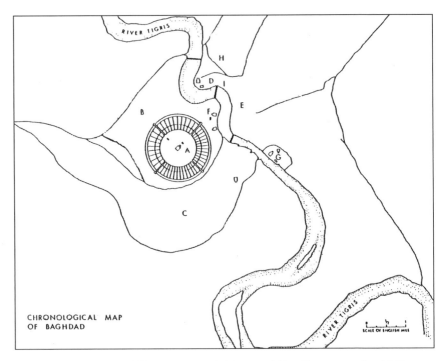

CHRONOLOGICAL MAP
OF BAGHDAD

Baghdad in the Early Middle Ages. Legend: (A) Round City. It was completed 762 C.E.
(B) Al-Harbiyah. A military suburb of Baghdad, it was begun before completion of
Round City. (C) Al-Karh. The great market area of the West Side, it was expanded in
774 C.E. (D) Al-Rusafah. The palace complex of the Caliph al-Mahdi, it was completed
776 C.E. (E) Al-Mukharrim. A residential district, possibly occupied as early as 769 C.E.,
it grew significantly after the development of al-Rusafah. (F) Al-Kuld. Al-Mansur's second residential palace built in 774 C.E. and occupied by the The later caliphs al-Rashid
and al-Ma'mun. (G) Dar al-Khilafah. The third major caliphal complex built in stages
after the Samarra interlude. (H) Al-Shammasiyah. Originally a staging ground for
military reviews and a camp ground, it was developed as a palace complex by the Buyid
emirs in the tenth century. (I) Bab al-Taq. The main commercial area servicing
al-Rusafah and the upper reaches of al-Mukharrim, it was probably developed as early
as 769 C.E. and greatly expanded in 776.

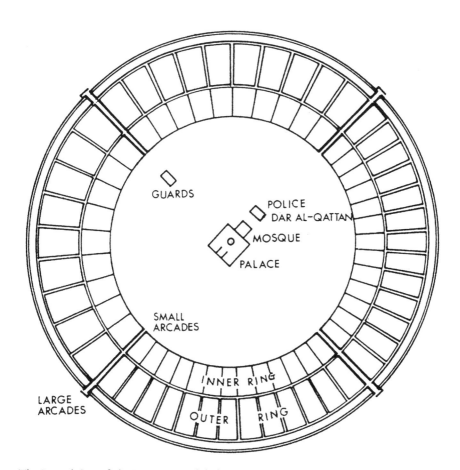

The Round City of al-Mansur at Baghdad.

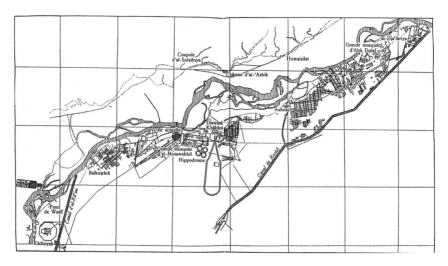

Map of Samarra.

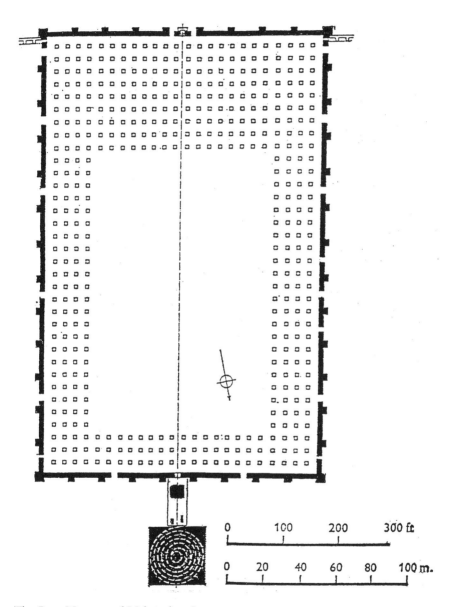

The Great Mosque and Malwiyah at Samarra.

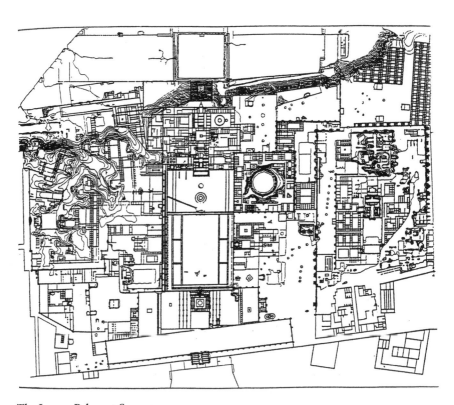

The Jawsaq Palace at Samarra.

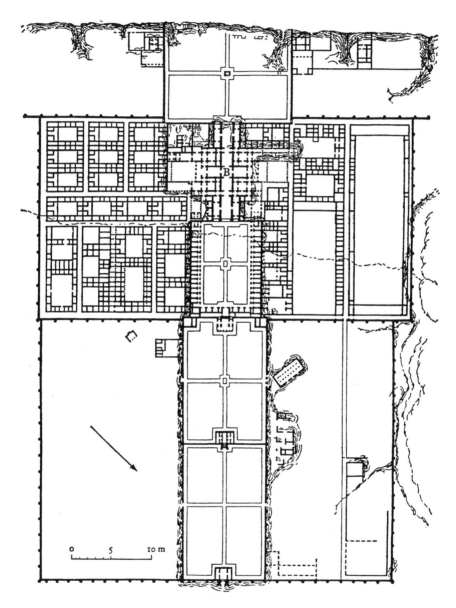

Balkuwara Palace at Samarra.

Selected Bibliography

The materials we have drawn upon to write book represent a lifetime of reading, research and reflection. To list all the books, monographs, and articles consulted over many decades and in various European and Near Eastern languages would have entailed a lengthy appendage to what has become perhaps the longest single essay ever written on the formative centuries of Islam. As this book was intended primarily for a general reading audience, we have carefully selected a bibliography limited in all but one instance to secondary sources in the English language, books and articles that will be generally accessible to an informed public. At times, as in the case of the chapters on Islamic law and theology, the complex subject matter called for the inclusion of more technical reading material.

Choosing which works to include and, more particularly which to exclude, was difficult, at times excruciatingly so. Readers seeking additional material will no doubt consult the more extensive bibliographies in the works listed here as well basic research tools such as the *Encyclopedia of Islam*, which has seen two editions with a third now underway; the *Encyclopedia of the Qur'an*; and the *Index Islamicus*, an ongoing project which contains a list of all articles published in European languages on Islamic subjects from the year 1900 on. In addition there are manuals to introduce readers to various tools of research in Islamic Civilization. No doubt, some specialists in Islamic studies, who are also a targeted audience for this book, would have preferred end notes or footnotes in addition to a most extensive bibliography, but the demands of the series in which this already massive work appears have made that impossible. We trust that readers familiar with our published work, most of which was intended for scholarly audiences, will be aware of the thoroughness with which have annotated our previous labors, drawing reference to both a wealth of secondary sources and primary texts from the Middle Ages. We hope that familiarity with our past efforts will inspire confidence in the current and highly reflective essay. Reflecting on this, we can cite Gustave E. von Grunebaum's words written toward the end of the Preface to his extended essay *Classical Islam*, a work cited in our Preface:

> Some of the facts, observations, and ideas presented in this book may seem to the specialist to be in need of documentary corroboration. The author . . . has decided for once to expose himself. . .in the interest of an unbroken narrative. . . . For the moment . . . he has adopted the immediate interests of a hypothetical readership, scholarly and lay, and the students in between. (p. 8)

Part I

Baneth, David H. "What Did Muhammad Mean When He Called His Religion Islam? The Original Meaning of *Aslama* and Its Derivatives." In *Israel Oriental Studies* 1 (1971): 183–190.

Bravmann, Meir. *The Spiritual Background of Early Islam*. Leiden, 1972.

Conrad, Lawrence. "Abraha and Muhammad: Some Observations Apropos of Chronology and Literary *Topoi* in Early Arabic Historical Tradition." In *Bulletin of the School of Oriental And African Studies* 50 (1987): 225–240.

Crone, Patricia. *Meccan Trade and the Rise of Islam*. Oxford, 1987.

Firestone, Reuven. *Journeys in Holy Lands*. Albany, 1990.

Hawting, Gerald R. *The Idea of Idolatry and the Emergence of Islam*. Cambridge UK, 1999.

Ibn Warraq [Ps.] (ed.). *The Quest for the Historical Muhammad*. Amherst NY, 2000.

Lammens, Henri. "La république marchande de la Mecque vers l'an 600 de notre ère." *Bulletin de l'Institut Egyptien* 5th series 4 (1910):23–54.

Lecker, Michael. *Muslims, Jews, and Pagans*. Leiden, 1995.

Motzki, Harald. (ed.). *The Biography of Muammad*. Leiden, 2000.

Newby, Gordon. *A History of the Jews of Arabia*. Columbia SC, 1988.

Peters, Frank M. (ed.). *The Arabs and Arabia on the Eve of Islam*. Ashgate Publishers USA and UK, 1998.

Ringgren, Helmut. *Islam, Aslam, and Muslim*. Lund, 1949.

Rodinson, Maxime. *Muhammad*. New York, 1971.

Watt, W. Montgomery. *Early Islam*. Edinburgh, 1990.

————. *Muhammad, Prophet and Statesman*. London, 1961.

————. "The Materials Used by Ibn Ishaq." In *Historians of the Middle East*. Edited by Bernard Lewis and Peter M. Holt. London, 1962, 23–34.

Part II

Adams, Robert M. *Land Beyond Baghdad*. Chicago, 1965.

Ayalon, David. *Islam and the Abode of War*. Variorum USA, 1994.

Brett, Michael. *The Rise of the Fatimids*. Leiden, 2001.

Bulliet, Richard W.. *Conversion to Islam in the Medieval Period*. Cambridge MA, 1979.

Crone, Patricia, and Martin Hinds. *God's Caliph*. Cambridge UK, 1986.

Dixon, 'Abd al-Ameer 'A. *The Umayyad Caliphate, 65–86/684–705*. London, 1971.

Donner, Fred McGraw. *Narratives of Early Islamic Origins*. Princeton, 1994.

Goitein, Shelomo D. "A Turning Point in the History of the Islamic State, Apropos of Ibn al Muqaffa''s Kitab al-Sahaba." In *Islamic Culture* 23 (1945): 120–135.

————. *Studies in Islamic History and Institutions*. Leiden, 1966.

Grabar, Oleg. "The Umayyad Dome of the Rock in Jerusalem." *Ars Orientalis* 3 (1959): 33–62

Hawting, G. R. *The First Dynasty of Islam*. London and Sydney, 1986.

Jafri, S. Hussein M. *The Origins and Early Development of Shi'a Islam*. London and New York, 1979.

Kennedy, Hugh. *The Early Abbasid Caliphate*. London, 1981.

————. *The Prophet and the Age of the Caliphates*. Harlow, UK, 2004.

————. *The Rise and Fall of Islam's Greatest Dynasty*. London, 2004.

Kohlberg, Etan. (ed.). *Shi'ism*. Ashgate Publishers USA and UK, 2003.

Lassner, Jacob. *The Middle East Remembered*. Ann Arbor, 1999.

————. *The Shaping of Abbasid Rule*. Princeton, 1980.

Lewis, Bernard. "An Interpretation of Fatimid History." In *Colloque internationale sur l'histoire du Caire (1969)*. Cairo, 1970.

————. *History—Recovered, Remembered, Invented*. Princeton, 1975.

————. "On Revolutions in Early Islam." In *Studia Islamica* 32 (1970): 215–231.

Momen, Moojan. *An Introduction to Shi'i Islam*. New Haven and London, 1985.

Omar, Farouk. *The 'Abbasid Caliphate, 132/750–170/786*. Baghdad, 1969.

————. *Abbasiyat: Studies in the History of the Early Abbasids*. Baghdad, 1976.

Robinson, Chase F. (ed.). *A Medieval Islamic City Reconsidered*. Oxford, 2001.

Sachedina, Abdalaziz Abdulhussein. *Islamic Messianism*. Albany, 1981.

Sanders, Paula. *Ritual, Politics, and the City in Fatimid Cairo*. Albany 1994.

Sharon, Moshe. *Black Banners From the East*. Jerusalem, 1983.

————. *Social and Military Aspects of the 'Abbasid Revolution*. Jerusalem, 1990.

Zaman, Muhammad Qasim. *Religion and Politics Under the Early 'Abbasids*. Leiden, 1997.

Part III

Abrahamov, Binyamin. *Islamic Theology: Traditionalism and Rationalism*. Edinburgh, 1998.

Azami, Muhammad Mustafa. *Studies in Early Hadith Literature*. Indianapolis, 1978.

———. *Studies in Hadith Methodology and Literature*. Indianapolis, 1977.

Baldick, Julian. *Mystical Islam*. New York, 1989.

Berg, Herbert. *The Development of Exegesis in Early Islam*. Curzon Publishers UK, 2003.

——— (ed.). *Method and Theory in the Study of Islamic Origins*. Leiden, 2003.

Burton, John. *An Introduction to the Hadith*. Edinburgh, 1994.

Calder, Norman. *Studies in Early Muslim Jurisprudence*. Oxford, 1993.

Cook, Michael. The Koran: *A Very Short Introduction*. Oxford, 2000.

Coulson, Noel J. *A History of Islamic Law*. Edinburgh, 1964.

Endress, Gerhard. "The Circle of al-Kindi: Early Arabic Translations of the Greek and the Rise of Islamic Philosophy." In *The Ancient Tradition in Christian and Islamic Hellenism*. Edited by G. Endress and R. Kruk. Leiden, 1997, 43–76.

Goldziher, Ignaz. *Introduction to Islamic Theology and Law*. English translation by Andras and Ruth Hamori. Princeton, 1981. Appeared in German as *Vorlesungen über den Islam*. Heidelberg, 1910.

———. *Muslim Studies*, vol.2. English translation annotated by Samuel M. Stern. London, 1971. Appeared in German as *Muhammedanische Studien*. Halle, 1890.

Hallaq, Wael B. *A History of Islamic Legal Theories*. Cambridge UK, 1999.

———. *The Origins and Evolution of Islamic Law*. Cambridge UK, 2005.

McAuliffe, Jane Dammen. *The Cambridge Companion to the Qur'an*. Cambridge UK, 2006.

Melchert, Christopher. *The Formation of the Sunni Schools of Law, 9th–10th Centuries*. Leiden, 1997.

Motzki, Harald. *The Origins of Islamic Jurisprudence*. English translation by Marion Katz. Leiden, 2002. Appeared in German as *Die Anfänge der Islamischen Jurisprudenz*. Suttgart, 1991.

Nagel, Tilman. *The History of Islamic Theology From Muhammad to the Present*. Princeton, 2000.

Rippin, Andrew. (ed.). *The Blackwell Companion to the Qur'an*. Oxford, 2006.

Schacht, Joseph. *An Introduction to Islamic Law*. Oxford, 1964.

Siddiqi, Muhammad. *Hadith Literature*. Islamic Texts Society, Cambridge UK, 1993.

Trimingham, J. Spencer. *The Sufi Orders in Islam*. London, 1971.

Vann Ess, Josef. *The Flowering of Muslim Theology*. Cambridge MA, 2008.

Watt, William M. *Bell's Introduction to the Qur'an*. Edinburgh, 1970.

———. *Islamic Philosophy and Theology*. Edinburgh, 1962.

Winter, Tim. *The Cambridge Companion to Classical Islamic Theology*. Cambridge UK, 2008.

Zaman, Muhammad Qasim. *Religion and Politics under the Early 'Abbasids*. Leiden, 1997.

Index

About the Authors

JACOB LASSNER (PhD Yale, 1963), Philip M. & Ethel Klutznick Professor Emeritus of Jewish civilization at Northwestern University, specializes in medieval Near Eastern History with an emphasis on urban structures, political culture and the background to Jewish-Muslim relations. He has been a member of the Institute for Advanced Study, and the Rockefeller Institute (Bellagio), and has held the Skirball Fellowship in Jewish-Muslim Relations at the Oxford Postgraduate Centre for Hebrew Studies. He has also held visiting professorships at the Universities of Michigan, California—Berkeley, Toronto, and Tel-Aviv. Among his publications are nine books, the most recent being *Jews and Muslims in the Arab World Haunted by Pasts Real and Imagined* (with Ilan Troen).

MICHAEL BONNER is professor of medieval Islamic history in the Department of Near Eastern Studies, University of Michigan, Ann Arbor, MI. He received his PhD in the Department of Near Eastern Studies, Princeton University, in 1987. His recent publications include *Jihad in Islamic History: Doctrines and Practices* (2006) and *Poverty and Charity in Middle Eastern Contexts*, coedited with Amy Singer and Mine Ener (2003). He has been a Helmut S. Stern fellow at the University of Michigan Institute for the Humanities and professeur invité at the Institut d'Etudes de l'Islam et des Sociétés du Monde Musulman, École des Hautes Études en Sciences Sociales, Paris, France and of Chaire de l'Institut du Monde Arabe, also in Paris. He was director of the University of Michigan Center for Middle Eastern and North African Studies in 1997–2000 and 2001–2003, and acting chair of the Department of Near Eastern Studies in 2007–08.

Recent Titles in
Praeger Series on the Middle Ages

Jews and Judaism in the Middle Ages
Theodore L. Steinberg

Materials, Methods, and Masterpieces of Medieval Art
Janetta Rebold Benton